"Considering the amount and quality of the legal gui... ...
Worse contains, it is probably the best value for the money, page for page, ...
popular publication on employment law in Canada today."

Richard A. Bailey
Vice President, Legal and Corporate Affairs
General Counsel and Secretary
Kraft Canada Inc.

"When the first edition of *For Better or For Worse* was published in 1996, it set a new standard in writing about law for the human resources profession. Astonishingly, the second edition exceeds even this."

Wayne McFarlane
Human Capital Leader, Canada
PricewaterhouseCoopers LLP

"The first edition of *For Better or For Worse* was a bull's eye. Employment, with its constant change, is a moving target. It looks as if Echlin and Thomlinson have hit dead centre again."

Darlene Brushett
Managing Director, Human Resources
BMO Nesbitt Burns

"Start on page 1 and read to the end. Or look into it for guidance on particular issues. Either way, *For Better or For Worse* covers a lot of front on employment law issues."

Michael Stern
President
Michael Stern Associates Inc.

"These two particular authors, Christine Thomlinson and Randy Echlin, make a great team. Who else has been so visible in books, looseleaf services and conferences over the past several years? Is there really any need to go anywhere else?"

Carol Wilding
National Director
Foster Parents Plan of Canada

"No human resources professional should be without a practical and accessible guide to employment law. More than any other book, *For Better or For Worse* is that guide."

Erwin Buck
Chief Financial Officer
MacLaren McCann Canada Inc.

"Of course it's important to know what the law says on an employment law issue when the issue comes up. But I also need to know what it means to me and what to do about it. Echlin and Thomlinson provide not just law, but practical management advice."

Myrna Cassidy
Director of Human Resources
Adecco Employment Services

"Randy Echlin and Chris Thomlinson have years of experience in advising front-line management on employment law. This was evident from the first edition, and is even more apparent now in the new revised and expanded second edition of *For Better or For Worse*."

Judy Kuehl
Manager of Corporate Human Resources
Intercon Security Ltd.

"*For Better or For Worse*, 2nd edition, is an easy-to-read reference book detailing a great deal of both legal and practical information for human resources professionals at all levels. As the name suggests, the book describes some excellent parallels to long-term relationships, making sense of a complicated field."

Margo Vanderland
National Human Resources Manager
Canada Colors and Chemicals Limited

"In the years since the publication of the first edition, Canadian human resources professionals have come to rely on Echlin and Thomlinson's *For Better or For Worse*, which is now the standard human resources legal guide. They can have even greater confidence in the second edition."

Vivian Springer
Director, Human Resources
TELUS Mobility

"Managing employees is challenging enough without the added worry of not knowing if you are on solid legal ground. With a copy of *For Better or For Worse* close at hand, managers and employment professionals can do their jobs with confidence."

Kathleen Kennedy
Director of Finance and Administration
GCI Communications Inc.

FOR BETTER
OR
FOR WORSE

A Practical Guide to Canadian Employment Law

Second Edition

160207

The Hon. Mr. Justice Randall Scott Echlin,
The Superior Court of Justice (Ontario)
Christine M. Thomlinson, B.A., LL.B.

with Foreword by
The Honourable Mr. Justice Frank Iacobucci

Aurora Professional Press,
a division of Canada Law Book Inc.
240 Edward Street, Aurora, Ontario L4G 3S9

National Library of Canada Cataloguing in Publication

Echlin, Randall Scott
   For better or for worse: a practical guide to
Canadian employment law / by Randall Scott Echlin,
Christine M. Thomlinson; with foreword by
Frank Iacobucci. – 2nd ed.

Includes bibliographical references and index.
ISBN 0-88804-402-X

   1. Labour laws and legislation – Canada.   I. Thomlinson,
Christine M., 1968-   II. Title.

KE3109.E24 2003   344.7101   C2003-900462-7
KF3320.ZA2E24 2003

To Ann, Libby, Rob, my mother, Madeleine, and my late father, Robert,
who have always believed in me.

Randy Echlin

To my family, Heath, Parker and Logan,
for supporting me through all the work that went into this project.

Chris Thomlinson

Foreword
to the First Edition

The former Chief Justice of Canada, The Right Honourable Brian Dickson, has written:[1]

> Work is one of the most fundamental aspects in a person's life, providing the individual with a means of financial support and, as importantly, a contributory role in society. A person's employment is an essential component of his or her sense of identity, self-worth and emotional well-being.

I heartily agree with these sentiments. It seems to me that work, along with family and education or training, is easily one of the most important influences of our lives. There is not only a symbiosis among these influences but also a synergy which defines and shapes us as human beings.

The authors have drawn an analogy between the relationships within marriage or family and work relationships. Whether the analogy is perfect or not is not the point; what is clear is that the importance of work has approached that of the family in modern society. This does not mean to say that work has replaced or taken precedence over family relationships; it cannot and should not. But we underestimate work if we fail to recognize its appropriate significance in our contemporary society.

In the legal world, the centrality of work is illustrated by the increased attention it has received, especially during my lifetime, from legislatures, courts, tribunals, practising lawyers and law teachers. We have witnessed many efforts to search for new ways to reflect society's views on the importance of work. These efforts have been made all the more challenging by expanding technology and societal innovations in a world of change and development. In fact, change has become a constant feature of modern society. We appear to be re-examining and reassessing all our core institutions and relationships, including those involving employment and work.

Against this backdrop, a book on the subject of employment law is most welcome. The authors describe their book in modest terms as simply a general

---

1   *Reference re: Public Service Employee Relations Act* (1987), 38 D.L.R. (4th) 161 at p. 199, [1987] 1 S.C.R. 313 at p. 368.

guide for employers; nonetheless, their specific advice and guidance are most instructive for key actors on the employment stage — human resources managers and senior executives. Moreover, like the authors, I agree that all decision-makers in employment areas will benefit from the book's messages not just on the legalities of employment but also on the moralities of the relationship.

That brings me to a major feature of the book which is deserving of special mention. Legal rules for much of human interaction largely represent only minimum requirements for human conduct. This book attempts to put the legal rules in their context; the authors acknowledge that forces outside the legal context are present and should be recognized and properly heeded. What is morally correct or fair should be the goal for which to strive in work relationships rather than the pursuit of the legal minimum which is dictated by the circumstances. Consequently, the authors' emphasis on keeping the legal rules in perspective is well placed.

I conclude by thanking and congratulating the authors for their effort and commitment, and I express the hope that readers will find their book useful and informative.

April 1996   The Honourable Mr. Justice Frank Iacobucci
                                              Supreme Court of Canada
                                                   Ottawa, Ontario

Preface

It was nearly nine years ago that Christine Thomlinson, then an articling student, suggested that there was a need for a book such as this. As has so often been the case, she was absolutely right! Through a mix of her enthusiasm, dedication, and plain old hard work, *For Better or For Worse: A Practical Guide to Canadian Employment Law* was first published in the fall of 1996. The idea for the content of this book arose from my involvement in teaching the employment law course at the University of Toronto for eight years. Chris went on to teach that course after I "retired", and another former colleague and co-author, Jennifer Fantini, is not only a graduate of that course, but also one of my former teaching assistants.

In this second edition, we have reprinted the original Foreword, prepared by The Honourable Mr. Justice Frank Iacobucci of the Supreme Court of Canada. We appreciate the unqualified and immediate support he has given to this project.

Much has happened in Canadian employment law over the past seven years. In fact, Mr. Justice Iacobucci has personally written two very significant decisions in *Wallace v. United Grain Growers Ltd.*,[1] and *McKinley v. BC Tel*.[2] Because of the impact of these decisions and others on the ever-evolving law in this area, it was felt imperative that this book be updated and a second edition be published.

Chris and I have been most gratified by the wide-ranging acceptance that the first edition received. It has been adopted as the textbook in a number of employment law courses. To that end, we made the commitment to all professors and instructors at the community college/university level (and will continue it) that if the book is used for an employment law course, Chris and I will make arrangements to personally come to that class and speak as guest lecturers on some aspect of the course. We cannot tell you how encouraging it is to have achieved the exceptional level of acceptance and sales with the first edition. We trust that this will continue going forward. Canada Law Book was again right in suggesting that our original work needed updating at this time.

---

1   (1997), 152 D.L.R. (4th) 1 (S.C.C.).
2   (2001), 200 D.L.R. (4th) 385 (S.C.C.).

Particular thanks to my colleagues, Brian Dingle, Sal Mirandola, Eva Krasa, Victoria Cowling and Benjamin Trister, and my former colleague, Geoff Morawetz, for their assistance in updating this second edition.

My Preface to the first edition thanked a number of people, and I will not repeat my comments again here except to continue to express my ongoing thanks to them and to Louise Dalhouse, my friend and former assistant and colleague, who worked with me for over 21 years.

I continue to be most grateful to my wife, Ann, who has supported me in every endeavour upon which I have embarked. Our two children, Libby, 18, and Rob, 14, have provided me with the kind of support only teenagers can supply. I look forward to watching, encouraging, and supporting them in their upcoming years at university and the careers that will follow.

Finally, I must note that nothing is more constant than change. When the first edition of this book came out, I was a member of an 11-person labour and employment department at Borden & Elliot. Later, I found myself the National Chair of a 50-person Labour and Employment Group at Borden Ladner Gervais LLP, one of Canada's largest full service law firms. This past April, I accepted an appointment as a Justice of the Ontario Superior Court of Justice, and left the active practice of law. As well, it was with considerable mixed emotions that I supported Chris when she decided to join with her friends, Janice Rubin and Melanie Manning, in creating Rubin Manning & Thomlinson LLP. I am as certain today as I was then that Chris will have a lifetime of active and significant contributions to the field of employment law. Her efforts in revising the first edition are apparent in the pages that follow. I owe much to Chris for her hard work, dedication, support, encouragement and friendship, which I will always greatly value.

Thank you.

Toronto, Ontario   Randy Echlin
May 2003

As daunting as the task of updating *For Better or For Worse* seemed when it was suggested, I think Randy and I both knew that the time had come. The 1997 Supreme Court of Canada decision, *Wallace v. United Grain Growers Ltd.*, was so significant that it is difficult to have any discussion about employment law today, be it with clients or opposing counsel, without making reference to the case. Once the legal implications of *Wallace* became clear, it was only a matter of time before we undertook the job of updating.

As was the case with the first edition, there are many to thank. I echo Randy's comments in respect of those he has already mentioned. Let me further extend our gratitude to the articling students at Borden Ladner Gervais LLP who assisted with the research: Brad Rafauli, Olivier Guillaume, Jenette Boycott and Tyler

Moore. Special thanks goes out to Brian Nicholson, Genny Na and Michelle Johal for their research and editorial assistance. The enthusiasm they all showed for the subject-matter was a constant source of inspiration.

As I reflect on the past year that I have been working on this book, I am still somewhat overwhelmed at the changes in my professional life. It is hard for me to believe that I started this second edition as a partner with BLG, and that I have now completed it as a founding partner of the newly created Rubin Manning & Thomlinson LLP. It seems somehow appropriate that, as Randy and I explore the employment relationship for the second time in the following pages, I should be embarking on a new working relationship myself. I am indebted to my friends and colleagues at BLG for supporting Randy and me in this endeavour, and equally grateful to my new partners, Janice Rubin and Melanie Manning, for helping me with my work overflow as I desperately worked to complete the project. Special credit also goes to Melanie for allowing me access to her own research for the purpose of updating the pregnancy and parental leave sections of the book.

Much has also changed in my personal life since the first edition. No one deserves more thanks in this undertaking than my husband, Heath, who has been unfailingly supportive throughout the past year. He has happily assumed the care of our two small children, Parker and Logan, *many* evenings and weekend afternoons. Not only has he never complained, but he has often suggested that he could do more if I needed extra time to work. I am truly blessed. For Parker and Logan, I hope that the stories we read together today will instill in them the love of reading that I gained from having those experiences myself as a child.

I have to say that, in leaving BLG and the ability to work with Randy on a day-to-day basis, I was certainly comforted by the fact that we continued to have this project in common. As I watch new members of our profession struggle to find a place for themselves, trying to learn how to be good lawyers without the benefit of role models and mentors, I know that I have been most fortunate. Over the years, Randy gave selflessly of his time, his opportunities and his contacts in order to support me in my growing career, and he continued to do so with others at BLG right up until the time he was appointed to the Bench. I will always be indebted to him. I owe much of the lawyer I am today to him, and I will always be honoured to call him my friend.

Toronto, Ontario   Christine Thomlinson
May 2003

Table of Contents

Table of Cases

Introduction

When we consider the amount of time that individuals spend working during their lifetimes, it is not surprising that employment relationships are often as important to us as our spousal and other personal relationships. Jobs are pivotal in our lives. They help to define who we are, and they provide us with an opportunity to demonstrate our abilities, thereby increasing our self-esteem and self-confidence. Given the personal investment we make in our work, it is often difficult for us to refrain from becoming emotionally attached to our employers and our colleagues. When employment difficulties arise, it is not unusual for employees to react in an emotional manner, and employers need to be prepared for this reality. This is why the "relationship" analogy seems particularly apt in the employment law context. There are many parallels to be drawn between the two. Ultimately, if employers approach their relationships with their employees as they might their personal relationships, there is a greater likelihood that employees will be treated with courtesy and respect and, hopefully, there will be more contented employees and more productive workplaces as a result.

This book is intended as a guide to assist employers as they navigate their way through the employment relationship. We recommend that employers and others using the book do not consider it an alternative to professional legal advice. As we indicate throughout, there are many points in the employment relationship where the specific facts of the situation will dictate the proper way in which a matter should be handled. As a guide, this book is designed to be comprehensive. However, it does not deal with all eventualities, and it is likely that employers and individuals will encounter difficulties which are not directly addressed in the text. In such cases, there is no substitute for proper legal advice. Often, incurring a minimal legal expense at the outset of an employment problem can save the employer significant legal liability down the road. If we have provided employers with enough information for them to make rational and cost-effective decisions as to the appropriate time to involve legal counsel in their employment problems, then we have achieved our purpose.

This book is designed to assist employers. We expect that those who might find this publication most useful are human resources managers and senior executives who deal on a day-to-day basis with the types of problems discussed. In fact, all company decision-makers will benefit greatly from reading this book. In our experience, it is often the human resources professionals who have a cursory understanding of employment law and a good sense of when to involve legal counsel. Other decision-makers in an organization, outside of the human resources specialization, will often make business decisions without being aware of the employment law implications, and it is these individuals who will benefit most. We also anticipate that this book will be of interest to others in the employment law field, such as employees and lawyers who deal in this area on an intermittent basis. Lastly, since the publication of the first edition, we have been pleased to learn that this book has been selected as required reading in many employment law classes. We have conducted guest lectures in many of these classes and are always willing to do so where a teacher or professor has been so kind as to refer to this text. We invite you to make the request, and we will try to oblige.

One of the things which readers will notice about this book is that there is considerable interrelation between different areas, with topics and issues arising over and over again throughout the text. This is not unusual in this area of law. Many of the principles may arise more than once throughout any given employment relationship. Employers need to be aware that simply because a particular phase of the employment relationship has passed does not mean that an issue has necessarily disappeared. Recognizing this fact often encourages employers to deal with problems in a prudent manner when they first arise so they are that much better prepared to deal with such matters should they arise again.

The issues dealt with in the text have been simplified in many areas. We have found that many legal concepts are misunderstood, and we attribute this to the fact that they have often been dealt with by lawyers for lawyers. We trust that, in approaching topics in the way that we have, we will impart some understanding of many basic employment law issues. The complicated aspects of these issues can be dealt with by legal counsel on a case-by-case basis, in the form of legal opinions sought when necessary. In approaching the subject in this way, we have attempted to clarify this ever-evolving area of law. The number of wrongful dismissal cases has increased tremendously in recent years, as companies face difficulties and employees become more aware of their rights. Many such cases would likely not have arisen had all parties been aware of their obligations under the law. Many cases are settled when these obligations are realized.

It should be noted that, with employment law as its subject-matter, this book was not meant to cover employees who are currently in a union relationship. Unionized employees are governed by many different rules, including applicable labour legislation and the terms of a specific collective agreement. Employers with employees who are covered by collective agreements should not rely upon the comments provided in this book except as they may apply to those members of the organization who are not covered by the collective agreement, such as management employees.

A large portion of the text deals with the legislation which governs the employment relationship. We caution employers against relying solely upon these sections of the book when problems arise. What we have sought to do in reviewing these pieces of legislation is to educate employers as to the types of issues which they might expect to be addressed by the particular legislation which is currently in place in their jurisdiction. We have approached the legislation in this manner in order to provide a guide which could be useful in the broadest manner. Employment legislation is extremely dynamic and can change greatly in a short period of time. By providing employers with the basic principles, we hope to alert employers as to what might be the rights and obligations in their jurisdiction. Any employer faced with a problem or a question should contact legal counsel to confirm whether its business is governed by any specific type of provision. Employers may also contact the relevant government department or agency for answers to these questions, and contact numbers have been provided in this regard (current to the date of publication).

The Province of Quebec was included in our review of employment law legislation. However, readers should be aware that, in terms of all judge-made law referred to in the book, Quebec has been excluded to the extent that it is governed by civil law, as opposed to common law. Common law finds its roots in England, while civil law is based in France and is premised on different principles. Lawyers are trained either to practise common or civil law, although certain lawyers obtain education in both. The common law applies in all provinces and territories, with the exception of Quebec, and it is the common law which is referred to in this book. Quebec employers should seek the advice of provincial counsel to determine whether the civil law plays any role in a matter before they rely exclusively upon the contents of this book.

This book is designed to encourage employers and employees to accept and honour their legal obligations to each other. Ultimately, there is no substitute for proper planning and preparation. Employment difficulties often cause much trauma and disruption in the workplace, so it can mean a big payoff if such matters are dealt with prudently. Much of the law of wrongful dismissal has arisen by virtue of employers' lack of sensitivity. This book provides instruction for employers in handling employment matters in a way which minimizes hostility and, hopefully, legal liability.

Part 1
The Courting

INTRODUCTION

The employment relationship, with all of its promise and perils, begins long before the employee ever walks in the door for the first day of work. In fact, for many human resources professionals, much of the hard work involves getting to that first day. To get an employment relationship off to a proper start, a significant investment of time, effort and emotion is required on the part of both the employer and the employee. Accordingly, as in any other relationship, both parties ought to treat the "courtship" process leading to employment very seriously.

Both employers and would-be employees should keep in mind, at this early stage of the process, their duties and obligations in such matters as filling out application forms, asking interview questions and discussing the terms of a job. A careful and informed approach during the courtship can do much to reduce the likelihood of problems arising over the course of the relationship. Carelessness in the courtship stage could, at the least, result in no engagement and, at the worst, result in significant legal exposure.

THE JOB OPENING

The employment relationship begins at the moment when the employer identifies an opening to be filled by a candidate for employment. Before the search for the ideal candidate begins, the employer can benefit from taking the time to consider the defining requirements of the position it is looking to fill. Too often, the employer rushes out immediately to fill a vacancy without taking the opportunity to reconsider the position. In many situations, the position which has been vacated differs greatly from the one which was initially filled, particularly in today's climate of economic and technological change. Duties and responsibilities are often altered or transferred between employees, resulting in marked changes to positions over time. For these reasons, the employer may wish to review the position in detail before interviewing applicants.

Job Descriptions

An accurate written job description has advantages and disadvantages. A list of duties and responsibilities will best ensure that the employer is able to identify the appropriate person for the job. It can also prove very useful for employers when, after having hired a successful candidate, it is realized that the employee is not performing as expected. In such a case, the employee's conduct or performance can be compared to the job description and, if he or she is not fulfilling the duties of the position, the employer may be able to take action to discipline or dismiss the employee. There is, however, a danger in being too specific in drafting job descriptions. In today's climate of changing jobs and changing duties, the employer may face liability for constructive dismissal if it tries to change an employee's duties or responsibilities from those contained within the employee's job description.[1] Employers are probably still wise to draft a job description to ensure that the employee is aware of what the job involves and cannot later question certain assigned duties. However, employers may wish to include a caveat within the job description which states that the job includes any additional duties and responsibilities as may be assigned by the employer. Depending upon the extent to which the employer attempts to alter the employment agreement, such a clause may not protect it against liability for constructive dismissal. The clause may, however, give the employer some latitude and none the less make employees more tolerant of such changes than they might otherwise be, given that they were put on notice that such changes could be expected.

A job vacancy allows the employer to consider the essential duties and responsibilities of the position and to detail them in an updated job description. The employer can take this opportunity to restructure the position, since the law of constructive dismissal may have prevented such restructuring while the position was occupied. Once the employer has considered the duties and responsibilities of the position and has set these out in a job description, the employer will then be in a position to consider the terms of employment for the position.

Terms of Employment

One of the most important terms which the employer must consider with respect to a position will be the remuneration to be provided to the successful candidate. Remuneration can include a host of different types of compensation, including but not limited to salary, commission, bonus (discretionary or performance/productivity-based), benefits, use of a company car and/or a car allowance, stock options, participation in a pension plan, club memberships and employee discounts.

---

1 See the discussion under the heading "Constructive Dismissal" in Part 4, "The Separation".

Employers choosing the pay level for an available position should be aware of the existence of legislation in every Canadian jurisdiction which requires employers to pay to both men and women an equal amount if they perform the same or substantially the same work.[2] In certain jurisdictions, this obligation also exists even if the work is not the same or substantially similar, so long as the work is equally valued by the employer. Employers in jurisdictions like Ontario may have yet a further obligation to comply with pay equity when setting pay scales for various positions.[3]

Employers that have reached the point of choosing a remuneration value for a vacant position should be aware of their potential obligation to set the pay rate in accordance with pay equity. Employers that wish to add new employees to their workplaces but do not want to run the risk of violating any pay equity legislation should first determine whether they are bound by pay equity. If they are so bound, in defining a position and framing recruitment plans, they should keep in mind that the way they treat the position may indicate what kind of evaluation the pertinent "job class" deserves and thus what kind of wages are appropriate for the position.

Once the employer has determined the appropriate compensation scale for the position, the employer should consider the type of engagement that it wishes to make with the successful employment candidate. The employer can hire an employee for an indefinite period, pursuant to either a written or an oral contract. However, the employer is also within its rights to enter into an employment relationship for a fixed period of time. The employer should consider the type of relationship most suitable for the job and should decide whether it will be hiring on a fixed or an indefinite basis. In fact, depending upon the position, the employer may not even wish to hire an employee. It may be more appropriate and advantageous for the employer to hire an independent contractor.[4] Of course, these decisions should not be set in stone, and they may be negotiated with a successful candidate. However, at this stage, it is useful to make a preliminary decision regarding this term of employment because it will likely have an impact on the way the position is advertised, on the individuals who apply and on the person ultimately chosen.

This also presents an opportunity for the employer to consider whether a full-time replacement is necessary for the position. Although an employer may already have determined that a certain position no longer requires a full-time employee, it was probably not in a position to alter the position while it was occupied by a full-time person. At this stage, before the employer begins looking for a replacement, it can address the question of whether a full-time person is necessary or whether the position should be more appropriately categorized as part-time. Even

---

2   See under the heading "Equal Pay for Equal or Similar Work, or for Work of Equal Value" in Part 3, "The Marriage".
3   See under the heading "Pay Equity" in Part 3, "The Marriage".
4   See under the heading "Types of Employees" in Part 2, "The Engagement".

if the employer is satisfied that the position continues to require full-time work, it may be possible for the employer to attract a broader spectrum of candidates by considering flexible employment opportunities, such as job sharing.

Employers who take advantage of the job opening and consider it an opportunity to re-evaluate the type of engagement they wish to enter into with the next employee will likely derive more long-term satisfaction from the relationship into which they ultimately enter.

ADVERTISEMENTS AND JOB APPLICATIONS

Once the employer has used the employment vacancy as an opportunity to consider the possible restructuring of the position, taking into account the job description, remuneration, the employment contract and the flexibility of the position, the employer is prepared to advertise the available position to potential candidates.

Human Rights Requirements for Job Advertisements

Recruiting new employees is a process fraught with potential pitfalls for the employer. Employers need to ensure that the "help wanted" advertisement does not contain any words or meanings forbidden by human rights legislation, yet employers also want to ensure that the advertisement reaches a sufficiently diverse group of potential applicants. At times, it may seem as if the actual task of finding a competent employee is the least of the employer's difficulties.

From the very beginning of the recruitment process, employers must consider a number of factors which may affect the future happiness and success of the employment relationship. In particular, there now exists a substantial body of human rights law, in every province and at the federal government level, which regulates what employers can communicate in their advertisements or recruitment literature. Ontario's *Human Rights Code*[5] contains a provision whose general language resembles that used in other provinces:

> 23(1) The right under section 5 to equal treatment with respect to employment is infringed where an invitation to apply for employment or an advertisement in connection with employment is published or displayed that directly or indirectly classifies or indicates qualifications by a prohibited ground of discrimination.

Prohibited grounds of discrimination include race, ancestry, place of origin, colour, ethnic origin, sex, sexual orientation, disability, marital status, family status, age and religion.[6] Most employers are conscientious and reasonable and would not even consider starting off an employment relationship with an act of

---

5   R.S.O. 1990, c. H.19 (as amended to 2002, c. 18, Sch. C).
6   See Appendix A, Table 10, for a comprehensive listing of the prohibited grounds of discrimination in each of the Canadian jurisdictions.

discrimination. Such reasonable employers hardly need to be reminded not to advertise a job in a way which intentionally and directly discriminates against certain individuals on the basis of some prohibited ground. However, by following precedent, echoing traditional views of certain jobs or simply failing to properly scrutinize "help wanted" advertisements, employers may indirectly discriminate against certain persons and thereby find themselves in violation of provincial or federal human rights legislation.

Employers drafting advertisements should keep in mind the Ontario Human Rights Commission's statement that human rights laws are "based on the principle that employment decisions should be based on the applicant's ability to do the job rather than on factors that are unrelated to job requirements, qualifications or performance".[7] In an advertisement, employers should avoid using any language which is not related to the employee's ability to do the job advertised. For instance, unless driving is actually required for a particular job, it would be improper to request that applicants have a driver's licence, since this might exclude some individuals on the basis of a handicap, such as blindness. Also, language which suggests a traditional view of the gender of the person performing the work should be avoided. For example, nurses need not be women, and construction workers need not be men.

Assuming that the advertisement's language is wholly legitimate, employers should also consider how and where they are advertising. It is appropriate to ensure that every person who might be interested in the job, from whatever background, has an equal and reasonable opportunity to see the advertisement and apply for the job. It is possible that an advertisement is being improperly targeted at some individuals, and being kept from others, because the employer wants to evade the requirements of human rights law. Human rights legislation prohibits advertising which indirectly classifies applicants according to a forbidden ground of discrimination. To avoid any problems which might arise, employers are well advised to make sure that an advertisement is well distributed or at least published somewhere that everyone might see it, such as a daily newspaper.

The preceding strictures do not mean that employers are prohibited from including in job advertisements any reasonable requirements which are directly related to the job. If a job requires the employee to drive on a regular basis, it is hardly unreasonable or discriminatory to note in the advertisement that the successful applicant must be able to drive.

Even where there are legitimate requirements, however, the employer should still pay attention to the language of the advertisement for two reasons. First, human rights legislation requires employers to make reasonable accommodation for employees' needs in certain instances. For example, an employer may prefer a workplace where every worker is male, but such a requirement would violate

---

7   Ontario Human Rights Commission, *Hiring? A Human Rights Guide*, 2nd ed. (September 13, 1999) (available at www.ohrc.on.ca), "1. Introduction".

human rights laws, and an advertisement containing that requirement would be improper. Secondly, there may be very legitimate requirements for a position, but employers should be careful not to draw stereotypical or wrongful conclusions about who might wish, or be able, to fulfil such requirements. For example, a manual labour position should not be advertised as being only for men simply because the employer thinks that women will be physically incapable of doing the work. This can be avoided by simply stating that the position involves strenuous physical work, such as lifting and carrying. After all, not all male applicants will be able to do such jobs, while some female applicants may be very well qualified.

The employer should be prepared to justify any job requirement as a *bona fide* occupational requirement in accordance with the test established by the Supreme Court of Canada[8] in 1999:

1.   Was the requirement adopted for a purpose rationally connected to the performance of the job?
2.   Was the requirement adopted in an honest and good faith belief that it was necessary to the fulfilment of that legitimate work-related purpose?
3.   Was the requirement reasonably necessary to the accomplishment of that legitimate work-related purpose, keeping in mind the employer's duty to accommodate to the point of undue hardship?

Designing Employment Applications

The problems involved in crafting proper job application forms differ somewhat from those involved in writing job advertisements. A company advertising for a position must avoid discriminatory language but can still specify the particular position it wants to fill. On the other hand, application forms are designed not only to ascertain whether the potential employee has the necessary qualifications for the job but to distinguish among the various applicants and select the best person for the job, at least on a preliminary basis. The questions contained in the employment application need to elicit more than basic information like the applicant's name and address. However, such questions give rise to a concern that applicants could be made to face unnecessarily intrusive and potentially discriminatory inquiries.

As with employment advertisements, employers should bear in mind that employment decisions should be based on criteria relating to the applicant's ability to do the job in question rather than on factors which are unrelated to job performance. This should serve as a reminder to ask questions which are narrowly related to the issue of whether the applicant is the best qualified person for the

---

8   See *British Columbia (Public Service Employee Relations Commission) v. BCGSEU* (1999), 176 D.L.R. (4th) 1 (S.C.C.), where an aerobic capacity requirement for firefighters was found to discriminate against women and could not be justified under the above three-part test.

job, rather than questions which veer off topic and pry into the applicant's life without gathering any relevant information. The employer should attempt to ensure that the application cannot be construed as discriminatory.

Human rights codes and other legislation dealing with employment applications typically bar application forms or any other "written or oral inquiry" which directly or indirectly suggests that the employer is considering prohibited grounds of discrimination. While the provinces and federal government differ in some areas, most of them share the following basic restrictions.

Race

All questions about an applicant's race are prohibited. Similarly, application forms should not ask questions which might point to the race or appearance of the applicant, and companies should avoid asking for photographs at the pre-hiring stage.

Religion or Creed

Direct questions about the applicant's religion or creed, or questions which might indirectly elicit information about the applicant's religion or creed, should be avoided. Since businesses have a reasonable duty to accommodate workers' religious practices, application forms also should not ask questions which might suggest that the company is attempting to evade its duty to accommodate such applicants. Employers will often include such questions in their employment applications, claiming that they are merely trying to elicit information about the type of accommodation which might be necessary for a potential employee. A human rights commission considering this justification for such inquiries may not be persuaded. Information necessary to accommodate employees' religious beliefs can be obtained after an individual has been offered the job. Any attempt to obtain the information before this stage will likely suggest that the employee is being judged on the basis of this information.

Gender

Since gender discrimination is a forbidden form of discrimination in every jurisdiction of Canada, application forms should most certainly avoid any questions designed to elicit the applicant's gender. Even though it may seem a simple courtesy, it is best to omit the common question asking how the applicant wishes to be addressed, i.e., Mr., Mrs., Ms (although in some jurisdictions, like Manitoba, it may be permissible to include such a question as long as it is marked "optional"). Inquiries regarding such pleasantries can always follow the application process should the applicant secure a job interview.

Age

The provinces and federal government allow an individual to work once he or she has reached the age of 18 or 19, and in many jurisdictions the retirement age is 65. Aside from ensuring that an applicant fits within these parameters, it is improper to ask any further questions about the applicant's age, such as his or her date of birth. A simple query as to whether the applicant is of legal working age will suffice.

National or Ethnic Origin/Ancestry or Place of Origin

The only question which should be asked by employers with respect to any of these categories is whether the applicant is eligible to work in Canada. Any question eliciting more information than this will be considered improper. Similarly, prohibited questions include those designed to elicit the nationality of the applicant, the nationality of his or her relatives or spouse, the applicant's native language or the applicant's place of birth. Asking for an individual's Social Insurance Number may elicit information about the person's place of origin or citizenship status. Such a question should be avoided until a conditional offer of employment has been made.

Marital Status

Questions designed to learn whether the applicant is married, single, divorced or widowed, or any other inquiry into the marital status of the applicant, will run afoul of human rights legislation and should be avoided. It may be appropriate to ask, where the job requires it, whether the applicant is willing and able to travel or to be relocated. In addition, where information is requested regarding emergency contact information, there should be no information requested regarding the relationship between the applicant and the emergency contact until after hiring or a conditional offer is made.

Disability

Treatment of physical or mental disabilities varies from jurisdiction to jurisdiction. While Ontario prohibits any questions at all on the subject, at least until the interview stage, many provinces allow application forms to inquire into whether there is anything which would affect the applicant's ability to perform any of the functions of the job which the applicant seeks or, more generally, whether the applicant feels that he or she would be able to perform the sought-after job.[9] This

---

9   For example, the Saskatchewan Human Rights Commission publication, *Employer's Guide to Application Forms and Interviews under The Saskatchewan Human Rights Code* (revised April 2001) (available at www.gov.sk.ca/shrc/appforms.htm), says that it is permissible to ask "Do you have a disability which will interfere with your ability to perform the job for which you have

question should be followed up by asking whether any accommodations could be made to allow the applicant to do the job. However, if this information is provided by the applicant and he or she is subsequently denied the position, there may be a natural suspicion and even allegation of discrimination. It may be worthwhile for an employer to wait until a job candidate makes the "first cut" before exploring this issue.

Family Status

This category focuses primarily on whether the applicant has children, as opposed to the marital status category's focus on the spousal relationship. Most jurisdictions prohibit questions about whether the applicant has children or about child care arrangements, although questions regarding the applicant's ability to meet job requirements of overtime, travel or shift work may be allowed. Questions relating to pregnancy are also forbidden. Employers should not ask whether the applicant is pregnant, or intends to have children, or how long she or he will remain in the job market.

Sexual Orientation

Questions about an applicant's sexual orientation, or questions which would elicit such information indirectly, are improper and should be omitted.

Drug or Alcohol Addiction

Generally, questions about whether an applicant suffers from an addiction are improper. In essence, these questions seek to discover whether the applicant has the medical disability of addiction, and such questions are thus prohibited. Questions designed to determine whether the applicant belongs to medical or patient organizations, which would include groups such as Alcoholics Anonymous, are equally inappropriate.

Criminal Record or Convictions

Some jurisdictions, such as British Columbia and Ontario, discourage or prohibit questions relating to the criminal record of an applicant. In Ontario, it is permissible to ask whether the applicant has ever been convicted of a criminal offence for which a pardon has not been granted, but little else. One exception applies: where the information is necessary because of the nature of the job, an inquiry will be allowed. For instance, if the job involves driving, it is reasonable

---

applied?" If the answer to that question is "yes", then: "What functions can you perform and what accommodations could be made which would allow you to do the work adequately?"

to ask whether the applicant has been convicted of any offences under the provincial highway traffic Act. If the job requires the employee to be bonded, this too would be a reasonable ground for inquiry. Otherwise, employers should exercise caution when asking questions in this area.

Height and Weight Requirements

Employers occasionally use height and weight requirements to screen potential employment candidates. Such requirements might appear neutral on their face but may contravene human rights legislation if they result in indirect discrimination against certain individuals. Height and weight standards are often traditionally based upon the average height and weight of white, Anglo-Saxon males, and the restrictions could discriminate against females or members of racial and ethnic groups who, on average, are physically smaller than white, Anglo-Saxon males. Employers should be wary of setting height and weight restrictions because there is little empirical research which indicates that physical stature alone is determinative of an individual's ability to perform the essential duties of a job which requires significant physical exertion.[10] Even where an employer is able to establish that the height or weight requirements are *bona fide*, the employer may still be required to accommodate a particular candidate's needs.

Driver's Licence

Requesting the production of a driver's licence at the employment application stage may serve to screen out applicants with disabilities who could otherwise be accommodated. The driver's licence may also reveal information about an individual's age or physical characteristics which may suggest that the person has a particular ethnic or racial background. If the employer requires that the successful applicant drive as an essential duty of the position, this requirement can be included in the advertisement for the job, and a request for a copy of the licence can be made for inquiry purposes after the applicant has been made a conditional offer of employment.

Nepotism or Anti-Nepotism

Jurisdictions such as Ontario may allow an employer to obtain information regarding the applicant's relationship to current employees of the employer for the purpose of satisfying an existing nepotism or anti-nepotism policy. Employers are well-advised to simply ask whether the applicant is related to a current employee, instead of asking for the applicant's relationship with the employee,

---

10   Ontario Human Rights Commission, *Policy on Height and Weight Requirements* (approved by the commission on June 19, 1996) (available at www.ohrc.on.ca).

unless this information is definitely necessary for the purpose of satisfying the policy.

Other

Other questions which may be found to be inappropriate include inquiries about the applicant's political beliefs and associations, and the applicant's social background and financial means.

Sample Employment Application

The preceding list of prohibitions may give the impression that the employer is powerless to find out much at all about the individuals with whom it may be entering into an employment relationship. In fact, the employer is free to seek a great deal of information from a potential employee on an application form, as long as the form does not pry into irrelevant and improper areas. The following questions should provide employers, who are drafting job application forms, with some idea of the questions which may be asked, as well as those questions which should generally be avoided.

- **Do ask:**   Please provide a person to be contacted in case of emergency.
- **Do not ask:** What is your relationship with this person?

- **Do ask:**   Are you able to perform the following duties [describe duties]? If not, what is the nature of any accommodation you require?[11]
- **Do not ask:** Please describe any disabilities you may have.[12]

- **Do ask:**   Are you legally entitled to work in Canada?
- **Do not ask:** What is your nationality? What is your Social Insurance Number? (This may contain information about a person's citizenship status; wait instead until after the position has been offered.)

- **Do ask:**   What is the highest level of education you have attained?
- **Do not ask:** What primary and secondary schools did you attend and when?

- **Do ask:**   What languages do you speak?
- **Do not ask:** What is your mother tongue?

- **Do ask:**   Are you willing and able to transfer to another city, town or province?[13]
- **Do not ask:** Are you married? Are you pregnant?

---

11   This may not be appropriate in all jurisdictions, such as Ontario.
12   In some jurisdictions, including Ontario, it is recommended that no questions at all be asked on this subject.
13   This question is allowed in most jurisdictions.

- **Do ask:**   What is your surname?
- **Do not ask:** What is your maiden name? What is your Christian name?

- **Do ask:**   Do you have any memberships in clubs or other organizations which do not reveal your gender, race, religion, ancestry or place of origin?
- **Do not ask:** Do you have any memberships in clubs or other organizations?

- **Do ask:**   Are you available for shift work? If not, what accommodations are necessary?[14]
- **Do not ask:** What is your religion?

Ultimately, an employment application may include the following set of questions:

- Name?
- Address and telephone number?
- Are you legally able to work in Canada?
- Are you between 18 and 65 years of age?
- Are you willing to relocate in this province?
- Education: Secondary School — highest grade completed, type of certificate or diploma obtained?
  Community College/University — name and length of program, degree awarded, work-related skills?
- Employment history? (It is permissible to ask for full details.)
- Personal interests and activities (civic, athletic, etc.)?

Employee Misrepresentation on Job Applications

It is not only employers who must be careful when dealing with employment applications. Prospective employees, too, must show some restraint. While there is no specific statute obliging an applicant to be honest on a job application form, if hired, an employee can face a severe penalty for his or her deception. The courts have held that dishonesty may constitute just cause for dismissal. Such acts of dishonesty can constitute just cause if they seriously prejudice the employer or if they reveal that the employee is untrustworthy. Resumé fraud, false or misleading answers on application forms and other attempts at misrepresentation suggest that the employee has been untrustworthy from the start. The discovery of falsified resumés or application forms can therefore result in summary dismissal.

What standard of accuracy is to be expected from a job applicant's resumé or job application? It is unlikely the courts would take too harsh a view of an inconsequential and inadvertent error, such as accidentally giving the wrong date for a previous job where nothing depends on the accuracy of the date. At the

---

14   This question is allowed in most jurisdictions.

opposite extreme, it is clear that misrepresentation about material aspects of the application will provide justification for summary dismissal. For example, a court found that dismissal was justified where a discharged employee's resumé had been written on the stationery of his former employer even though he had been dismissed by that employer, since the stationery implied he still held the job. The resumé also stated that the employee was still working for his former employer and was about to be relocated to Vancouver and that he had taken a course in business management at the University of Toronto, none of which were true.[15] There are also cases which are not as extreme but which may none the less entitle the employer to dismiss for cause, such as if the applicant portrays himself or herself as competent or an expert in a particular field and then turns out to be incompetent. In such cases, this misrepresentation has justified the employer's summary dismissal of the employee.[16]

The applicant should not let interest in a job seduce him or her into any significant inaccuracy or misrepresentation on a resumé or job application. Employers may strive to underscore the importance of honest applications and strengthen their ability to dismiss dishonest workers by including a provision, at the end of job application forms, which discourages such dishonesty. The provision should state that the applicant attests that all information contained in the application is true and that the applicant understands that a false statement may disqualify him or her from employment, or constitute grounds for immediate dismissal if the employer later learns that information contained in the application or resumé is inaccurate.

INTERVIEWING

The interview provides the employer with an opportunity to meet the potential candidate and get a sense of the individual's suitability for the particular position. In many cases, the employer will have elicited all relevant job-related information from the employment application and the employee's resumé. The job interview is used to determine if the individual is compatible with the working environment and is a suitable "fit". However, some employers may pay minimum attention to the application process and will use the interview to determine if the employee has the appropriate qualifications for the position. Regardless of the purpose of the interview, employers need to exercise caution at this stage of the courting process as well.

---

15 *Cornell v. Rogers Cablesystems Inc.* (1987), 17 C.C.E.L. 232 (Ont. Dist. Ct.).
16 *Bridgewater v. Leon's Manufacturing Co.* (1984), 6 C.C.E.L. 55 (Sask. Q.B.).

Human Rights Requirements and Guidelines

As with advertisements and applications, employment interviews are subject to the requirements of provincial and federal human rights legislation, which is designed to ensure that applicants are not discriminated against on any prohibited grounds, such as race or gender. However, unlike other parts of the recruitment process, interviews are "live", and the interviewer is required to think on the spot. It is therefore even more important that interviewers have a clear understanding of what they are permitted by law to ask of job applicants so that the employment relationship can start off on the right foot and so that those who are not hired can be sure that they were not rejected for discriminatory reasons.

Interviewers should concentrate on eliciting only that information which will help them make an informed decision about whether the candidate is the right person for the job and whether accommodation will be required. Such questions as "How old are you?" or "Are you married?" may be everyday pleasantries but, in the context of the job interview, they may lead the applicant to believe that he or she is being rejected for improper reasons. A reasonable and cautious approach will avoid long-term problems. It may be wise for employers to develop a standard set of questions which will be asked of every interviewee. There can then be no suggestion that a particular applicant was singled out for discriminatory treatment. It may also be helpful for interviews to be conducted by teams. This allows for a variety of input into the decision-making process and may avoid inherent biases. It will also prove helpful in the event that a discrimination complaint is made because all members of the team will be able to corroborate evidence of what took place during the interview.

Many employers are under the impression that it is acceptable to ask questions regarding the prohibited grounds of discrimination so long as the information elicited from the applicant does not form the basis for denying employment. The problem is, once the employer *has* the information, it is often very difficult to make a hiring decision without any consideration of it. Human rights law is clear that so long as the information plays some part in the decision (it does not have to be the sole reason), the decision will be considered to be discriminatory. In addition, and more importantly, in jurisdictions like Ontario, human rights legislation contains an express prohibition against making written or verbal inquiries that might classify an applicant on the basis of a prohibited ground of discrimination. In other words, it may be illegal just to ask the question.

The following categories merit special attention from interviewers and human resources professionals.

Race/Ancestry/Ethnic Origin/Place of Birth/Sex

Generally speaking, questions touching on such subjects are not permissible. However, some service organizations and special interest employers may be permitted to ask such questions, where these traits may be useful and necessary requirements for the job in question. For instance, a group working with children of a particular ethnic heritage or a job at a women's shelter might entitle the employer to inquire into a candidate's heritage or to make an assessment of the applicant's gender.

Religion or Creed

Similarly, questions regarding religion or creed are not permitted, although it may be reasonable to ask if any accommodation of an individual's religious beliefs will be required. For example, retail employers may need to ask about a candidate's recognition of the Sabbath to determine an applicant's ability to work on weekends. A denominational school may also be permitted to inquire into the religion of the applicant where the job requires the applicant to discuss religion with students or to communicate certain religious beliefs to them.

Disability

It is forbidden to discriminate against individuals on the basis of disability. If the issue is raised by the applicant during the interview, the interviewer should simply inquire about whether the candidate has any disabilities directly related to the performance of the particular job and what kind of accommodation would be required for the individual to perform the job satisfactorily. Employers are generally required by human rights legislation to accommodate employees, short of undue hardship.

Citizenship

Questions about the candidate's citizenship should be limited in most cases to whether the applicant is legally entitled to work in Canada. For some jobs, such as senior executive positions, further questioning about the applicant's citizenship may be appropriate, as there may be certain restrictions on the applicant's ability to assume the position based on provincial or federal corporations legislation.

Criminal Record or Convictions

As with employment applications, where the job requires the employee to be bonded, it is certainly reasonable to ask questions to ensure that the applicant is qualified. Similarly, if the job involves driving, it is proper to ask whether the interviewee has any convictions under the provincial highway traffic Act. Otherwise, the interviewer should confine questioning to inquiries as to whether the applicant has a record of any unpardoned criminal convictions.

Marital/Family Status

Many employers often fall prey to asking prohibited questions about marital or family status. This is rarely done intentionally; these issues are often raised in an effort to make small talk during the interview. However, employers must be aware that, even by asking innocent questions on these subjects, they can be giving the applicant the impression that these issues are of concern to the employer and may be violating human rights laws. Rather than asking questions about the applicant's marital status or whether he or she has children, employers should confine themselves to asking, where necessary, whether the applicant will be able to perform the work required according to the scheduled work hours and whether he or she can work overtime. Again, employers may be required to accommodate a particular individual in this regard. It may be appropriate for the employer to inquire into the applicant's marital or family status if the employer serves a particular group identified by marital status, such as single women.

Driver's Licence

The interview is an appropriate place for the employer to discuss with an applicant the fact that driving is a requirement of the position. If the candidate has a disability which in some way restricts the candidate's ability to fulfil this requirement, the employer must explore the possibility of accommodation of the candidate's disability. A copy of the applicant's driver's licence should not be requested until after a conditional offer of employment has been made.

Age

Questions about the applicant's age are generally inappropriate and should be avoided, apart from the simple inquiry as to whether the candidate is of legal working age. Further questions about age may be relevant for the determination of pension and other such benefits, but these can wait until after the individual has been offered a position.

Sample Interview Questions

When planning interviews, it may be helpful for employers to keep the following general guidelines in mind.

- **Do ask:** Will you be able to work the number of hours required in this job?
- **Do not ask:** How much time do you require to devote to your children? Do you plan on having children?

- **Do ask:** Are you eligible to work in Canada?
- **Do not ask:** Where are you from?

- **Do ask:** Is there anything which might prevent you from doing the job as we have described it? Is there any accommodation you may require?
- **Do not ask:** Do you have any disabilities?

- **Do ask:** Have you ever been convicted of an offence under the *Criminal Code* which has not been pardoned? We need our employees to be bonded. Will this be a problem for you for any reason?
- **Do not ask:** Have you ever been arrested or convicted?

Negligent Misrepresentation[17]

Relationships based on false promises or misinformation eventually end unhappily. In the employment context, that means that the parties can end up in court, resulting in unnecessary pain and expense. This can occur when interviewers make false or inaccurate claims about a job in the course of encouraging an applicant's interest in a position. If these promises result in the applicant taking a new job, only to discover that he or she took the job based on inaccurate information and has suffered a loss because of it, the employer may face significant liability. Such circumstances have been referred to as cases of "wrongful hiring".

This issue was dealt with by the Supreme Court of Canada in the case of *Queen v. Cognos Inc.*[18] Mr. Queen was a Calgary-based chartered accountant who responded to a newspaper advertisement, placed by Cognos Inc., looking for an accountant to help in the development of a computer accounting program. Mr. Queen was in a secure position and making a decent salary when he responded to the advertisement. Nevertheless, he was contemplating a change. During his interview with Cognos, he was told that the position they had in mind was an important one; the accountant would play a central role in the project, the staff working on the project would double in time and the successful candidate would be involved throughout the whole development stage. He was not told that the nature of the position and the budget were subject to further approval. He took the job and the company subsequently decided to cut funding of the project,

---

17 For further discussion of this topic, see under the heading "Negligent Misrepresentation" in Part 2, "The Engagement", and Part 5, "The Divorce".
18 (1993), 99 D.L.R. (4th) 626 (S.C.C.).

making Mr. Queen's position a far less significant one. Mr. Queen was ultimately dismissed 18 months after having been hired. Mr. Queen sued the company for negligent misrepresentation. He claimed that he would not have accepted the position were it not for Cognos' representations about the scope and viability of the project. He had been assured that the project was a reality and that his involvement with it would be on a permanent basis.

The Supreme Court of Canada held that an interviewer has a duty to take reasonable care to avoid making misleading statements. Here, the interviewer failed in this duty by misrepresenting the security of the job to Mr. Queen and by misleading him about the nature of the position, since the interviewer knew the company's managers had not yet approved the project's budget. Though the contract signed by Mr. Queen contained a disclaimer which allowed the company to reassign or dismiss him, that did not save the company from liability for making false promises about the nature of the job, such as the size and importance of the project. Cognos was required to pay damages for Mr. Queen's lost income, the loss he suffered on the purchase and sale of his new home in Ottawa, emotional stress, costs and the expenses incurred by Mr. Queen in finding a new job.

According to the *Queen* decision,[19] the following factors are necessary to establish negligent misrepresentation:

1. The person making the representations to an applicant must have a "special relationship" with him or her sufficient to give rise to a duty of care.
2. The representation must be untrue, inaccurate or misleading.
3. The person making the misrepresentation must have been negligent.
4. The applicant must have relied on the misrepresentation in deciding to take the job.
5. The reliance must have caused the applicant to suffer a loss.

A company and its representatives are under a duty of care, during the pre-employment interview, to exercise reasonable care and diligence in making representations regarding the employer and the employment opportunity being offered. The Supreme Court further noted that it is not enough for company representatives to be honest in their representations; they owe a duty to ensure that such representations are accurate and not misleading. *Queen* also suggests that a disclaimer clause in an employment contract, which makes clear, before the employee joins the organization, the risks the employee can expect, may narrow liability.

The *Queen* case serves as a powerful reminder to employers to be careful what they promise during a courtship. However, companies will not always be liable for promises which go awry. Courts will reject negligence claims where the misrepresentation does not meet the criteria set out in the *Queen* case. For instance, if a manager says that a job will likely be available soon on the basis of

---

19   *Supra*, at p. 643.

past experience and present knowledge but, due to matters outside of the manager's control, the job does not materialize, it is unlikely that a court will find the manager or the company negligent for having made this misrepresentation.

Of course, it also holds true that the employee must have relied upon the misrepresentation in question when deciding to switch jobs. If the inaccurate information was irrelevant to the employee's decision to move, or if the employee is experienced in the particular market and made his or her own investigation of the information provided by the prospective employer, then the new employer may not be liable for misrepresentation.[20]

Nevertheless, prudent employers will be careful not to make overreaching promises at the interview stage. This is especially true if the company is aware of any reasons why it may not be able to follow through on its promises. If there are aspects of a job which the employer is unsure of or which are subject to change or approval, the employer should be candid about such circumstances. Of course, the employer may simply wish to use the interview to assess whether the applicant is suitable and may save any discussion of terms until the contract stage. However, once a discussion of the job begins at the interview, the employer would be wise to be frank and open when trying to woo the potential employee.

Inducement[21]

The facts in the *Queen* case suggest another issue which should concern both employees and employers at the courting stage of the employment relationship: the inducement of an individual who is currently working for one company to take a position with another company. Individuals who are lured from one job to another may be happy to be rid of their former employer. Nevertheless, they are still sacrificing the security of existing employment. Often, they give up more than just security; they give up seniority, benefits or the chance of advancement. Employees such as Mr. Queen may also be enticed to a new job which requires that their families uproot themselves and move to a new location.

The issue of inducement should be of concern to employers for two reasons. First, where an employer lures an individual from another firm through aggressive recruiting techniques or promises of job security, higher income or a chance at advancement, and the employee is then fired or constructively dismissed and sues for wrongful dismissal, the courts may award pay for a longer period of reasonable notice.[22] This concept was explained by Justice Iacobucci in the Supreme Court of Canada decision, *Wallace v. United Grain Growers Ltd.*:[23]

---

20 See *Grant v. Oracle Corp. Canada Inc.* (1995), 8 C.C.E.L. (2d) 1 (Man. C.A.), affg 90 Man. R. (2d) 206 (Q.B.).
21 Also sometimes referred to as "allurement" or "enticement".
22 See the discussion under the heading "Inducement" in Part 2, "The Engagement".
23 (1997), 152 D.L.R. (4th) 1 (S.C.C.).

> ... many courts have sought to compensate the reliance and expectation interests of terminated employees by increasing the period of reasonable notice where the employer has induced the employee to "quit a secure, well-paying job ... on the strength of promises of career advancement and greater responsibility, security and compensation with the new organization"...
>
>   .   .   .   .   .
>
> In my opinion, such inducements are properly included among the considerations which tend to lengthen the amount of notice required.[24]

As was also pointed out, not all inducements will carry equal weight. The significance of the inducement in question will vary with the circumstances of the particular case.

The court will consider any factors which might indicate that the employee was induced to leave a good position, at some loss, to take the new job, including such things as:

1. The employee formerly ran his or her own business.
2. The old job was secure.
3. The employee rejected other and better job offers due to this employer's enticement.
4. The employee was required to move to take the new job (although employees who relocate frequently will find it more difficult to make this claim). The employee will not automatically be granted a longer reasonable notice period simply because he or she left one job to take another.

If the employer can show that there was no significant degree of enticement or allurement, or if the new job lasts several years before going sour, it is less likely that a court will accept an allurement argument. However, in one case,[25] even where the Chief Executive Officer of a hospital had been employed for six years, the Court found inducement and awarded 30 months' pay in lieu of notice. In this case, the plaintiff did not apply for the job, but was rather approached by a headhunter. He was flown from Moncton, New Brunswick, to Peterborough, Ontario, to interview for the position, and when he rejected the job offer, it was enhanced in order to quell any of his outstanding concerns. As was provided in that case, the length of time an employee has served following inducement is just one of the factors the courts should consider in determining the degree of weight to be applied to the factor of inducement.

The second reason employers should be cautious of alluring or enticing employees to join their organizations is that such allurement often brings with it representations which may be misleading and can form the basis for a negligent

---

24 *Supra*, at p. 30, citing Christie *et al.*, *Employment Law in Canada*, 2nd ed. (Toronto: Butterworths, 1993), at p. 623.
25 *Kilpatrick v. Peterborough Civic Hospital* (1998), 36 C.C.E.L. (2d) 265 (Ont. Ct. (Gen. Div.)), supp. reasons 79 A.C.W.S. (3d) 685 (Ont. Ct. (Gen. Div.)), revd on other grounds 174 D.L.R. (4th) 435 (Ont. C.A.).

misrepresentation claim. If new employees are lured from one job to another but the new employer has been careful to be honest about any eventualities, such as the possibility that a job will be subject to budget approval or that the employee will be considered probationary for the first six months, then the mere fact that the job switch ultimately costs the employee may not be a source of liability for the new employer. However, if these employees arrive at their new positions and find that the managers who enticed them to leave their old jobs were less than honest and candid, employers may expect trouble. In addition to pay in lieu of reasonable notice, employers may be liable for paying the cost of any losses, such as the costs of moving or buying (and, in some cases, selling) a new home, suffered by an employee as a result of negligent misrepresentation.

Employers dealing with individuals who are thinking about switching jobs should be careful that their efforts to induce that person to "jump ship" do not involve promises that the employer cannot keep. Where a promise is subject to conditions such as budgetary approval, or where the company wishes to reserve the right to modify a job description or to terminate the employee during the probationary stage, it should make its intentions clear before the employee is hired.

Medical Testing/Drugs and Alcohol

Employers are justly concerned about the health of prospective employees and about whether they have any addictions which might adversely affect their health and, more importantly, their ability to perform the essential duties of the job in a safe and efficient manner. A decision to hire someone is a decision to invest in that person's future. An employer does not want to reject a number of people who might have been productive for many years, only to hire and train someone whose health or lifestyle hampers his or her ability to work. In particular, employers who are aware of studies showing the severe drop in productivity and effectiveness which accompanies a drug or alcohol addiction are not eager to start up employment relationships with such individuals. Due to concerns that such fears have led employers to make unfairly discriminatory decisions at the hiring stage, human rights legislation places limits on the degree to which employees can be tested for medical conditions or for drug or alcohol addictions at the pre-employment stage.

Depending upon jurisdiction, employers are not powerless, at the application and/or interview stage, to ask questions which may provide information regarding prospective employees' potential health problems. Although it is not permissible to inquire into the details of an applicant's medical condition or to ask questions which suggest that the employer will discriminate on the basis of any medical condition, it is appropriate to ask potential employees whether there is any reason they will not be able to perform the job duties as set out and whether the employer will be required to accommodate the individual. If the employer wishes to go a step further and engage in medical testing, certain restrictions apply.

Employers should refrain from engaging in any medical testing until they have decided to hire a particular individual. Such testing should be scheduled after the successful candidate has been offered the position. The offer of employment may be conditional upon a medical test which indicates the individual's ability to perform the job in a safe manner. Medical testing may involve either a general pre-employment routine examination or a test more specifically related to the requirements of a particular position. Either way, employers should follow several basic guidelines to avoid review by the applicable human rights governing authority. Where the examination is designed to test whether the candidate can perform the position's essential requirements, the examination should be rationally related to the needs of the job and not one which would uncover irrelevant medical matters. If the employer chooses to proceed by way of a general pre-employment physical, then such tests should be given to all employment candidates and not be reserved for only a select few, particularly those with disabilities. Finally, each examination should be assessed on an individual basis, rather than treating test subjects as a class.

Once the employer has conducted a pre-employment medical examination, the exercise becomes significantly more complicated if the employer obtains information it does not like. At this stage, if the employer wishes to deny employment to the applicant on the basis of the applicant failing to fulfil certain medical job-related criteria, or on the basis that the applicant requires a clean bill of health in order to perform the job, the employer will be required to satisfy the three Supreme Court of Canada conditions discussed earlier:[26]

1.   The requirement was adopted for a purpose rationally connected to the performance of the job.
2.   The requirement was adopted in an honest and good faith belief that it would achieve the legitimate work-related purpose.
3.   The requirement is reasonably necessary to the accomplishment of the legitimate work-related purpose, keeping in mind the employer's obligation to accommodate to the point of undue hardship.

If these criteria cannot be fulfilled, the employer may have difficulty denying the position to the applicant. For this reason, many employers choose to dispense with pre-employment medicals altogether, other than in the most exceptional circumstances.

Since the Ontario Court of Appeal decided a case involving the drug testing policy of Imperial Oil,[27] it has generally been thought that pre-employment drug

---

26   *British Columbia (Public Service Employee Relations Commission) v. BCGSEU* (1999), 176 D.L.R. (4th) 1 (S.C.C.).

27   *Entrop v. Imperial Oil Ltd.* (2000), 189 D.L.R. (4th) 14 (Ont. C.A.).

testing in Canada is extremely problematic. Although the case itself dealt with the effect that Imperial Oil's policy had on an existing employee, the Court of Appeal had occasion to comment upon other components of the policy, including a provision which allowed for pre-employment drug testing. Writing for the Court, Justice Laskin held that pre-employment and random drug testing were violations of the Ontario *Human Rights Code* and were not permissible. The fatal flaw in respect of such testing was that, while a positive drug test confirmed the presence of a substance in the body, it could not consequently be proven that the individual suffered any form of impairment at the time of the test. While the same problem was not found to exist with respect to alcohol testing (the Court finding that a breathalyzer test could demonstrate impairment), the Court only commented on random alcohol testing for safety-sensitive positions, finding it to be justified providing the sanctions for a positive test were individually tailored. In light of this, it is recommended that any employer considering the implementation of a drug or alcohol testing policy obtain specific legal advice with respect to the policy and its enforceability, given the legal complexities associated with this area.

Checking References

If employers choose to ask for references from prospective employment candidates, they should understand that in some circumstances they may be obliged to check them. Although this area of law is only sparsely developed in Canada, it appears that, at least in cases where it would be reasonably necessary to check an applicant's employment references, and where the employer's failure to do so has led to adverse consequences, the employer may be held liable for the improper acts of its employee.

It is certainly the case in the United States that damages may be awarded against an employer who knew or should have known that an employee was unfit for work, and thus exposed others to an unreasonable risk of harm. For instance, in one case,[28] it was found that a security guard company ought to have checked on an employee's history after it received reference evaluations from former employers which contained mixed comments about his competence. Once employed, the guard proceeded to collaborate with thieves to rob an establishment guarded by the employer company. Courts in the United States have also awarded damages against the employers of a bartender and a bank security guard.[29]

Similarly, in one Ontario case,[30] two bouncers at a bar viciously beat a customer in the parking lot, causing him severe and permanent brain damage and rendering

---

28 *Welsh Manufacturing, Division of Textron, Inc. v. Pinkerton's Inc.*, 494 A.2d 897 (R.I. Sup. Ct. 1984).

29 *Murphy v. State Wine & Spirit Co.*, 212 Mass. 285 (Sup. Jud. Ct. 1912); *Langill v. Columbia*, 289 So.2d 460 (Fla. Dist. C.A. 1974).

30 *Downey v. 502377 Ontario Ltd.*, [1991] O.J. No. 468 (QL) (Gen. Div.).

him incapable of working or managing his own affairs. In addition to the liability imposed against the bouncers, the Court noted that their references had not been properly checked by the employer bar. One of the bouncers had lied on his application, omitting that he had previously been convicted of wounding. Although the Court held that there may have been an effort to contact one former employer, the application form was not appropriately marked, suggesting that, for the most part, the employee's references had not been checked. The Court held that the bouncers' backgrounds should have been checked and that the employer was liable for not having done so.

These cases do not necessarily suggest that employers must ask for references, though of course references can be helpful in making successful hiring decisions. Nor do these cases suggest that every unchecked reference will lead to liability. However, where the nature of the job is such that the employee could cause harm to third parties (for example, bouncers, security guards or lifeguards), and where the employer asks for references, the employer may face liability if the references go unchecked and damage is suffered as a result. Indeed, regardless of whether the employer asks for references, if the job could foreseeably result in the employee causing harm to the public or to other workers, the employer should be satisfied that the employee's background and qualifications are suitable for the position. If an employer requests references with the intention of checking them, it may be wise to accompany the reference request with a request for the employee's permission to make the necessary inquiries. In fact, with the introduction of privacy legislation in Canada,[31] there may currently (for federally regulated employers) and, by 2004, ultimately (for provincially regulated employers) be a statutory requirement to obtain consent before collecting employee information from references. For this reason, employers would also be prudent to establish a procedure for so doing. There can then later be no argument that the applicant was not aware that the references would be checked.

HEADHUNTERS, SEARCH FIRMS AND EMPLOYMENT AGENCIES

Many employees are not hired directly by their employer at all, but instead find work through the use of employment agencies or "headhunters". While employment agencies may provide large numbers of lower level workers on a temporary or longer term basis, executive recruiters often specialize in securing employment for more senior managers and executives. While this may take away from the company's initial courting responsibility, it does not necessarily remove the company's potential liability for whom and how it hires. Generally, employment agencies which contract to provide temporary labour for businesses stand in the role of employer with respect to their temporary workers. However, search

---

31 *Personal Information Protection and Electronic Documents Act*, S.C. 2000, c. 5 (as amended to 2002, c. 8).

agencies or headhunters which help put employers and would-be employees together do not act as the successful candidate's employer, and therefore potential liability for improper pre-employment processes remains primarily with the employer. This was certainly the finding in *Kilpatrick v. Peterborough Civic Hospital*,[32] where the Court commented as follows on the hospital's attempt to defend the case on the basis that its recruiter had not been authorized to make the representations he did:

> Whether or not McMonagle had any authority of the Board of Directors is of no instance. During the negotiations, he acted as agent for the hospital and any representations he made leading to reasonable inferences to be drawn by Kilpatrick would have been binding upon the hospital.

Employers should ensure that the agent they select to be responsible for hiring on their behalf has complied with all of the human rights laws which apply to the pre-employment process. The employer cannot use an employment agency to evade its legal obligations to hire fairly and impartially, without discrimination. Most human rights legislation forbids both the placing of orders with employment agencies which would contravene such legislation, and the acceptance of such orders. Thus, employers must make it clear to employment agencies or headhunters, either in their contracts or in correspondence, that they expect the agency to comply with all relevant legislation, including the applicable human rights code. Human resources professionals should also know that employment agencies fall under the jurisdiction of legislation in each province which requires that they be properly licensed, that they do not act for both employer and employee (and thus that they do not charge two fees for their services) and that their fees be fixed or approved by the province. Employers might also seek to secure an indemnity for any liability or costs incurred by the employer arising out of unauthorized statements or representations on the part of the recruiter.

---

32 (1998), 36 C.C.E.L. (2d) 265 (Ont. Ct. (Gen. Div.)), at p. 269, supp. reasons 79 A.C.W.S. (3d) 685 (Ont. Ct. (Gen. Div.)), revd on other grounds 174 D.L.R. (4th) 435 (Ont. C.A.).

Part 2

The Engagement

INTRODUCTION

Having reached this stage in the employment relationship, the employer has chosen an employment candidate and is prepared to offer this individual a position within the employer's organization. At this point, there are many considerations for the employer. The employer needs to be aware of the potential minefields when offering the position to the individual. The employer and employee will also want to take some time to consider the manner in which they wish to establish the employment relationship, whether it will be a true "employment" relationship or whether another alternative is more suitable, such as an independent contracting or partnership relationship. Finally, before the employee commences work, the employer should seriously consider affirming the terms of employment in an employment contract. Such a document need not be complex but may serve to reinforce some of the more important aspects of the employment relationship which is to follow.

HIRING

Potential Minefields in the Hiring Process

After the conclusion of the recruitment or courting phase of the employment relationship, the employer usually reaches a point where it has identified a suitable candidate and is ready to offer this individual a position within the employer's organization. There are a number of potential minefields which an employer should seek to avoid when engaging in the actual hiring of an employee.

Inducing Breach of Contract

If the candidate is offered a position by the employer and, in order to accept that position, the individual breaks an existing employment contract with his or her current employer, this former employer may not only have a potential claim against its former employee for breach of contract, but it may also have a claim against the new employer, based upon the tort of inducing breach of contract.

In order to make a successful claim of inducing breach of contract against the employee's current employer, the former employer would have to show that:

1. A valid contract existed between itself and the employee.
2. The current employer knew of the existence of this contract.
3. The current employer intended to wrongfully procure a breach of this contract.
4. Such a breach was in fact procured.
5. The former employer suffered damage as a result of this contract breach.[1]

This is not a particularly easy test to meet; the former employer will be required to show that the current employer acted fraudulently or in bad faith in inducing the contract breach. The current employer will have a valid defence against the claim if it can show that, in offering employment to the candidate, it acted *bona fide* and in the best interests of the company. If an individual officer, director or employee of the company is the target of the claim, it will also be necessary for that individual to show that he or she acted within the exercise of his or her authority as a company representative.

An example of such conduct might find "Newco" recruiting and offering a position to "Pat". Pat is the best salesperson at "Oldco", and Oldco is in direct competition with Newco. If Pat were to accept the position with Newco, and Oldco is able to demonstrate that Pat was hired not for the good of Newco, but rather for the specific reason of causing harm to Oldco and eliminating it as a competitor, Oldco might be able to sustain a claim of inducing breach of contract against Newco.

A similar situation arose in the Manitoba Court of Appeal case, *Neal Bros. v. Wright*.[2] In that case, the former employer, Neal Bros., sued Wright, an ex-employee who had left Neal Bros. to start his own competitive enterprise. Neal Bros. alleged that Wright had induced breaches of the employment contracts between Neal Bros. and two of its salespersons after Wright hired these two employees for the new operation. The Court found in favour of Neal Bros. and held that the two salespersons would probably not have left Neal Bros. were it

---

1   *Butler v. Dimitrieff* (1991), 38 C.C.E.L. 139 (Ont. Ct. (Gen. Div.)), revd 49 A.C.W.S. (3d) 1177 (Ont. C.A.). This case was overturned on appeal, on the basis that the facts did not support a finding of liability for inducing breach of contract. See also *McFadden v. 481782 Ontario Ltd.* (1984), 5 C.C.E.L. 83 (Ont. H.C.J.).

2   [1923] 4 D.L.R. 998 (Man. C.A.). See also *Ernst & Young v. Stuart* (1997), 144 D.L.R. (4th) 328 (B.C.C.A.), where the accounting firm Arthur Andersen & Co. was found liable for inducing breach of contract when an Ernst & Young partner left to join Arthur Andersen. The trial judge found that Arthur Andersen knew that the partner was required to provide notice to Ernst & Young pursuant to contract and that he had not done so, and found this to be a wrongful interference with contractual relations. The Court of Appeal did not disturb this finding, and damages were assessed against Arthur Andersen in the amount of $75,000.

not for the inducement of Wright. The effect of these salespersons going to join a competitor resulted in damage to Neal Bros., and the Court awarded $2,500 to compensate for this damage.

If the candidate is currently employed elsewhere, it may be wise for the employer to inquire as to whether the employee is currently operating under an employment contract with the other employer. This may serve to alert the employer to a potential claim against it for inducing breach of contract, if the employer proceeds to offer the individual a position. However, the employer may also intentionally refrain from making such inquiries in order to avoid satisfying the condition which requires that the current employer have actual knowledge of the existence of a contract between the former employer and the employee. Generally speaking, in those circumstances where an employer makes a legitimate offer of employment to an individual based on the individual's suitability for the position, and this decision is made for the good of the company, it will be difficult for a former employer to prove the *mala fides* or intent necessary to make a successful claim for inducing breach of contract. Cautious employers can attempt to avoid any potential liability for inducing breach of contract by including in the employee's contract or the offer letter a sentence or paragraph clearly stating that the employee was not induced to enter into employment with the current employer. Obviously, such a statement will be of little value to the employer if the employee was clearly induced but, in a less clear case, such a statement can suggest that the employer did not intend to induce.

Enforceability of Restrictive Covenants and Employment Contracts

If the potential candidate is currently employed elsewhere and the employer does choose to engage the candidate in a discussion of his or her current employment contract, the employer may wish to examine any restrictive covenants within the terms of the employee's existing contract. This will be particularly important if the employer acts in competition with the individual's current employer and if there is a concern that the individual might somehow be restricted in the performance of employment duties with the new employer.

It is not uncommon for written employment contracts to contain restrictions on competition, solicitation of employees or customers, or the use of confidential information. This is particularly the case within sensitive industries, such as those in which trade secrets and confidential information are highly proprietary, or where the employer's business is largely dependent upon customer contacts or highly skilled employees. An employer considering hiring a certain individual may be particularly concerned about whether the individual's ability to perform the employment duties might be restricted by the individual's existing employment contract. For example, the individual may have signed a contract with his or her current employer agreeing that he or she would not enter into competitive employment for some period of time after the end of the employment relationship, or the individual may have agreed that he or she would not take any of the employer's customers or any fellow employees if leaving to pursue other employment. Depending upon the reasons for choosing the candidate in question, the existence of any of these types of restrictions may be of paramount concern to the employer offering the position.

Even if the employee's current employment contract contains such restrictions, it is not necessarily the case that the restrictions will be enforceable, such that the employee would be liable for breaching them. Generally speaking, any covenant which constitutes a restraint on trade is unenforceable.[3] However, such restrictive covenants in employment contracts may be found to be enforceable if they are reasonable in the circumstances. If the restrictive covenant does more than protect the employer's legitimate proprietary interests and, in so doing, unduly restrains the employee's ability to engage in the free trade of his or her employment services, then the covenant will likely be held to be unenforceable. In general, a court considering enforceability will examine the legitimate interest being protected, the scope of the protection, and the duration and geographic extent of the restriction.[4] If the court finds that the employer has gone beyond the bounds required to protect its proprietary rights, any such restrictions will be held to be unenforceable.

An employer who considers offering a position to a candidate will want to be aware of any restrictions which may currently hinder the employee's ability to perform the responsibilities of the position being offered. If the candidate is subject to restrictions which will limit his or her ability to perform, the new employer may wish to seek legal advice to determine whether the employee will be liable for breaching the restrictive covenants contained within the employee's current employment contract. Such a legal opinion will assess the likelihood that a court would find the restrictive covenants in question to be enforceable. Despite a legal opinion which states that such restrictions will likely be unenforceable, an employee who is subject to such restrictions may not be willing to join the new employer in breach of the contract without the new employer agreeing to assume any liability to which the employee may be subject if he or she is sued for breach of contract. Depending upon the value of the employee and the likelihood of a lawsuit, providing such indemnification may be used as a bargaining chip in the negotiation of an employment contract. However, employers who do not wish to incur this liability may also attempt to negate this possibility by including in the employee's contract a clause which states that the employer will not be subject to any restrictive covenants which may bind the employee and will not be liable for any damages resulting from the employee's breach of such restrictive covenants.

---

3   See the discussion under the heading "Restrictive Covenants" in Part 5, "The Divorce".
4   See the commentary under the heading "Determining the Reasonableness of a Restrictive Convenant" in Part 5, "The Divorce", for a comprehensive description of these factors.

Negligent Misrepresentation

Employers offering a position to a candidate for employment should be wary of misstating the conditions of employment to make the position appear more enticing. As the Supreme Court of Canada held in the case of *Queen v. Cognos Inc.*,[5] so long as the following elements of a negligent misrepresentation claim are present, a plaintiff will be successful in such a case:

1. There must exist a "special relationship" between the parties resulting in a duty of care.
2. The representation made must be untrue, inaccurate or misleading.
3. The misrepresentation must be made negligently.
4. The negligent misrepresentation must be relied upon.
5. The party relying upon the negligent misrepresentation must suffer some damage.

In the case of *Lewis v. Coles*,[6] Mr. Lewis was employed in a long-term position in Ontario, earning in excess of $50,000, when his friend, Mr. Coles, offered him a job as a business manager in British Columbia. The position involved selling products such as undercoating, insurance and financing to purchasers of motor vehicles, and the income was based solely on commission. Mr. Lewis took the position only after he was assured by Mr. Coles that he would earn no less than $50,000. The Lewis family moved to British Columbia. Unfortunately, Mr. Lewis was only able to earn half of what he had been promised. After six months, he returned to Ontario with his family and sued Mr. Coles for negligent misrepresentation.

Mr. Justice Josephson held that all of the *Queen* requirements for negligent misrepresentation had been met in this case. There was a special relationship giving rise to a duty of care in that Mr. Coles was offering Mr. Lewis a position with his company in a field where Mr. Coles had special expertise and knowledge. The representation made to Mr. Lewis with respect to the potential income of the position was untrue and was made negligently. Mr. Lewis relied upon this misrepresentation in accepting the position and moving to British Columbia. However, it was also held that Mr. Coles was only liable to Mr. Lewis for 30% of his damages, as Mr. Lewis should have taken steps to check the information

---

5   (1993), 99 D.L.R. (4th) 626 (S.C.C.). See also under the heading "Negligent Misrepresentation" in Part 5, "The Divorce", for a discussion of the tort of negligent misrepresentation.

6   (1992), 47 C.C.E.L. 302 (B.C.S.C.). See also *Lenarduzzi v. P.B.N. Publishing Ltd.* (1995), 9 C.C.E.L. (2d) 238 (Ont. Ct. (Gen. Div.)), where it was held that the defendant employer was liable for negligent misrepresentation after having offered the plaintiffs substantially higher earnings than what was paid in their current positions, and having made promises of stable employment. The representations turned out to be untrue when the plaintiffs were all dismissed within one month. Justice Jenkins awarded the plaintiffs, in addition to damages for wrongful dismissal, an amount of $25,000 each to compensate for the negligent misrepresentation.

being provided to him by Mr. Coles. In this case, Mr. Lewis was seen to have contributed to the negligence.

To minimize liability for negligent misrepresentation, employers should pay particular attention to the individuals with whom an employment candidate comes into contact during the hiring process, and such individuals should be instructed regarding restrictions on what they should be representing to the employment candidate. Obviously, the fewer interviews, and the fewer company representatives involved in the recruitment process, the less likely it will be that the employer will lose control of representations made to a candidate. However, establishing such limitations is often impractical.

Anticipatory Breach

Anticipatory breach occurs when a party repudiates its contractual obligations before they fall due. This can be done either through express language or conduct, or as a matter of implication from what the party has said or done. Both employers and employees can be liable for anticipatory breach of contract, although this is more common for employers as it is often their company plans which change and eliminate job opportunities. For example, if an employer hires an employee from out of town to join the employer's organization, and the employer communicates to the employee, before he or she begins work, that the position is no longer available, the employee may be entitled to sue for anticipatory breach of contract. The employee would need to show that an offer was made and accepted. If the employer demonstrated conduct which amounted to a total rejection of the employment contract, and there was lack of justification for such conduct, the employee might succeed in a claim for damages. Whatever the employer does must make it clear that the employer no longer intends to be bound by the provisions of the contract which it entered into with the employee.

If the employee believes that the employer has communicated that it no longer intends to be bound by the employment contract, the employee should clearly indicate to the employer that he or she has "accepted" the employer's conduct as repudiation of the employment contract before making alternate arrangements. If the employee were to assume that the employer intended to breach the employment contract, and went on to find other employment, the employer might later sue the employee for breach of the employment contract if the employer was subsequently in a position to fulfil the terms of the contract. By "accepting" the repudiation, the employee avoids any future obligations that he or she may have pursuant to the contract and may be in a position to sue for damages if the employee has suffered as a result of the anticipatory breach of contract.

If the employer can justify the repudiation of the employment contract, then this may serve as a defence to the claim of anticipatory breach of contract. For example, if the employee was hired to act as manager of a bank, and is charged and convicted of misappropriation of funds prior to commencing employment, the employer may be able to prove that there was cause for breach of the employment contract yet to be performed.

In the case of *Levi v. Chartersoft Canada Inc.*,[7] Mr. Levi was offered the position of marketing and sales manager for Chartersoft by Mr. Lee, the company's president. Mr. Lee was anxious to find someone for this position because he was planning to market a computer graphics software package which the company had recently developed. Mr. Levi was securely employed elsewhere when he accepted the position with Chartersoft. After the employment contract was signed, but before Mr. Levi started work, Mr. Lee decided that Mr. Levi did not project the appropriate image for this product, given the inappropriate manner in which he acted and dressed. The day before Mr. Levi was to start work, Mr. Lee told him that there was no job available for him. The trial judge held that the company had made serious errors in its hiring of Mr. Levi. The company should have taken more time to ensure that Mr. Levi was the right person for the job before requiring him to leave his secure employment. The contract entered into was for a fixed term of one year. Mr. Levi was awarded damages in the amount of one year's salary.

It is important for employers to be aware of the potential for a claim of anticipatory breach of contract lest employers assume that, simply because the employment engagement has not yet started, the employer has no obligations to the employee. If there exists the possibility that the employer may not be able to offer the employee secure employment, the employer may wish to offer a position on a conditional basis. This way the employer will be protected in the event that the employment opportunity does not materialize and will avoid what might otherwise be liability for anticipatory breach of contract.

Inducement

Employers are potentially exposed to risk when they try to recruit an employee away from secure employment elsewhere. If the employee is ultimately hired and goes on to have a somewhat lengthy career with the employer, the application of the doctrine of "inducement" will diminish as time passes. However, if the employee is lured away from secure employment elsewhere and is led to believe that he or she will be engaging in lengthy employment but is then abruptly dismissed without cause, the employer may not be entitled to rely on the employee's short period of service to justify a minimal severance package.

An employee in such a situation will be entitled to reasonable notice of the dismissal or pay in lieu thereof.[8] The appropriate period of reasonable notice is always dependent to some degree on the employee's length of service. However, where the employee has been lured away from secure employment elsewhere,

7 (1994), 8 C.C.E.L. (2d) 10 (Man. Q.B.).
8 See under the heading "Reasonable Notice" in Part 5, "The Divorce".

some courts will not necessarily adopt the employer's argument that the employee's length of service is minimal. If the court accepts that, were it not for the inducement of the employer, the employee would likely still have his or her secure employment elsewhere, it may also be inclined to recognize or give credit for the employee's former service when determining the appropriate reasonable notice period. This can have serious legal implications where an employer finds itself liable for substantial damages for an employee of very short service.

Employers wishing to avoid the possibility of being liable for such damages awards should address the issue of inducement and length of service at the commencement of the employment relationship. Employers can try to negotiate a contractual provision indicating that the employee's prior service will specifically not be recognized. The employer may try to draw attention away from this as a term of the contract by merely stating it within the offer letter. Naturally, the employee will oppose having no recognition of former service. If the employer is particularly interested in this employee, then the parties may ultimately have to reach a consensus as to how the issue will be handled. A possible solution might have the parties agreeing to fixed notice periods in the event of dismissal of the employee, with the chosen notice period being a compromise in terms of the amount of former service that it represents.

Use of Headhunters

Many employers use headhunters when doing their recruiting, and such employers are often not aware that, even if it is the headhunter who does the recruiting on the employer's behalf, inducement may still be an issue if the employee is dismissed shortly after having been hired. The fact that the headhunter did the recruiting does not relieve the employer of its potential liability in the area of inducement.

Similarly, if the headhunter makes any misrepresentations on the employer's behalf during the recruitment process, the employer may still be liable for negligent misrepresentation even though it did not actually make the misrepresentations. In such circumstances, a court will view the misrepresentations of the headhunter to be the misrepresentations of the employer.

Employers need to be aware of their potential liability for the actions of the headhunters they hire, so that they can be diligent when giving instructions to such headhunters. Particularly prudent employers may wish to enter into contracts with their headhunters which specifically set the boundaries of what the headhunters can say and do within the recruitment process, and will perhaps even go so far as to transfer to the headhunter, in the form of an indemnity, responsibility for any liability arising out of the recruitment. With such a contract in place, the employer will be in a much better position if the employee ultimately sues because the headhunter can then be sued for breach of contract.

DEFINING THE EMPLOYMENT RELATIONSHIP

Types of Employees

One of the threshold issues in employment law relates to whether an individual is considered to be an "employee". Employees may be entitled to sue for wrongful dismissal and may also have available to them many of the rights and remedies discussed elsewhere in this book. Many individuals may not technically be employees because of the nature of their particular employment relationship. Aside from these individuals, most other potential employees have the option of entering into an employment relationship or entering into an independent contracting relationship. Independent contractors are becoming more and more popular in today's markets, with individuals enjoying the flexibility which contracting has to offer and employers enjoying the simplicity and the minimized obligations, both financial and legal. Subject to any existing contractual provisions, an employee will generally have more and broader legal rights and remedies than an independent contractor.

Independent Contractors

An employer-employee relationship is distinct from that of principal and independent contractor. It is the individual who must establish that he or she is an "employee". The issue of whether a person is an independent contractor or an employee will be determined largely on the basis of the facts of each case. It will be necessary for a court to determine whether a particular individual is an "employee" for the purpose of sustaining a wrongful dismissal action. There are various factors which a court will consider in this regard. However, it may also be necessary for an individual to prove that he or she is an employee and not an independent contractor for the purpose of taking advantage of the remedies available pursuant to various statutes, such as employment standards and human rights legislation. Generally speaking, such statutes will contain a definition of "employee" which must first be examined to see whether the individual qualifies. In addition, referees and boards of inquiry considering statutory breaches will often adopt the common law tests and consider the factors relevant to whether or not there is an employment relationship.

There are many factors which might suggest an employment relationship over that of an independent contracting relationship, and many of these relate to the employment relationship tests. However, specifically in relation to independent contractors, courts will often be inclined to view the relationship as one of principal and independent contractor where the individual sets the hours, maintains control over the work done, provides his or her own tools and equipment, is subject to minimal company supervision and has the ability to perform work for other employers so long as it does not interfere with the existing contract with the employer.

Employers often believe that they can control whether certain individuals will be viewed as employees or independent contractors simply by making an explicit recital, within the written contract entered into, that the individual is either one or the other. This is not a foolproof method. When faced with such contractual provisions, courts and other authorities will rarely rely on them as proof of either the existence or absence of an employment relationship. More often than not, a court will view the recital as proof of the relationship which the parties intended to enter into, but will then go on to consider whether the parties did in fact enter into such a relationship. Similarly, the fact that individuals have incorporated themselves or declared themselves to be self-employed for tax purposes is not determinative of their legal status as an independent contractor. It will simply be yet another factor to be considered by a court in its ultimate determination.

Employers should pay particular attention to the way in which their employment relationships are structured, particularly if they intend to rely on their classification of certain individuals as independent contractors for the purpose of relieving themselves of certain statutory obligations. For example, employers are required to deduct income taxes, employment insurance and Canada Pension Plan premiums from employees' salaries. They also have obligations pursuant to employment standards legislation to pay overtime and vacation pay. If the employer has structured its relationships to avoid these obligations, the employer must be careful to ensure that this is done in an effective manner, or it may later be liable for any deductions or payments not made pursuant to statute if the government authority subsequently disagrees with the employer's position. Employers considering such schemes should consult their legal counsel for the purpose of obtaining a legal opinion or perhaps seeking advance rulings from the relevant government authority.[9]

Dependent Contractors

Increasingly, the courts have also recognized an intermediate class of contractors. While such contractors may not be considered employees, neither can they truly be considered "independent" contractors. The status of their relationship with the employer is sufficiently durable and close to that of an employee that the courts have found such individuals to be entitled to reasonable notice. Factors

---

9   For a more comprehensive discussion of the specific factors that the Canada Customs and Revenue Agency (formerly Revenue Canada), a court, or some other regulatory body might consider in determining whether an individual is an employee or an independent contractor, reference can be made to a pamphlet published by Canada Customs and Revenue Agency, entitled *Employee or Self-Employed?* (Ottawa: October 1998; updated February 4, 2002) (available on-line at www.ccra-adrc.gc.ca).

which have been considered relevant to the finding of such "dependent" contractors include the individual's length of service, the type of restrictions imposed against acting for competitors, the degree of exclusivity, and the time and resources the individual has devoted to the company. In other words, the courts tend to look for indications of a relationship of a more permanent nature.

For example, in *Aqwa v. Centennial Home Renovations Ltd.*,[10] the plaintiff was an "independent sales agent", with a written agreement with the defendant employer which allowed either party to terminate the contractual relationship at any time without notice. When the employer did abruptly terminate the contract after approximately one year and a half, the plaintiff sued, claiming damages for wrongful dismissal or, in the alternative, damages for breach of contract.

The trial judge noted that a traditional employer/employee relationship did not exist in this case, but that what did exist was "a modern-day emerging relationship which is more closely allied to the employment relationship than it is to the traditional independent contractor relationship".[11] Although the plaintiff had declared himself, for tax purposes, to be self-employed, and his income was totally dependent upon his efforts, the Court examined many other factors akin to those present in a traditional employment relationship, such as the fact that the plaintiff was trained by the employer, was "urged" to attend employer sales meetings, and was required to follow the employer's procedures as set out in a company manual. As such, this was held to be an appropriate case in which to imply a contractual provision requiring the employer to provide the plaintiff with reasonable notice of the termination of the contract. The trial judge did note, however, that the amount of pay in lieu of notice to be awarded was to reflect the fact that the parties had agreed to establish an independent contractor relationship from the outset, and therefore an award that would otherwise be provided to a wrongfully dismissed employee in the circumstances would be too high. The plaintiff was ultimately awarded five times the average monthly commissions he earned.

Agents

Generally, agents are not considered to be employees, but rather independent contractors, and thus are not entitled to reasonable notice. At first glance, this distinction may appear straightforward; however, making this distinction in practice may prove to be rather difficult. For example, the particular job title does not necessarily resolve the issue. Courts have been divided as to whether insurance

---

10 (2001), 12 C.C.E.L. (3d) 97 (Ont. S.C.J.).
11 *Supra*, at para. 14.

or real estate "agents" should be considered "employees" or "agents" at law.[12] Factors which weigh in favour of an individual being treated as an agent include remuneration on the basis of commission, a lack of entitlement to receive fringe benefits, and the opportunity to work with other businesses. In contrast, where an individual is prohibited from acting for competitors, a court may find that the individual is an employee because he or she falls under the employer's control. Put another way, the distinction between an agent and an employee often turns on the extent to which the individual has committed to devoting his or her full attention and service to the employer and has forsaken all other means of compensation.

Directors

The law is clear that a director is not a servant of a corporation, and thus not an employee. As a result, in most cases, a director is not entitled to be given reasonable notice of his or her dismissal from the position. However, if the director also acts as an employee, the individual may still be entitled to reasonable notice with respect to his or her other position within the company. Where the director holds other positions which are part of the duties of a director (such as chairperson or chief executive officer), so long as no contract of employment can be established, the director would still not be entitled to reasonable notice of dismissal.

Shareholders

The fact that a dismissed employee is also a major shareholder of the company is of no consequence to the individual's entitlement to reasonable notice of dismissal. The individual will still be entitled to the rights and remedies open to dismissed employees.

Partners

A partnership is defined as two or more persons who have entered into a business agreement in common with a view to profit. A person forming part of a partnership cannot be said to be an employee of the partnership. Where it becomes less clear as to whether an individual has a right to reasonable notice of dismissal is in a situation where two parties have entered into business together but have never classified the venture as a partnership *per se*. If one individual then takes

---

12 It was held in *Re/Max Ontario-Atlantic Canada Inc. v. Registrar of Real Estate & Business Brokers* (1986), 33 D.L.R. (4th) 125 (Ont. H.C.J.), affd 55 D.L.R. (4th) 320n (Ont. C.A.), that real estate "salesmen" could be employed as independent contractors, while in *Jaremko v. A.E. LePage Real Estate Services Ltd.* (1989), 60 D.L.R. (4th) 762 (Ont. C.A.), affg 39 D.L.R. (4th) 252 (Ont. H.C.J.), a real estate salesperson was held to be an employee.

control of the finances, and pays a salary to the other while merely drawing from the company funds for himself or herself, this may be viewed as an employment relationship as opposed to a partnership. Ultimately, when determining the type of relationship between the parties, the court will look closely at the nature of the relationship, the provisions of the partnership agreement and the intention of the parties. This issue can also arise in the context of profit sharing arrangements. There is a presumption at law that profit sharing arrangements are indicative of partnerships. However, a court will base its ultimate decision on the intent of the parties.[13]

Joint Venturers

A joint venture is a one-time business arrangement between two or more persons with a view to profit. As in the case of partnerships, where the venture is entered into by two individuals who plan to share equally in the profit of the venture, this will not be viewed as an employment relationship. However, there may be situations where one individual involved in the venture plays a role more akin to that of an employee and is involved in the venture on a day-to-day basis, performing regular duties. Even if the individual can be considered to be an employee, it is possible that the joint venture contract contemplates the dismissal of such individual. In such instances, the individual may still not be entitled to a common law reasonable notice period.

Ministers

Traditionally, church ministers have not been considered employees of their given churches, nor of the broader administrative authority of the denomination. The relationship between the minister and his or her organization has been considered to be one of a clerical or ecclesiastical nature, with a spiritual essence, and is not intended to create an employment relationship.[14] However, there have also been cases where the courts have been able to find a basis upon which to award such individuals damages for wrongful dismissal. In one case, a United Church minister successfully sued for wrongful dismissal, and at trial it was held that:

> ... an ordained minister of the defendant church is dependent upon the defendant church for his position, and I believe that he or she is to be considered an employee

---

13 Individuals who believe that they may already be partners, or who are in the process of establishing a partnership, should pay particular attention to the specific partnership legislation which exists in their jurisdiction. This legislation will define a partnership and, if it applies to the parties' relationship, will set out a regulatory scheme of which the parties should be aware.

14 *Lewery v. Salvation Army in Canada* (1993), 104 D.L.R. (4th) 449 (N.B.C.A.), leave to appeal to S.C.C. refused 107 D.L.R. (4th) vii.

for purposes of determining whether the employment has been wrongfully terminated.

The plaintiff was discharged by the defendant church in a manner which did not
conform to the [church's published] Manual. I think the Manual, for this purpose at
least, can be considered as being analogous to a form of contract of employment
governing the relationship of an employee and an employer.[15]

Mr. Justice Carruthers found that the minister was an employee of the church and
was entitled to reasonable notice of his dismissal on that basis. On appeal,
however, the case was decided on its facts and not on the basis of the existence
of an employment relationship. The Court of Appeal was reluctant to hold that
there exists an employment relationship between ministers and their churches.[16]

Employee of a Not-for-Profit Corporation

Many not-for-profit organizations are under the misconception that they are
not bound by the law relating to wrongful dismissal and that they have the ability
to dismiss employees without notice. Similarly, many such organizations are of
the view that they are free from the obligations set by employment standards
legislation because of the moral importance of the work that they do. There is no
question that not-for-profit organizations are engaged in important work but there
is also little question that they are still employers and are subject to all of the
legal obligations arising as a result.

Crown Employees

Historically, Crown employees have held their positions at the "pleasure of the
Crown", meaning that the Crown has the right to dismiss its employees at will,
without notice and without any further liability. This principle has been extended
to include a broad array of Crown corporations and agents, and represents a
substantial exception to the right of employees to receive reasonable notice of
their dismissals.

Overall, the courts have been very critical of the Crown's ability to terminate
its employees at will and thus tend to look for any circumstances which would
rebut such a presumption.[17] The Crown's prerogative to dismiss without notice
can be displaced by a contract of employment which demonstrates that the
employee may have some right to notice upon termination. For example, a

---

15 *McCaw v. United Church of Canada* (1988), 51 D.L.R. (4th) 86 (Ont. H.C.J.), at p. 114, vard 82
    D.L.R. (4th) 289 (Ont. C.A.).
16 See also *David v. Congregation B'Nai Israel* (1999), 44 C.C.E.L. (2d) 302 (Ont. Ct. (Gen. Div.)),
    in which it was held that a rabbi was entitled to damages for wrongful dismissal equivalent to 30
    months' reasonable notice when his contract with the synagogue was found to be unenforceable.
17 See *Nicholson v. Haldimand-Norfolk (Region) Board of Police Commissioners* (1978), 88 D.L.R.
    (3d) 671 (S.C.C.), and *Molloy v. Ontario (Human Rights Commission)* (1992), 41 C.C.E.L. 101
    (Ont. Ct. (Gen. Div.)).

contract which provided that the employee could not be fired on the basis of illness was held by the British Columbia Supreme Court to be sufficient evidence that the employer had waived its right to terminate at will.[18] Furthermore, when the Crown enters into a collective agreement with a union, it loses its right to terminate at will. Federal and provincial statutes governing public employees may also restrict the scope of the common law rule.

In the case of *Wells v. Newfoundland*,[19] a commissioner for the Newfoundland Public Utilities Board had his position eliminated by statute due to a decrease in workload for the board. Mr. Wells was not offered a position with the new board constituted pursuant to the statute, and was not offered any compensation. He sued for wrongful dismissal. The Supreme Court of Canada was asked to consider whether Mr. Wells could be entitled to pay in lieu of notice of dismissal in light of the fact that he was a servant of the Crown.

The Supreme Court held that Mr. Wells had an employment contract with the Crown, and that it was a term of that contract that he would serve until the age of 70, subject to good behaviour. Since no misbehaviour was alleged, the Court held that the government was in breach of the contract and that Mr. Wells was, therefore, entitled to damages. This would have been the case if Mr. Wells had been employed in the private sector, and it was held that, as an employee of the Crown, his status should be no different. The Court identified the difficulty in reconciling the old approach that such employees were subject to the feudal conditions of serving at the pleasure of the Crown, with the modern environment of mutual contractual obligation. Justice Major wrote:

> ... it is time to remove uncertainty and confirm that the law regarding senior civil servants accords with the contemporary understanding of the state's role and obligations in its dealings with employees. Employment in the civil service is not feudal servitude. [Mr. Wells'] position was not a form of monarchical patronage. He was employed to carry out an important function on behalf of the citizens of Newfoundland. The government offered him the position, terms were negotiated, and an agreement reached. It was a contract.[20]

Based on the foregoing, Mr. Wells was awarded damages to compensate him for his loss as a result of the breach of contract on the part of the government.

Testing for an Employment Relationship

The existence of an employment relationship can be a very important determination for an employee seeking to establish an employer's liability for wrongful dismissal. Likewise, an employer may wish to avoid liability for wrongful dismissal, or other obligations which it might have to individuals classified as

---

18   *McLean v. Vancouver Harbour Commissioners*, [1936] 3 W.W.R. 657 (B.C.S.C.).

19   (1999), 46 C.C.E.L. (2d) 165 (S.C.C.).

20   *Supra*, at p. 178.

employees, and will attempt to do so by establishing that the relationship between the parties is other than an employer-employee relationship. This issue cannot be determined merely according to the individual's or the employer's perception. Nor can such a determination be made on the basis of the existence of a contract or job description which refers to the individual as an employee. Rather, this question involves a complex series of tests which have been developed by the courts over time.

These tests are meant to assist in the determination of whether an individual is an employee, and thus whether he or she can sue for wrongful dismissal. They were designed to facilitate a court's analysis of the essence of the relationship between the parties. The principle tests are:

- (a) the control test;
- (b) the fourfold test;
- (c) the "organization" test; and
- (d) the permanency test.

Courts have also developed an alternate test which involves an application of many of the factors used in each of the other four tests.

The Control Test

This test was the first to be developed and was based on the traditional view that the employment relationship has four significant factors:

- (1) the employer's authority to select an individual for employment;
- (2) the employer's ability to determine the means of payment (wages or other remuneration);
- (3) the employer's control and direction over the employee with respect to the type, manner and timing of work; and
- (4) the employer's right to discipline the employee.

The control test developed by virtue of the assessment that, of the enumerated factors, the employer's ability to control the employee's work is the most important. The theory is that the less control the employer has over the individual's work and how it is to be done, the less likely it is than an employment relationship will be found.

For example, if an individual hired to work for the employer is also able to work for other establishments and has no quotas or set working hours, it is unlikely that an employment relationship would be found to exist on an application of the control test. In contrast, a television advertising salesman who was eventually paid only by commission was nevertheless held to be an employee because he was still subject to the close direction, control and supervision of the employer television station and was required to make a daily written report of his

activities.[21] In a similar situation, involving a sales representative who was paid
only by commission, with daily tasks and direction given by the company as to
where and to whom to sell, the Court found that the salesman was an employee
even though the employer had always considered him to be an independent
contractor.[22]

Where the employer maintains control over the employee, the type of remuneration the employee receives, whether it be by piecework, by commission, from a
third party or paid out to a third party, will not, generally speaking, significantly
affect the presumption that the individual is an employee. It should also be
noted that, in the case of professional or highly skilled employees, control is an
insufficient indicator of employment status, given that many such individuals are
not subject to significant supervision due to the specialized nature of their training
or the independent nature of their responsibilities.

The Fourfold Test

As in the case of professional employees, it soon became apparent that the
control test was not always sufficient to determine an employment relationship.
The fourfold test was developed as a result of the inability of the control test to
make a proper characterization in all cases. The fourfold test involves the measure
of the following four factors, of which control is one:

(1) control (the greater degree of control the employer exercises over the
work performed, the more suggestive of an employment relationship);

(2) ownership of tools (in an employment relationship, the employer generally supplies the equipment and tools required to perform the work);

(3) chance of profit (the greater the degree to which the employer controls
the amount earned by the individual, the more this suggests an employment relationship); and

(4) risk of loss (where the employer assumes all or most of the risk of loss,
such as in a case where an individual assumes no financial risk and is
paid for services regardless of the financial health of the business, this is
suggestive of an employment relationship).

This test is said to be driven by the overall question: "Whose business is it?" The
greater detail required by this test assists in determining whether the individual is
working for himself or herself or is simply engaged in service for the employer.

In the oft-cited case of *Montreal v. Montreal Locomotive Works Ltd.*,[23] the
question was whether the defendant company was in occupation of certain premises so as to be taxable in the material periods. That issue depended on whether,

---

21 *Goldberg v. Western Approaches Ltd.* (1985), 7 C.C.E.L. 127 (B.C.S.C.).

22 *Mayer v. J. Conrad Lavigne Ltd.* (1979), 105 D.L.R. (3d) 734 (Ont. C.A.).

23 [1947] 1 D.L.R. 161 (P.C.).

during these periods, the company was operating merely as a manager or agent of the government, or whether it was carrying on business on its own behalf as a principal. This was not an employment law case, but the Privy Council relied on the tests established at common law for determining whether individuals are employees. The Privy Council noted that, in earlier cases, a single test, such as the presence or absence of control, was often relied on to determine whether the situation was one of master and servant. However, it was held that control in itself is not always conclusive and, in more complex conditions of modern industry, more complicated tests often have to be applied. Therefore, the fourfold test was proposed and applied and has since been referred to over the following half-century of jurisprudence in this area of the law.

The "Organization" Test

The "organization" test, also known as the economic dependency test or the integration test, adds yet another factor to be considered by the courts when determining whether an employment relationship exists. This test endeavours to determine whether the person's work is an integral part of the business or merely accessory to the business. Generally, this test is viewed as another factor to determine the issue of employment status, together with the control test and the other factors set out in the fourfold test.

When applying this test, the court examines the degree to which the worker is integrated into the company's activities. For instance, if the individual's duties and efforts are a vital part of the business, or if the individual is economically dependent on one establishment, then it is more likely that the individual will be viewed as an employee rather than as a self-employed person.

For example, a doctor who practised his specialty from a hospital was given support staff, office space and a fee for his administrative duties. This was his only office, and most of his compensation came from fees charged to patients. The doctor was found to be an employee of the hospital on the basis that he administered a department which was an integral part of the hospital's operations, the hospital benefited directly from his administrative duties and the staff and equipment were the property of the hospital.[24]

The organization test often appears to be somewhat of a "test of last resort" for a court wishing to interpret a particular relationship between a company and an individual as an employment relationship. Even if a court is unable to find that an individual satisfies the other tests required to be classified as an employee, it is not uncommon for the court to apply a "smell test" and to determine, on the basis of the organization test, that the individual's role was so integral that he or she must be viewed as an employee.

---

24   *Koch v. Ottawa Civic Hospital* (1979), 3 L. Med. Q. 204 (Ont. H.C.J.).

The Permanency Test

One final factor which can be added to the list of those which a court will consider in determining whether or not a given individual is an employee is the degree to which the individual's tenure with the employer company is of a permanent nature. This test focuses on the durable nature of the relationship. Factors which may indicate a more permanent type of relationship include the fact that the individual is selected or trained, that he or she was recommended to the employer or that the individual is under continuing supervision. The application of this test would allow a person who might otherwise be viewed as an independent contractor with very long service to be classified by a court as an employee of the company.

The Combining Factors Approach

Certain more recent cases have moved away from applying any one of these tests and have endorsed instead an approach which involves applying all relevant factors, taken from any of the tests, to ultimately determine whether the individual performing services does so as a person in business for himself or herself. According to this approach, the object is to search for the total relationship as between the employer and the individual, and no one of the tests will suffice. The court will examine all possible factors, recognizing that not all will be relevant or have equal weight in every case. Certain factors are more important in certain situations.[25]

THE EMPLOYMENT CONTRACT

Written versus Unwritten Contracts

Once the employer and the prospective employee have decided to form an employment relationship, they must next ask whether they wish to have a written or an unwritten contract govern this relationship. A written contract of employment is a formal document which sets out all the terms of the parties' relationship, and may include the duties the employee is expected to perform, the benefits he or she will receive in return and the means by which the parties can end their relationship. If the parties come to an oral agreement about the employment relationship but do not set any of this down on paper, or in the event that the employment relationship develops in the absence of the parties formally considering any terms of employment, then the parties will be bound by what is

---

25 *Wiebe Door Services Ltd. v. M.N.R.*, [1986] 3 F.C. 553 (C.A.), as referred to and endorsed by the Supreme Court of Canada in *671122 Ontario Ltd. v. Sagaz Industries Canada Inc.* (2001), 204 D.L.R. (4th) 542 (S.C.C.).

known as an unwritten (or verbal) employment contract. Regardless of whether the employee and employer negotiate any of the terms of the relationship, and whether they subsequently set any agreed-to terms to paper, they may still be bound by a valid employment contract.

When disputes arise within the context of unwritten employment contracts, a court will ordinarily read in a number of implied contractual terms between the parties, based on what it believes the parties *would* have agreed to had they sat down and negotiated a written contract. Most unwritten employment contracts are seen to include an implied term that the employee will be provided with reasonable notice upon dismissal, or pay in lieu of such reasonable notice. Other terms may also be implied into the unwritten employment relationship depending upon the circumstances.

In the early part of this century, written employment contracts were quite rare, given that the balance of power between the parties more often than not favoured the employer. With the emergence of larger sports and entertainment contracts in the 1950s and 1960s, and of senior executive contracts in the 1970s and 1980s, written employment contracts have become increasingly popular. Written employment contracts have also been viewed as a way to introduce some certainty into the field of employment law, which has, in the last 20 years, been involved in much upheaval and development.

In the same way that it is often felt that discussion of a prenuptial agreement between a couple engaged to be married suggests some lack of faith in the permanency of the relationship, so too parties felt it impossible to develop a warm employment relationship in the wake of discussions of legal terms, signatures and talk about termination and severance. In recent years, however, employers and employees alike have come to realize that there are benefits to be gained by both if there exists a clear, written document which lays out in some detail the terms of their relationship. By agreeing early on as to what they can expect from each other, both employer and employee can avoid expense and uncertainty if disputes arise in the future.

Employers faced with the inconvenience of drafting an employment contract (or the possibility of retaining legal assistance for the purpose of doing so) often question whether there is anything of value to be gained by the use of written employment contracts. There is often a misconception that written employment contracts are only to be used when a very senior executive's employment is being considered. Naturally, contracts are useful in such situations, but they are equally useful in setting the parameters of the employment of lower level employees as well. If the prospect of drafting complex agreements for each and every employee, from the chief executive officer to the cleaning staff, seems overly daunting, employers should remember that written employment contracts can be as simple as an initial letter sent offering the position, setting out some of the terms, and requesting the employee's acceptance of these terms. In the case of a lower level employee, these terms might include hourly wage and hours of work, while more senior executives will require terms dealing with more comprehensive compensation schemes and performance standards.

Written employment contracts can be of great value to employers for a number of reasons. First, a written contract can provide a valuable level of security for the employer and help avoid the possibility that a court will award costly damages against the employer in the event of a wrongful dismissal action. Rather than leaving it open for a court to decide on the amount of reasonable notice to which an employee is entitled on dismissal (and having to incur substantial legal costs in representation to reach that point), the employer may insert a provision into the employment contract which sets out exactly how much money or notice the employee will receive if he or she is dismissed without cause. Employers concerned about their competitive position may also insert into the agreement a clause which guarantees that the employee will not compete with it for an agreed-upon period of time after the employee leaves the company. Employers similarly concerned about inventions, confidentiality or customer lists can establish, within their employment contracts, protection against misuse of these assets.[26] In addition, an employer may use the employment contract to outline the employee's duties and required level of performance. If the employee does not fulfil these duties or fails to meet the required standard set out in the contract, then the employer will be able to justify dismissal by arguing that the employee has breached the terms of the employment contract. In short, the written employment contract offers the employer a way to set out its expectations of the employee, to preserve its freedom to make decisions in its own best interest and to limit its costs if the relationship goes sour down the road.

Although it may appear that entering into such agreements favours the employer, there are, in fact, also substantial benefits to be gained by employees who enter into written employment contracts. In particular, by ensuring that the contract clearly sets out the employee's duties and role within the organization, employees can protect themselves from sudden changes in their employment. In the face of a negotiated term defining the employee's position, a change could be viewed as a breach of contract. In the absence of such a contractual clause, it will be up to a court to determine whether the change made to the employment relationship went to a fundamental term of the employment relationship and thus constituted constructive dismissal. For example, if an employee has accepted a job because it is in a particular geographical location, then he or she would be well-advised to include a term in the employment contract which protects the employee from geographical relocation. In the absence of such a clause, it is open for a court to hold that geographical relocation was not a fundamental term of the employment relationship and that the employee was expected to make such moves in the course of employment. Similar clauses dealing with the employee's

---

26 See under the heading "Restrictive Covenants" in Part 5, "The Divorce", for a discussion of the restrictive covenants which are used in such circumstances.

position, duties, office location, hours, remuneration and benefits can be written into the agreement and a subsequent change in any of these areas will be considered a breach of the contract entitling the employee to an award in damages.

Employment contracts can also help the employee avoid a last-minute dispute about his or her entitlement on dismissal. While such a provision has obvious benefits for the employer, the employee will also have much more leverage to negotiate a favourable severance package before the relationship begins, as goodwill is at its highest and the parties have a vested interest in coming to an agreement. Generally speaking, interrupting the honeymoon phase of the employment relationship to agree on a written contract may result in a much healthier relationship for both parties and spare them a stormy divorce.

Drafting the Contract

The sheer number of potential clauses in the regular employment contract makes it clear that, in drafting a contract, the parties should consider what it is that they want out of the particular employment relationship and then draft the contract with those goals in mind. Furthermore, both parties should give some thought to issues which may later result in disputes (such as the scheduling of vacations or the payment of bonuses), in order to ensure that both employer and employee accurately understand what is expected of them and what they may expect in return. Before drafting and signing an employment contract, there are a number of particular considerations which should be kept in mind by both employers and employees.

All contracts, including employment contracts, require three elements before they will be recognized by the courts:

(1) an offer;
(2) acceptance of the offer; and
(3) what is known as "consideration".

Offer and acceptance need not be formal and may be fulfilled by a simple conversation between the parties, but many employers will send a written offer of employment to the prospective employee and ask him or her to sign and return it. "Consideration" is not the same as what is normally understood by use of the term, but instead has a special legal meaning. Essentially, both parties must have given up something in exchange for the bargain reached. This is easily visualized in an ordinary contract for the sale of goods, where the vendor gives up the goods and the purchaser gives up the money. In the employment context, consideration typically takes the form of the promise given by the employee to work and the promise given by the employer to pay for such services.

Given this definition of "consideration", employers may run into trouble ensuring the validity of employment contracts entered into with existing employees. In certain instances, it has been held that employment contracts entered into after an employee has commenced employment may be void for lack of consideration,[27] since the parties made their promises before the employee started work and no new consideration passed to validate the contract when it was signed. This problem may be corrected if the employer provides something, such as a promotion, additional remuneration or a signing bonus, when entering into an agreement with an existing employee. However, employers should still be cautious in entering into such contracts, since such changes may still not fulfil the "consideration" requirement if they are annual pay raises or promotions which the employee can show would have been received even if the contract had not been entered into.

To further ensure that the employment contract being entered into between the parties is valid, employers should ensure that there is no evidence of unfairness or improper effort to influence the prospective employee. Courts will refuse to uphold a contract which was signed as a result of coercive pressure or undue influence by one party, though they are reluctant to do so without evidence of significant pressure.[28] The employee should be given a chance to read and understand the contract before signing it and, to this end, should also have an opportunity to seek independent legal advice concerning the contract. Employers are wise to forward a draft employment contract to the employee well in advance of the employee's first day of work, so the employee is given ample opportunity to consider the terms of the contract, seek advice, discuss with the employer potential problems and sign the contract before the employment relationship starts.

Employment contracts should be drafted in clear and unambiguous terms. Since written contracts are often drafted by employers, those responsible should be aware of a legal concept known as *contra proferentem*, which deals with situations where courts are forced to interpret contracts which are ambiguous on their face. In such situations, courts interpret any ambiguities in the contract against the drafter of the agreement. So, for example, if an employer has drafted a contractual term which is vague in that it may have two possible interpretations, a court will often accept the interpretation which is most favourable to the employee, the logic being that had the employer wanted to ensure the other interpretation it could have been more explicit in drafting the agreement.

Employers should also endeavour to keep their employment contracts up to date and in accordance with any changes made to the employment relationship. If employers allow the contracts to slide so the contracts no longer reflect the

---

27 *Francis v. Canadian Imperial Bank of Commerce* (1994), 120 D.L.R. (4th) 393 (Ont. C.A.), varg 41 C.C.E.L. 37 (Ont. Ct. (Gen. Div.)).

28 *Puiia v. Occupational Training Centre* (1983), 43 Nfld. & P.E.I.R. 283 (P.E.I.C.A.), revg 43 Nfld. & P.E.I.R. at p. 291 (P.E.I.S.C.).

employees' current working relationships, the contracts may be invalid and unenforceable.[29] Both the employer and the employee should retain a copy of any executed employment contract.

Finally, employers drafting employment contracts must turn their attention to several statutes. First, if the parties intend to include in the contract a clause providing for notice or pay in lieu of notice of dismissal, the termination provisions of the relevant employment standards legislation must be considered. Employers must ensure that, when determining the amount of notice or pay to which an employee will be entitled upon dismissal, the employee is provided with at least as much notice as, or more notice than, that required by the legislation. The Supreme Court of Canada, in *Machtinger v. HOJ Industries Ltd.*,[30] held that the employer could not evade the minimum notice requirement under the legislation by contracting out of it. Moreover, as an incentive for employers to contract for at least the minimum reasonable notice period required under the statute, the Court held that the employees were entitled not to the mere statutory minimum notice pay in such a case, but rather to the common law reasonable notice period. In this case, the two employees in question were awarded seven and seven and a half months' notice respectively instead of the four weeks to which they were entitled under the legislation.

Employers who make regular use of employment contracts should be particularly aware of the minimum notice requirement in their contractual termination provisions. One problem which often arises is that employers provide the minimum notice required by statute for the employee in the first year of service and subsequently forget to update the notice provision after the minimum amount has changed due to the employee's increasing years of service. Employers should either ensure that contracts are updated regularly in this regard, or they may wish to consider including some type of sliding scale in their notice provisions, thereby providing for an increased period of notice in relation to the employee's increased period of service.

In addition, when drafting employment contracts, employers should consider the relevant provincial statute of frauds or similar legislation. For example, according to Ontario legislation,[31] fixed term contracts which relate to a period in excess of nine years may be invalid.[32] The Ontario statute has no application to contracts of indefinite hire, as it contemplates only those agreements which are of a fixed term.

A short note or a letter of hire which is agreed to by the employee may constitute a valid employment contract. Employers drafting their own contracts

---

29 *Wallace v. Toronto-Dominion Bank* (1983), 145 D.L.R. (3d) 431 (Ont. C.A.), leave to appeal to S.C.C. refused 52 N.R. 157n; *Allison v. Amoco Production Co.* (1975), 58 D.L.R. (3d) 233 (Alta. S.C.); *Nardocchio v. Canadian Imperial Bank of Commerce* (1979), 41 N.S.R. (2d) 26 (S.C.).
30 (1992), 91 D.L.R. (4th) 491 (S.C.C.), revg 55 D.L.R. (4th) 401 (Ont. C.A.).
31 *Employers and Employees Act*, R.S.O. 1990, c. E.12 (no amendments), s. 2.
32 *Horton v. Rio Algom Ltd.* (1995), 9 C.C.E.L. (2d) 180 (Ont. Ct. (Gen. Div.)).

should ensure that these agreements contain the following minimum requirements:

- the names of the parties to the employment agreement;
- the date on which the contract begins;
- the position which the employee will assume and a description of his or her duties if necessary to define the position;
- the duration of the employment contract; and
- some indication that consideration was given, whether expressly or by implication.

Though following all this advice may seem unnecessarily inconvenient, there are advantages, especially if the parties have negotiated a strong employment contract. In *Wallace v. Toronto-Dominion Bank*,[33] the Ontario Court of Appeal held that, even where a term of an employment contract is harsh, the employee may still be bound by it, as long as the contract is clear and unambiguous, was agreed to by the employee without pressure or undue influence by the employer and the terms of the contract are not so onerous or blatantly unfair as to require the court's intervention. Since courts may be less inclined to uphold a harsh contract in cases where the employee is unsophisticated, employers can only benefit by making sure that the circumstances surrounding the signing of an employment contract appear fair and reasonable. That way, the employer will have the support of the courts when it most needs it.

Contractual Terms Used in Employment Contracts

Every employment situation presents different needs and priorities for both the employer and the employee. For example, some employees may wish an agreement which protects them against relocation, while others are happy to move, and some employers may not be as concerned about the size of the employee's prospective severance package as they are about extending the payout over time to encourage the employee's search for a new job. Those who employ large numbers of workers in relatively menial, transient tasks may wish to keep their contracts short and simple, in keeping with the informal nature of the business. Employers who recruit individuals for high-paying senior positions will consider it well worth the effort to put together a detailed document with a number of specific provisions regarding a host of different issues.

Remuneration

An essential part of every employment contract is the provision laying out how much the employee is to be paid for his or her services, and how and when such

---

33 *Supra*, footnote 29.

payments are to be made. The pay provision can range from a very simple statement of the worker's hourly wage or annual salary to an elaborate compensation scheme for more highly placed personnel, which may include commissions or bonuses, either mandatory or discretionary. Before drafting an employment contract, an employer should become familiar with the relevant employment standards legislation pertaining to minimum wage, timing of payment of wages, maximum hours and overtime pay. Employers cannot escape these legislated standards by contracting out of them, and any contract which attempts to do so is likely to be found to be unenforceable.

Employers should also consider the issue of future increases in the employee's remuneration. These increases may be provided for in the contract, and doing so may avoid later problems. Specific regular increases may be provided for, but more conservative employers may wish to simply state that the employee's pay will be raised each year according to the annual Cost of Living Adjustment or according to changes in the Consumer Price Index. It is also possible to leave things somewhat more open by simply stating that the employer will raise (or reduce) the employee's remuneration each year in accordance with an annual performance evaluation to be conducted on or around a specified date. Employers experiencing periods of fiscal restraint may wish to omit this term altogether from their contracts so as to avoid the possibility that such clauses will be viewed as a commitment to effect a salary review.

Term

Employers will wish to consider whether the contract will be for a fixed term or for some indefinite period. Despite the fact that an employment relationship is being entered into for an indefinite period, many employers still see the value in putting many of the terms down on paper. In such circumstances, either the issue of the term of the contract will not be addressed, or the contract will explicitly state that it is for an indefinite period. In other cases, employers prefer to use employment contracts for fixed periods of time and will wish to define the term of the agreement.

A fundamental employment law principle is that a contract of employment for an indefinite term is terminable only if reasonable notice is given. This principle is not absolute; it is a presumption that is rebuttable if the contract of employment clearly specifies some other period of notice, whether express or implied.[34] This principle does not, however, apply to fixed term contracts. If an employee's contract is not renewed at the conclusion of a fixed term, the employee is not dismissed or terminated. Rather, the employment simply ends in accordance with the terms of the contract.[35]

---

34   *Machtinger v. HOJ Industries Ltd.*, *supra*, footnote 30.
35   *Chambly (Ville) v. Gagnon*, [1999] 1 S.C.R. 8.

The courts require unequivocal and explicit language in a contract before they will deprive an employee of his or her right to reasonable notice. Any ambiguities in the contract will be interpreted against the interests of the employer, on the assumption that it was the employer that prepared the contract. For example, in *Ceccol v. Ontario Gymnastic Federation*,[36] the plaintiff, Ms Ceccol, was employed by the federation for almost 16 years, pursuant to a lengthy series of one-year contracts. When the federation advised her that her contract would not be renewed for the upcoming year, it purported to rely on the fact that Ms Ceccol had been employed pursuant to a one-year contract, and it gave her notice accordingly. Ms Ceccol sued, claiming reasonable notice at common law representative of her 16 years of service. The Ontario Court of Appeal held that the federation's contracts did not contain the clear and unambiguous language necessary to deny Ms Ceccol reasonable notice at common law. As Mr. Justice MacPherson stated, writing for the Court:

> Employers should not be able to evade the traditional protections of the [*Employment Standards Act*] and the common law by resorting to the label of "fixed term contract" when the underlying reality of the employment relationship is something quite different, namely, continuous service by the employee for many years coupled with verbal representations and conduct on the part of the employer that clearly signal an indefinite term relationship.[37]

In light of the *Ceccol* case, employers are cautioned against using fixed term contracts unless the employment is truly expected to be for only a fixed period of time. The dangers of attempting the use of fixed term contracts where the employment will, in fact, be for an indefinite term are apparent. Any such attempt should be made only with the assistance of legal counsel.

If the contract is to be for a fixed period of time, the employer should give some thought to the renewal process for the contract, unless the contract is to govern a one-time project. Because fixed term contracts are often used to limit the employer's liability in the event of dismissal and will often contain a termination provision, the employer needs to be careful to keep track of the expiry date of such contracts. If a contract expires and the employee continues on with the organization, the employment relationship proceeds under the governance of the common law, and the employer may no longer be able to take advantage of the limited liability. A way to avoid this eventuality would be to include in fixed term contracts an automatic renewal provision, but employers must also be careful in using such clauses. If an employer is planning not to renew a given employment contract but accidently misses the expiry date, the employer may find the contract automatically renewed and will now be committed to a relationship which could have been avoided. Ultimately, employers should consider how they wish to set

---

36   (2001), 204 D.L.R. (4th) 688 (Ont. C.A.).

37   *Supra*, at para. 26.

up their contracts and then take care to monitor the expiration and renewal of all fixed term contracts.

Termination

Considering the termination issue at the inception of the employment agreement may raise a dark cloud at the beginning of the relationship, but it may also save the parties much aggravation and legal expense at a later time when the relationship turns stormy. Settling termination issues early on, by contract, significantly reduces the risk of a court imposing its own view of what constitutes dismissal for cause or reasonable notice for the dismissed employee.

Like those dealing with remuneration, termination provisions may range from the very simple to the more complex. A simple provision may state that the employee is entitled to eight weeks' notice of dismissal, or eight weeks' pay in lieu of notice, while a more complicated provision may contemplate additional notice and severance pay for each of the employee's additional years of service with the company. It should be recalled that the termination provision must provide for at least the minimum notice or pay required by the relevant employment standards legislation. One simple way to attempt to ensure this is to include in the contract a provision which states that the employee will be entitled to the greater of the notice specified in the contract and the amount of notice provided for in the applicable employment standards legislation. However, any such provision will need to be prepared with great care. If it is drafted by the employer and open to multiple interpretations, it is likely to be the interpretation that favours the employee that will be preferred by the court.[38]

The parties may also wish to include some definition of "just cause", that is, those actions on the part of the employee which will be considered a fundamental breach of the employment contract and which can lead to dismissal without requiring that reasonable notice or pay in lieu of notice be given. Setting out various grounds which justify dismissal for cause is useful for a number of reasons. The employer can let the employee know what the expectations are with regard to his or her behaviour. The employer's interests can be guarded by broadening the scope of behaviour for which the employee can be fired at no cost to the employer, while the employee can attempt to restrict such grounds in order to confine dismissal to a series of certain discrete events. Employers may wish to set reasonable annual performance standards or to single out certain kinds of misbehaviour or failures to meet company policy as constituting just cause for dismissal. The contract should also declare that anything which would fall under the common law definition of "just cause" will constitute just cause for dismissal under the contract.

---

38 *Christensen v. Family Counselling Centre of Sault Ste. Marie and District* (2001), 12 C.C.E.L. (3d) 165 (Ont. C.A.).

In addition, the parties should consider whether they intend that any pay in lieu of notice set out in the contract will be paid irrespective of whether the employee mitigates his or her damages by finding suitable alternate employment within the notice period. Employers who assume that they will not be required to make further payments under the employment contract after the dismissed employee finds another job should be aware of cases such as *R. v. Mills*.[39] In that case, the Alberta Court of Appeal found that a contractual provision substituting six months' salary for reasonable notice could be treated as creating a contractual right to the money. Thus, even if an employee found other employment during the notice period, the employee would still be entitled to the whole payment from his or her former employer. It is possible, however, that a court might, in the absence of any consideration of the issue of mitigation in the employment contract, imply a term providing that the employer is only responsible for pay in lieu of reasonable notice up to the point at which the employee secures alternate employment.

Employers who are willing to provide the dismissed employee with a lump sum payment which will not be affected by subsequent mitigation are often in a position to negotiate a somewhat smaller amount as a result. However, employers who are not financially able to absorb a lump sum payment may be interested in arranging for continuing payments of the employee's salary for a predetermined notice period. In the event of such continuing payments, employers may also be interested in providing for some sort of percentage payout in the event that the employee finds other work during the notice period. For example, it is not uncommon for a contract to provide that the employee will receive salary continuance for a specific period of time, up to the point at which the employee secures alternate employment. At this point, the employee will be entitled to receive a percentage of any amount remaining to be paid throughout the rest of the notice period (often 50%). Such a clause provides incentive for the employee to seek other employment since he or she will receive a windfall in so doing, and it provides some relief to the employer in the event that the employee is marketable.

Any amount to which an employee becomes entitled pursuant to an employment agreement will be considered to be due to the employee at the time of dismissal. Therefore, an employer may have a great deal of difficulty trying to get an employee to sign a release in exchange for the payment of this contractual entitlement. The employee could rightly take the position that the contractual sum is payable irrespective of whether he or she signs a release, and refuse to do so. Even if an employer is able to obtain a signed release at this time, the enforceability of such a release is questionable, given that the employee has been offered nothing new in exchange for signing, and therefore the release is likely lacking requisite consideration. An employer who wishes to obtain a release waiving the employee's right to take any action against the employer upon payment of the

---

39   [1986] 5 W.W.R. 567 (Alta. C.A.).

contractual sum, would be well advised to provide for a clause in the agreement which specifies that the employee will be required to sign a release prepared by the employer before he or she will be entitled to receive the termination payment.

Lastly, an employer might also want to include in the contract a clause which provides how much notice the employee is required to give if he or she chooses to resign employment. When a court, in the absence of such a clause, is determining how much notice an employee should have given, the court will generally consider how much time the employer would need to find a replacement for the employee. Employers might consider using this as a guide when drafting such clauses. However, regardless of the foregoing, the authors' view is that clauses requiring between two and four weeks' notice on the part of the employee are more or less the norm.

Some employers choose not to deal with termination in their employment contracts, preferring instead to rely on termination policies contained within a company employment manual. Such an approach should be exercised with caution, based on a decision of the Ontario Court of Appeal, *Christensen v. Family Counselling Centre of Sault Ste. Marie and District*.[40] In the *Christensen* case, the employer attempted to rely on its termination policy instead of providing the plaintiff with reasonable notice of her dismissal. The trial judge reviewed the termination policy carefully and found it to be unclear and capable of multiple interpretations. She held that, in such a case, the interpretation that would be chosen would be that which favoured the employee. Here, this result allowed the plaintiff to claim damages for wrongful dismissal despite the existence of the termination policy. Both the trial judge and the Court of Appeal confirmed that the common law principle entitling an employee to reasonable notice of his or her dismissal is a presumption, rebuttable only if the contract or policy clearly specifies some other period of notice. Even if the employer in *Christensen* had been clear in the writing of the policy, a further issue would have arisen as to whether the employee was aware of and/or understood the policy. Based on *Christensen*, employers considering the implementation of termination policies should ensure that such policies are carefully prepared and very clear. Employers should also consider how they can ensure that employees are aware of, understand and agree to the contents of the policy. In this regard, an employer should make sure that new employees are provided with a copy of the employment manual before commencing employment, and the employee should be required to sign an acknowledgment, referencing the policy, before starting work. Employers may wish to take the extra precaution of specifically reviewing the policy with the employee, and making a note of this discussion in the employee's file or having the employee initial the policy following this review. In such a case, the employer will be better able to defend a later claim that the employee was not bound by the policy.

---

40 *Supra*, footnote 38.

Job Description

A job description can be an essential part of the employment contract for both employers and employees, though both parties face the difficult job of drafting a description which achieves a delicate balance between ambiguity and specificity. The benefit of a job description clause lies in the fact that it permits the employer and employee to reach a clear understanding of what work will be expected. The employee will know the limits of the work which is expected, while the employer will be reminded of exactly what the employee is obliged to do.

A job description should be detailed enough to diminish misunderstandings or disputes regarding the employee's function and detailed enough to give the employer grounds for finding that the employee, by failing to live up to the job description, has breached the employment contract. At the same time, employers will wish to retain some flexibility by keeping the description sufficiently fluid so as to allow for modification of the employee's duties without giving the employee grounds to claim that he or she has been constructively dismissed. To this end, employers may wish to include a clause which explicitly states that the employee's duties and title may be modified by the employer, subject to advance notice. By contractually retaining the discretion to demote the employee or reduce remuneration in certain circumstances, the employer reduces the risk of a court finding that a constructive dismissal has taken place.

Probationary Period

Similar to the circumstances which result in couples living together in common law relationships prior to entering into marriage, employers often want the opportunity to test the employment relationship with a particular employee before committing to it on a more permanent basis. Employers who wish to gauge the employee's competence and suitability for a job should secure this by establishing a probationary period. The provision of such a period will enable the employer to have a set amount of time in which to assess the employee and to dismiss the employee if the relationship is found to be untenable. The employment contract provides the ideal vehicle by which to set out the existence of a probationary period and its terms. The contract should clearly state that the employee understands that a probationary period of a set period of time, during which either party may end the relationship under certain circumstances, will precede full-time employment. Employers who fail to make clear the existence of a probationary period may be subject to the common law reasonable notice requirements in the event that they wish to dismiss a probationary employee.

Provincial employment standards legislation often sets out a period of time for which an employee must have been employed before he or she is entitled to statutory notice. In Ontario, this period is three months, and many Ontario employers believe that there exists an implied probationary period of three months as a result.[41] Although an employee who has been employed for less than three months in Ontario may not be entitled to statutory notice, this does not prevent a court from finding that an employer owes to such an employee, upon dismissal, some amount which represents reasonable notice at common law.[42] Employers who wish to take advantage of probationary periods should explicitly provide for them within the terms of the contract and set out the conditions which apply to such probationary periods.

As mentioned earlier, employment contracts must comply with the minimum notice requirements set out in the relevant employment standards legislation. This requirement continues to apply even if a probationary period is included within the employment contract. For example, in Ontario, an employer is entitled to provide within the employment contract that the employee may be dismissed without notice during the probationary period so long as the period is three months or less. However, if the probationary period is longer than three months, the contract must provide for at least the statutory minimum notice to be given to the employee upon dismissal for reasons other than for cause.

Employees may not be receptive to the idea of a probationary period. In the case of more senior employees, it may be necessary to proceed without a probationary period in order to reach an agreement. If the contract is drafted to allow the parties to use the probationary period as a mutual time in which to try each other out, it may seem more equitable to the employee. However, employers should keep in mind that a probationary period is merely a period of time in which employees seek to prove the extent and suitability of their abilities. Employees who are not prepared to meet this challenge and accept a probationary period may be sending a message that their ability to perform in the position is questionable.

Employers should ensure that the contract provides for circumstances in which dismissal can take effect during the probationary period. There is case law which suggests that, in order to dismiss an employee during the probationary period, the employer must be able to show some objective evidence of the employee's inability to perform or lack of suitability.[43] The employer may wish to reserve its right to dismiss for reasons other than those contemplated within the probationary period, and this can be provided for within the contract. It is not clear whether a court will recognize such a reservation of rights over and above the case law in this area, but the contract will, at a minimum, show that the parties contemplated the probationary employee's dismissal in a variety of circumstances.

---

41 See Appendix A, Table 4.
42 See under the heading "Reasonable Notice" in Part 5, "The Divorce".
43 *Mison v. Bank of Nova Scotia* (1994), 6 C.C.E.L. (2d) 146 (Ont. Ct. (Gen. Div.)), supp. reasons 6 C.C.E.L. (2d) 159 (Ont. Ct. (Gen. Div.)); *Markey v. Port Weller Dry Docks Ltd.* (1974), 47 D.L.R. (3d) 7 (Ont. Co. Ct.).

Employers often question what an appropriate probationary period might be. The answer varies depending on a number of factors. The amount of time reasonably needed to assess the employee's performance should be considered. For instance, a relatively short period may be all that is required to assess a factory line worker, given the repetitive nature of the work, while a much longer period may be needed to assess the competence of a professional employee.

Employers will also want to set periods which take into account the possibility that the employee may become ill or take holidays during the probationary period. Courts have generally not been supportive of unilaterally imposed probationary periods, and employers may have difficulty enforcing periods which have been extended to compensate for unforeseen contingencies. If the employer finds that it needs to extend the probationary period, then such an extension should be mutually agreed upon between the parties. However, despite such apparent agreement, courts may still rule against the validity of the period if it can be shown that the employee felt that there was no alternative but to agree to the proposed extension.

In general, employers should endeavour to obtain as long a probationary period as is reasonably necessary to assess the employee's performance. Probationary periods can always be shortened or waived as the relationship progresses if it is found that the employee is suitable and meets all of the requirements of the position. For morale-boosting purposes, employers should consider finding some way to recognize that an employee has completed the probationary period and achieved regular full-time status within the organization.

Management Rights

It may be worthwhile for an employer to attempt to include a general clause reserving management's ability to make unilateral changes to the employment relationship, despite the inclusion of specific provisions to this effect within other parts of the agreement. Such general clauses will not necessarily bind the employee in every case, but they may make courts less inclined to interpret contracts too strictly on their terms. Such clauses are most likely to survive and have effect if they are moderately worded and reserve only the right to make "reasonable" changes or if they provide that advance notice of any change is to be given to the employee.

Service to the Best of One's Abilities

One contract term employers often choose to insert in an employment contract is some form of pledge that the employee will do the job to the best of his or her abilities. Though this general clause may have little legal impact on the employment relationship, it may serve ancillary functions. First, it will remind the employee of his or her obligations to the company and, secondly, it may help to define what is expected of the employee under the contract, thereby providing support for the employer in the event that the employee is dismissed for failing to demonstrate a proper commitment to the job. However, such clauses are by no means a perfect shield against wrongful dismissal claims.

Relocation

Employers, especially those with national or international offices, may wish to provide for geographical relocation of the employment within the terms of the contract. Where the employer thinks it may one day require the worker to switch offices, cities or even provinces or countries, then it is in the employer's best interests to say so at the outset of the relationship. In the absence of such a clause, it is possible that a court may, on the strength of the evidence before it, be willing to find an implied contractual term allowing for relocation of an employee.[44] However, rather than relying on the possibility of achieving this result in court,[45] employers are better off to provide for the possibility of relocation within the employment contract. Conversely, if the employer does not wish to preserve the right to relocate, or if the employee expresses strong resistance to the possibility of such a move, the contract can also provide that the employment relationship will be fixed to one geographical location.

Benefits

For employees whose jobs carry other benefits, the employment contract is an excellent place to set out the extent of the benefits package and any conditions associated with it. Benefits clauses can address a number of issues. For example, with respect to vacation, employers may wish to set out the allowed number of days, whether these can be taken at will or are subject to scheduling rules and whether paid vacation time can be accumulated or carried forward from year to year. The use of a company car, or company reimbursement for work-related use of the employee's own vehicle, may be provided for. Any other benefits granted to the employee should also be discussed and set out in the contract, particularly with respect to whether the employee is entitled to any of them upon dismissal, be it with or without cause. It may also be worthwhile to discuss the company's treatment of expenses.

With respect to any benefits being provided to the employee, the employer will want to ensure that any applicable eligibility periods are clearly set out in the

---

44 See *Smith v. Viking Helicopter Ltd.* (1989), 24 C.C.E.L. 113 (Ont. C.A.), in which the Ontario Court of Appeal found that the relocation of an executive from Ottawa to Montreal did not create a breach of the contract.

45 Because, in some cases, courts have held that the requirement to relocate was tantamount to dismissal: see *Morris v. International Harvester Canada Ltd.* (1984), 7 C.C.E.L. 300 (Ont. H.C.J.).

employment contract or initial letter of hire. In doing so, the employer can ensure that if some normally insurable event occurs prior to eligibility, there can be no question of the employee's awareness that he or she would not be covered in such a situation. It is often possible to waive such eligibility periods and, if this is done, this should also be clearly stated in the contract, and a diligent employer will obtain written confirmation from the relevant insurer.

"Entire Agreement" Clause

The "entire agreement" clause offers employers a valuable opportunity to eliminate potential disagreements and simplify disputes about the terms of employment governing a relationship. Most employment contracts are signed only after an initial process of interviews, discussions and some degree of bargaining over contractual terms. Out of this process, certain terms are reflected in the agreement, others are specifically excluded and some are often not discussed at all. Occasionally, however, something which was discussed and agreed to is not explicitly reflected in the agreement. Parties often question whether such a promise still forms part of the employment agreement and often, when such circumstances arise, it is a judge who will make the ultimate determination.

Rather than go to the expense and difficulty of resolving these matters in court, the parties may wish to include an "entire agreement" clause within the contract to ensure that it is agreed between them that *all* promises made are adequately reflected in the agreement. By this clause, the parties agree that the contract being signed constitutes the whole and entire agreement between the employee and employer, and that it supersedes any discussions, negotiations or documents which came before it. This clause should alert all parties and the court alike to the fact that the discussion and negotiation phase of the relationship is now over and the only words which should be considered are those contained within the written contract.

While an entire agreement clause may protect against court challenges in certain circumstances, it must be remembered that it will not offer a perfect defence against the employer's words and deeds during the creation of an employment relationship. An employer who knowingly makes false or unrealistic promises to a prospective employee may be guilty of negligent misrepresentation. Such was the case in *Queen v. Cognos Inc.*,[46] in which Mr. Queen was misled about the future economic health and status of the company (and thus his job security) during the job interview process. When he signed the employment contract, he approved a clause noting that the agreement superseded all previous talks. However, it was held that the contract did not bar Mr. Queen from suing for negligent misrepresentation. Accordingly, even when an employer uses an

---

46 (1993), 99 D.L.R. (4th) 626 (S.C.C.). See the prior discussion of this case under the heading "Negligent Misrepresentation" in Part 1, "The Courting".

entire agreement clause, the employer will not necessarily be protected from
everything done prior to executing the contract.

Inducement

If an employee has been recruited from another company, he or she may wish
to negotiate a term into the agreement which specifically recognizes past service
for the purpose of employment with the new employer. For example, if Ms Jones
is being recruited by Newco away from Oldco where she has been for 15 years,
she might be in a position to insist that Newco recognize her 15 years of service in
her new relationship for the purpose of benefits and termination. Any agreement
regarding inducement should be explicitly provided for in the employment contract. On the other hand, Newco may not wish to recognize Ms Jones' 15 years of
service and may specifically wish to provide that Ms Jones is deemed to have
commenced employment on the day she began with Newco. This may close the
door on Ms Jones later arguing to a court that, because of the inducement,
recognition should be made of her previous service.

Independent Legal Advice

Employers are not often anxious to have their employment contracts reviewed
by employees' lawyers. However, to the extent that an employee has been provided with an opportunity to seek and receive independent legal advice regarding
the terms of the contract, it will be more difficult for the employee to later argue
that the agreement was signed under duress or by mistake, or that the employee
failed to understand what was being signed. The employer may wish to include a
provision in the contract which states that the employee has been provided with
ample time and opportunity to seek independent advice before signing the contract. Such a clause may be particularly important where the employee is somewhat unsophisticated and might not otherwise be aware of his or her right to
question the terms being offered by the employer. However, where the employee
is sophisticated, he or she may be held to the terms of the contract even if
independent advice is not sought.[47]

Non-Competition/Non-Solicitation/Non-Disclosure

Employers often perceive the value in their business to lie either in their
relationships with their customers or in their confidential information. Given that
employees often have access to sensitive information (including customer lists)
which is vital to the conduct of the employer's business, employers are often

---

47   *Wallace v. Toronto-Dominion Bank* (1983), 145 D.L.R. (3d) 431 (Ont. C.A.), leave to appeal to
     S.C.C. refused 52 N.R. 157n.

concerned that such information could be used by an employee to his or her own advantage during or after employment. Employers can attain a degree of protection from problems in this area by having employees sign a clause acknowledging that they will preserve the company's essential secrets and will not compete against the company or solicit its clients. This form of a clause is known as a restrictive covenant, and can be contained within an employment agreement or form the basis for a separate agreement. However, courts generally view clauses which restrict an employee's ability to work as in restraint of trade, and such a clause will often be struck down unless the employer can show that it was reasonable in the circumstances. Employers interested in securing this type of protection should consider this matter seriously before an employee starts work, as it is often much more difficult to enforce a restrictive covenant entered into during the course of an existing employment relationship.

Employers should also consider restrictive covenants from the flip side. If an employee is being hired because of his or her relationships with clients at a competing employer, or because an employee possesses certain information about the industry, the employee, in accepting employment with the employer, might be in breach of an existing restrictive covenant. In such a case, if the former employer is looking to commence an action against the employee for breach of the restrictive covenant, it is not unusual for the hiring employer to be named, in any such litigation, as having induced the breach of the contract. In order to avoid any unexpected liability upon hiring new employees, the employer might wish to include a clause in the contract whereby a new employee declares that he or she is not under any existing obligations created by *previous* non-competition or other restrictive covenants.

Intellectual Property Ownership

Similarly, for some employers, there exists tremendous concern that the value of the business lies in the intellectual property created by employees during the normal course of business. If an employee, during the course of employment, develops or invents something which ultimately becomes profitable for the employer, there can often be a dispute as to the ownership of the intellectual property. Simply because the employee works for the company does not always mean that ownership in intellectual property lies with the employer. To avoid problems in this area, many employers retain lawyers skilled in intellectual property to draft comprehensive agreements, making clear all the contemplated circumstances in which intellectual property might be developed, and specifying where the ownership will lie in each such circumstance.

Mandatory Retirement

Occasionally, employers will wish to include provisions which state that the employee will be required to retire upon reaching a certain age. Such provisions must be very carefully drafted, as a poorly drafted provision attempting to confirm that the employee is not being guaranteed employment past a certain date may be viewed as having promised employment up to that date. Employers not wanting to be tied to any particular employee for a given period of time are best to seek legal advice if considering the inclusion of such a clause. Employers would also be wise to seek the advice of employment law counsel in their jurisdiction before attempting to set a mandatory retirement age, so as to fully gauge the human rights implications of so doing. In jurisdictions such as Ontario, the human rights legislation defines "age" as those ages between 18 and 65. Therefore, an Ontario employee dismissed pursuant to a proper mandatory retirement policy could not seek the protection of the *Human Rights Code*,[48] alleging discrimination on the basis of age. However, in other jurisdictions where "age" is defined differently or not at all, there may be human rights consequences associated with the adoption of a mandatory retirement policy.

Choice of Law

Where a company hires an employee to do work in another province or country, or where an individual from another province or country is hired to work in the employer's jurisdiction, the parties may face the problem of determining the appropriate law to apply to the contract. While this issue may have no importance during the life of the employment contract, it can very easily determine the outcome of a disagreement if the relationship falls into dispute.

For example, if an Ontario company hires an American to work in its New York office (being paid in U.S. dollars and paying U.S. taxes), but the American regularly does work in the Ontario office, which law will apply in the event that the employee is wrongfully dismissed? Canadian law requires that reasonable notice be given for dismissal without cause, while New York law provides that the employer may terminate the relationship at will.[49] The employer can deal with such issues by putting a "choice of law" clause in the contract. Such a clause simply states that the contract shall be interpreted according to the laws of the jurisdiction agreed upon by the parties. If, however, the clause in no way relates to the parties, and appears to a court to be an attempt on the part of the employer to secure a contractual interpretation which is favourable to the employer and unfairly prejudicial to the employee, then the court may be inclined to rule against the validity of such a term or the contract as a whole.

Employers should also be aware that, in the absence of a choice of law clause, courts will interpret the contract according to the law of the jurisdiction which has the closest and most substantial connection to the parties. For instance, in the

---

48   R.S.O. 1990, c. H.19 (as amended to 2002, c. 18, Sch. C).
49   *Hill v. W.P. London & Associates Ltd.* (1986), 13 C.C.E.L. 194 (Ont. H.C.J.).

Hill case,[50] the Court found that the employment contract should be interpreted according to New York law and that the former employee was not entitled to the protection of Ontario's law of reasonable notice. In a case where a Canadian employee opened a branch office in Chicago, however, his contract remained subject to Canadian law.[51]

Severability Clause

No matter how carefully a contract is drawn up, sometimes problems or errors do occur. In that event, it may well be better to save the rest of the contract rather than allow a court to invalidate the whole document to the employer's potential detriment. This can be provided for by way of the insertion of a clause which states that, in the event that a contractual provision is invalidated by a court, it will not be taken as affecting the validity of the rest of the document. Instead, the clause will be "severed" from the rest of the contract and a judicially imposed substitute accepted, while the rest of the document remains in force.

Liquidated Damages

Employers may wish to consider whether the contract should include a clause which provides that the employee pay a sum of money in the event of a breach of the contract. Drafting such a clause is a delicate process, and legal advice should be sought. Liquidated damages clauses are often difficult to distinguish from penalty clauses, which are unenforceable. Employers are entitled to calculate a pre-estimate of their damages in the event that the employee breaches the contract and to require the employee to pay this sum. However, if the clause constitutes a penalty for breach, it will be void. Simply designating a clause as a "liquidated damages" clause will not prevent a court from carefully examining the clause and finding that it is, in fact, a penalty clause. Clauses which are not extravagant or unconscionable, in that they do not far exceed what the employer would suffer in the event of a breach, and clauses which provide for the payment of a lump sum upon the happening of one event are more likely to be viewed by a court as being liquidated damages clauses.

Wage Deductions

In the event that the employee owes a debt to the employer (such as payment for personal telephone calls, unpaid corporate credit card bills or other expenses), employers may wish to preserve their ability to deduct such moneys from any unpaid amounts owed to the employee in the event of dismissal. Many provincial

---

50 *Supra.*
51 *Campbell v. Pringle & Booth Ltd.* (1988), 30 C.C.E.L. 156 (Ont. H.C.J.).

Acts, including Ontario's *Employment Standards Act, 2000*,[52] impose certain limits on such wage deductions unless they are expressly agreed to by the employee. Thus, a clause reserving the employer's ability to make wage deductions, where necessary and as long as they do not interfere with the relevant legislation, will be of great assistance to the employer seeking to recover such moneys after the employment relationship has been severed.

Waiver Clause

A waiver clause allows the employer and employee to make occasional changes in their working relationship without changing the terms of the employment contract. The parties can include in the contract a clause which acknowledges that, if either party waives a condition of the employment agreement on one occasion, this does not constitute an indefinite or permanent waiver of such a condition.

Employment Manuals

Where an employer has a large number of employees and wants to modify elements of its relationship with all of them without having to sit down and negotiate a new employment contract with each employee, one way to do so is through the use of an employment manual or handbook. The manual ensures that each employee has ready access to the terms of employment and provides an easy vehicle for the employer who wishes to change or add to its understanding with its employees.

The use of the employment manual requires some care. Employers often believe that, when trouble with an employee arises, they can dig into the storage room, dust off the employment manual and point the employee to some provision which he or she may not have seen in years, if at all. In cases where the handbook was not made an integral part of the employment relationship from the beginning, and was unilaterally introduced or modified without notice or an opportunity for the employees to agree or disagree with the changes, the courts have found that the manual does not bind employees and cannot be used.[53]

In order to properly guarantee the effectiveness of the employment manual, employers should make sure employees know from the outset that the manual carries effective contractual terms governing their relationship. If there is an employment contract, it should make reference to the manual and indicate that the employee is bound by the terms contained in the manual. Furthermore, any changes made to the manual must be announced and should be reasonable. Changing the office hours from nine-to-five to midnight-to-seven may not be

---

52   S.O. 2000, c. 41 (as amended to 2002, c. 18, Sch. J), s. 13.
53   *Ewasiuk v. Estevan Area Home Care District 9 Inc.* (1985), 9 C.C.E.L. 267 (Sask. Q.B.).

seen as being contemplated in the employee's agreement to be bound by the manual. A cautious employer may wish to follow the policy of the bank in *Wallace v. Toronto-Dominion Bank*,[54] ensuring that employees sign a document each year acknowledging that they have read and that they understand the manual. However, depending upon the circumstances, even this step will not necessarily provide the employer with an ironclad position.

EXECUTIVE EMPLOYMENT CONTRACTS

General

While the executive employment contract is based on all of the same principles which are at work in contracts with lower level employees and contains many of the same terms, the complex pay and benefits packages which are often involved in recruiting qualified executives typically require a more detailed contract. The executive employment contract may be cut from the same cloth as other employment contracts, but it is usually a much more sophisticated document, closely tailored to each individual relationship. While the majority of the terms discussed in the preceding section dealing with general employment contracts will often be included in an executive employment contract, there are a number of terms which are specific to the executive-employer relationship.

Terms

Duties and Performance

Job descriptions are not as commonly used in executive employment contracts and, when they are, the executive's duties are often left sufficiently broad so as to incorporate all responsibilities which might be expected in the execution of the position. Employers often have very high expectations of executives, given the larger stake which is placed in their employment. For this reason, executive employment contracts often make some provision for the measurement of performance, whether it be a comprehensive performance review or some remuneration scheme which is performance-driven.

Benefits

Since the merger and acquisition days of the 1980s, benefits have rapidly become a significant part of the executive's overall compensation. When taken together, such benefits as pay bonuses, pensions and stock options can amount to a sum which is greater than the executive's base salary. Courts have become more

---

54 *Supra*, footnote 47.

willing to treat these benefits as an integral part of the executive's employment contract. Bonuses can be dependent on the executive's performance or the company's performance, or both, and can be mandatory or purely at the discretion of the employer. The details of the bonus scheme should be clearly set out in the contract, or reference should be made within the contract to an annexed written bonus plan. Similarly, the parties may wish to reference within the contract both the employer's registered pension plan and any supplemental or "top-hat" plans which the employer provides for the benefit of executives. Finally, the details of any stock option plans or "phantom" plans provided for the benefit of the executive should be set out in the contract or referenced as an appendix.

An employer may be asked by its executives to establish a retirement compensation arrangement ("RCA") for their benefit. RCAs are provided for in the *Income Tax Act* (Canada),[55] and most funded supplemental pension plans constitute RCAs under that Act. Contributions by an employer to an RCA are not subject to the monetary limits which apply to registered pension plans and are generally fully deductible to the employer in the year that they are made. However, all contributions to an RCA and all income (including capital gains) earned in the RCA are subject to a 50% refundable tax which is required to be remitted to the Canada Customs and Revenue Agency. This tax is refunded to the RCA when benefits are paid out of the RCA on the basis of $1.00 of refund for every $2.00 paid out. The employee pays tax on benefits received by him or her out of the RCA, at normal graduated rates, in the year the benefits are received. The establishment of an RCA requires the appointment of a trustee and involves ongoing administrative costs and tax filings.

Employers should consider placing a clause in the executive contract which explicitly addresses what will happen to benefits in the event of dismissal. The employer and employee may agree that benefits will continue after dismissal for a period of time, or they may agree that benefits will cease upon dismissal. The employer and employee may agree that benefits will continue depending on whether the dismissal is with or without cause. Finally, they may agree that benefits will be paid in a lump sum, or will be paid over time, or some combination of these two. Executives often wish to capture the tax advantages of a one-time payment upon dismissal. Therefore, an employer who is able to afford a lump sum termination payment may be able to bargain for a smaller benefits package in exchange for the lump sum payment.

It is to both parties' benefit to contemplate the future of the executive's benefits in the event of dismissal and to provide for this within the terms of the employment contract. A generously or carelessly written employment contract may create an unshakeable obligation on the employer to compensate for benefits in the event of dismissal. If this is not what the employer intends, then the right to modify or terminate the executive's benefits should be expressly reserved, at least

---

55   R.S.C. 1985, c. 1 (5th Supp.) (as amended to 2002, c. 9).

in the event of certain occurrences, such as dismissal for cause. If an employer intends to attach conditions to the payment of benefits to the executive, the contract is the place to do so in order to ensure that a court does not view the benefits as an integral part of the executive's overall compensation package.

Perks

Just as the lower level employee might be entitled to certain special benefits, such as the use of a car, so too the executive will likely seek a number of "perks" in the position, such as a company car, use of a driver, a cellular telephone, a club membership or even use of a company jet. Given the importance of such perquisites to many executive employees, they should be provided for in any employment contract to ensure that no disputes later arise, especially in the event of dismissal. In recent years, more and more unusual perks have continued to make their way into employment contracts, including free car washing, attendance at a spa and provision for children's education expenses. The contract should make reference both to the conditions and entitlements which accompany the perks *during* employment and to whether the right to the perks continues, if only temporarily, or ceases abruptly at the end of the employment relationship.

Stock Options

The giving of stock options as a term of employment became increasingly popular throughout the 1990s and, in particular, with the rise to fame of the "dot.com" industry. Although the provision of the stock options themselves might be mentioned in an employment agreement, the specific terms governing the grant are usually dealt with in a separate stock option agreement. Employers should be aware, however, that the law dealing with stock options is evolving at a rapid clip, and there have been cases dealing with what happens to the options when employment terminates. Those preparing such stock option agreements will need to familiarize themselves with these cases in order to ensure that the agreements properly provide for what happens to the options when employment terminates.[56]

Golden Parachutes

While the executive employment contract will often resemble, for the most part, the regular employment contract, the "golden parachute" is unique to upper-echelon employees. In essence, the golden parachute provides a series of benefits to an executive upon a change in control of a business, to be paid on termination

---

[56] For a more comprehensive discussion of this issue, see under "Stock Option Plans" in Part 5, "The Divorce".

or when the executive resigns. The parachute serves two functions. First, a lucrative parachute offers a substantial incentive for senior executives who are being recruited by a company. More importantly, however, the golden parachute offers a way for the directors of a company to ensure that the executive will manage the company in a conscientious and disinterested way, in the event of a change of control, by guaranteeing that the executive will be well rewarded no matter what happens.

The rationale behind the provision of golden parachutes within executive employment contracts is that the executive negotiating on behalf of a company which is embarking on a change of control will be best able to represent the needs of the company and maximize the return to the shareholders if he or she is unconcerned as to the ultimate effect of the change of control on his or her position within the company. Golden parachutes have also received criticism from those who argue that an executive who will be well compensated despite the outcome of a change of control will not have enough at stake to do the job properly. Still, golden parachutes are widely believed to be useful, in at least some executive positions, and are now a firmly entrenched part of the executive employment landscape.

While employers and executives can negotiate their own golden parachute package, a typical package may include the following elements:

(a) a salary payment substantially in excess of what the executive would receive if the common law level of payment in lieu of reasonable notice were to be relied upon;

(b) benefits;

(c) stock options; and

(d) other elements, such as club memberships, insurance or career counselling.

Another term which occasionally appears in golden parachute packages is the "back to the future" clause which allows the executive to receive a pension or other retirement benefits from a certain specified date, which may stretch as far back as 40 years prior to the date of the contract. This would allow the executive to receive a pension based on 40 years of work for the company, despite the amount of time that the executive has actually worked for the company.

The size of golden parachutes can be limited by including some kind of mitigation provision which may either offer a smaller lump sum payment on termination, instead of a larger payment made over time, or provide for some reduction in the amount paid by the employer in the event that the executive finds alternate employment after dismissal. Unless an explicit mitigation clause is included in the contract, courts may read a golden parachute clause as giving an executive the absolute right to the benefit package, regardless of how soon other work is found.

It is generally recommended that golden parachutes be drafted to provide for a maximum payout of 24 months' compensation in the event that the parachute is triggered. Although courts have considered and endorsed the rare case in excess of 24 months, golden parachutes have been largely free of judicial consideration, and the more excessive the golden parachute, the more likely a court will question its enforceability. Also, for practical purposes, it does an executive little good to negotiate a parachute which is so excessively lucrative that the employer will be disinclined to pay it out in the event that it is triggered. To the extent that a parachute can be agreed to which is reasonable and accepted by both parties, the executive will not be faced with the prospect of asking a court to endorse the parachute.

Golden parachutes are only triggered by the occurrence of certain events. Generally, the parachute can be set off for one of three reasons:

1. There is a change in control of the corporation.
2. The employee resigns for "good reason" (or something which closely resembles a constructive dismissal).
3. The employee is dismissed by the new corporation.

Some contracts will include all of these triggers, many will be set up with some sort of a double trigger and a few others will require only a single triggering event. No matter which combination of options is chosen, it is important to define the triggers within the employment contract so that both parties know when the parachute will "open".

"Change in control" for the purpose of a golden parachute may mean any significant change in the ownership or organizational structure of the company, such as a takeover or merger. Factors which may constitute a change in control and trigger the parachute include a change of directors involving the majority of the board, a change in ownership of the corporate shareholdings, a change of personnel among the top executives or the delisting of the company from a stock exchange.

Most parachutes contemplate the employee's dismissal by the new employer after a change in control. Other parachutes can also be triggered by the resignation of the employee. Employers will wish to be particularly careful in defining those circumstances in which an executive's resignation can trigger the opening of the parachute. Often this is done by providing that the parachute will be triggered by resignation for "good reason". "Good reason" typically refers to the kinds of changes which would allow the employee to take the position that he or she had been constructively dismissed.[57] These would be changes to fundamental terms

---

57 See under the heading "Constructive Dismissal" in Part 4, "The Separation", for a discussion of constructive dismissal.

of the employment relationship and might include a change in job title, responsibilities or reporting relationship, a forced relocation to another city or country, or a reduction in pay.

Corporations that draw up executive employment contracts which include golden parachutes should be aware of the duties they owe under Canadian corporate law. Three separate provisions of both the *Canada Business Corporations Act*[58] and the applicable provincial business corporations legislation may affect the legitimacy of the golden parachute. First, the directors may set the remuneration of any director, officer or employee of the company, subject to corporate articles, by-laws or unanimous shareholder agreements. Thus, the corporate articles, agreements and by-laws should be checked for anything which might affect the drafting of a golden parachute. Secondly, if the executive is a director or officer of the corporation, he or she must disclose the terms of the contract to the board of directors, and the contract must be approved.[59] Thirdly, directors and officers owe a duty of care towards the corporation, meaning that they must act prudently, honestly and with the best interests of the corporation in mind. Obviously, this duty extends to the drafting of employment contracts. Directors who are involved in setting or approving the pay level of senior officers and who do not bargain with the company's interests firmly in mind may open themselves up to future liability under provincial or federal business corporations legislation.[60]

Golden parachutes should be drafted with care and specificity to ensure that they cannot be challenged and that both the executive and the employer understand the terms of the package. In particular, the parties should keep the following in mind when engaged in the drafting of such contractual provisions:

- If a golden parachute clause is to be included in an executive's employment contract, this should be done *as soon as possible* and certainly long before there are any hints of a takeover or other change of control within the company.
- Particularly where directors and officers are involved in setting, approving or receiving benefits packages such as golden parachutes, they must display a lack of self-interest and remember their duty to act in the corporation's best interests. This may militate against extremely large benefits packages which would not appear to be in the company's best interests.

---

58 R.S.C. 1985, c. C-44 (as amended to 2002, c. 9).
59 See also the applicable securities legislation and requirements to disclose the existence of such agreements within prospectuses.
60 See *Rooney v. Cree Lake Resources Corp.* (1998), 40 C.C.E.L. (2d) 96 (Ont. Ct. (Gen. Div.)), where it was held that the severance payout owed to the executive was unenforceable due to the fact that it was inherently unfair and unreasonable. Justice Dilks held (at para. 52) that "one must examine all the surrounding circumstances" when determining if a particular contract is fair and reasonable to the corporation, "including the purpose of the agreement and its possible ramifications for the corporation".

- Where directors and officers receive golden parachutes, their contracts should be disclosed to and approved by the board of directors and the shareholders, and such contracts should be reasonable and fair to the company.
- The terms and conditions of the parachute (including benefits, how they are to be paid, triggering events) should be set out in detail to ensure that both parties understand their rights and obligations.[61]

Golden Handcuffs

Employers will occasionally negotiate provisions known as "golden handcuff" clauses. In the same way that golden parachutes provide substantial benefits if the executive *leaves* the company in the event of a change in control, golden handcuffs aim to keep favoured executives by paying substantial benefits as long as the executive *stays* with the company. Such benefits end when the executive leaves the company. In addition to keeping in mind the same considerations which apply to the provision of golden parachutes, employers should ensure that the golden handcuff clause clearly delineates that the benefits are temporary. Otherwise, the employer runs the risk that a court may rule that these benefits are actually part of the employee's basic compensation and thus subject to inclusion in a consideration of money owing in lieu of reasonable notice. Examples of golden handcuffs include deferred bonuses or stock options and interest-free or low-interest loans. Golden handcuffs may be useful in industries where there is a high turnover rate among executives or key employees, or where a shaky company wishes to retain stability and ward off mass departures. For example, after a number of traders left a brokerage firm, the company instituted a multi-million-dollar golden handcuff package. As a result, the firm was able to retain its top traders for an extended period of time.

Arbitration Clause

With the increasing complexity of disputes arising out of executive employment contracts, many employers and executives make provision in the contract for arbitration of potential disputes. Arbitration is meant to provide the parties with a binding decision made by a neutral decision-maker, who is mutually agreed to by the parties. Such a dispute resolution mechanism has the potential advantages of being quicker and less costly than the normal court process and confidential (such hearings can be specified to be held in private, with their results kept confidential), and can be determined by someone with a particular specialty in the area of employment law.

---

61 For a more comprehensive discussion of golden parachutes, see Stikeman, Elliott, *Executive Employment Law* (Markham: Butterworths, 1993), Chapter 11.

Immigration Issues

Given the increasingly global nature of the corporate environment, it is no surprise that companies often seek to hire or transfer executives from around the world. As a result, employers often question their obligations when it comes to hiring or transferring foreign executives to a Canadian office. Given the exacting requirements of the laws and regulations concerning immigration, this section should not be taken as a definitive guide; in situations involving immigration of employees, it is always advisable for employers to consult with legal counsel. This section will provide guidelines for the questions and issues which should be discussed with an expert if the occasion arises.

Two separate distinctions are important when considering the immigration of executive employees. First, a difference exists between Canada's immigration laws of universal application and the preferential immigration provisions of various treaties to which Canada has subscribed, such as the North American Free Trade Agreement ("NAFTA") and the General Agreement on Trade in Services ("GATS"). Secondly, there is a distinction to be drawn between immigration of employees for a temporary period and immigration of employees on a permanent basis.

Before beginning the immigration process for a foreign employee or potential employee, the employer would be wise to question whether there are any criminal convictions in the individual's history. Criminality is a basis on which entrance to Canada can be denied, and the employer would be wise to discover it before investing in the process. In addition, visitors to Canada who will be engaging in employment in Canada in an occupation which deals with public health and education concerns will be required to obtain medical clearance from Health and Welfare Canada by way of an immigration medical examination.

Subject to certain exceptions, all persons seeking entry to Canada for employment on a temporary basis must have an employment authorization to enter the country. An employment authorization is not required where the individual can be classified as a "business visitor".[62] In theory, securing an employment authorization involves two distinct steps. First, an application must be made in Canada to Human Resources Development Canada for "job validation". Secondly, if the application for job validation is successful, then the person in respect of whom the job validation was granted may apply for an employment authorization, and it will likely be granted. However, a large number of employment authorizations are obtained without the job validation process first having been followed, since there are many exceptions to this two-step process which can be utilized.

---

62 The persons who qualify as "business visitors" are defined separately in the immigration provisions of universal application, NAFTA and GATS. Where an individual satisfies the definition and is covered by the respective provisions or treaty, then he or she will be exempt from the Employment Authorization requirement.

The job validation process is a purely administrative one and involves the employer (or its legal counsel) writing to and persuading Human Resources Development Canada that granting the job validation is justified in the circumstances, keeping in mind that the result of a job validation is the hiring of a foreign worker over a Canadian one. Justification may be advocated on any ground; however, it is most often successfully made out by presenting a successful labour market argument (that is, there was no one qualified in Canada willing to fill the position) or by arguing that the employment validation will be of benefit to Canada through the creation of employment opportunities or increased export revenues. Generally speaking, job validation is costly, time-consuming, uncertain and subject to the bias of the employment counsellor making the decision, who naturally favours the employment of Canadians over foreign workers. Where possible, it is recommended that this step be avoided.

There are a number of exceptions to the job validation requirement. First, under the immigration provisions of universal application, job validation is unnecessary where the employer is effecting an intra-company transfer of one of its senior managers or executives.[63] A similar exception to the job validation requirement exists under NAFTA, although the definition of "management" is broader and covers a wider class of employees, and the assignment can continue for an aggregate of up to seven years. Under NAFTA, the definition of "transferee" also includes persons who have "specialized knowledge" of their employer's proprietary technologies, processes, products and/or services. However, in such cases, transfer is limited to a maximum of five years. To qualify for the NAFTA exemption to enter Canada, the foreign employee must be a United States or a Mexican citizen and must have been employed by the company in a qualifying capacity for at least one full year within the preceding three-year period. Similar provisions also exist in GATS, but intra-company assignments are limited to an aggregate of three years.

In addition to transferring existing employees to Canadian operations, employers may also be able to hire new employees while still taking advantage of exceptions to the job validation requirement. Under NAFTA, professionals, including economists, engineers, management consultants and computer systems analysts, are exempt from the job validation requirement. In all such cases, however, there are minimum educational or experience credentials which the professional will be required to satisfy before being eligible for the exemption. A similar exemption exists under GATS, although the definition of "professional" is extremely narrow, presenting limited opportunities for employers to take advantage of this exemption.

In addition to these exceptions to the job validation requirement, Canada subscribes to other international treaties which also provide exceptions to the requirement. Employers would be wise to seek the advice of experienced legal

---

63 This is referred to as the "E-15" exemption.

counsel to learn about their various options when considering the immigration of a foreign worker for a temporary purpose.

Employers may also wish to hire and bring foreign workers to Canada on a permanent basis. Such individuals must apply to Citizenship and Immigration Canada for permanent resident ("landed immigrant") status and will be subject to a quasi-judicial selection process. Canada's selection criteria for permanent resident status are designed to assess whether the applicant will be able to become "successfully established" in Canada. This determination is, of course, imperfect and is made by applying statutorily prescribed criteria and seeing how the applicant measures up against what is colloquially known as the "points system". Values or "points" are allocated to such categories as education, experience and language ability. This process is made easier if the applicant already has a permanently validated offer of employment before the application for landed immigrant status is filed. It should be noted, however, that there are risks inherent in an employer supporting an individual in an application for permanent residence. First, the process is an expensive one and, even more importantly, once the individual has been awarded landed immigrant status, he or she is not tied to the employer and may terminate the employment relationship with impunity. Thus, it is often preferable for an employer to first endeavour to bring a foreign worker to Canada on a temporary basis and test the relationship before agreeing to assist the employee in obtaining permanent resident status.

Part 3

The Marriage

INTRODUCTION

The employer and employee have now entered into an employment relationship; the "marriage" has begun. The length of the relationship is dependent upon a host of factors, ranging from the employer's treatment of the employee to the individual personality of the employee. While many employment relationships will be extremely successful and will continue for many years, there will be problem employees in any workplace, and there will be employers who do not live up to their legal obligations to their employees.

Human resources publications tend to contain very extensive coverage on this period in the employment relationship. Unlike human resources professionals, lawyers are not often consulted during the "marriage", when the employment relationship is strong. This Part does not outline how human resources departments should be structured or how personnel policies should be created. Rather, it attempts to highlight the various pieces of legislation which govern the employment relationship, and the legal issues which arise during the term.

Employers who do not comply with the applicable employment legislation are not necessarily hard-hearted, but are often just unaware of their obligations. Since this is rarely an excuse for non-compliance, we have attempted, in this Part, to alert employers to many of their statutory obligations. The material in this Part is very general and is not provided for the purpose of setting out the law as it pertains to each Canadian employer. Rather it is offered as a guide to help employers become aware of the types of responsibilities and obligations they might expect to apply in their workplaces. Employers facing any of the situations discussed in this Part are advised to consult with their local legal counsel to obtain an opinion regarding the particular law which applies to their situation in their jurisdiction.

CONSIDERATIONS DURING THE EMPLOYMENT RELATIONSHIP

Like all marriages, successful employment relationships require hard work. Even the most conscientious employer will be aware that not all employment relationships will be successful because the employee variable cannot necessarily be controlled by the employer. Employers who no longer see each employment relationship through rose-coloured glasses have begun to realize that preventive measures can be taken during the employment relationship. Such measures will serve either to prolong the employment relationship or to better prepare the employer for separation or divorce.

Performance Reviews and Employee Evaluations

Large employers often have a formal procedure in place to review an employee's performance on a regular basis. An evaluation form is completed, and employees are provided with feedback regarding the quality of their work. The benefits of performance reviews from a productivity standpoint are obvious. They serve to ensure that employees are made aware of problems with their performance and that such problems are corrected, if possible. They certainly serve as positive reinforcement for those employees who are performing optimally. Performance reviews are also important from a legal standpoint because they may, in certain circumstances, provide the foundation for a dismissal for just cause.[1] It is advisable for *all* employers to implement some system of performance reviews, which can be as informal as having regular meetings with individual employees to discuss performance. Such meetings should be documented.

Performance reviews which are honest and identify potential and actual problems assist employees by drawing such problems to their attention and assist employers by either eliciting improved performance or by potentially laying the foundation for a dismissal for cause if serious problems are not corrected. Employers are strongly encouraged to approach performance reviews with a view to providing the most honest evaluation possible. The following scenario is all too common: an employer finally decides that an employee's performance leaves the employer no alternative but dismissal. The employee is dismissed, sues for wrongful dismissal and the first thing that the employer's legal counsel discovers in the employee's personnel file is a series of glowing performance reviews. In such a case, it becomes practically impossible for the employer to sustain a dismissal for cause, and the employer may face significant legal liability for wrongful dismissal. If there are problems with the employee's performance, these should be indicated on the review form, and goals should be set for the correction of such problems.

Many employers conduct performance reviews at the same time as employees' salary reviews. This is not advised. Most salary reviews result in an employee's salary being increased, even if this is limited to a cost of living increase. In the face of a raise in salary, an employee is likely to disregard any accompanying

---

1   See the discussion under the headings "Behaviour Which May Constitute Just Cause" in Part 4, "The Separation", and "Just Cause" in Part 5, "The Divorce".

negative feedback regarding his or her performance. If the employer wishes any constructive criticism to register with the employee, the employer should hold a separate performance review for the purpose of discussing the employee's performance problems.

Where possible, employers should implement the use of a standard form in conducting performance reviews. This will go a long way towards ensuring that these meetings are conducted in a uniform manner. In addition to assessing problems, the review form can include achievements and goals, all of which can be revisited at the next review to determine whether goals have been achieved and problems corrected. The form should gauge the employee's strengths and, in particular, the employee's weaknesses, as this will invite supervisors and managers to list troublesome areas. The form should include a place where the employee can respond to the contents of the review and a place for the employee to sign indicating that he or she has been provided with a copy of the form. It is not necessary for the employee to indicate agreement with the contents of the form. So long as the employee has been provided with a copy of the form, it will be difficult for the employee to later allege that the employer failed to bring such performance problems to the employee's attention.

Additional Documentation

When an employee's performance problems become so serious that the employer begins to consider dismissing the employee for cause, the first question that the employer's legal counsel will ask relates to the nature of the paper trail which the employer has built up concerning the employee's difficulties. It is advisable to document every significant incident of misconduct which occurs during the employment relationship, even if this means recording incidents outside of the regular performance review system. This includes seeking documentation from those individuals who may have witnessed a particular incident, be they employees, members of management or even customers.

For example, in a situation involving a hospital technician who was dismissed for just cause (namely, poor performance and attitude), documentation was obtained from each staff member and patient who was present or who witnessed the technician's conduct or behaviour in respect of each reported incident. The employee's manager called a meeting after every report of misconduct on the part of the technician, and copies of the witnesses' statements were referred to during these meetings. In addition to the technician and the department manager, also present at each of these meetings was at least one of the technician's supervisor or the quality control representative. The manager, supervisor and quality control representative took notes at each of these meetings, documenting in detail what the technician was told about her performance. All of this documentation was obtained in addition to the employee's regular performance reviews which reflected the ongoing problems. When the employee was dismissed, the hospital had a binder of material supporting its position that the employee was dismissed for cause. Not only did the compiled material constitute overwhelming evidence in support of the employee's dismissal for cause, but it also proved instrumental in refreshing the witnesses' memories when the technician ultimately sued for wrongful dismissal.

Salary Reviews

Although salary reviews are generally driven by an employee's performance, salary and performance reviews are unrelated and should be conducted separately. If the reviews must be conducted together, then the employer should make every effort to distinguish between a salary increase and a performance review in which problems are indicated. Unless the problems are clearly brought to the employee's attention independently of the increase in salary, the employee may later claim that he or she believed that there were no problems with performance, based on the salary increase.

Many employers maintain a practice of providing annual increases in salary to productive or exemplary employees. Such generosity is virtuous but is not necessary and may cause problems for the employer down the road. In the absence of employment contracts providing for such, employers are under no obligation to provide employees with regular salary increases. Doing so can expose an employer to liability in a case where the employer subsequently wishes to dismiss an employee. Take, for example, a financial services firm which flourished during the 1980s. All employees who were with the employer during this time received extremely generous salary increases. By the time the recession began in the early 1990s, the employees' salaries had achieved such astronomical proportions that, when the employer wished to downsize, it found it could not afford to do so because it could not afford severance packages based on the employees' current salaries. It solved the problem by providing the employees with advance notice of pay decreases, but this had a profound effect on employee morale and could have been avoided had the employer refrained from getting carried away with pay increases during the boom years. Discretionary bonuses could have been provided instead, reflecting exceptional performance in any given year.

Pay decreases are becoming more common these days, especially in organizations like the one just described. Employers should be cautious when considering the implementation of pay reductions, as remuneration has been held to be a fundamental term of the employment contract and a decrease could be construed as a constructive dismissal.[2] Courts have been somewhat more sympathetic to the plight of employers in recessionary times and may be more willing to accept a pay decrease if it is moderate and the decrease is applied consistently to all

---

2   See under the heading "Change in Remuneration" in Part 4, "The Separation".

employees. However, if the pay decrease is considered fundamental to the employment relationship, then the employer will be required to provide the employee with reasonable notice of the change[3] in order to allow the employee to seek alternate employment. If the employer is unable to provide reasonable advance notice of the change and the employee is unwilling to accept the change, then the employer may wish to dismiss the employee immediately by providing pay in lieu of reasonable notice of dismissal.

Updating Employment Contracts and Personnel Policy Manuals

A potential problem which employers often encounter is the lapse of employment contracts. Employment contracts which provide for a set notice period which is less than that provided for in the relevant employment standards legislation will be void.[4] Employment contracts for fixed terms where the terms have expired provide little protection.[5] In such cases, employers who attempted to ensure that their legal exposure for pay in lieu of reasonable notice was limited in the event of dismissal have been surprised to learn that the provisions in their contracts could not be enforced. Where such contracts have lapsed, the employment continues outside of the parameters of the contract and is governed by the common law, which may entitle the dismissed employee to a much greater notice period than was provided for in the contract. This can have substantial implications for employers.

To ensure that such contracts do not lapse, employers need to put in place a system which notifies them that employment contracts are in need of updating or renewal. Some form of a diary or notification system will ensure that reminders are provided. This system can be as simple as marking renewal dates on a calendar or as sophisticated as some computer programs which record such dates so that the user will be reminded of the dates in the future. In either case, it is advisable to have a backup system in place, such as providing a secretary or assistant with these dates as well.

Instead of maintaining a notification or diary system, employers might wish to draft contracts which make provision for certain eventualities such as a lapse in the term of the contract. In the case of an employee whose service will eventually require a notice provision in excess of that currently being provided, the employer might wish to include in the contract a sliding scale formula for notice instead of a set notice period. For example, the employer might choose a formula such as one week of notice for each year of service. Employers should confirm that the formula chosen will not result in any employee receiving less than the employment standards minimum in the event of dismissal. One way around this might

---

3   See under the heading "Reasonable Notice" in Part 5, "The Divorce".
4   See under the heading "Employment Standards Legislation" in Part 5, "The Divorce".
5   See under the heading "Term" in Part 2, "The Engagement".

be to simply provide that the employee will, at the very least, be entitled to the minimum amount of notice provided for in the relevant employment standards legislation, plus some additional amount.

In situations involving fixed term contracts, employers can seek to prevent a lapse of the contract by providing for automatic renewal within the terms of the contract. This can be helpful in situations where the employer wishes to remain bound by the terms of the contract but is concerned that the fixed term of the contract may lapse without a new contract being drafted. However, employers implementing such clauses should do so cautiously. For every employee whom the employer wishes to keep pursuant to the terms of the contract, there is likely to be another whose contract the employer does not wish to renew. If such an employee's contract lapses and the contract includes an automatic renewal clause, the clause will be triggered and the employment will continue for another term. The employer in such a case may find it cannot then dismiss the employee without liability. Ideally, employers should stay abreast of the renewal dates of contracts so that decisions can be made regarding renewal and contracts can be renewed only where this is desired.

One of perhaps the easiest ways to avoid the hassle involved with recording and staying abreast of contract renewal dates is to refrain from the use of fixed term employment contracts altogether. Many employers are often of the view that, unless a contract is for a fixed term, it cannot be terminated. This is not so. An employment contract can be for an indefinite term and, none the less, be subject to a termination clause contained within the contract. In this way, the employer can enter into an agreement with an employee which will last for the length of the employment relationship and will only end when the termination clause contained within the agreement is invoked. Employers that choose to use indefinite term contracts should still periodically review the nature of the employment relationship, and might consider updating the contract or replacing it where it is clear that the employment relationship which existed at the time the contract was entered into no longer exists, as might be the case where the employee has received a significant promotion or has been reassigned, or where the employee's duties have been dramatically altered.

Employment policy manuals can prove to be a useful method of communicating to employees the acceptable practices and procedures within the organization. Assuming that each employee received a copy of the policy manual when he or she joined the company, and was requested to agree to the terms before joining, the question arises as to how the employer can subsequently implement a policy change during the employment term. Examples of such changes include altered hours of operation, a change in the reimbursement of expenses, or a modified vacation policy. The employer will have minimal difficulty implementing such a change if the change does not result in a breach of employment standards legislation and if the change is not so fundamental that it can be considered a constructive dismissal. Constructive dismissal occurs when the employer unilaterally changes any fundamental term of the employee's contract evincing an intention to no longer be bound by the contract.[6] So the question facing an employer is whether or not the change being contemplated is fundamental to the affected employees' contracts. If the change is inconsequential, as it may be in a case where the employer wishes the lunch hour to begin 15 minutes later, then this may not be fundamental and the employer may be entitled to implement such a change without incident. However, if the employer decides to implement a more serious change, then it may wish to take precautions, assuming that constructive dismissal may be alleged.

The change should be proposed to the employees, and they should be asked to consent. To ensure that they have agreed, employers are wise to require the employees to read and sign the changed policy so that their consent is recorded. If the employees are unwilling to accept the change, and the change is a fundamental one, then the employees must be provided with reasonable notice of the change, so that they may seek other employment if they are unwilling to work under the new policy. The employer should determine the longest notice period which would apply in relation to any of its employees and then notify the employees in writing that the change will be implemented when the notice period expires. If the employer cannot wait for the expiration of the notice period before implementing the change, to limit legal liability the employer can provide pay in lieu of reasonable notice of dismissal to those employees who are unwilling to accept the change. Obviously, the least expensive alternative is to give the employees the maximum amount of notice possible of impending changes. For this reason, employers considering changes to policies should finalize such changes as far in advance of the implementation date as possible so that the employer can take advantage of any advance notice provided when determining what, if any, pay in lieu of notice must be provided to the employees.

Conscientious employers will want to ensure that employees are familiar with company policies and that such policies are implemented, enforced and applied consistently amongst all employees. In so doing, employers will have greater success in ensuring that such policies will be viewed as enforceable.

Promotions and Probationary Periods

Employees who consistently perform at an optimum level for their employers will often be considered for a promotion when one becomes available. If the employee accepts the promotion, it will usually entail new duties and responsibilities, regardless of whether the promotion is accompanied by a consequent increase in remuneration. Employers often proceed under the misconception that, if the employee does not prove to be suitable for the new position, the employer may simply dismiss the employee without notice because the employee has proven

---

6   See under the heading "Constructive Dismissal" in Part 4, "The Separation".

incapable of performing the duties of the position. In fact, this is not the case, and employers should be prepared to return an employee to his or her former position in the event that the employee does not succeed at the new position. If the employer wishes to dismiss an employee who has not succeeded at a promoted position, and the employer is unable to substantiate a dismissal for cause, the employer will be required to follow the regular rules which apply to dismissal without cause in order to avoid legal liability. The employer must provide the employee with reasonable notice of the dismissal or pay in lieu of notice. An employee will often accept a promotion because of its increased prestige, but employers should also be cautious of forcing an employee to accept a promotion. If the promotion involves increased duties and responsibilities and the result is a fundamental change to the employee's contract, this could be classified as a constructive dismissal, and the employer will wish to proceed as advised in any constructive dismissal situation.[7]

At the opposite end of the spectrum from employees who are being considered for promotion are those whose performance is causing such concern that the employer is contemplating putting them on probation. The imposition of a probationary period during the employment relationship can also be viewed as a constructive dismissal, since the employer could be seen to be unilaterally changing a fundamental term of the employment relationship. If the probationary period is imposed in good faith, as part of a progressive discipline program, and the employee consents, the employer is less likely to face liability for having imposed the period. However, the employer should be prepared to provide the employee with the full probationary period in which to demonstrate an improvement in performance.

Alternate Work Arrangements

Alternate work arrangements have become more popular in recent years, with employees appreciating the flexibility which part-time work, flexible hours, working at home, work-sharing programs, telecommuting and independent contracting allow. In light of the growing trend towards widespread implementation of these alternate work arrangements, many employers are being asked by employees to allow such arrangements. With the exception of an employer's duty to accommodate pursuant to human rights legislation,[8] employers are not required to provide any such arrangements.

Despite there being no requirement for employers to provide such arrangements, other than where human rights legislation so requires, such arrangements can prove beneficial in many instances, given the positive effect they have on workplace morale. In certain circumstances, it simply will not be feasible to allow

---

7   See under the heading "Constructive Dismissal" in Part 4, "The Separation".
8   See under the heading "Duty to Accommodate" later in this Part.

such arrangements, as in a brokerage situation where constant client coverage is required.[9] In other cases, if the employee's request is workable for the employer, such programs are worth considering as they can have a profoundly positive impact on the morale and attitude of the individual involved, as well as on the workplace as a whole. In addition, participation in such programs can serve to send a message to the community that an employer is progressive and willing to recognize the special needs of its workforce.

In some cases, it is the employer who seeks to implement such programs in its workplace. Again, the employer must beware of potential liability for constructive dismissal. For example, in the case of an employee who starts employment on a full-time basis and is subsequently told that his or her hours are being cut down to part-time status, or that the employee is now required to share his or her position with another employee, this is likely to be viewed by a court as a constructive dismissal, as it may constitute a unilateral fundamental change to the employment relationship. Employers should provide sufficient notice of such changes as to constitute reasonable notice and should seek employee consent, or be willing to provide an employee with pay in lieu of notice of dismissal if the employee is unwilling to work under the changed conditions.

Employee Attendance

The issue of employee absences is one which plagues employers, given the current human rights regime and the duty of the employer to accommodate certain employees. If an employee requests a leave of absence, irrespective of the length, the employer may be required to provide such leave if to do so would accommodate the employee's special needs and would not push the employer to the point of undue hardship.[10] Employers need only be concerned with those requests which relate to an employee's special needs. For example, if the employee requests the leave because of a disabling condition, the employer may be required to provide it so as to avoid a human rights complaint that the employer failed to accommodate the employee's disability. Similarly, an employer may be required to provide leaves of absence for employees because of their unique religious, parental or familial concerns. An employer is not required to provide a leave of absence where there are no adverse human rights implications, as in a case where the employee wishes to extend his or her vacation. Unless the employee has scheduled a leave of absence by using vacation days, employers are not required to pay employees for days not worked. This does not detract from the fact that such absences can be extremely disruptive to the workplace, especially if they are unpredictable.

---

9   Even such legitimate reasons may not remove the requirement that the employer provide accommodation if such is required by human rights legislation.
10   See under the heading "Duty to Accommodate" later in this Part.

It is not unusual for each workplace to have at least one employee whose attendance is abysmal. In many cases, despite the existence of a company policy providing for a set number of paid sick days, employers will continue to pay employees for days taken off in excess of those provided for in the policy if the employee calls in sick. One way to test the employee's illness is to threaten to cut off the employee's salary for sick days taken in excess of those stipulated in the policy. However, the employer runs the risk that such employees will then present themselves for work while sick, exposing other employees to potentially contagious illnesses. The employer may also open itself up to a potential human rights complaint if the effect of such an action is to discriminate against the employee on the basis of disability. The employer may try establishing a sick day policy which allows for a minimum number of paid sick days, with any additional days being at the employer's discretion. This may serve to discourage those employees who feel they are entitled to take all available sick days, whether or not they are actually sick. Employers might also attempt to control employees' attendance problems by establishing an employee assistance program, implementing an employee help line, providing flu shots or providing employees with health club membership subsidies. Employers should also consider whether an employee will be required to present a medical certificate before being entitled to a sick day under the policy.

Access to Employee Records

Personnel records kept by the employer are the property of the employer, and the employer is entitled to retain these records, even after the employee leaves the organization. However, where it was once thought that an employer had no legal obligation to allow an employee access to his or her personnel file, there is now legislation in the federal jurisdiction which requires such disclosure in certain circumstances.

The *Personal Information Protection and Electronic Documents Act* ("PIPEDA")[11] provides, in Schedule 1 (with which all federally regulated employers are required to comply), that individuals must be given access to that personal information which the organization has collected. In addition, the individual has the ability to challenge the accuracy and completeness of the personal information and have it amended as appropriate. Schedule 1 of PIPEDA does contemplate that an organization may not be able to provide access to all the personal information it holds about an individual. Specifically, Schedule 1 provides:

> Exceptions to the access requirement should be limited and specific. The reasons for denying access should be provided to the individual upon request. Exceptions may include information that is prohibitively costly to provide, information that contains references to other individuals, information that cannot be disclosed for

---

11   S.C. 2000, c. 5 (as amended to 2002, c. 8).

legal, security, or commercial proprietary reasons, and information that is subject to solicitor-client or litigation privilege.[12]

Although PIPEDA currently applies only to those employers who are federally regulated (banks, telecommunications companies, airlines, etc.), it also provides that it will come to apply to all Canadian employers as of January 1, 2004, unless similar provincial legislation is enacted in the meantime. Despite the fact that, for a remaining short period of time, some employers may still have an ability to deny their employees access to their personnel records, based on the PIPEDA implementation schedule, unless some exceptional reason exists for not producing the employee's file, it is generally recommended that such records be disclosed, since employees rarely request disclosure of such records unless they are required for some important purpose. Unfortunately, disclosure is often denied because of the employer's suspicion that the records are being sought for the purpose of obtaining information to support a lawsuit against the employer. Even in such a case, if the employer has kept adequate records, there is no reason to deny the request, particularly if the contents of the personnel record might discourage the employee from bringing a claim. All information relevant to a lawsuit, including the personnel file, must be produced during the course of a lawsuit, so if the employer declines the request at this stage, and invites a lawsuit, it will be required to produce the information in any event.

A related issue which often arises concerns the employer's obligation with respect to employee medical records which the employer may have in its possession. Such records typically come into existence in the case of mandatory pre-employment medical examinations or in cases where employers keep a company doctor or an occupational health and safety doctor on staff. Generally, staff doctors will only be required to produce such records in limited circumstances.[13] For example, where the doctor discovers that an employee has a reportable or communicable disease, he or she may be required to report this disease to the local health unit, pursuant to the relevant health protection legislation. A doctor may also be required, pursuant to highway traffic legislation, to report any individuals who, in the doctor's opinion, are suffering from a condition which makes it dangerous for that person to operate a motor vehicle. In addition, doctors may be required to report to the local authorities where they learn that a serious crime, such as murder, rape, robbery or kidnapping, has been committed or is about to be committed. Although this may be a breach of the doctor's duty of confidentiality, the doctor will likely be protected for having made such disclosure

---

12 *Ibid.*, Schedule 1, s. 4.9, "Principle 9 – Individual Access".
13 If it could be argued that such records are like those kept at a medical institution, then a court may have a right to order production in other circumstances, such as where the patient has authorized disclosure: see *Frenette v. Metropolitan Life Insurance Co.* (1992), 89 D.L.R. (4th) 653 (S.C.C.).

in the interests of the protection of society.[14] Finally, a doctor will be required to produce any information sought pursuant to a subpoena, unless the doctor can claim that the information is privileged by virtue of the relationship between the doctor and patient.[15]

Company doctors also often question how their obligation to the employer can be reconciled with their obligation to the various employees or "patients". In the course of an examination, a doctor is often in receipt of confidential information regarding an employee, and the doctor may be liable if such information is disclosed. However, the employer will have hired a company doctor for the purpose of obtaining medical information about the employees, and it will likely come as an unpleasant surprise if a company doctor takes the position that employee medical information is confidential. Whether or not the doctor-patient relationship exists when a doctor is examining an employee for the employer will depend largely upon the nature of the examination. Company-employed doctors may be retained for the purpose of conducting an examination of a job applicant or an employee for some employment-related purpose, such as the determination of whether the employee is physically able to perform the duties of the job. In these situations, it is generally believed that the doctor assumes the role of examiner rather than therapist and the doctor's primary duty is to the employer rather than to the patient/employee. However, where a patient is attended by a staff doctor who is employed to provide services for the employees, the doctor's primary duty may not be to the employer. The person or entity to whom the primary duty is owed will likely depend upon the unique facts of each case. Employers might wish to consider establishing a policy for the disclosure of medical information if they have a company doctor on staff. If all employees are informed by the company doctor prior to an examination that information obtained during the examination may be provided to the employer, and the employee consents to the examination on this basis, it will be difficult for the employee to later argue that the duty of confidentiality was breached. Employers may wish to require employees to sign a consent form or may wish to post notices to this effect in the examination or waiting room.

HUMILIATION OR HARASSMENT OF THE EMPLOYEE

Occurrences of harassing behaviour in the workplace are on the rise and often prompt employers and employees to consider their legal rights in the presence of

---

14 *Halls v. Mitchell*, [1928] 2 D.L.R. 97 (S.C.C.); *Tarasoff v. Regents of University of California*, 17 Cal.3d 425 (1976).

15 Although it is considered dishonourable and indiscreet for a doctor to reveal professional confidences, and such disclosure may expose the doctor to disciplinary action, courts have generally been reluctant to extend a privilege for doctor-patient communications: see *Halls v. Mitchell*, *supra*; *R. v. Burgess*, [1974] 4 W.W.R. 310 (B.C. Co. Ct.); *Torok v. Torok* (1983), 44 O.R. (2d) 118 (S.C.).

such behaviour. If an employer treats its employee in a manner which is humiliating or tantamount to harassment, the employee may feel that he or she has no option but to resign the employment. If, in such a case, the conduct on the part of the employer is such as to amount to a repudiation of the employment relationship, then the employee may have a cause of action against the employer. Employees in these situations have resigned their employment and made successful claims that they were constructively dismissed.[16] The court will consider the conduct in question and determine whether the facts indicate conduct inconsistent with the express or implied conditions of employment. This determination can differ from case to case, depending on the societal standards in place in the jurisdiction at any given time. As in any constructive dismissal case, the conduct will be judged objectively and not on the basis of what the employee perceived or felt.

Employees who, in the workplace, are subject to harassment which is rooted in some statutorily prohibited ground of discrimination, such as sex, race or sexual orientation, should be aware that this type of conduct may be prohibited by human rights legislation. Such employees should first consider complaining to their employers or immediate supervisors, as this kind of harassment may constitute just cause for summary dismissal, and the employer may, after an investigation, put a quick stop to the behaviour by terminating the harasser. If this does not happen, or if the harassed employee does not feel that his or her problem is being addressed, a further option may be to issue a complaint with the human rights commission in the given jurisdiction. Human rights commissions generally have broad powers to investigate and remedy complaints and to create harassment-free workplaces by necessary means. It may also be possible for employees to seek a monetary award from their employer if they have suffered pain or mental anguish as a result of the harassing behaviour.

Courts have recognized that a victim of harassment may make a claim against the employer or the harasser in tort, in circumstances of assault or intentional infliction of nervous shock.[17] Courts have also recognized that, if a victim of harassment is dismissed for having complained about the harassment or for refusing to accept sexual advances made by an employer, he or she may have a valid claim for wrongful dismissal.[18] However, the courts have not accepted that a separate cause of action based on harassment alone is available to a harassment victim, particularly in a case where the harassment is based on a ground of discrimination prohibited by human rights legislation. In such cases, courts have

---

16 *Berg v. Cowie* (1918), 40 D.L.R. 250 (Sask. C.A.); *Paitich v. Clarke Institute of Psychiatry* (1988), 19 C.C.E.L. 105 (Ont. H.C.J.), affd 30 C.C.E.L. 235 (Ont. C.A.).

17 See *Boothman v. Canada*, [1993] 3 F.C. 381 (T.D.); *Clark v. Canada*, [1994] 3 F.C. 323 (T.D.); *Kulyk v. Toronto Board of Education* (1996), 139 D.L.R. (4th) 114 (Ont. Ct. (Gen. Div.)).

18 See *Tremblett v. Aardvark Pest Control Ltd.* (1987), 16 C.C.E.L. 306 (Ont. Dist. Ct.), and *Gagne v. Smooth Rock Falls Hospital* (1991), 39 C.C.E.L. 281 (Ont. Ct. (Gen. Div.)), affd (unreported, March 3, 1997, Ont. C.A.).

held that claims should more appropriately be made with the relevant human rights commission.[19]

Although sexual harassment has been at the forefront of workplace issues in recent years and, as a result, many employers and employees have had some experience in dealing with the problem, many others are still unaware of the breadth of prohibited sexual conduct in the workplace. When the term "sexual harassment" is heard, employees are often envisioned being offered career advancement in exchange for sexual favours, while the many other types of behaviour which can be considered sexually harassing are not always appreciated. Sexual harassment has been defined as "unwelcome conduct of a sexual nature that detrimentally affects the work environment or leads to adverse job-related consequences for the victims of the harassment".[20] Such behaviour may include sexual remarks, unwelcome touching, inappropriate jokes, sexual requests or suggestions, staring, making comments about a person's appearance, and the display of sexually suggestive pictures, drawings or slogans. To constitute harassment, the conduct must be known or ought reasonably to be known to be unwelcome. It may be a defence for a harasser to argue that he or she did not know that the behaviour was offensive. However, the behaviour will be viewed on an objective standard and, if it is determined that the harasser should have known that the conduct was unwelcome, the individual will be liable.

Given the concern about sexual harassment in the workplace, some employers feel that they should take steps to restrict all sexual relations between employees. It does not appear that this is necessary. Even human rights adjudicators have recognized that the purpose of sexual harassment legislation is not to prevent relations between employees, unless the social contact engaged in is coerced or compelled, or an employee's refusal to participate may result in a loss of employment benefits.[21] In the case of *Dooley v. C.N. Weber Ltd.*,[22] Mr. Dooley was fired for having engaged in sexual relations with two female subordinates. The Court could not find that Mr. Dooley's behaviour had an adverse effect on the business and thus found in Mr. Dooley's favour.

While it may not be necessary for employers to place an outright ban on sexual relations between employees, particular attention should be paid to relations between supervisors and their subordinates. The power differential between such

---

19 See *Seneca College of Applied Arts & Technology v. Bhadauria* (1981), 124 D.L.R. (3d) 193 (S.C.C.); *A. (N.) v. C.F.P.L. Broadcasting Ltd.* (1995), 9 C.C.E.L. (2d) 56 (Ont. Ct. (Gen. Div.)).
20 *Janzen v. Platy Enterprises Ltd.* (1989), 59 D.L.R. (4th) 352 (S.C.C.), at p. 375.
21 *Bell and Korczak (Re)* (1980), 80 C.L.L.C. ¶18,006 (Ont. Arb. Bd.).
22 (1994), 3 C.C.E.L. (2d) 95 (Ont. Ct. (Gen. Div.)), affd 80 O.A.C. 234 (C.A.), leave to appeal to S.C.C. refused 89 O.A.C. 318n.

employees often makes it difficult to distinguish between consensual and non-consensual relations.[23] Such relationships may not affect the employer's business, as in the *Dooley* case, but they do have the potential for severely damaging employee morale. If such relationships are made public, others in the workplace are likely to feel ignored relative to the subordinate who is involved with the supervisor and are likely to suspect favouritism. Employers considering implementing policies restricting employee relationships would be well-advised to concentrate their efforts on relationships between supervisors and subordinates.

Employers may be held liable for their employees' acts of harassment in the workplace and should therefore act diligently once they are made aware of the existence of workplace harassment in their organizations. The Supreme Court of Canada has held that the principle of vicarious liability applies to an employer;[24] that is, employers may be responsible for the unauthorized discriminatory acts in which their employees engage during the course of employment. Generally speaking, if the employer has actual or constructive knowledge of harassment, the employer must take reasonable action to promptly eradicate the harassment.

The first step which every employer should take to prevent harassment in the workplace is to develop and implement a workplace harassment policy.[25] Such a policy should, at a minimum, provide the following:

(a) an explanation of the underlying philosophy of the policy;
(b) some definition (not necessarily exhaustive) of the prohibited conduct;
(c) a warning as to the penalties which will be invoked for a violation of the policy;
(d) a procedural guideline for the filing of complaints pursuant to the policy; and
(e) an outline of what one might expect to occur once a complaint has been filed.

In order for a workplace harassment policy to be effective, all employees should be educated regarding the policy, and the policy should be strictly enforced.[26] Employers should consider two separate education sessions regarding the policy. The first should educate all employees regarding the types of behaviour

---

23 See *Bannister v. General Motors of Canada Ltd.* (1998), 164 D.L.R. (4th) 325 (Ont. C.A.), and *Simpson v. Consumers' Assn. of Canada* (2001), 209 D.L.R. (4th) 214 (Ont. C.A.), leave to appeal to S.C.C. refused 214 D.L.R. (4th) vi, where, in both cases, a finding was made that the dismissal of a supervisor for having engaged in sexual misconduct with a subordinate was justified.

24 *Robichaud v. Canada (Treasury Board)* (1987), 40 D.L.R. (4th) 577 (S.C.C.).

25 In fact, pursuant to the *Canada Labour Code*, R.S.C. 1985, c. L-2 (as amended to 2002, c. 9), s. 247.4, all federally regulated employers are required to issue a policy statement concerning sexual harassment.

26 See *Hinds v. Canada (Employment & Immigration Commission)* (1988), 24 C.C.E.L. 65 (Can. Trib.), and *Bannister v. General Motors of Canada Ltd.* (1994), 8 C.C.E.L. (2d) 281 (Ont. Ct. (Gen. Div.)), revd on other grounds 164 D.L.R. (4th) 325 (Ont. C.A.), as examples of cases where courts frowned upon employers who had harassment policies in place which were neither implemented nor enforced by the employers.

which are prohibited, and the second should educate supervisors and managers on how to recognize and control harassment, and how to effectively implement the policy.

Although the object of a harassment policy is to achieve a harassment-free workplace, it will not always be successful. If an incident occurs, employers are encouraged to consider the following:

1. Employees with harassment complaints should be instructed to issue those complaints with a contact person who, where possible, is someone outside of their department.

2. It is wise for companies to designate at least two contact persons to receive such complaints, so that employees can take their complaints to the person with whom they feel most comfortable.

3. Complainants should be instructed to make written notes of the incident as soon as possible after it has taken place, and to include the names of possible witnesses.

4. Upon receipt of a complaint, the employer should measure the reported behaviour against the harassment policy and determine whether an investigation is merited.

5. If an investigation becomes necessary, the investigator chosen should be someone who is independent of the area in which the complainant works and who has experience with personnel and human rights legislation.

6. The investigation should come across as fair and unbiased, which may require particular alterations to the investigation format. For instance, if the complaint is one of sexual harassment, then the employer may consider using two investigators, one male and one female, while an investigator of a particular race may be required if the complaint is one of racial harassment.

7. While the investigation is being concluded, consideration should be given to implementing interim measures in the workplace. For example, it may be necessary to suspend the alleged harasser with pay, or to arrange for a transfer or some reassignment of reporting relationships for a temporary period of time.

8. The investigator should meet with both the complainant and the alleged harasser, as well as any relevant witnesses, and every attempt should be made to keep all information collected during the investigation confidential.

9. The investigation should be conducted as quickly as possible, and the complainant should ultimately be informed of the outcome of the complaint, regardless of whether any action is taken against the harasser.

Dealing with a complaint appropriately when it first arises can go a long way towards resolving the issue in an amicable way in furtherance of the employment relationship.

Workplace Violence

The issue of harassment in the workplace is also of increasing concern to employers who are beginning to see incidents of workplace violence as one of the most troublesome problems they run the risk of facing. The role that harassment has played in some of these incidents of violence provides a powerful motivator for employers to be on rigorous alert for any signs that harassment may be present in the workplace. For example, an incident at Sears Canada in southwestern Ontario in 1996 found a woman shot dead by a manager she worked with after she had been the victim of his prolonged sexual harassment. In the Ottawa incident at OC Transpo in April 1999, Pierre LeBrun entered his former workplace and opened fire, killing four of his former co-workers, and wounding two others, before killing himself. The post-incident investigation revealed that he had been the victim of significant ridicule and harassment in the workplace, primarily as a result of a speech impediment. Whether or not harassment was experienced by the ultimate victim or perpetrator of violence, the fact is that it can play a role, and it puts an organization at considerable risk.

Employers seem generally quite motivated to eliminate the risk of violence in the workplace. Putting aside the issue of legal obligation, many employers have no doubt realized that a scared and anxious workforce is not the most productive workforce. On the legal side, there is no question that employers also have an obligation to ensure that they maintain a violence-free workplace. This obligation may arise either as a result of the common law of negligence, or pursuant to some statutory regime. The two most common sets of statutes seen to govern areas of workplace violence are occupiers' liability Acts and occupational health and safety Acts.

An employee who is a victim of violence in the workplace (or the employee's family) might choose to bring a claim against the employer, alleging that the employer failed to take all reasonable steps to protect the employee. As such, the employer might be held to be liable to the employee as a result of the common law of negligence. "Negligence" has been defined as the omission to do something which a reasonable person, guided upon those considerations which ordinarily regulate the conduct of human affairs, would do, or the doing of something which a prudent and reasonable person would not have done.[27] A company might be found to be negligent if it unintentionally omits to do that which a reasonable person would have done, or does that which a person taking reasonable precautions would not have done.

To be successful in a negligence claim against an employer, an employee would have to show the following on a balance of probabilities:

1. The employer owed a duty of care to the employee.

---

27   *Blyth v. Birmingham Water Works Co.* (1856), 11 Exch. 781.

2.   The employer breached the standard of care owed to the employee.
3.   The employer's breach was the proximate cause of the employee's injury.
4.   The employee suffered actual damage or loss as a result of the injury.

The first part of the fourfold test will likely be met in making a negligence claim, as it has been held that an employer has a general duty to take reasonable care for the safety of its employees and to provide a safe system of work.[28] The standard of care will be judged against the measure of reasonableness.

An example of this potential liability can be seen in a decision from the United States, *Clark v. Carla Gay Dress Co., Inc.*[29] In this case, Ms Clark had recently separated from her husband, and she claimed that she had warned her supervisor that her husband had beaten her and was a drug addict. One day, her husband appeared at her workplace and requested a visit with Ms Clark to discuss a visit with their child. Ms Clark's supervisor noted that Mr. Clark seemed friendly. Ms Clark first refused to meet with her husband, but agreed on a second request in order to avoid a scene. After a discussion lasting a few minutes, Ms Clark attempted to return to work. At that moment, her husband grabbed her wrist, pulled out a gun, chased her to another room, and shot her in the head. The employer was ultimately found not to be liable because it could not have reasonably foreseen the violent incident. Even if Ms Clark had spoken to her supervisor about her husband, there was no warning that she feared for her safety or wished that he be removed from the premises. Also, Mr. Clark had appeared friendly when he attended for his visit. On the basis of all of these factors, the Court was satisfied that the employer could not have foreseen that allowing Mr. Clark to enter the premises would put Ms Clark at risk.

In addition to the common law, the duty to provide a safe workplace arises under statute. Under occupiers' liability legislation, an employer will be seen to be an "occupier" if it is in physical possession of the premises or has responsibility for and control over the condition of the premises or the activities carried on there. If an employer is seen to be an occupier, then the employer will owe a statutory duty to provide safe premises for all who enter. By definition, this duty can extend beyond that owed to employees, to include a duty to all those who enter the premises: suppliers, volunteers, customers, members of the public, etc. In order to be found liable under occupiers' liability legislation, an employer would have to have engaged in roughly the same type of negligent conduct as that described earlier in this section. Essentially, it will be up to the victim or his or her family to demonstrate that the employer failed to take reasonable care. Employers that do business in areas that put their employees at unusually high

---

28   *Carriere v. Board of Gravelbourg School District No. 2244 of Saskatchewan* (1977), 79 D.L.R. (3d) 662 (Sask. C.A.).
29   178 Ga. App. 157 (Ga. App., 1986).

risk, or employers with knowledge of specific risks, will likely be held to a higher standard of care.[30]

Lastly, occupational health and safety legislation in Canada works to ensure the safety of workers and sets out obligations for employers to prevent and remedy health and safety hazards in the workplace.[31] Generally speaking, it may be possible for employees to make use of occupational health and safety legislation as a way to prevent violence in the workplace. Take, for example, the case of *O.P.S.E.U. v. Ontario (Ministry of the Solicitor General and Correctional Services)*,[32] in which a group of prison guards refused to escort prisoners into the jail's exercise yard on a particular day when staffing levels had dropped. On this day, guards had also been asked to escort a prisoner outside the jail for medical reasons, making the remaining guards particularly concerned about the possibility of being overcome by the prisoners due to lack of staff. The Ministry of Labour determined that the guards had had legitimate concerns for their safety, and found the employer's instructions to the guards to carry out the yard exercises, when staffing levels had dropped below the established safe levels, constituted a failure on the part of the employer to take every precaution reasonable in the circumstances for the protection of the workers, in accordance with the applicable occupational health and safety legislation.

An employer faced with a risk of violence in the workplace is not only wise to obtain legal advice and determine the extent of the employer's duty to protect the workforce, but it may also be advisable for the employer to contact the police and secure their assistance in attempting to reduce the chances of or prevent a violent incident. In this regard, an employer may be able to assist an employee make use of certain measures available under the *Criminal Code* of Canada,[33] such as the laying of charges or the obtaining of a peace bond (restraining order).

Alcohol Liability

As an extension of the duty to provide a safe workplace, employers should also be aware that courts are increasingly willing to attach liability to employers who do not take responsibility for employee consumption of alcohol. Those employers who provide employees with alcohol, or who sponsor events at which alcohol is served, are particularly at risk. Take, for example, the case of *Jacobsen v. Nike Canada Ltd.*,[34] where an employer supplied a cooler of beer to its employees

---

30 See, for example, *Allison v. Rank City Wall Canada* (1984), 6 D.L.R. (4th) 144 (Ont. H.C.J.), and *Q. v. Minto Management Ltd.* (1985), 15 D.L.R. (4th) 581 (Ont. H.C.J.), affd 34 D.L.R. (4th) 767n (Ont. C.A.), in which two companies were held liable for not having taken reasonable steps to ensure the safety of their tenants, in part because both companies were found to have had information suggesting that they were at a higher risk for crime.

31 See under the heading, "Occupational Health and Safety Legislation" later in this Part.

32 [1997] O.O.H.S.A.D. No. 97 (T. Wacyk).

33 R.S.C. 1985, c. C-46 (as amended to 2002, c. 22).

34 (1996), 133 D.L.R. (4th) 377 (B.C.S.C.).

during working hours. When one of the intoxicated employees became injured in an accident while driving home after work, the employer was found liable for negligence. The Court held that the duty owed by an employer is equivalent to that owed by commercial vendors of alcohol to patrons of an establishment. Because Nike provided the alcohol and then effectively required employees to drive home from its remote work location, it was essentially making drinking and driving a condition of work. Nike had a responsibility to not only watch for signs of impairment, but also to take proactive steps to prevent employees from driving while impaired. It fundamentally failed in these duties.

Employers should be equally wary of the office Christmas party or any work-related social function where alcohol is served. In *Hunt (Litigation Guardian of) v. Sutton Group Incentive Realty Inc.*,[35] a Sutton employee became intoxicated at the office afternoon Christmas party. She left the party in the early evening, only to subsequently spend approximately three hours with some co-workers continuing to drink at a nearby bar. When she left the bar and attempted to drive home, she was involved in an accident in which she suffered severe brain damage. She sued her employer in negligence, alleging that Sutton had failed to properly safeguard her from harm. Justice Marchand of the Ontario Superior Court of Justice agreed, finding that the duty to protect employees extended beyond the employer's premises. The employer admitted that he had known that Ms Hunt was intoxicated at the party, and it was held that he could have reasonably foreseen that possible harm could come to her when she left the party. The employer should have taken positive steps to prevent Ms Hunt from driving home. Even though the employer offered taxi rides to all employees generally, this was considered not to be enough. Specific mention was also made of the open and unsupervised bar, which meant that the employer could not monitor the consumption of alcohol by employees.[36]

In light of the *Nike* and *Sutton* decisions, employers who provide alcohol to employees, or who sponsor events where alcohol will be consumed, should consider taking a number of steps as a means by which to minimize their potential liability:

---

35 (2001), 196 D.L.R. (4th) 738 (Ont. S.C.J.), revd 215 D.L.R. (4th) 193 (Ont. C.A.). On appeal, a new trial was ordered as the result of a finding that the trial judge had improperly charged the jury. The Court of Appeal also expressed concern regarding the trial judge's decision that Sutton was partially responsible for Ms Hunt's injuries, but felt that it had insufficient evidence before it to make any conclusive findings in this regard.

36 Compare with *John v. Flynn* (2001), 201 D.L.R. (4th) 500 (Ont. C.A.), leave to appeal to S.C.C. refused 210 D.L.R. (4th) vi, in which an employer was found not responsible for the injuries suffered by a third party who was involved in a car accident with an employee of the company. The employee had come to work intoxicated and continued to drink, on breaks in the parking lot, throughout his shift. After work, he drove home, had a beer, and then got into his car and had an accident in which the plaintiff was injured. The Ontario Court of Appeal was not prepared to accept that the employer owed a duty of care to a third party for the activities an employee engaged in after work, particularly where there was no evidence that the employer had even been aware that the employee had been intoxicated when he left work.

1. Send the message to employees that consumption of alcohol is a personal choice, and try to ensure that no employee attending the event feels pressured to drink.
2. Provide safe transportation (rides or complimentary taxi chits).
3. Plan an event where consumption of alcohol is not the primary activity.
4. Do not use an open bar, which allows for self-service. Rather, allow only designated servers to pour alcohol.
5. Ensure that alcoholic beverages are secured and that only authorized personnel have access.
6. Ensure that all servers are 18 years of age or older, and have received some training in the identification of intoxicated individuals.
7. Establish procedures for measured servings of alcohol.
8. Consider issuing limited numbers of drink tickets to employees instead of allowing employees unlimited servings. (This is not foolproof. Employees who wish to drink more than their ticket allotment will normally be able to obtain extra tickets.)
9. Serve food as well as alcohol.
10. Consider hiring additional security or other staff to assist in the detection of intoxicated individuals.
11. Stop the service of alcohol at a time well before the end of the event, and continue with service of non-alcoholic beverages to the end of the event.

EMPLOYMENT STANDARDS LEGISLATION

General

For many years, the employment relationship was viewed as a simple contract between a master and servant, and thus the parties were free to establish whatever contractual provisions they desired. In reality, however, terms were almost exclusively dictated by the employer, who possessed the most power in the bargaining of terms. To compensate for the employer's perceived unfair bargaining advantage, each of the provinces and territories enacted employment standards legislation.[37] The *Canada Labour Code* deals in Part III with employment standards for federally regulated organizations. Employment standards legislation represents direct statutory intervention and regulation of the employment contract and has established minimum standards which apply to all relationships between employers and employees.

Employment standards legislation applies only to employer-employee relationships and thus may not apply to other types of relationships, such as those

---

37 For a more comprehensive discussion of employment standards in Ontario, see E.M. Roher, *The Employment Standards Guide* (Scarborough: Carswell, 2001 – looseleaf), and R.M. Parry, *Employment Standards Handbook*, 3rd ed. (Aurora: Canada Law Book Inc., 2002 – looseleaf).

involving independent contractors, partners or consultants. When determining whether a party is an employee for the purpose of the application of employment standards legislation, reference will first be made to the relevant definitions contained in the legislation. Employment standards referees have also been known to refer to the common law tests used to determine whether a certain party is an employee.[38]

Employers will occasionally enter into relationships with individuals where it is suggested that the individual is an independent contractor for the purpose of attempting to avoid the application of employment standards legislation. As is the case under the common law, such arrangements may not always be effective. If a decision-maker reviewing the relationship finds sufficient evidence of an employment relationship, employment standards legislation may be found to apply to the relationship, despite the parties' stated intention to the contrary.

Except as noted in the applicable legislation, employment standards legislation applies to every employment contract, whether oral or written, express or implied. Employers and employees are prohibited from entering into any agreement wherein they purport to contract out of certain provisions of the relevant employment standards legislation. For example, an employer may not come to an agreement with its employees that they work overtime for their regular wages.

Employment standards legislation is intended to provide minimum standards only. Where an employer has agreed to provide some greater benefit than that set out in the employment standards legislation, the employer will be bound by this promise and will not be entitled to fall back on the minimum standards set out in the legislation. Employers also have significant obligations, under employment standards legislation, to keep accurate records regarding their employees, including records of wages paid, hours worked and holidays accrued. Failure to keep such records could expose employers to substantial liability, as employment standards referees will often defer to the word of the employee in the event that an employer has not kept accurate records to support its position.

Employers are required to pay to their employees all outstanding wages. Wages are defined in employment standards legislation to include any monetary remuneration payable to an employee by an employer under the terms of the employment contract. In Ontario, wages are meant to include any payments made under the employment standards legislation, and any allowances for room and board, but are not meant to include tips and gratuities, discretionary gifts or bonuses or travel allowances or expenses. In Ontario, overtime pay, vacation pay, living allowances and bonuses paid pursuant to an incentive plan have also been held by referees to constitute "wages".

---

38 *Cambrian College (Re)* (unreported, November 11, 1991, E.S.C. 2940, Joyce); *Scholze (Re)* (unreported, February 10, 1994, E.S.C. 94-34, Muir). See under the heading "Testing for an Employment Relationship" in Part 2, "The Engagement", for a discussion of these common law tests for employee status.

Employers should be very wary of retaining any portion of an employee's wages as payment for some outstanding moneys owed by the employee to the employer. In Ontario, for example, such withholding is prohibited unless authorized by statute, by court order or in writing by the employee. This would apply, for example, to a situation where an employer wished to deduct from the employee's wages an amount:

(a) outstanding from personal use of a company credit card;
(b) representative of an overpayment of wages;
(c) resulting from cash shortages attributable to the employee; or
(d) arising due to the fact that an employee took vacation time prior to its actual accrual.

Public Holidays

Employment standards legislation in all jurisdictions states that employees must be provided with certain designated days off as public holidays and that employees must be paid for these days, despite the fact that the employees did not work on these days. The jurisdictions vary somewhat in their provision of the particular days which represent public holidays.[39] Employees are not prohibited from working on public holidays; the legislation merely provides for their minimum entitlement in the event that they do work on such days. In many cases, employers can require employees to work on a public holiday as long as the employee is properly compensated for doing so. In Newfoundland, New Brunswick and Ontario, only those employees in certain industries can be required to work on public holidays. In Ontario, these industries include hotels and tourism, restaurants and taverns, hospitals and continuous operations.

In certain jurisdictions, employees are required to fulfil a minimum service requirement before they are entitled to paid public holidays. While there are no such requirements in Manitoba, Nova Scotia, Ontario or Saskatchewan, there is a three-month (or 90-day) requirement in New Brunswick, a 60-day requirement in Quebec and a 30-day requirement in the other jurisdictions.

Employees in British Columbia, Manitoba, Newfoundland, Nova Scotia, Prince Edward Island and the federal jurisdiction will not be entitled to a paid public holiday if the employee has not worked 15 of the 30 days preceding the statutory holiday. In addition, employees will not be entitled to a paid public holiday if they are absent without authorization on either the working day preceding or following the public holiday[40] or if they do not work on the public holiday after they have been asked or scheduled to do so.[41]

---

39 See Appendix A, Table 1.
40 Except those employees in British Columbia or Saskatchewan or under federal jurisdiction.
41 Except in British Columbia, Quebec, Newfoundland and Saskatchewan.

Generally speaking, employees are meant to receive paid public holidays even if a holiday falls on a non-working day for an employee (such as on a weekend or a day off or during an employee's vacation). In most circumstances, the employee in such a case will be entitled to take a paid holiday at some other time, normally before the employee's next annual vacation. Most jurisdictions also provide for the substitution of public holidays and allow employees to take a paid public holiday on another working day if they choose to work on the actual public holiday.[42]

An employee who does not work on a public holiday is entitled to be paid for the day. Employment standards legislation in most jurisdictions contains provisions which set out the calculation of "public holiday pay", which, for example, in Ontario, is equal to the regular wages and vacation pay earned by the employee in the preceding four weeks, divided by 20. Employers should be aware of these calculations because, as can be seen from the Ontario calculation, it is not technically compliant to simply pay the employee his or her regular wages for the day.

Employees who do work on public holidays are entitled to receive public holiday pay plus an extra amount as compensation for the service provided on the holiday.[43] In the majority of jurisdictions, employees who work on public holidays receive public holiday pay plus a premium equivalent to one and a half times their regular rate of pay.[44] In Newfoundland and Quebec, employees do not receive a premium payment for working on a public holiday. Instead, in addition to receiving their regular wages for the holiday, such employees will receive a payment to compensate them for working the hours on the holiday (calculated based on the employee's regular wages) or may receive extra time off. Time worked on public holidays is not to be taken into account when calculating an employee's entitlement to overtime pay.

Certain employees may be exempt from the public holiday provisions of employment standards legislation. For example, in Ontario, many professionals, as well as firefighters, taxicab drivers, seasonal tourism employees and certain students, are exempt from the public holiday provisions of the *Employment Standards Act, 2000*.[45]

---

42 Those jurisdictions which do not so provide include Alberta, Quebec and Prince Edward Island.

43 In many provinces, the employee may also choose to take another day as the public holiday in lieu of any additional compensation. This option is not available in Saskatchewan or the Yukon. In British Columbia, the provisions are complex but, like other provinces, contemplate an employee receiving compensation for the public holiday (whether by way of regular wages or a day off at a later date) as well as compensation for the hours actually worked on the holiday, which includes a premium payment.

44 Exceptions to this include Quebec, Newfoundland and British Columbia. In British Columbia, employees will typically receive one and a half times their regular wages, but may earn up to double their regular wages in circumstances where they work in excess of 11 hours on a public holiday.

45 S.O. 2000, c. 41 (as amended to 2002, c. 18, Sch. J).

Minimum Wage

Minimum wage legislation was enacted early in the 20th century in response to increasing discontent amongst employees whose wages were failing to keep up with the increased cost of living. All jurisdictions, including the federal jurisdiction, have enacted regulations governing the provision of minimum wages to certain employees. The fact that most jurisdictions have established the minimum wage by way of regulation or order allows for regular amendments to be made to the minimum wage with minimal inconvenience and administration.[46] Minimum wage rates do change from time to time, although advance notice will usually be given by the government ministry responsible. The rates in existence in any jurisdiction at a given time are most significantly affected by the current government.[47]

Minimum wage legislation is meant to apply to all employees in a jurisdiction, including those employees who are not paid on a hourly basis. It is the employer's responsibility to ensure that minimum wage compliance is achieved, and this may require some calculation for those employees who are not paid on an hourly basis. While tips and gratuities are not normally taken into account when an employee's minimum wage is calculated, in Quebec there exists a separate minimum for employees who usually receive gratuities.

Certain jurisdictions provide for wages lower than the established minimums to be paid to young persons,[48] students[49] or persons serving liquor.[50] Most jurisdictions also allow for the deduction from an employee's earnings of expenses associated with providing the employee with room and board, even if this deduction brings the employee's earnings to a level below that set out as the required minimum wage.[51] Some jurisdictions allow an employer to deduct the cost of supplying and cleaning uniforms from the employee's wages, but employers are

---

46 The exceptions to this are Nunavut and the Northwest Territories, where the minimum wage is set out in the employment standards legislation itself.

47 See Appendix A, Table 2, for a listing of the minimum wages.

48 In the federal jurisdiction and in the Yukon, the minimum wage only applies to employees 17 years of age and older, while in Newfoundland, it applies only to employees 16 years of age and older. In the Northwest Territories and Nunavut, the minimum wage varies, depending upon whether an individual is 16 years of age or older. In Nova Scotia, certain farm labourers under 16 years of age are also exempt.

49 Ontario has a special minimum wage for students under 18 years of age whose hours do not exceed 28 in a week. Other specific students may be generally exempt from the minimum wage provisions of the legislation.

50 This is provided for in the Ontario legislation.

51 In the federal jurisdiction, Ontario, Alberta, Manitoba, Nova Scotia, Prince Edward Island, Quebec, the Northwest Territories, Nunavut and the Yukon, the legislation stipulates a maximum amount which an employer is entitled to attribute to room and board in making such a deduction.

not entitled to make these deductions if to do so would bring the employee's wages to a level below that of the required minimum wage.[52]

Many jurisdictions make some provision for employees to receive remuneration if they are called in to work, even if they do not work or only work for a short period of time. This is referred to as "call-in pay" and is meant to protect workers from being called in at an employer's discretion only to discover that no work exists. In such cases, the call-in pay provisions ensure that the employee receives some compensation for his or her trouble, and attempt to ensure that employers do not call employees into work unnecessarily. With the exception of New Brunswick, where no provision is made for call-in pay, all jurisdictions stipulate that an employee who is called in will receive a minimum number of hours' pay for being called in, regardless of whether or not the employee actually works for the minimum period.[53]

Certain employees are exempt from the minimum wage and call-in provisions of the employment standards legislation. In Ontario, for example, many professionals, as well as certain students and trainees and superintendents or janitors who reside in the building, are exempt from receiving minimum wage under the provisions of the *Employment Standards Act, 2000*.

Hours of Work and Overtime Pay

To ensure that employees are not required to work excessive hours, all jurisdictions have enacted provisions which limit the number of hours which employees may work on a day or in a week.[54] In most jurisdictions,[55] employees are to receive premium payment for any hours worked in excess of these standard hours and, in some jurisdictions, maximum hours have been set, over which an

---

52 Such deductions are allowed in Alberta, British Columbia (in certain circumstances), Manitoba, Nunavut and the Northwest Territories. In Nova Scotia, the employer is entitled to deduct below the minimum wage level if the working apparel is of woollen or similar material and requires dry cleaning. This deduction is prohibited in certain industries in Saskatchewan.

53 In the federal jurisdiction, Alberta, Manitoba, Newfoundland, Ontario, Prince Edward Island and Quebec, the minimum pay is three hours' wages; in the Yukon, the minimum pay is two hours' wages; in the Northwest Territories and Nunavut, the employee will be paid four hours' wages so long as the work was not scheduled in advance. In Saskatchewan, an employee who reports to work receives a lump sum of remuneration (which is currently equivalent to three hours' wages). In British Columbia, an employee who just shows up for work is entitled to minimum pay of two hours' wages and will be entitled to four hours' wages once he or she begins to work (unless the work is suspended for reasons beyond the employer's control). In Nova Scotia, employees are entitled to minimum pay of three hours' wages only if they are called in for non-regular working hours.

54 Appendix A, Table 3, contains a listing of standard and, where applicable, maximum hours, as well as overtime rates for each of the various jurisdictions, current to the date of publication.

55 As can be seen in Appendix A, Table 3, in some jurisdictions, overtime payments are calculated as a percentage of minimum. Theoretically, depending on how much an employee earns in these jurisdictions, the overtime payment may not represent a "premium".

employee is not permitted to work under any circumstances unless authorization of the ministry is sought and obtained.

Employers may be exempt from maximum hours provisions in certain circumstances. For example, many jurisdictions, including Ontario, Alberta, Manitoba, Saskatchewan, Nova Scotia, Nunavut and the Northwest Territories, allow employees to work past the maximum hours in the case of an accident or emergency. However, there may be limits and specifications as to what constitutes an accident or emergency. For example, in Ontario, extended hours are only permitted in so far as they are required to "avoid serious interference with the ordinary working of the employer's establishment".[56]

Certain jurisdictions, including Alberta, Nova Scotia, Prince Edward Island, Nunavut, the Northwest Territories and the federal jurisdiction, also allow employers to vary working hours, in some fashion, by making an application to the appropriate government ministry or department. If an employer is not content with the restriction set out in the legislation dealing with hours of work, inquiries should be made to the relevant authorities to learn whether an exception can be made which suits the employer's operation.

Employers are required to pay their employees overtime pay for all hours worked in excess of the standard hours in a week. In most jurisdictions, the overtime rate is equal to one and a half times the employee's regular rate of pay. Thus, an employee who earns $10 per hour will be entitled to $15 for each hour of overtime work performed. In some provinces, the employee will only be entitled to one and a half times the minimum wage set in the province.[57]

Generally speaking, employers cannot force their employees to work overtime and cannot take any disciplinary action against an employee who chooses not to work overtime. In establishing an employee's consent to work overtime, it will not be sufficient for an employer to simply point to the employee's job application and the general expression of a willingness to work overtime contained therein. Nor should the employer look to the fact that the employee has previously worked overtime. Express consent to work the particular overtime in question must be obtained. In certain jurisdictions, in the case of an emergency situation, employers are entitled to require their employees to work overtime without prior consent.[58]

Employers in certain jurisdictions, including the federal jurisdiction, Quebec, Ontario, British Columbia, Manitoba, Saskatchewan, the Northwest Territories, Nunavut and the Yukon, are permitted to average or stagger hours of work over a number of weeks. In some cases, this may require ministerial consent and/or the employees' consent. This enables employers to require employees to work in

---

56 *Employment Standards Act, 2000* (Ontario), s. 19.
57 See Appendix A, Table 3, for a list of the overtime rates in each jurisdiction.
58 These jurisdictions include Manitoba, Saskatchewan, Ontario and the federal jurisdiction.

excess of standard hours without overtime pay in a given week. However, employees will be entitled to overtime pay if the average number of hours for the specified period of time exceeds standard hours.

In virtually all jurisdictions, an employer may increase daily hours in order to provide for a compressed work week. However, this type of arrangement may require the consent of the employee or the union, if there is one. Ministerial consent may also be required for a compressed work week. In order to achieve a compressed work week, days where the hours worked exceed the statutory maximums may still be subject to a maximum number of additional hours, and any hours worked in excess of the maximum may be subject to overtime pay.

In many provinces, certain classes of employees are exempt from the hours of work and overtime provisions. The majority of jurisdictions, including Ontario, exempt professionals and students in professional training, supervisors and managers, certain salespeople, and agricultural employees or farm labourers. As well, Ontario, the Yukon and British Columbia exclude firefighters from the standard and maximum hours requirements. In Ontario and Saskatchewan, construction workers are not subject to the provisions. Municipal police officers, domestic servants and janitors, public servants, trappers and fishers are also excluded in some other jurisdictions.

A number of jurisdictions have separate provisions or legislation regarding the hours of work for youth employees.[59] A number of jurisdictions, such as Ontario, Quebec, Nova Scotia, Alberta and British Columbia, have also established separate schedules governing the hours of work for employees in various industrial undertakings.[60]

In certain jurisdictions, instead of paying an employee for his or her overtime hours worked, an employer can compensate for overtime by providing the employee with one and one-half hours of paid time off work for each hour of overtime worked.[61] However, both the employer and the employee must agree to such an arrangement, and the paid time off work must be taken within a specified period of time from the period of time in which the overtime was earned. In the majority of provinces, paid time off work must be taken within three months of entitlement. However, British Columbia provides that paid time must be taken within six months, while Quebec and the Yukon provide for a 12-month period. Although Ontario employees are entitled to receive paid time off within three months after it is earned, with the employee's consent, a 12-month period is permitted.

---

59   These jurisdictions include Nova Scotia, Alberta, Quebec, New Brunswick, the Northwest Territories, Nunavut, Prince Edward Island and the federal jurisdiction. Manitoba and British Columbia have provisions which require ministerial permission to employ a "child", as defined in the legislation.

60   This has also been done in the federal jurisdiction for motor vehicle operators, in Manitoba for workers in the construction industry, in Saskatchewan for highway workers, newspaper employees and others, and in the Yukon for domestics, farm workers and others.

61   These jurisdictions include Alberta, British Columbia, Manitoba, Ontario, Quebec and the Yukon.

Employers should ensure that, when paying employees for overtime hours, there is some indication made, both in the books and to the employee, of the portion of the payment which is designated as pay for overtime. In the absence of records indicating that specific payment for overtime has been made, employment standards referees have also been known to designate payments to employees as gratuitous and have required employers to pay overtime, even if the employer believed that such payment had already been made.

The importance of employers' keeping accurate records of the hours worked by employees cannot be overstated. If an employee makes a claim for unpaid wages or overtime, and the employer has no records to counter the claim, the employment standards referee must decide what hours the employee worked. It is not uncommon for referees, in such circumstances, to defer to the employee's recollection.

Required Rest Days

Employers are required by law to provide their employees with a minimum of one full day or 24 consecutive hours of rest per week according to employment standards legislation.[62] In jurisdictions like Ontario and Alberta, employers may have more flexibility in providing time off, in that in Ontario and Alberta, instead of having to provide one day off in each one-week period, employers are allowed to provide two consecutive days off in each two-week period and, in Alberta, employers can provide three consecutive days off in a three-week period or four consecutive days off in a four-week period. In the Yukon, employees are entitled to two full days of rest per week, as are employees in Saskatchewan if the employer's establishment employs more than 10 people. The majority of jurisdictions also require that the rest period be on Sunday whenever possible.[63]

There are a number of exceptions and exemptions to the day of rest requirements. Certain employees may be exempt from the required rest provisions, including managers, supervisors, professionals, persons engaged in farming, watchpersons, firefighters and employees engaged in work of an emergency nature. Where particular employees are not exempt from the day of rest provisions of the relevant legislation, in certain jurisdictions,[64] the law provides that the appropriate governing body can issue a permit exempting certain establishments from the regulations or authorize an alternate or flexible work arrangement.

---

62 However, in British Columbia, employers must provide 32 consecutive hours of rest to all employees.

63 This includes the federal jurisdiction, New Brunswick, Newfoundland, Nova Scotia, Prince Edward Island, Saskatchewan, the Northwest Territories and the Yukon. Alberta, British Columbia and Quebec do not require that the rest period be on a Sunday.

64 Including British Columbia, Manitoba, New Brunswick and Saskatchewan.

The federal *Lord's Day Act*[65] prohibited commercial dealings or paid employment on Sunday, but was struck down as unconstitutional in that it sought to compel religious observance.[66] This statute appeared to discriminate against non-Christians and to prohibit non-Christians from carrying on otherwise lawful, normal activities on Sundays. Since the declaration of the unconstitutionality of the *Lord's Day Act*, a number of jurisdictions, including Ontario, Manitoba, New Brunswick, Nova Scotia, Prince Edward Island, Quebec and the Northwest Territories, have either taken steps to establish new retail business closing legislation and/or repealed their provincial equivalent of the *Lord's Day Act*. In Ontario, Sunday opening became legal in late 1991 under the *Retail Business Holidays Act*.[67] Ontario businesses can now remain open on a Sunday unless Sunday is a "holiday" as defined by the *Employment Standards Act, 2000*. However, in Ontario, even on a holiday, small stores, tourist area businesses and other designated businesses can open and even large stores may open on a holiday Sunday if they close on a different day for religious reasons.

Most jurisdictions still have legislation restricting the type of work which may be done on a Sunday, although such statutes may now be of relatively limited effect as they are essentially lists of exemptions to mandatory Sunday closing rules. Often exempt are small convenience stores, drug stores, gas stations, flower, fruit and vegetable stands, newsstands and laundromats, as well as hotels, restaurants and other businesses offering services to tourists. In addition, sporting events and other recreational and amusement activities are often permitted to take place on a Sunday.

Where an employer is not exempt from the relevant Sunday observance legislation, it may be entitled to apply for a permit from the appropriate governing body, stating that the employer's business is exempt. In certain provinces, such as British Columbia, Saskatchewan, Manitoba, Ontario and Quebec, municipalities may be entitled to regulate the opening and closing of shops and services on Sundays. Also, in some jurisdictions, including Ontario, Manitoba and Prince Edward Island, employers may be permitted to open on Sunday if the employer's business was closed on another day of the week. Employees, such as those in Ontario, Manitoba and New Brunswick, may be protected from having to work on a Sunday through the legislated provision of a right to refuse to perform such work. Employers in these jurisdictions are prohibited from dismissing or disciplining employees who refuse to perform work on a Sunday.

---

65   R.S.C. 1970, c. L-13.
66   See *R. v. Big M Drug Mart Ltd.* (1985), 18 D.L.R. (4th) 321 (S.C.C.).
67   R.S.O. 1990, c. R.30 (as amended to 2002, c. 17).

Termination of Employment

Individual Termination

According to employment standards legislation, employers are entitled to terminate the employment of an individual at any time, so long as the individual is provided with notice of the dismissal. The amount of notice required is mandated by statute and differs from jurisdiction to jurisdiction. Generally speaking, the amount of statutory notice to which an employee is entitled is dependent upon the length of the employee's service with the employer. The exception to this generalization is Manitoba, where an employer is required by statute to provide an employee with notice equivalent to only one pay period, unless the employer has established its own practice as to the termination of employment. To qualify, a Manitoba employer is required to provide each person in its establishment with written notice of the terms of the termination practice which it wishes to implement and must keep a notice of this practice posted in a prominent place. Thirty days after complying with these requirements, the employer's practice will be considered to be in effect.[68]

An employer usually has the choice of providing an employee with the required written notice, terminating employment immediately and paying the employee his or her regular wages for the required period in lieu of written notice, or using some combination of advance notice and pay in lieu. Pay in lieu of notice is considered to be the amount that the employee would have earned if he or she had worked normal hours during the notice period, or may be calculated based on some set period of time.[69] In some jurisdictions,[70] it is specifically stated that overtime is not to be factored into a calculation of the employee's normal or regular wages for the purpose of calculating pay in lieu of notice. Where an employee does not work regular hours for the purpose of calculating pay in lieu of notice, some method of averaging will be required to determine the employee's entitlement. In certain jurisdictions, like Ontario and Alberta, provision is made for such an averaging procedure. In Ontario, for example, an employee's regular wage will be determined by calculating the employee's average weekly wage based on the employee's last 12 weeks of employment.[71]

A majority of jurisdictions[72] expressly prohibit an employer from changing the terms or conditions of the employment contract during the notice period; the

---

68 Appendix A, Table 4, sets out the notice periods applicable to termination of an individual's employment in each of the various jurisdictions, current to the date of publication.

69 In British Columbia, for example, the amount provided is the employee's average weekly wage earned in the eight weeks preceding dismissal.

70 These jurisdictions include Ontario, Saskatchewan, Nova Scotia, Prince Edward Island, Quebec and the federal jurisdiction.

71 *Employment Standards Act, 2000* (Ontario), s. 61(1.1).

72 Including the federal jurisdiction, Ontario, Alberta, British Columbia, the Northwest Territories, Nova Scotia and the Yukon.

employee is to be paid all wages and benefits to which he or she would have been entitled had he or she not been terminated. In a case where the employee has been provided with pay in lieu of notice, and his or her employment has been terminated immediately, the employer is generally entitled to consider the employment terminated and to discontinue the employee's benefits.[73]

Employees who have experienced some interruption in their service with the employer often question whether this interruption will negate their prior service when determining length of service for the purpose of the appropriate notice period calculation. In fact, a number of jurisdictions make provision for continuous service in the event of an interruption in service. For example, in jurisdictions like Alberta, Ontario, Nova Scotia, Nunavut and the Northwest Territories, an interruption in service will be ignored for the purpose of the termination provisions of employment standards legislation if the interruption is not longer than the period specified in the statute or regulations. In many cases, this period is approximately three months, except in Saskatchewan, where this period is 14 days.

Where an employer has sold a business, it is generally not necessary to provide the employees with notice of termination if the purchasing employer is planning to continue their employment. The majority of jurisdictions provide for continuous employment in such circumstances, which means that the employee will continue to be employed unless given notice of termination prior to the sale by the selling employer or after the sale by the purchasing employer. In the event that the purchasing employer wishes to provide such an employee with notice of termination, such notice must be calculated taking into account the employee's former service with the selling employer.

In the event of the bankruptcy of an employer or the appointment of a receiver, employers should consult legal counsel in their jurisdiction to determine whether their employees should be provided with notice of termination. In British Columbia,[74] for example, where a bankruptcy, appointment of a receiver or some other insolvency-type event takes place, the employer is required to provide employees with notice of termination or pay in lieu of notice.

Employers should be cautious of continuing an employee's employment after the statutory notice period has expired. In a number of jurisdictions, such as the federal jurisdiction, Alberta, British Columbia, New Brunswick, Newfoundland, Nova Scotia, the Northwest Territories, the Yukon and Nunavut, employment standards legislation provides that if an employee continues to work past the

---

73   Exceptions to this include Ontario and the Northwest Territories, where employees are entitled to the benefits coverage they would have received had they remained employed throughout the notice period, regardless of whether they are provided with pay in lieu of notice.

74   *Employment Standards Act*, R.S.B.C. 1996, c. 113 (as amended to 2002, c. 42), s. 65(1)(d).

expiry of the notice of termination, then that notice is no longer valid.[75] Thus, if an employer still wishes to terminate an employee after the notice period has expired and after the period set out in the statute, the employer is required to provide the employee with fresh notice of termination, taking into consideration the additional service of the employee since the original notice was provided.

In certain jurisdictions, including Alberta, Manitoba, Newfoundland, Nova Scotia, Quebec, the Yukon and Prince Edward Island, employees are required to provide their employers with statutory notice of termination if they wish to end the employment relationship. This notice is usually less than that which an employer is required to provide according to employment standards legislation, but may be the same depending upon the jurisdiction. In those jurisdictions where there is no statutory requirement to give the employer notice of the decision to quit, employees should be aware that there may still exist a requirement to provide reasonable notice of termination at common law.

There are a number of exceptions to the notice requirements. In general, a seasonal, temporary or term employee does not receive notice. However, in jurisdictions such as Ontario, British Columbia, Manitoba, Nova Scotia and the Yukon, a term employee may be entitled to notice if the employee works for some period after the expiry of the term. For this reason, employers should again be cautious of allowing term employees to continue to work beyond the expiry of the term unless the employer is willing to risk the possibility of having to provide the term employee with statutory notice or pay in lieu of notice.

Employees who refuse reasonable alternative work, or are terminated for just cause or other misconduct, may also not be entitled to written notice of termination or pay in lieu thereof. In addition, the notice requirements may not apply if the employment contract becomes impossible to perform due to a fortuitous or uncontrollable event.[76]

In the vast majority of jurisdictions, employment standards legislation stipulates that an employee who is temporarily laid off is not entitled to statutory notice of termination, as a temporary layoff does not constitute a termination. The length of an acceptable temporary layoff varies by jurisdiction. It may be several days or as great as a number of weeks or months. Employers considering the layoff of employees would be wise to consult local employment law counsel to determine the legal implications of laying off employees for a given period of

---

75 Generally speaking, it is sufficient for the employee to work past the expiry of the notice period. However, in New Brunswick, the employee must have worked for an additional month past the original termination date before the notice will be deemed to be ineffective and, in Nova Scotia, the employee must have worked for an additional period equivalent to the length of notice originally provided.

76 For example, in *Data Business Forms Ltd. (Re)* (unreported, February 3, 1988, E.S.C. 2312, Dissanayake), the contract became impossible to perform by virtue of the employee's refusal to join the union and, in *Bodega Ltd. (Re)* (unreported, March 25, 1983, E.S.C. 1389, Black), the contract also became impossible to perform where the employee left work two days after receiving notice, stating that he was planning to quit anyway.

time. Although temporary layoffs will not entitle employees to notice of termination, employees will be entitled to notice if the layoffs become permanent. Some jurisdictions, including Ontario, Alberta, Newfoundland, the Yukon, British Columbia, Manitoba, Nova Scotia, Nunavut and the Northwest Territories, state that a layoff will be deemed a termination and the notice period will apply if the layoff continues for an extended period of time. In Ontario, Newfoundland and the Yukon, for example, an employer must give the employee notice or pay in lieu thereof if the layoff exceeds 13 weeks in a period of 20 consecutive weeks.

Mass Termination

Governments have recognized that employers will often be terminating large numbers of employees at a time as a result of the closing of an operation or downsizing. With the exception of Prince Edward Island, all jurisdictions have enacted employment standards provisions which deal with the termination of large numbers of employees. If an employer wishes to terminate a certain number of employees, and this qualifies as a mass termination for the purpose of the legislation, the employer will generally be required to provide its employees and/or the Minister or Director of Employment Standards with notice of the termination.[77] Where notice must be given to the employees, these periods generally apply to all employees regardless of the length of their employment.[78] In jurisdictions where there is no requirement that notice be given to employees in such circumstances, or in Prince Edward Island where there are no mass termination provisions, employers are required to comply with the individual termination provisions when terminating large numbers of employees. British Columbia, Saskatchewan and the federal jurisdiction are unique in that employees terminated pursuant to the mass termination provisions are entitled to both mass termination notice *and* any individual notice to which they are entitled under the legislation.

The mass termination provisions generally apply when a set number of employees are being dismissed within a short period of time (typically four weeks).[79] Generally speaking, the same exceptions which apply to the provision of individual notice of termination also apply to mass termination, in that term employees or employees guilty of misconduct are not entitled to notice. A number of jurisdictions, including the Northwest Territories, Nunavut and Newfoundland, stipulate that an employer may not terminate employees prior to the expiry of the notice period. This differs from British Columbia where employers are allowed to

---

77 The requisite notice periods are summarized in Appendix A, Table 5.
78 Exceptions to this include Newfoundland, Nova Scotia and Manitoba (where employees with less than one month of service are exempt), as well as Ontario (where employees with less than three months of service are exempt).
79 Both the requisite number of employees and the relevant time periods are set out in Appendix A, Table 5.

terminate groups of employees immediately and provide them with payment in lieu of notice.

The applicable employment standards legislation and the Ministry or Department of Labour will typically have very strict requirements regarding the form and substance of the notice to be given to both the employees and the government. In the case of a mass termination, employers should contact the Department or Ministry of Labour, Employment Standards Branch, to ensure that they are fully advised of all of the necessary requirements for effecting proper notice.

As well as providing the Minister or Director of Employment Standards and the employees with notice, a number of jurisdictions, including the federal jurisdiction, British Columbia, Manitoba and Quebec, also state that the employer may be required to participate in a joint planning committee along with employee representatives. The purpose of this committee is to establish an adjustment program to ease the effects of the termination and to assist employees in finding alternate employment.

Payment of Wages upon Termination

Each of the various Canadian jurisdictions has its own requirements regarding the payment of a terminated employee's wages.[80] All of the jurisdictions have also set up a program to assist employees in recovering any unpaid wages. However, the limitation period during which an employee can bring a claim is different in each jurisdiction, and some jurisdictions have established a ceiling on the amount that an employee is entitled to recover.[81]

Severance Pay

Although often, any and all payments made to employees at termination are referred to as "severance pay", for the purposes of this discussion, severance pay means payments required by statute which are received over and above any statutory notice obligations. In Ontario and the federal jurisdiction, employment standards legislation provides that certain employees may be entitled to receive an extra payment, in addition to termination pay, upon termination. According to the *Canada Labour Code*, all employees with 12 consecutive months of service are entitled to severance pay of the greater of two days' pay for each completed year of service or five days' pay. In Ontario, only those employers who terminate more than 50 employees in six months or less due to a plant or operation closing, or those who have a $2.5 million or more payroll, are liable to pay severance. Furthermore, all severance payments are restricted to those employees with five or more years of service. Like the federal jurisdiction, severance payments in

---

80 These are summarized in Appendix A, Table 6.
81 The relevant limitation periods are also set out in Appendix A, Table 6.

Ontario are also based on service and closely approximate one additional week's pay for each year of service, up to a maximum of 26 weeks' additional pay.

Employees will be excluded from receiving severance pay in many of the same circumstances where they would be excluded from receiving notice of termination. They may be disentitled if they are dismissed for just cause, if they refuse a reasonable alternative offer of employment or if they are guilty of wilful misconduct, disobedience or neglect of duty. Employees cannot be given notice in lieu of statutory severance, as severance payments must actually be paid. However, it may be possible for Ontario employers to implement an instalment plan for the payment of severance pay. Such a plan requires the approval of the Director of Employment Standards and cannot extend for more than three years after the termination.

The Concept of "Stacking"

Employment standards legislation provides for notice of termination or pay in lieu and, in some jurisdictions, also provides for the payment of statutory severance pay. What, for a period of time, was considered unclear was whether these amounts were payable in addition to an entitlement that an employee had to reasonable notice of his or her dismissal, or pay in lieu. Employment standards legislation does not make reference to the entitlement to common law reasonable notice and, as a result, it has been up to the courts to attempt to determine whether there is a right on the part of employees to have the statutory amounts "stacked" on top of the entitlement to reasonable notice.

Since a decision of the Ontario Court of Appeal in 1996, this question now appears to be settled. In the case of *Stevens v. Globe and Mail*,[82] one of the questions before the Court of Appeal was whether the Globe and Mail was entitled to deduct from wrongful dismissal damages owed to Mr. Stevens an amount that had already been paid to Mr. Stevens on account of statutory severance pay. The Court of Appeal conducted an extensive review of the legislation and the applicable case law and ultimately concluded that the severance pay that Mr. Stevens had already received should, in fact, be deducted. This case now stands for the principle that there exists "no stacking" in regards to an employee's dual entitlement to statutory and common law notice and/or severance. An employee who receives pay in lieu of notice of his or her dismissal will be considered to have also received his or her statutory entitlements, assuming they are less than the reasonable notice provided. Similarly, an employer can fulfil its obligations to a dismissed employee by providing sufficient advance notice of the dismissal, provided the statutory notice is subsumed in the overall notice period.

---

82   (1996), 135 D.L.R. (4th) 240 (Ont. C.A.).

Employers considering fulfilling their statutory and common law obligations through the provision of advance working notice should be aware that in jurisdictions such as Ontario, where there exists a statutory severance obligation, such amounts must, if owed, be actually paid to the employee.

Statutory severance pay cannot be rolled into a common law reasonable notice period if the employer is providing working notice. The employer will be required to pay any necessary statutory severance pay upon termination despite having fulfilled its common law reasonable notice obligations. However, in Ontario, if the employer and employee consent, statutory severance can be paid in instalments for up to a period of three years.[83]

Pregnancy and Parental Leave

Pregnancy Leave

All jurisdictions make provision for women who have fulfilled a minimum service requirement to take pregnancy leave[84] around the time when they are to have a baby. Although this leave is meant to be unpaid, in most jurisdictions employees are entitled to have their benefits continued throughout the leave.[85] Employees on pregnancy leave may also be entitled to claim employment insurance for the period of time they are on unpaid pregnancy leave. Employees may be entitled to pregnancy leave even if the pregnancy terminates or the baby is stillborn.

To be eligible for pregnancy leave, employees in most jurisdictions must have worked for the employer for some minimum period of time.[86] Prior to taking pregnancy leave, employees must provide their employers with written notice of their intention to take leave.[87] In some jurisdictions, employees are required to submit, in addition to written notice of the intention to take pregnancy leave, a medical certificate certifying the fact of the pregnancy and specifying the expected birthdate. In the remaining jurisdictions, employers are entitled to request such a medical certificate.

Employees are entitled to begin pregnancy leave prior to the actual birth of the baby, but most jurisdictions specify the earliest date on which an employee is entitled to commence leave.[88] In certain jurisdictions, an employee may be required to take some minimum period of time off following the birth of the baby,

---

83 *Employment Standards Act, 2000*, ss. 64 and 66.
84 This is referred to as "maternity leave" in some jurisdictions.
85 Of those jurisdictions that require employers to continue benefits plans during the employee's leave, only British Columbia, Ontario and the federal jurisdiction require employers to continue making contributions to the plans.
86 These minimum eligibility requirements are set out in Appendix A, Table 7, as is the length of leave to which an employee is entitled.
87 The amount of notice required is also set out in Appendix A, Table 7.
88 These dates are set out in Appendix A, Table 7.

and this may or may not be included in the normal leave entitlement. The employee may be required to submit a request if she wishes to return to work prior to this minimum period of time after the delivery date, and may be required to produce a medical certificate ensuring her fitness to return. In particular jurisdictions, like Ontario, Newfoundland, Saskatchewan and Prince Edward Island, for example, employees will be entitled to a full six weeks following delivery even if they might not otherwise be so entitled because of the amount of leave taken prior to delivery. Jurisdictions like the Northwest Territories, Nunavut and Manitoba provide a pregnant employee with extra time equal to the period between the expected and actual dates of delivery if such is necessary as a result of the baby being born after the expected delivery date. In such cases, the extended amount of time is added to the end of the pregnancy leave.

Most jurisdictions provide for an exception to the notice requirement under special circumstances, such as early delivery, complications, miscarriage or still-birth. An employee who goes on pregnancy leave in such an emergency situation is generally required to provide her employer with a medical certificate within a specified period of time after stopping work. In Ontario, this notice must be provided to the employer within two weeks of the commencement of the leave.

Legislation in British Columbia and Saskatchewan contains provisions whereby pregnancy leave can be extended for medical reasons. In addition, most provinces permit an employee to return to work before the required period has expired as long as the employee has a doctor's written permission. Ontario permits an employee to change the beginning and end dates of her pregnancy leave as long as she provides her employer with sufficient notice. Specifically, with respect to the start of the leave, to choose an earlier date, the employee must give the employer two weeks' written notice before the earlier date. To choose a later date, the employer must be notified in writing two weeks before the original start date. To choose an earlier end date for the leave, the employee must give the employer four weeks' written notice before the earlier date. To choose a later end date, the employer must be notified in writing four weeks before the original end date.

In the federal jurisdiction and in Quebec, pregnant employees may request job modification or reassignment if continuing in the current job or working conditions would pose a health risk to the employee or the unborn child. In the vast majority of jurisdictions, employers are entitled to require employees to take early leave if the pregnancy impairs their job performance. However, this is generally a last resort and is typically only utilized if reassignment or job modification is unworkable.

In a case where an employee is taking either pregnancy or parental leave, employment standards legislation provides that the employee's right to work is protected and the employee is entitled to return to his or her job at the completion of the leave. Where it is not possible for an employer to provide the employee with the same job after the leave, the employee must be provided with a comparable job with equivalent wages and benefits.

Employers will not necessarily be able to avoid the requirement that an employee be reinstated after pregnancy or parental leave by simply suspending their operations. In certain jurisdictions, the employer will be required to reinstate such an employee according to applicable reinstatement provisions once operations resume. Employers are also not entitled to take any reprisals against employees who intend to or have taken pregnancy or parental leave. Such employees may not be dismissed, suspended, laid off or otherwise discriminated against because they have become pregnant or because they have sought to or have exercised their right to take pregnancy or parental leave.

Most Canadian jurisdictions address, in some form, the protection an employee on pregnancy or parental leave has relating to service and seniority. However, these protections vary widely by jurisdiction. In some provinces, like Ontario, the legislation makes clear that a period of leave is to be included in a calculation of length of employment to determine an employee's rights, regardless of whether the employment is active or not. In other jurisdictions, the legislation might provide for continued benefits and service accrual throughout the leave, where in others, it may simply be that the leave will be counted for seniority purposes.

Parental/Adoption Leave

All jurisdictions also provide for an unpaid leave of absence to be taken when an employee becomes a new parent. This includes adoptive parents, who are meant to have the same rights to parental leave as birth parents. However, in Newfoundland, Saskatchewan and Prince Edward Island, employees are none the less entitled to special adoption leave in addition to parental leave. British Columbia also allows the natural and adoptive parents of children with special needs an extended leave. In those jurisdictions where provision is made for parental leave, attention should be paid to the statutory definition of "parent" to determine whether an employee is entitled to the leave. In Ontario, for example, the definition of "parent" is very broad and includes an individual "who is in a relationship of some permanence with a parent of a child and who intends to treat the child as his or her own".[89] In most jurisdictions, parental leave is available to *both* parents of a newborn or of a newly adopted child.

As in the case of pregnancy leave, the jurisdictions vary widely with regard to the length of time allowed for parental leave and the length of time an employee must have worked before being entitled to take parental leave.[90] As with pregnancy leave, employees will typically be entitled to return to work before the expiry of the leave if they provide their employers with the requisite notice or medical certificate.

---

89 *Employment Standards Act, 2000*, s. 45, definition "parent".
90 The various entitlements and requirements for parental leave are set out in Appendix A, Table 8, including the amount of notice which must be provided to an employer before the leave can be taken.

All jurisdictions specify the period of time during which parental or adoption leave must commence.[91] In most jurisdictions, a biological mother planning to take parental leave is required to begin the leave immediately after her pregnancy leave, unless the employee and employer agree otherwise. While certain jurisdictions contemplate that a situation may arise where the employee is ready to commence parental leave immediately after pregnancy leave, but the child is hospitalized at this time, employees should be careful when considering a decision to delay a leave. In jurisdictions such as Manitoba, Ontario and Prince Edward Island, this may have no effect on the length of the leave, while in other jurisdictions, employees may end up with a reduced parental leave.

As is the case with pregnancy leave, the notice which an employee is obligated to provide to his or her employer with respect to the intention to take parental or adoption leave can be excepted in the event of special circumstances, such as the early delivery or placement of a child. An employee will still be entitled to parental leave as long as he or she provides the employer with sufficient notice. For example, Ontario requires an employee to give notice within two weeks of stopping work. Other jurisdictions may permit an employee to extend parental leave if a medical emergency arises.

Other Leaves of Absence

Many jurisdictions make provision for additional leaves of absence. Employees in British Columbia, New Brunswick, Ontario and Quebec are entitled to between three and 10 days of unpaid leave each year to meet the responsibilities associated with the care, health or education of a child in the employee's care or in the care of any member of the employee's family. In Ontario, this is referred to as "emergency leave",[92] and is actually more broadly defined to include personal illness, injury or medical emergency, or death, illness, injury, medical emergency or urgent matter relating to a whole host of specified individuals who have some type of relationship with the employee, familial or otherwise. In Quebec, employees are also entitled to take unpaid leaves for medical examinations related to pregnancy. Fathers in Quebec are entitled to five days of paternity leave within 15 days of the birth of their children. Part of this leave may be with pay if the employee meets a minimum service requirement of 60 days. Employees adopting children may be entitled to a similar leave exclusive of any parental leave to which the employees may be entitled.

In the majority of jurisdictions,[93] employees are entitled to bereavement leave of between one and five days in the event of the death of a member of their immediate or extended family. Bereavement leave may or may not be with pay,

---

91   These periods are also set out in Appendix A, Table 8.
92   This only applies to employees whose employer regularly employs 50 or more employees.
93   Including the federal jurisdiction, British Columbia, New Brunswick, Newfoundland, Nova Scotia, Prince Edward Island, Quebec, Saskatchewan and the Yukon.

depending on the jurisdiction and on the length of time the employee has been working. Certain jurisdictions[94] also allow for employees to take leaves of absence due to illness or injury. In the federal jurisdiction, employers are required to have a wage replacement plan in place so that employees on sick leave receive wages which are equivalent to their regular wages. In many jurisdictions,[95] employees are permitted (in some cases pursuant to separate legislation governing jury duty) to take time off work to perform jury duty or to take time off work if they are summoned or subpoenaed to appear in court as a witness. Finally, in Quebec, employees may take advantage of "special occasion leave" to receive one paid day of absence for their own wedding and one unpaid day of absence for the wedding of a member of the employee's immediate family.

Employers are also required to provide all employees with four consecutive hours' leave to allow employees to cast their vote in a federal election. These hours may be granted at the convenience of the employer. Only those employees who are qualified to vote in a federal election are entitled to this leave. In addition, all of the provinces and territories have separate elections legislation which entitles employees to time off work in order to cast their vote in a provincial or territorial election. The length of time allowed varies between jurisdictions. Several of the jurisdictions[96] have also enacted similar legislation allowing for time off work to vote in municipal elections. Generally speaking, employers are not to deny their employees the opportunity to vote, nor are they to punish their employees for doing so. Employers who impose such penalties may find themselves guilty of an offence and subject to a fine or imprisonment or both.

Vacations and Vacation Pay

All employees in Canada are entitled to take vacations from their employment and are entitled to be paid a minimum amount during that time. The length of vacation to which an employee is entitled will depend upon the jurisdiction and the employee's length of service.[97]

Employees are meant to receive both their vacation entitlement and any statutory holidays so that, if a holiday falls within an employee's annual vacation, the employee will either be entitled to extend the vacation by one day or to take an additional holiday prior to the employee's next annual vacation.

In general, an employee must have completed one year of employment before he or she will be entitled to take a paid vacation. Quebec and New Brunswick calculate vacation entitlement based on a specific date or "reference year". In Quebec, the relevant period runs from May 1st to April 30th, whereas in New

---

94 Including the federal jurisdiction, Newfoundland and the Yukon.
95 Including Nova Scotia, Alberta, British Columbia, Manitoba, Ontario, Newfoundland, Prince Edward Island, Quebec and Saskatchewan.
96 Including Alberta, New Brunswick, Ontario, Quebec and the Yukon.
97 The various vacation entitlements are set out in Appendix A, Table 9.

Brunswick vacation entitlement is calculated using the employee's service as of the end of June. Nevertheless, both provinces allow an employee who has not completed a full year of service as of the set date to receive one day of vacation for every month worked, up to a maximum of two weeks. Other jurisdictions, such as Alberta, British Columbia, the Northwest Territories, the federal jurisdiction and Nunavut, allow for employers to set up a common anniversary date against which to measure all employees' vacation entitlement. In Saskatchewan, an employer who wishes to establish a uniform date of vacation entitlement must provide employees with one and one quarter days' vacation for each month of service. To qualify for 12 months of service in Newfoundland, employees must have worked a requisite percentage of their normal working hours[98] within the preceding year, and they must have worked at least 90% of their normal working hours in the preceding year in order to receive vacation time with pay.

Although an employee may not be entitled to take a paid vacation until after 12 completed months of employment, with certain limited exceptions, employees' vacation entitlement begins to accrue as soon as they commence employment. In British Columbia and Newfoundland, employees must work for five days before they begin accruing statutory vacation time, while in the Yukon, employees must fulfil a minimum 14-day service requirement before they begin to accrue vacation time. Although many employers will allow their employees to take vacations before they have actually been earned, employers should be cautious of such a practice. In jurisdictions such as Ontario, if an employee ceases employment before having earned all of the vacation already taken, the employer is not allowed to set off the employee's wages to account for such vacation.[99]

Employees who are entitled to vacations pursuant to employment standards legislation are also entitled to be paid for such vacations. In general, employees are entitled to receive 2% of their annual earnings for each week of their statutory vacation entitlement. According to this formula, someone earning $50,000 would receive $1,000 for each week of their vacation entitlement. In Saskatchewan, employees are entitled to receive during their paid vacation pay equivalent to what they would have earned for one regular work week. This amounts to a sum somewhat less than that received by those employees in other jurisdictions who earn 2% of annual earnings per week of vacation. Employers should pay particular attention to the definition of "annual earnings" (or "wages" or "salary", as the case may be) for the purpose of calculating an employee's vacation pay. Depending upon the jurisdiction, certain remuneration amounts, such as tips, gratuities, overtime, bonuses or commissions, may or may not be included in the vacation pay calculations.

---

98 "Normal working hours" is defined as the number of hours that an employee might reasonably expect to work in the type of work in which the employee is engaged.

99 In Ontario, there are circumstances in which such set-off can be made, such as with the written authorization of the employee.

With the following exceptions, employers are generally required to pay vacation pay to their employees in advance of the employee's vacation. In Alberta, vacation pay may be paid on the employee's next regularly scheduled payday. In British Columbia, vacation pay is due at least seven days preceding the annual vacation period, while in the federal jurisdiction and Saskatchewan, an employer must pay vacation pay within the 14 days preceding the vacation.

A majority of provinces require an employer to provide an employee with his or her vacation within 10 months of entitlement. However, Alberta, British Columbia, Quebec and Saskatchewan provide that an employee must receive his or her vacation within 12 months after it becomes due. New Brunswick and Prince Edward Island dictate that an employee must receive his or her vacation within four months.

If employment is terminated before an employee becomes entitled to his or her annual vacation, the employee receives whatever vacation pay is applicable depending on the employee's service at the time of termination. In some jurisdictions,[100] the employer is required to pay to the employee his or her outstanding vacation pay upon termination, while other jurisdictions require the payment to be made within a certain period following the termination, ranging from three days to 14 days, depending upon the jurisdiction.[101]

Certain jurisdictions may allow employees to postpone their vacations or waive their rights to them altogether in certain circumstances. For example, employees in Nova Scotia are permitted to waive their entitlement if they have worked less than 90% of the regular hours available during the last year. Employees in the Northwest Territories may be permitted to waive vacation leave in exceptional circumstances upon making a joint employer-employee application to the Department of Labour. In Saskatchewan and the Yukon, employees are permitted to receive payment in lieu of vacation time. In Ontario, employees and employers are permitted to make arrangements regarding payment in lieu of vacation, but such arrangements must be approved by the Director of Employment Standards. Although employers are generally not permitted to give payment in lieu of vacation time, in Quebec, if an employer closes its operations for two weeks to give employees their annual vacations, those employees entitled to three weeks' vacation may make a request to receive payment for their third remaining week of vacation.

---

100 Including Alberta, Manitoba, Newfoundland, the Northwest Territories, Nunavut and the federal jurisdiction.

101 This payment must be made within six days in British Columbia if the employee terminates the employment relationship and within two days if the employer terminates the employment relationship. The payment must be made within seven days in the Yukon, within 10 days in Nova Scotia and within 14 days in Saskatchewan. In Prince Edward Island, the payment must be made before the end of the next regular pay period and, in New Brunswick, it must be made at the time of final pay. In Ontario, the payment can be no later than seven days after the employment ends or the day that would have been the employee's next payday.

Employers generally maintain the right to dictate when employees can take their annual vacations. Although it is rare for employers to simply announce to employees when their allotted vacation will take place, employment standards legislation does give employers this right. This might prove useful in circumstances where an employer shuts down for given periods throughout the year and expects its employees to take holidays during these shutdown periods. Employers may also be required to provide employees with a certain requisite amount of notice of any vacation period dictated by the employer. For example, in Alberta, Newfoundland and the federal jurisdiction, employers are required to give at least two weeks' notice, while in Quebec and Saskatchewan, four weeks' notice must be given. In Nova Scotia and New Brunswick, an employer is required to give one week's notice, while in Manitoba, it is 15 days.

Some jurisdictions also protect employees from having their employers dictate that their vacations be taken in small pieces. In Alberta, Newfoundland, Nova Scotia, Ontario, Prince Edward Island and Saskatchewan, employees are permitted to take their vacation in one unbroken period if they wish, although in virtually all of these provinces, the annual vacation may be broken down into several shorter periods if this is what the employee requests. British Columbia, Manitoba and Ontario employment standards legislation actually goes so far as to specify that employees cannot be required to take their annual vacations in periods of less than one week.

As in the case of overtime, employers should keep complete and accurate records of all vacation pay paid to employees. Where such payments are made, it should be clear to employees that these payments represent vacation pay. In the absence of clear records and the appropriate designation of payments, employers run the risk of having such payments classified as gratuitous by employment standards officers, and employers may be ordered to pay vacation pay.

Particular employees may be exempt from the vacation pay provisions, including professionals, students training for certain professions, certain farm labourers, fishers, salespersons, municipal police officers and public servants, depending upon the jurisdiction. Employers should always ensure that the employee whose vacation entitlement they are considering is not excluded from vacation entitlement pursuant to the relevant employment standards legislation.

Homeworkers

Employers in British Columbia, Manitoba, Ontario and Saskatchewan who employ individuals who work out of their homes should be aware of the presence, in the applicable employment standards legislation, of specific provisions which deal with "homeworkers". In Ontario, "homeworker" is defined as "an individual who performs work for compensation in premises occupied by the individual primarily as residential quarters but does not include an independent contractor".[102] Manitoba defines "home work" as "work that an employee performs at his or her home, but does not include the sale of goods or services".[103]

Manitoba employment standards legislation provides that employers who employ individuals to do home work must maintain a record of the names and addresses of all such employees, their wages and a description of their work. This information must be made available to the Director of Employment Standards upon request. The Director of Employment Standards can establish conditions and limitations on an employer with respect to the wages of a homeworker.

British Columbia's legislation stipulates that an employer must provide the Director of Employment Standards with information required to keep a register of employees who work in private residences. In Ontario and Saskatchewan, an employer must keep its own register of information regarding homeworkers, including their names, addresses, wages and benefits.

HUMAN RIGHTS LEGISLATION

General

Human rights legislation was designed to be of general application and to protect individuals against many types of discrimination and human rights violations.[104] However, all human rights legislation also deals specifically with discrimination and other human rights issues which arise in employment. Governments appear to have recognized that, without proactive governing legislation, employers may not take the initiative in seeking to eradicate discriminatory behaviour in the workplace.

Human rights legislation is remedial and is therefore meant to be given the interpretation which will best ensure that its objectives are attained.[105] The legislation is meant to emphasize problem solving and the compensation of victims, not the punishment of offending employers. Employers should be aware that they are not entitled to enter into contracts with their employees which absolve them of their human rights obligations[106] and that they are not entitled to take reprisals

---

102 *Employment Standards Act, 2000* (Ontario), s. 1.
103 *Employment Standards Code*, S.M. 1998, c. 29 (C.C.S.M. c. E110) (as consolidated to December 15, 2002), s. 80(1).
104 For more comprehensive discussions of human rights, see Mr. Justice W. Tarnopolsky and W.F. Pentney, *Discrimination and the Law* (Scarborough: Carswell, 2001 – looseleaf), B.A. Grosman and J.R. Martin, *Discrimination in Employment in Ontario: A Guide for Employers and Employees* (Aurora: Canada Law Book Inc., 1991), R. Zinn and P. Brethour, *The Law of Human Rights in Canada: Practice and Procedure* (Aurora: Canada Law Book Inc., 2000 – looseleaf), or L. McDowell, *Human Rights in the Workplace: A Practical Guide* (Scarborough: Carswell, 1999 – looseleaf).
105 *Action Travail des Femmes v. Canadian National Railway Co.* (1987), 40 D.L.R. (4th) 193 (S.C.C.).
106 *Winnipeg School Division No. 1 v. Craton* (1985), 21 D.L.R. (4th) 1 (S.C.C.).

against employees who attempt to exercise their rights under human rights legislation.

Discrimination

Human rights legislation across Canada prohibits discrimination in employment. An employer cannot refuse to employ or refuse to continue to employ an individual on any of the prohibited grounds of discrimination.[107] This prohibition against discrimination extends to any terms or conditions or any aspect of employment. Many jurisdictions, such as Ontario, British Columbia, Manitoba, Nova Scotia, New Brunswick, Prince Edward Island and Saskatchewan, also include employment agencies in their prohibition against discrimination; an employment agency or employment bureau cannot refuse to refer someone on any enumerated grounds or discriminate against a prospective employee in any other manner.

Both direct and indirect discrimination are prohibited by human rights legislation. Direct discrimination occurs when an employer adopts a rule or practice which on its face discriminates against an individual on the basis of one of the prohibited grounds of discrimination.[108] For example, if an employer denies a woman employment for the specific reason that she is a woman, this is direct discrimination and is prohibited conduct.

The prohibition against discrimination also includes indirect discrimination,[109] which occurs when an employer adopts a rule or practice for legitimate business reasons which is on its face normal and will apply equally to all employees, but which has a discriminatory effect, upon a prohibited ground, on one employee or a group of employees. A discriminatory effect is brought about when a rule imposes, due to some special characteristic of a group or an individual, obligations, penalties or restrictive conditions which are not imposed on other members of the workforce.[110] For example, indirect discrimination was found to have occurred in the *Bhinder* case,[111] when employees were required to wear hard hats on the job. In that case, it was held that, although the employer was not specifically prohibited from requiring employees to wear hard hats, the requirement had the indirect effect of discriminating against certain individuals who, according to

---

107 These prohibited grounds are summarized in Appendix A, Table 10.
108 *Ontario (Human Rights Commission) v. Simpsons-Sears Ltd.* (1985), 23 D.L.R. (4th) 321 (S.C.C.).
109 Also known as constructive or adverse-effect discrimination.
110 *Ontario (Human Rights Commission) v. Simpsons-Sears Ltd.*, *supra*, footnote 108.
111 *Bhinder v. Canadian National Railway* (1985), 23 D.L.R. (4th) 481 (S.C.C.).

their religion, could wear only turbans on their heads.[112] Since the Supreme Court of Canada held, in the case of *Ontario (Human Rights Commission) v. Simpsons-Sears Ltd.*,[113] that it is not necessary that there be an intent to discriminate in order for a court or tribunal to find that human rights legislation has been violated, the prohibition against indirect discrimination exists in all jurisdictions. However, in the human rights legislation of jurisdictions like Ontario and Manitoba, indirect discrimination is expressly prohibited.

For quite some time, it was accepted that different approaches were necessary for justifying a case of discrimination, depending upon whether the discrimination was direct or indirect. In 1999, a unanimous Supreme Court of Canada considered this distinction in *British Columbia (Public Service Employee Relations Commission) v. BCGSEU*[114] (the *Meiorin* decision), and determined that it was no longer workable. As far as the Supreme Court in *Meiorin* was concerned, the underlying purpose of human rights legislation is not served by treating one type of employment-related discrimination differently than the other.

Tawney Meiorin was a female firefighter, employed by the British Columbia government, who was dismissed from her employment when she failed to pass a series of aerobic fitness tests. On her behalf, her union grieved her dismissal, alleging that she had been discriminated against on the basis of her sex. Justice McLachlin, writing for the Court, enunciated a new three-part test which was meant to apply, going forward, to all cases of both direct and indirect discrimination. Specifically, an employer attempting to justify a discriminatory practice would be required to show three things:

(1) that the standard was adopted for a purpose rationally connected to the performance of the job;

(2) that the standard was adopted in an honest and good faith belief that it was necessary to the fulfilment of that legitimate work-related purpose; and

(3) that the standard was reasonably necessary for the accomplishment of that legitimate work-related purpose. In order to fulfil this last criterion, an employer would also be required to show that it was impossible to accommodate the individual employee(s) without imposing undue hardship on the employer.

---

112 In the *Bhinder* case, it was affirmed that this rule had the indirect effect of discriminating against a group of people on the basis of their religion. However, in *Bhinder*, the Supreme Court of Canada found that the indirect discrimination was justified as a *bona fide* occupational requirement ("BFOR"). This decision was later overruled by the Supreme Court of Canada in *Central Alberta Dairy Pool v. Alberta (Human Rights Commission)* (1990), 72 D.L.R. (4th) 417 (S.C.C.). There, the Court held that, where a rule has an adverse discriminatory effect, the appropriate response is to uphold the rule in its general application and consider whether the employer could have accommodated the adversely affected employee without undue hardship.

113 *Supra*, footnote 108.

114 (1999), 176 D.L.R. (4th) 1 (S.C.C.).

In the *Meiorin* case, the government's aerobic requirement ultimately failed the third component of the test because there existed insufficient proof that the standard was reasonably necessary for the safe and efficient work of a firefighter.

This unified approach is actually consistent with human rights legislation in certain jurisdictions, such as Ontario, Manitoba and the Yukon, which legislation provides that, in certain circumstances, a *bona fide* occupational requirement ("BFOR")[115] cannot be proven without first showing that accommodation to the point of undue hardship is impossible. What is now clear, based on *Meiorin* (and the companion *Grismer* decision),[116] is that employers in general will have a difficult time establishing justification for a case of discrimination in employment.

Discrimination in Advertisements, Job Applications and Interviews

Most jurisdictions also specifically prohibit discrimination with respect to the recruitment of employees. It is discriminatory to publish or display an advertisement for employment which indicates any preference, specification or limitation based on a prohibited ground of discrimination. As well, it is generally the case that employment applications and written or oral inquiries will be considered discriminatory and an infringement of human rights legislation if they indicate any limit or preference based on a prohibited ground of discrimination. Employers engaged in the process of drafting employment advertisements or applications may wish to contact their local human rights commission to determine whether any guidelines or policies exist which may assist employers in this endeavour, as is the case in Ontario and Quebec.

Special Employment

In the majority of jurisdictions,[117] an employer may be exempted from treating all persons equally in employment where the employer is a religious, philanthropic, educational, fraternal, political or social institution or organization, is primarily engaged in serving the interests of persons identified by a prohibited ground of discrimination, and employs only or gives preference in employment to persons similarly identified, if the qualification is a reasonable and *bona fide* qualification because of the nature of the employment.[118] For example, if an organization in Ontario, established for the purpose of educating members of a racial minority on aspects of their culture, wished to hire as instructors only

---

115 In some jurisdictions, this is also referred to as a *bona fide* occupational qualification ("BFOQ").
116 *British Columbia (Superintendent of Motor Vehicles) v. British Columbia (Council of Human Rights)* (1999), 181 D.L.R. (4th) 385 (S.C.C.).
117 With the exception of Alberta, Manitoba, New Brunswick and the federal jurisdiction.
118 The prerequisite that the qualification be reasonable and *bona fide* is not required in all jurisdictions, but is included in the legislation of Nova Scotia, Ontario and Prince Edward Island.

members of this particular racial minority, it could seek to do so pursuant to the provisions of the Ontario *Human Rights Code*.[119] The requirement that an instructor be a member of the racial minority would only be upheld if it was a reasonable and *bona fide* requirement due to the nature of the employment.

Special Programs

All jurisdictions, with the exception of Alberta, make some specific provision for affirmative action, stipulating that affirmative action programs are not discriminatory. For instance, the Ontario *Human Rights Code* asserts that the right to equal treatment with respect to employment is not infringed by an affirmative action program which is designed to relieve hardship or economic disadvantage, is designed to assist disadvantaged persons and groups in achieving equal opportunity or is likely to contribute to the elimination of the infringement of those individuals' rights. Similarly, the British Columbia *Human Rights Code*[120] provides that a program or activity approved by the Human Rights Council whose object is to improve the conditions of disadvantaged individuals is not discriminatory. The relevant provisions in the federal jurisdiction are applicable to all matters within federal authority and are quite broad. They state that an affirmative action plan or program is not discriminatory, nor does it require approval by the Canadian Human Rights Commission.

Discrimination with Respect to Benefits

Exceptions are also granted with respect to employee benefits plans. In general, retirement, pension and group insurance plans which discriminate on the basis of age are not considered to be discriminatory. In certain jurisdictions,[121] the legislation may also permit an exemption on the basis of additional prohibited grounds, such as marital status, physical disability and sex. In jurisdictions such as the Northwest Territories and the Yukon, no provision is made for any benefits plan exemptions whatsoever and, in the federal jurisdiction, the exemption regarding age does not extend to insurance plans. Employers considering the implementation of such plans should carefully review the provisions of the relevant human rights legislation to determine whether any potentially discriminatory aspects of the particular plan are exempted.

---

119 R.S.O. 1990, c. H.19 (as amended to 2002, c. 18, Sch. C), s. 24(a).
120 R.S.B.C. 1996, c. 210 (as amended to 2001, c. 15).
121 Including Ontario, Alberta, New Brunswick, Prince Edward Island, Nova Scotia and British Columbia.

Exemptions

Although a number of exemptions to human rights legislation have already been discussed, each jurisdiction's legislation may contain other exemptions for employees or programs. In many jurisdictions, exemptions are made for domestics employed in a private home or living with their employer. Similarly, there are often exemptions for farm employees. In Ontario, employers may be entitled to refuse applicants on the basis of prohibited grounds of discrimination if the primary employment duty will be attending to the medical or personal needs of the employer, an ill child or an aged, ill or infirm spouse or relative. The Ontario *Human Rights Code* also allows employers to grant or withhold employment to the spouses, children or parents of the employer or an employee.

Harassment

All jurisdictions prohibit harassment in employment. Harassment is any demeaning or offensive conduct or behaviour. To constitute a violation of human rights legislation, harassment must be connected to some prohibited ground of discrimination, such as sex, sexual orientation, age, disability, race, religion, colour or creed. Whether or not the individual who engaged in the conduct intended to harass or offend the victim is irrelevant for the purposes of human rights legislation. A violation can exist if the victim is offended by the harasser's conduct, regardless of the intent. Although many think only managers or supervisors instigate harassment, it is no less a violation of human rights legislation when engaged in by co-workers.

In the federal jurisdiction, Ontario, Quebec, New Brunswick, the Yukon, Nova Scotia, Manitoba[122] and Newfoundland, sexual harassment of employees in the workplace is specifically prohibited.[123] Where sexual harassment is not specifically prohibited in a jurisdiction's human rights legislation, it will be found to be prohibited within the prohibition against sex discrimination. The Supreme Court of Canada has supported an Ontario Board of Inquiry decision confirming that sexual harassment is indeed sex discrimination.[124]

The conduct which is prohibited by sexual harassment provisions of human rights legislation generally includes any unwelcome or objectionable sexual solicitations, advances or demands, or any comment, gesture or conduct of a sexual nature which is known or ought reasonably to be known to be unwelcome. In a

---

122 The Manitoba *Human Rights Code*, S.M. 1987-88, c. 45 (C.C.S.M. c. H175) (as consolidated to December 15, 2002), actually contains more general language pertaining to harassment.

123 In the federal jurisdiction, sexual harassment is also dealt with in detail in the *Canada Labour Code*, while in Prince Edward Island, the matter is discussed in the *Employment Standards Act*, S.P.E.I. 1992, c. 18 (as amended to 2000 (2nd), c. 7).

124 *Janzen v. Platy Enterprises Ltd.* (1989), 59 D.L.R. (4th) 352 (S.C.C.), applying *Bell and Korczak (Re)* (1980), 80 C.L.L.C. ¶18,006 (Ont. Bd. Inq.).

number of jurisdictions, including Ontario,[125] sexual harassment also includes "a sexual solicitation or advance made by a person in a position to confer, grant or deny a benefit or advancement to the person where the person making the solicitation or advance knows or ought reasonably to know that it is unwelcome". This extends to any reprisal or threat of reprisal against a victim for having rejected the advances of an individual in a position to confer, grant or deny a benefit or advancement to the victim.

The prohibition against harassment extends not only to employers but also to their employees and agents. Employers not diligent in seeking to eradicate sexual harassment from their workplaces may be found to be vicariously liable for the acts or omissions of their employees. In jurisdictions like Manitoba, New Brunswick, Prince Edward Island, the Yukon and the federal jurisdiction, the human rights Act may specifically set out this vicarious liability or state that employers have a positive obligation to take reasonable efforts to prevent sexual harassment. In the absence of a specific provision, the employer may still be found to be vicariously liable for the actions of its employees based on the Supreme Court of Canada decision in *Robichaud v. Canada (Treasury Board)*.[126] However, any proactive steps taken by the employer to deal with harassment in the workplace may have an impact on the court's or tribunal's decision as to the remedy to be awarded to the victim. A lesser remedy may be awarded where it is found that the employer took some action to prevent the culpable behaviour.

Duty to Accommodate

In addition to the common law duty to accommodate, which arises in certain circumstances, in a number of jurisdictions, such as Manitoba, Ontario, the Yukon and the federal jurisdiction, human rights legislation imposes an obligation on the employer to make specific accommodation in special circumstances. For example, in Ontario, in a case of discrimination, there will not be a BFOR if the group or individual can be accommodated without undue hardship on the employer. In many jurisdictions, employers will also be specifically required to accommodate the special needs of those with mental or physical disabilities before such persons can be discriminated against in employment.

Employers have encountered difficulties in determining exactly what is meant by the term "undue hardship" and will likely continue to do so, as the exact definition will depend largely upon the circumstances of each particular case. The Supreme Court of Canada has, however, had several opportunities to provide some guidance in this area. We do know that more than mere negligible effort is required to satisfy the duty to accommodate. The use of the term "undue" implies that some hardship is acceptable; it will only be "undue" hardship which satisfies

125 *Human Rights Code* (Ontario), s. 7(3)(a).
126 (1987), 40 D.L.R. (4th) 577 (S.C.C.).

the test.[127] We also know that there are particular factors which will be considered in the determination of undue hardship. The legislation generally sets out that costs, health and safety requirements and any outside sources of funding will be considered. Other factors which may be considered include the disruption of a collective agreement, the morale of other employees and the interchangeability of the workforce and facilities.[128]

A further issue which often arises with respect to the duty to accommodate is what role, if any, the employee has to play in assisting the employer with the accommodation. First, it is incumbent upon the employee to express to the employer the need to be accommodated. Except in cases where the need to accommodate is obvious, employers will not be seen to have a duty to accommodate if they are not aware of the employee's need for accommodation.[129] In the Supreme Court of Canada case, *Central Okanagan School District No. 23 v. Renaud*,[130] Mr. Justice Sopinka stated that individuals have a duty to assist in securing appropriate accommodation. This duty does not entail a responsibility to propose changes to the workplace rules, but rather involves taking reasonable steps to facilitate the solution proposed by the employer. Employees are not entitled to perfect solutions. If the accommodation is reasonable, the employer's duty is discharged, regardless of whether the employee turns down the accommodation offered.[131] Ultimately, the employer's actions will be measured against the undue hardship test and a determination will be made as to whether the employer did enough under the circumstances.[132]

Administration

Human rights legislation is enforced by a human rights commission in all of the jurisdictions, except the two territories where the ministry retains control. In Ontario, the Ontario Human Rights Commission oversees the implementation and enforcement of the *Human Rights Code*. When employees feel that they have been discriminated against or have been subject to a violation of their human

---

127 *Per* Sopinka J., writing for a unanimous court in *Central Okanagan School District No. 23 v. Renaud* (1992), 95 D.L.R. (4th) 577 (S.C.C.), at p. 585.

128 *Central Alberta Dairy Pool v. Alberta (Human Rights Commission)* (1990), 72 D.L.R. (4th) 417 (S.C.C.), at p. 439.

129 See *Strauss and Liquor Licence Board of Ontario (Re)* (1994), 22 C.H.R.R. D/169 (Ont. Bd. Inq.), and *Emrick Plastics v. Ontario (Human Rights Commission)* (1992), 90 D.L.R. (4th) 476 (Ont. Div. Ct.).

130 *Supra*, footnote 127.

131 *Supra*, at p. 593.

132 For more assistance in understanding what is required to fulfil the duty to accommodate, employers can contact the Human Rights Commission or governing body in their jurisdiction (see Appendix C – Government Contacts). For example, the Ontario Human Rights Commission has published *Policy and Guidelines on Disability and the Duty to Accommodate* (approved November 23, 2000), and *Policy on Creed and the Accommodation of Religious Observances* (approved October 20, 1996).

rights, they contact the governing body and issue a complaint. The procedure for doing so is set out in the relevant human rights legislation. In most jurisdictions,[133] the legislation allows others besides the complainant to bring the complaint before the commission. Employers may similarly make inquiries with human rights governing bodies if they are concerned that an action they are considering taking or a company policy may be in violation of employee rights.

Human rights legislation in a number of jurisdictions contains limitation periods for the bringing of human rights complaints. In jurisdictions such as Manitoba, Newfoundland, the Yukon and Ontario, employees are expected to issue a human rights complaint within six months of the event which gives rise to the complaint. In the federal jurisdiction, Alberta, British Columbia, New Brunswick and Prince Edward Island, such complaints need only be brought within 12 months. However, the commission may grant an extension and allow the complaint to be issued if it is filed after the limitation period has expired, in circumstances where the complaint is brought in good faith and results is no prejudice to any other parties involved.

Once a complaint has been issued, the process followed by the governing body will vary by jurisdiction but, in general, a human rights officer will follow up a complaint with some kind of investigation. These officers typically have very broad powers of investigation. They may be entitled to order the production of documents, request interviews with potential witnesses, enter premises and generally cause a considerable amount of disruption in the workplace. Since there is typically no cost involved when a complainant wishes to issue a human rights complaint, thereby commencing the investigation process, employers should be aware of the potential disruption which such investigations can cause. Employers wishing to avoid these investigations may seek to deal with potential human rights violations in a more proactive manner.

All human rights legislation empowers the governing body to try to effect a settlement between the parties either during the investigation or after. In some jurisdictions, these settlement discussions take the form of voluntary or mandatory mediation. Generally, the provincial statutes also contemplate that, if no settlement can be agreed upon, and the complaint is seen to have merit, a board of inquiry or human rights tribunal may be appointed to hear the matter. In the event that a board of inquiry or tribunal is appointed, there will be a full administrative hearing to decide whether the employee's rights have been violated. In many jurisdictions, such as Alberta, Ontario, Manitoba, Nova Scotia, Saskatchewan and the federal jurisdiction, the legislation specifies that the commission, the complainant and the employer will be proper parties to the hearing. It is likely that this will be the case even where the legislation does not so specify. The board of inquiry or tribunal will hear all evidence and render a decision.

---

133 With the exception of New Brunswick, Prince Edward Island, the Northwest Territories and the Yukon.

Remedies

The board of inquiry or tribunal also has certain powers with respect to granting remedies in the event that the hearing is decided in the employee's favour. In all jurisdictions, the board of inquiry or tribunal may make any order necessary to put a stop to and rectify the discrimination. These are often referred to as "cease and desist" orders. As part of this order, an employer could be required to reinstate the employee, pay a compensatory monetary award, apologize or do anything else to bring itself into compliance with the legislation, such as implementing policies or conducting education seminars. In certain jurisdictions, the tribunal also has the power to make a monetary award of damages if the employer's discriminatory conduct was wilful or reckless, or if the victim suffered humiliation, mental anguish or loss of self-respect.[134] In addition, in most jurisdictions, employers who discriminate may be guilty of an offence and liable on summary conviction to a fine, ranging from $100 for an individual employer in Newfoundland and the Northwest Territories to $50,000 in the federal jurisdiction for all employers who are not individuals.

EQUITY LEGISLATION

Equal Pay for Equal or Similar Work, or for Work of Equal Value

All jurisdictions have legislation containing provisions which are meant to ensure that female and male employees receive the same compensation for performing similar or substantially similar work.[135] Generally speaking, employers cannot pay a female employee less than a male employee who works for the same employer and does similar or substantially similar work.[136] In considering the meaning of "similar or substantially similar" work, courts have held that this does not necessarily mean work which is identical.[137]

Provisions which guarantee equal pay for equal, similar or substantially similar work ensure that employees are paid the same for work which is identical, similar or substantially similar. Certain jurisdictions have provisions which go one step further and ensure that employees receive equal pay for work of equal value. This

---

134 In Ontario, an employee may recover up to a maximum of $10,000 under this heading. In the federal jurisdiction and Saskatchewan, the amount is $5,000, while in Manitoba it is $2,000 for an individual and $10,000 in all other cases.

135 These provisions may be contained in either human rights or employment standards legislation.

136 Pursuant to the Newfoundland and Labrador *Human Rights Code*, R.S.N.L. 1990, c. H-14 (as amended to 2001, c. N-3.1), female employees must also be given training and advancement opportunities, pension rights and insurance benefits which are equal to those made available to male employees in the same establishment.

137 *R. v. Howard* (1970), 13 D.L.R. (3d) 451 (Ont. C.A.); *Riverdale Hospital v. Ontario* (1973), 34 D.L.R. (3d) 289 (Ont. C.A.).

allows jobs to be measured in terms of their value to the employer and ensures that jobs which are equally valued receive equal pay.

In Quebec, the relevant provision makes reference to "equivalent" work, as opposed to similar work. The use of the word "equivalent" actually means that, in Quebec, employers are required to provide equal pay for work of "equal value". The Yukon *Human Rights Act*[138] contains a similar provision with respect to work of equal value which applies to the public sector only.[139] The *Canadian Human Rights Act*[140] (the "C.H.R.A.") applies to all federal undertakings or matters coming within Parliament's jurisdiction and deems it discriminatory for an employer to establish or maintain wage differences between male and female employees in the same establishment if they perform work of "equal value".

The C.H.R.A. outlines four factors on which the value of work is to be assessed:

(1) skill;
(2) effort;
(3) responsibility; and
(4) conditions associated with the work performed.

The remaining jurisdictions also identify factors which must be used to determine whether employees' work is similar or substantially similar. In the Manitoba *Employment Standards Code*, these factors are the kind or quality of work and the amount of work required of, and done by, the employees. The legislation in the Northwest Territories and Nunavut recognizes the jobs, duties or services that employees are called upon to perform as part of the decision of whether male and female employees engage in similar work. With the exception of Alberta, the remaining jurisdictions cite the factors identified in the C.H.R.A., as does Prince Edward Island, which also considers education and experience when assessing whether work is similar or substantially similar.

Despite the prohibition against paying female employees less than male employees for performing similar or substantially similar work, there are some reasons which justify a difference in compensation. The equal pay provisions in many jurisdictions state that it is not discriminatory for an employer to base a wage differentiation on the following grounds: seniority, merit systems and a system based on quantity or quality of production. Equal wage guidelines pursuant to the C.H.R.A. state further that differentiation in pay based on formal appraisal systems, red circling, rehabilitation or training assignments, internal shortages of labour skills, and regional wages, is not discriminatory, while the Quebec *Charter of Human Rights and Freedoms*[141] dictates that differentiation

---

138 S.Y. 1987, c. 3 (as amended to 1998, c. 11).
139 However, the Yukon employment standards legislation still prohibits all employers from discriminating against male or female employees by paying them different wages where they perform similar work.
140 R.S.C. 1985, c. H-6 (as amended to 2002, c. 7).
141 R.S.Q., c. C-12 (as amended to 2002, c. 34).

based on experience, years of service and overtime is also not discriminatory if such criteria, along with seniority, merit and productivity, are common to all personnel. Rather than specify factors which would justify a difference in pay, the legislation in the Northwest Territories and Nunavut states that a difference in pay based on any factor other than gender will not render the wage differentiation discriminatory if that factor would normally justify such a difference.

The C.H.R.A. specifically states that an employer cannot reduce wages on the basis of gender. A number of jurisdictions echo this sentiment and their equal pay provisions state that wages cannot be reduced in order to bring the employer into compliance with the equal pay provisions. The Saskatchewan *Labour Standards Act*[142] asserts further that an employer cannot decrease an employee's rate of pay because the work is performed only by employees of the same sex. Finally, the Manitoba *Employment Standards Code* provides that an employee's acceptance of lower wages is not a defence to an action with respect to a violation of equal pay for equal work provisions, nor does it act either as a bar to that employee's right to lay a complaint under the Code or as a defence to prosecution pursuant to the Code.

If an employee believes that he or she is being paid in contravention of the equal pay for equal work provisions of the appropriate provincial legislation, the required procedure to be followed and the remedy available to the employee will depend on the legislation which contains the prohibition. For example, in Ontario, this provision is contained in the *Employment Standards Act, 2000*. Subject to the application of the *Pay Equity Act*,[143] the employee would pursue recourse as he or she would any suspected violation of the *Employment Standards Act*.

Pay Equity

In addition to equal pay for equal work provisions in employment standards and human rights legislation, and in addition to the equal work for equal value provisions in Quebec and the federal jurisdiction, some provinces have enacted specific pay equity statutes. The fundamental rationale for pay equity stems from the premise that, in general, women are segregated into a narrow range of occupations and, as a result of gender discrimination, their work in these occupations has traditionally been undervalued. Pay equity is further based on the notion that occupational groupings or "job classes" in organizations tend to be either male-dominated or female-dominated, and compensation for the female-dominated job classes is artificially depressed on the basis of unwarranted systemic sex discrimination.

The pay equity model is based on the concept that employees should be paid equally for work which is of "equal value" to the employer, not just for work

---

142   R.S.S. 1978, c. L-1 (as amended to 2002, c. 54).
143   R.S.O. 1990, c. P.7 (as amended to 2002, c. 17, Sch. C).

which is similar or substantially similar. For example, the equal pay for equal work model would never result in an employer being required to provide equal pay to an office clerk and a factory line worker, due to the difference in the type of work done by each employee. However, according to the pay equity model, it could be determined that these employees perform work which is of equal "value" to the employer and thus deserve equal pay.

There exist, in certain jurisdictions, provisions which provide for equal pay for work of equal value. Although this is the premise on which the pay equity model is based, these jurisdictions do not have pay equity. In the federal jurisdiction and the Yukon public sector, employees can complain if they believe that the equal pay for work of equal value provisions are being violated. However, in provinces with pay equity schemes, the governments have recognized that wage discrimination against women is endemic to the economy and requires a positive and systemic remedy. Here, wage discrimination is not only prohibited, but employers are faced with positive obligations to scrutinize their pay practices and ensure that they comply with the legislation.

Pay equity legislation requires an employer to evaluate the work performed by employees and to divide the workforce into job classes, so that the job classes can be considered to determine whether they are male-dominated or female-dominated. Employers must value each of the job classes, compare like classes and then endeavour to compensate each female job class with a wage rate comparable to that of the male job class performing work of equal value.

In Ontario, pay equity is governed by the *Pay Equity Act*, which requires employers to compensate equally male and female employees for work which is of equal value to their employers, even if the men and women are performing different jobs. According to the Act, every employer with 10 or more employees must establish and maintain compensation practices that provide for pay equity in an owner's "establishment", which is defined as all the employees employed within a geographic division.[144] Pay equity will be achieved when every female job class in the establishment has been compared to a job class or job classes under one of the various comparison methods, and any adjustment to the job rate of each female class which is indicated by the comparison has been made.

To achieve the purposes of Ontario's *Pay Equity Act*, jobs must be grouped into job classes based on the positions in an establishment which have similar duties and responsibilities, require similar qualifications, are filled by similar recruiting procedures and have the same compensation schedule, salary grade or range of salary rates. The classes are then identified as female, male or gender-neutral, and job information is collected with respect to the female and male classes. A female-dominated job class is generally one in which at least 60% of the positions are held by women, while a male-dominated job class is generally one in which at least 70% of the positions are held by men. In identifying whether a particular

---

144 *Pay Equity Act*, s. 1, definition "establishment".

job class is male-dominated or female-dominated, regard must also be had to the historical incumbency of the job class and the gender stereotypes which exist in the fields of work to which the classes pertain.

Job value is determined by measuring the demands that a particular job makes on workers. The determination is based on evaluating common job features which are relevant to job performance, without taking into account the individual worker. Although there are a number of different job evaluation methods which can be used to measure job value, the evaluation system used must be capable of determining value of work by applying four criteria:

(1) skill;
(2) effort;
(3) responsibility; and
(4) working conditions.

Once the jobs in an establishment have been grouped into classes and the classes have been valued, employers must compare the value of female job classes with the value of male job classes. Employers are required to use a "gender-neutral comparison system" to determine whether pay equity exists for jobs of equal value. The component parts of a gender-neutral comparison system, each of which must be gender-neutral for the system as a whole in order to be considered valid, are:

(a) the accurate collection of job information;
(b) the choice of a mechanism to determine how values will attach to the job information;
(c) the application of the mechanism to determine the value of the work performed; and
(d) the actual comparison.

When all of the job classes have been valued, the values must then be compared for the purpose of achieving pay equity. The compensation levels of job classes are not to be compared with those in external labour markets, but rather are to be compared with those within the internal organization which have been found to possess equal value. The *Pay Equity Act* recognizes that there will not always be job classes which can be compared and makes provision for alternate methods of comparison in such cases. Generally speaking, where it is necessary to use such an alternate method, the Pay Equity Commission must be contacted.

Once job classes which are similarly valued have been compared, it will become clear that an adjustment in wages may be necessary if the compensation levels are not equal for jobs with equal value. However, there are acceptable reasons for compensation differences. These acceptable differences may result from formal seniority systems, temporary training assignments, formalized merit pay, red circling and skills shortages. However, these exceptions must apply to both men and women equally and an employer must be able to justify them.

If job classes of equal value have different compensation levels which cannot be justified by one of the exceptions listed in the legislation, it will be necessary to make adjustments for compensation differences. Compensation adjustments are to be made once a year, but employers may limit annual pay equity adjustments to 1% of their previous year's total Ontario payroll. As in the case of equal pay for equal work provisions, reductions in pay are not permitted for the purpose of achieving pay equity.

When pay equity has been achieved, employers have an ongoing responsibility to ensure that they maintain equitable, gender-neutral compensation practices in their establishments. In Ontario, if an employee believes that an employer is in contravention of the *Pay Equity Act*, that employee (or a group of employees) may file a complaint with the Pay Equity Commission. A commission review officer will investigate the complaint and attempt to effect a settlement. If one cannot be achieved, the matter may be referred to the Pay Equity Hearings Tribunal. Both the tribunal and the review officer have broad powers to make orders which require employers to comply with the pay equity legislation. It is an offence for an employer to fail to comply with such orders or to attempt to penalize employees for exercising their rights under the *Pay Equity Act*. Upon conviction of such an offence, an employer can be liable for a fine of up to $5,000 if the employer is an individual and $50,000 in any other case.

Manitoba, New Brunswick, Nova Scotia, Prince Edward Island and Quebec all have separate pay equity legislation which is similar to that in Ontario in most respects. However, besides Ontario, only Quebec's *Pay Equity Act*[145] applies to both private and public sector employees. Pay equity legislation in the other provinces has limited application. The Manitoba *Pay Equity Act*[146] applies only to that province's Crown entities, civil service, large health care facilities and universities. With some exceptions, the New Brunswick *Pay Equity Act*[147] implements pay equity in the province's public service. The Nova Scotia *Pay Equity Act*[148] applies to civil servants, highway workers, corrections employees, certain hospital employees, Crown corporations, public sector corporations, hospital and school boards, universities and municipalities. In Prince Edward Island, the *Pay Equity Act*[149] applies to the government, the Crown, colleges and universities, hospitals and nursing homes, and other organizations receiving government funds. On September 11, 1990, the British Columbia provincial government announced a $40 million pay equity program for the province's civil servants.

---

145 R.S.Q., c. E-12.001 (as amended to 2001, c. 26).
146 S.M. 1985-86, c. 21 (C.C.S.M. c. P13) (as consolidated to December 15, 2002).
147 S.N.B. 1989, c. P-5.01 (as amended to 1994, c. 52).
148 R.S.N.S. 1989, c. 337 (as amended to 2000, c. 28).
149 R.S.P.E.I. 1988, c. P-2 (as amended to 1995, c. 28).

Affirmative Action

Affirmative action is a comprehensive, result-oriented plan adopted by an employer as a remedy for employment discrimination, with special emphasis on systemic discrimination.[150] Although affirmative action is probably best known for its acceptance in the United States, Canadian examples include the implementation of employment equity programs and those provisions contained in human rights legislation which, although discriminatory, allow for the creation of special programs designed to redress past discrimination experienced by members of a particular class or group. The Supreme Court of Canada has also recognized affirmative action as an effective means by which to deal with systemic discrimination, which has been defined as:

> . . . discrimination that results from the simple operation of established procedures of recruitment, hiring and promotion, none of which is necessarily designed to promote discrimination. The discrimination is then reinforced by the very exclusion of the disadvantaged group because the exclusion fosters the belief, both within and outside the group, that the exclusion is the result of "natural" forces, for example, that women "just can't do the job" . . . To combat systemic discrimination, it is essential to create a climate in which both negative practices and negative attitudes can be challenged and discouraged.[151]

In the case of *Action Travail des Femmes v. Canadian National Railway Co.*,[152] a complaint was brought that the company had engaged in policies or practices discriminating against women in employment in the St. Lawrence region. The Supreme Court of Canada recognized the problem of systemic discrimination and the need for proactive measures to combat the problem. As a result, the imposition of a mandatory affirmative action program by the human rights tribunal was upheld, requiring the company to ensure that one of every four new employees in the blue collar category in the St. Lawrence region be a woman until women comprised 13% of that job category.

The effect of all of these legislated pronouncements is to permit the occurrence of otherwise discriminatory action in order to improve the plight of individuals who have traditionally been disadvantaged and/or discriminated against. In addition, the otherwise discriminatory conduct attempts to relieve the disadvantages that these individuals have historically experienced and to ensure that opportunities are equally available to all members of society.

---

150 See the definition suggested by the Affirmative Action Division of the Canadian Employment and Immigration Commission (1979), cited in Mr. Justice W. Tarnopolsky and W.F. Pentney, *Discrimination and the Law* (Scarborough: Carswell, 2001 – looseleaf), at p. 4-142.
151 *Action Travail des Femmes v. Canadian National Railway Co.* (1987), 40 D.L.R. (4th) 193 (S.C.C.), at p. 210.
152 *Supra.*

Employment Equity

The purpose of employment equity is to develop and implement a variety of employment practices which will improve the status of certain designated groups. Its goal is to provide these groups with an equal opportunity in employment without direct or systemic discrimination. In addition, barriers to employment are removed with the anticipation that this will result in equal representation of the designated groups in the workplace. Where human rights legislation seeks to prohibit discrimination, employment equity legislation goes one step further, requiring employers to take positive, proactive measures in the workplace to remove barriers and make the workplace more equitable.

The *Employment Equity Act*[153] is federal legislation which applies to anyone who employs 100 or more employees in connection with a federal work, undertaking or business, and included in its realm is any corporation established to perform a function or duty on behalf of the Canadian government. This includes the federal public service, the Canadian Forces and uniformed members of the Royal Canadian Mounted Police. However, the Act does not apply with respect to any work, undertaking or business of a local or private nature in the Yukon or the Northwest Territories. The designated groups to which the Act applies are women, aboriginal people, persons with disabilities and visible minorities. Members of visible minorities are persons other than aboriginal people and will be determined if individuals identify themselves or allow themselves to be identified as non-Caucasian in race and non-white in colour. Persons with disabilities will be determined if they consider themselves to be or believe that employers consider them to be disadvantaged in employment due to an impairment.

Under the federal *Employment Equity Act*, an employer has four duties. First, the employer must consult with employee representatives regarding the implementation of employment equity. To this end, employee representatives are permitted to ask questions and submit advice regarding the implementation of employment equity. Secondly, the Act requires the employer to identify and eliminate workplace barriers which prevent the employment of designated groups. Thirdly, the employer must then institute positive policies and practices and make reasonable accommodation efforts to ensure that the designated groups obtain a degree of representation in the portion of the workforce from which the employer may reasonably be expected to draw employees. Fourthly, the employer is required to prepare a plan which sets out the goals to be achieved during the year and a timetable for implementation of employment equity, as well as an annual report.

The enactment of the federal *Employment Equity Act* clarifies that the obligation to implement employment equity does not require an employer to take a particular measure to implement employment equity where this would cause

---

153 S.C. 1995, c. 44 (as amended to 2002, c. 8).

undue hardship on the employer. This obligation also does not require the employer to create new positions, to promote or hire unqualified individuals, or to contradict the merit principle.[154]

The annual report which employers are required to file consists of several prescribed forms. On one form, the employer and the industrial sector(s) in which its workers are employed must be identified. On a second form, the distribution of all employees must be classified by occupational category, indicating the designated groups in each category. An additional form requires the employer to account for the distribution of all designated groups in each salary range. Further forms require the employer to account for employees hired, promoted and terminated with respect to their designated group, sex and occupational category. Finally, the employer must provide a description of what measures were taken to implement employment equity, including results achieved and a description of the consultations between the employer and its employee representatives concerning the implementation of employment equity. Upon completion, an employer must certify the forms as to their accuracy and ensure that an annual report is available for public inspection.

The federal *Employment Equity Act* provides that a copy of the employer's annual report must be received by the Minister of Employment and Immigration by a designated date. An employer who fails to file such a report may be liable for a monetary penalty not exceeding $10,000 for a single violation, and up to a maximum of $50,000 for repeated violations.[155] The Minister then has an obligation to forward all such employer reports to the Canadian Human Rights Commission, and the commission may initiate an investigation on the basis of information in the reports which indicates that discrimination may exist in the workplace. Under the C.H.R.A., the commission, private individuals or groups of individuals can also commence complaints if there are reasonable grounds to suspect systemic discrimination in the workplace.

Quebec is the only jurisdiction that has enacted employment equity legislation similar to that in the federal jurisdiction.[156] In Quebec, the Act applies to women, aboriginal peoples, visible minorities because of their race or skin colour, and persons whose mother tongue is neither French nor English and who belong to a group other than the aboriginal peoples group or the visible minorities group. In other jurisdictions, many employers have employment equity programs in place and are actively working toward removing workplace barriers for the four designated groups. The federal government has a non-legislated Federal Contractors Program which ensures that all contractors who supply goods and services to the federal government, have 100 employees or more, and are bidding on contracts

---

154 *Employment Equity Act* (Canada), s. 6.

155 *Ibid.*, s. 35(3).

156 "Act respecting equal access to employment in public bodies and amending the Charter of Human Rights and Freedoms", R.S.Q., c. A-2.01 (no amendments).

of $200,000 or more, achieve and maintain a fair and representative workforce.[157] In Ontario, the repeal of the province's two-year-old employment equity legislation in 1995 led to the announcement of the "Equal Opportunity Plan", a service and support program for employers wishing or continuing to implement employment equity.

OCCUPATIONAL HEALTH AND SAFETY LEGISLATION

General

Occupational health and safety legislation is aimed at regulating workplace safety standards and first arose to address the rise in industrial accidents and unsafe working conditions.[158] Today, most jurisdictions have comprehensive occupational health and safety legislation which generally applies to all sectors of the economy. Any separate provisions which are unique to one industry are typically enacted through regulations. Occupational health and safety legislation differs from workers' compensation legislation, which is designed to deal with issues arising after the occurrence of workplace accidents and injuries, in that occupational health and safety legislation is aimed at the prevention of such accidents and injuries.

The various statutes generally strive to centralize the administration of occupational health and safety laws under one authority. In Ontario, for example, this authority is the Ministry of Labour, as it is the Ministry or Department of Labour in many jurisdictions. In British Columbia, however, the Workers' Compensation Board bears the responsibility for the administration of occupational health and safety. Specific issues are therefore addressed in the provisions of that province's *Workers Compensation Act*.[159] In the federal jurisdiction, it is the *Canada Labour Code* which contains health and safety provisions, and it applies to employers and employees of federal works and undertakings.

Modern occupational health and safety laws are a collection of the three following types of provisions:

(1) general health and safety provisions applicable to most workplaces;
(2) provisions which apply to certain industries, such as mining and construction; and

---

157 Quebec has a similar program requiring contractors with 100 or more employees, bidding on contracts of $100,000 or more, to implement affirmative action.

158 For a more comprehensive discussion of occupational health and safety in Ontario, see N.A. Keith, *Canadian Health and Safety Law: A Comprehensive Guide to the Statutes, Policies and Case Law* (Aurora: Canada Law Book Inc., 2001 – looseleaf); N.A. Keith, *Ontario Health and Safety Law: A Complete Guide to the Law and Procedures, with Digest of Cases* (Aurora: Canada Law Book Inc., 2001 – looseleaf).

159 R.S.B.C. 1996, c. 492 (as amended to B.C. Reg. 267/2002).

(3) hazard-oriented provisions which address problems with respect to spe-
     cific hazards or substances.

Occupational health and safety legislation is concerned with the prevention of
accidents and disease and with the deterrence and penalization of those who
violate occupational health and safety standards.

    The legislation in a majority of the jurisdictions provides for the creation of
advisory groups composed of both management and labour representatives, as
well as health and safety professionals. These groups are meant to establish
programs for the instruction of occupational health and safety principles and to
promote awareness for the need of such principles in the workplace. In general,
these bodies act as advisory groups to the Minister of Labour.

Duties and Rights

    Occupational health and safety legislation in all jurisdictions is consistent in
that it sets out certain duties and rights which all those covered by the legislation
have in certain circumstances. This is consistent with the theory of internal
responsibility, which suggests that it is those within the workplace who are best
able to assess workplace hazards and health and safety issues, and to design and
implement solutions. Not only do employees and employers have certain duties,
but, depending upon the jurisdiction, there may be duties placed upon others
playing some role in the workplace, such as supervisors, contractors, suppliers,
owners and directors.

Employers' Duties

    All employers are required to take certain precautions and measures with
respect to occupational health and safety, and are generally responsible for ensuring the health and safety of all employees and workers on their premises. Employers are also required to provide employees with proper equipment and protective
devices and to ensure that these items are maintained in good working order. In
addition, employers are obligated to provide workers with proper health and
safety instruction, information and supervision, especially with respect to the
use of tools, equipment and hazardous materials in the workplace. In Ontario,
employers have an explicit duty to hire only competent supervisors. There may
also be a general requirement to post and make available to employees the
relevant occupational health and safety legislation and to prepare a policy or code
of practice regarding safe working procedures.

Employees' Duties[160]

All provincial occupational health and safety legislation imposes obligations on employees to take proper precautions in the workplace in order to protect their personal health and safety and that of others. These obligations include the duty to wear and use protective clothing and to use workplace equipment properly so as not to endanger oneself or other employees, to report known hazards or violations of the applicable legislation to supervisors or employers, to refrain from performing work which poses imminent danger to others, and to co-operate with the health and safety committee or representative and any other person exercising a right under the applicable legislation. In addition to these and other general duties, workers will also be subject to more specific duties and regulations which apply to their particular industry.

Duties of Others

Employers and employees may not be the only individuals on whom duties are placed by occupational health and safety legislation. In Ontario, duties are imposed on supervisors who must ensure that employees use protective devices properly, are aware of potential and actual dangers in the workplace and know what measures of protection to exercise. British Columbia similarly places obligations on its supervisors under the occupational health and safety regulations. A general duty to ensure that there is compliance with the Ontario legislation is also imposed on Ontario architects and engineers. In many jurisdictions, contractors have this same duty and, in addition, a duty is imposed on suppliers to ensure that the materials they provide are safe to work with and in good condition. Finally, in jurisdictions such as Ontario and Saskatchewan, a duty is imposed on project owners to determine whether any designated substances or hazards exist on the site.

Employee Rights

(i) Right to Know

In order that each employee receive that to which he or she is entitled pursuant to occupational health and safety legislation, that being the right to healthy and safe working conditions, it is necessary for all employees to have the right to obtain information, training, supervision and instruction on all matters pertaining to occupational health and safety in the workplace. For example, employees are

---

160 While there is no question that these duties are owed by employees, in some jurisdictions, such as Ontario, the emphasis is placed not on "employee" duties, but rather on "worker" duties, so as to clearly send the message that occupational health and safety is the responsibility of everyone working on a site, including, for example, independent contractors.

entitled to be aware of any inspection or other orders made in accordance with occupational health and safety legislation. Also, in accordance with the Workplace Hazardous Materials Information System ("WHMIS"), employees maintain the right to know about hazardous substances and materials in the workplace.[161]

(ii) Right to Refuse Work

Occupational health and safety legislation also provides employees with the general right to refuse work where such refusal is warranted. For instance, all jurisdictions permit employees to refuse work if they are likely to be immediately endangered by the equipment or physical conditions of the workplace, or if the conditions present are life-threatening. Workers may also be entitled to refuse work where a violation of the relevant legislation may cause them to suffer some form of injury or where they believe there is some degree of risk involved in the work which is not imminent or life-threatening but which is dangerous none the less. In Alberta and British Columbia, employees are obligated to refuse unsafe work. With limited exception, it is not necessary that the unsafe conditions actually exist, so long as the employee has reason to believe that they do. In many jurisdictions, employees may be disentitled to refuse to work if to do so would endanger or jeopardize the life, health or safety of another worker.

Once employees have refused to work, they must, however, report the workplace dangers to their supervisor or employer, who is then obligated to investigate the problem. If the worker is satisfied with the results of the investigation, he or she returns to work. If the worker is not satisfied with the investigation which follows, the workplace's health and safety committee or its representative may be required to look into the matter. Where an employee remains dissatisfied with the recommendations or changes made to remedy the conditions of concern, the government agency responsible for health and safety may be contacted. An inspector or officer will then investigate the matter and render a decision as to whether or not the employee's concerns have been adequately addressed.

In Ontario, in addition to employees, health and safety committee members also have the right to issue stop work orders. A bilateral stoppage occurs if at least two certified members of the workplace occupational health and safety committee, including one representative each of labour and management, agree that a particular problem exists. They can then require the employer to cease production or the use of particularly dangerous equipment. In certain circumstances, a unilateral stoppage may occur where one certified member alone orders the employer to cease production or the use of the equipment. This could occur where dangerous conditions exist or where a contravention of the legislation creates a situation which could seriously injure a worker. If an employer takes the position that the certified member was reckless or used bad faith in exercising his

---

161 See under the heading "Toxic Substances" later in this Part.

or her power to effect a unilateral work stoppage, a complaint may be filed with an adjudicator who must then decide whether or not the committee member acted properly.

In Quebec, the legislation also makes provision for a worker to request a "protective reassignment" in two circumstances:

(1) where the worker is pregnant or nursing; or

(2) where the worker is exposed to a contaminant.

In order to support a protective reassignment, a worker will be required to provide his or her employer with a medical certificate supporting the worker's contention that the working environment poses a threat to the health or safety of the worker, the unborn child or a nursing child.

(iii) Right to Participate

In an effort to make worker health and safety the joint responsibility of employees and management, all jurisdictions make provision for the creation of joint occupational health and safety committees, comprised of representatives of both workers and management. The mandate of such committees includes identifying any dangerous or hazardous situations in the workplace, making recommendations with respect to the improvement of safety and work conditions, and handling employee complaints regarding unsafe conditions in the workplace. Committees also have certain powers which may include the right to deal with health and safety complaints from workers, the right to participate in health and safety inspections or investigations, the right to establish worker educational or training programs and the right to request information from employers.

In a number of jurisdictions, including Manitoba, Ontario, Saskatchewan, the Yukon, Nova Scotia and the federal jurisdiction, employers may be required to have a health and safety representative in situations where the employer is exempt from creating a joint health and safety committee. Such representatives cannot be members of management and are typically chosen or elected from among the workplace employees. Health and safety representatives have the same general rights and duties as those of health and safety committees, including the carrying out of workplace inspections to identify potential hazards and the investigation of complaints with respect to unsafe conditions.

Enforcement of Employee Rights

To ensure that employees exercise their right to refuse work in unsafe conditions, every jurisdiction provides some protection for workers who seek to exercise their rights under occupational health and safety legislation. The degree of protection will depend upon the jurisdiction and may range from protection for refusing unsafe work to protection for reporting problems or violations, requesting information or doing anything in compliance with occupational health and safety legislation.

If an employee is disciplined, discharged or otherwise reprimanded for exercising a right provided for by occupational health and safety legislation, there are a number of avenues the employee can take in pursuing a remedy. The employee may be entitled to issue a complaint with the relevant labour board, as is the case in Ontario, Manitoba, Newfoundland, Prince Edward Island and the federal jurisdiction. In such a case, it will be up to the employer to show that the particular reprisal was justified. If the employee works in a workplace organized under a collective agreement, then he or she will be required to choose either to pursue the labour board route, if it is available, or to proceed to arbitration pursuant to the provisions in the collective agreement.[162] In proceeding by way of arbitration, the employee's interests are represented by his or her union, and costs will be involved. In contrast, the labour board route is free (with the exception of any legal representation which may be retained). In jurisdictions like British Columbia, the governmental agency with power to administer occupational health and safety legislation may have the power to issue orders requiring employers to rectify improper employer reprisals. In addition, all jurisdictions provide for prosecution of offending employers, although this remedy is unlikely to satisfy an employee who contends that the employer has violated the reprisal provisions of the legislation. Prosecutions may result in the placing of sanctions on the employer, but sanctions are unlikely to have any effect upon the situation of an employee who has been unfairly treated. Finally, employees may be able to take action pursuant to the common law. If an employee has been wrongfully dismissed, he or she may be entitled to commence an action against the employer. However, proceeding by way of litigation is expensive, lengthy and risky.[163] Employees would be wise to consider other available routes before turning to the common law in a situation such as this.

Toxic Substances

Many jurisdictions have special legislative provisions which deal with the use of toxic substances or biochemical agents. In particular, these provisions often deal with the permitted maximum exposure to such substances, inventory control, analysis of substances in accordance with accepted standards, and use and control of the substances in the workplace. For example, in jurisdictions such as Ontario, Prince Edward Island, New Brunswick, Newfoundland, Manitoba, Nova Scotia and Quebec, employers are required to make and maintain an inventory of all

162 Arbitration of such a matter is not available within the federal jurisdiction.
163 See the discussion under the heading "When the Dismissal Leads to Litigation" in Part 5, "The Divorce".

hazardous materials and physical agents in their workplaces. Furthermore, Ontario manufacturers must inform the Director of Occupational Health and Safety of any intention they have to produce or distribute new biochemical agents. The Director of Occupational Health and Safety must supply instructions with respect to how toxic substances or biochemical agents may be handled in the workplace, and employers are then required to post the instructions in the workplace for the employees' benefit.

In addition, all the provinces and territories have regulations concerning the Workplace Hazardous Materials Information System, most commonly known as "WHMIS". WHMIS is a nationwide occupational health and safety program which is designed to protect workers by providing them and their employers with pertinent information about hazardous materials or substances which are being used in the workplace. The system requires standard information about hazardous substances to be given to employers from producers, suppliers and importers. The employers are then expected to relay the information to their employees who ultimately use the materials. The transfer of information is effected by means of proper cautionary labelling, detailed data on the composition, properties, potential dangers and suggested emergency treatment procedures associated with the hazardous materials, and the effective training of workers and supervisors who use the hazardous substances.

Reporting Workplace Accidents or Injuries

All jurisdictions impose an obligation on employers to report workplace injuries and accidents to the designated administrative agency or department. There will generally be immediate reporting requirements in the case of fatal or very serious accidents or injuries, whereas less serious accidents or injuries will typically only need to be reported within a set period of time, which varies between jurisdictions and depends upon the nature of the accident or injury. Employers are also usually required to report the occurrence of workplace accidents or injuries to the health and safety committee or representative. In addition, employers are required to report any known occurrences of occupational illnesses or diseases suffered by employees.

In jurisdictions such as British Columbia and the federal jurisdiction, the employer will be required to conduct an investigation of the accident or injury, whereas in other jurisdictions an inspector may be dispatched to conduct an investigation once notice of the accident has been received from the employer. Employers are generally not entitled to disturb the accident site until after an investigation has been conducted, whether it be by the employer or by an investigation officer. However, an exception is usually made if preserving the accident site would result in risk to the health and safety of other workers.

Investigations

All occupational health and safety legislation provides for the appointment of officers or inspectors who must investigate complaints of hazardous conditions or accidents in the workplace. The powers of these individuals are broad. For instance, in the course of an investigation, they are generally entitled to enter a workplace with or without notice, require production of any drawings, specifications or documents, examine equipment, review books and make inquiries of current or former employees. In addition, an inspector or officer may order compliance with the relevant legislative enactment and may even issue a stop work order if he or she is of the view that employees are endangered by the workplace conditions. Many jurisdictions require employers to post in the workplace copies of these orders or other inspectors' notices. Employers and employees are also generally required to give all reasonable assistance to enable an inspector or officer to carry out his or her duties, and are typically prohibited from obstructing or hindering such investigations.

The orders of officers or inspectors can generally be appealed to an adjudicator or a board set up by the respective occupational health and safety authorities. Although a number of jurisdictions provide the right to appeal the decisions of such adjudicators or boards to the courts, in jurisdictions like Ontario, British Columbia, New Brunswick and the federal jurisdiction, such decisions are final and not subject to appeal. An officer or inspector may also order that an employee suspected of having contracted an occupational disease undergo a medical examination. A number of jurisdictions provide for a chief occupational medical officer who has the same powers as any other officer or inspector.

Offences

In most jurisdictions, a violation of occupational health and safety legislation is a summary conviction, quasi-criminal offence, as is the violation of an order of an inspector or officer. Individual corporations are subject to fines if found guilty, while individuals may be incarcerated, fined or both. It is also generally the case that any violation by a manager, agent, representative, officer, director or supervisor of a corporation is equivalent to a violation by the corporation itself, although the respective individuals might be held liable as well.

In some jurisdictions, occupational health and safety legislation makes specific provision for the defence of due diligence to be available to an individual or a company charged with an offence. For example, in Ontario, in certain circumstances, the legislation provides for a defence if the accused can prove that every precaution reasonable in the circumstances was taken. Even in jurisdictions where the legislation does not explicitly provide for such a defence, it may be available to an accused based on the application of the common law.[164]

---

164   *R. v. Sault Ste. Marie (City)* (1978), 85 D.L.R. (3d) 161 (S.C.C.); *R. v. Chapin* (1979), 95 D.L.R. (3d) 13 (S.C.C.).

Regulations

All the provinces and territories have enacted regulations regarding occupational health and safety standards with respect to specific industries, such as petroleum drilling, construction and mining. In addition, there are usually regulations regarding the use of blasting and the allowable noise level of explosives and industries generally. There are also provisions governing first aid, sanitary, hygiene and ventilation standards in working establishments, and workers who work alone. With respect to toxic substances, there are often provisions regarding particular chemical hazards and materials, such as asbestos and sulphur, as well as regulations which limit the permissible concentrations of airborne contaminant substances.

Other

The legislation of both Saskatchewan and British Columbia contains provisions which address the issue of violence in the workplace. In Saskatchewan, an employer is required to provide a policy statement regarding violent occurrences and how they are to be handled. In British Columbia, an employer must provide a risk assessment plan regarding violence, and all violent incidents must be reported in the same manner as industrial accidents. Furthermore, a British Columbia employer is required to inform an employee of any risk of violence in his or her employment. However, neither the Saskatchewan nor the British Columbia provisions are applicable to violence which occurs between employees in the course of their employment. Such occurrences are dealt with by the criminal law process or other similar avenues.

With incidents of workplace violence on the rise, there would seem to be an increased likelihood that workplace violence will be seen more and more as an occupational health and safety issue and the threat of violence as a workplace hazard. As a result, future years may see more legislation looking to regulate and protect against violence in the workplace.

Similarly, it has been suggested that harassment poses an equally dangerous physical workplace threat, and one which should be under the ambit of occupational health and safety legislation. Since the majority of incidents of workplace harassment relate to one of the prohibited grounds of discrimination, properly within the jurisdiction of those government bodies established to deal with human rights violations, we have seen little willingness to date to sweep harassment issues into the occupational health and safety purview. However, if harassment at large continues to be a significant workplace problem, more ministries and Departments of Labour may begin to take an interest in this area.

WORKERS' COMPENSATION LEGISLATION

General

Workers' compensation legislation is meant to address industrial accidents or injuries which occur while workers are performing their duties as instructed by their respective employers. Workers are entitled to compensation if their accidents or injuries arise out of and in the course of employment. This legislation operates on the premise that it would be unjust to require workers to commence lengthy and expensive court proceedings before they can obtain compensation for their injuries. Instead, workers' compensation schemes have little or no regard for blame, fault or negligence and provide injured employees with access to compensation and benefits from an accident fund. In general, workers' compensation is compulsory, and employees cannot waive their right to compensation under the scheme.

All provinces and territories have workers' compensation legislation, which generally applies to all employees in the jurisdiction.[165] Employees of provincial or territorial governments will similarly be covered by the workers' compensation legislation in their jurisdiction. Employees of the federal government are governed by the *Government Employees Compensation Act*.[166] This legislation provides compensation for the injuries and accidents of federal government employees according to the benefits scale set out in the provincial or territorial workers' compensation legislation which would apply if the worker were employed in private industry.

By virtue of the workers' compensation system, there exists no right of action for compensation resulting from a workplace accident or injury. Thus, employees cannot sue their employers for damages relating to their injuries. However, Ontario, British Columbia, Manitoba, New Brunswick, Prince Edward Island and Nova Scotia do provide that, in certain circumstances, employees may be entitled to bring an action for injuries suffered in the course of employment. For example, Ontario employers who participate in neither the collective liability scheme nor the individual liability scheme under Part I of the *Workplace Safety and Insurance Act, 1997*[167] can be sued for negligently maintaining defective works, machinery and/or buildings. They are also liable for any negligence on the part of their employees. Where a third party, such as a supplier or a contractor, is involved in a claim, workers or their dependants may also be in a position to elect to either sue the third party or receive workers' compensation. If the worker elects to

---

165 Within each jurisdiction, there may be certain exceptions to the legislation, such as farm labourers, domestics, casual workers or homeworkers.

166 R.S.C. 1985, c. G-5 (as amended to 2002, c. 7).

167 S.O. 1997, c. 16, Sch. A (as amended to 2002, c. 18, Sch. J).

receive compensation, the workers' compensation board may be entitled to maintain an action against the third party on behalf of the worker. In addition, provisions with respect to individual liability provide that any contributory negligence on the part of the injured employee will be taken into account. This is in contrast to the general workers' compensation principle of no fault compensation.

Each jurisdiction has a governing body responsible for the accident fund and for dealing with workers' compensation claims, both at the initial claim stage and in an appeal capacity. In the majority of jurisdictions, these are referred to as workers' compensation boards.[168] The workers' compensation board may also act as an advisory board and may implement research and training programs for health and safety. Most jurisdictions[169] have a specific body which hears appeals, such as the Workplace Safety and Insurance Appeals Tribunal in Ontario. In New Brunswick, Newfoundland, Nova Scotia and Prince Edward Island, decisions of the workers' compensation board can be appealed to the courts. In all other jurisdictions, the workers' compensation board maintains exclusive jurisdiction to hear all matters, and matters can only proceed to the courts by way of judicial review.

Collective Liability and the Accident Fund

Workers' compensation schemes are generally based on collective liability, that is, employers are required to pay premiums into an accident fund, and it is out of the fund that legitimate claims will be paid. Jurisdictions like Ontario, Manitoba and Quebec are based on a two-tiered system wherein two groups of employers are created. Employers in the first group are subject to collective liability based on their class or subclass. Employers in the second group are self-insured and must pay the cost of their accidents, although they are still subject to workers' compensation legislation. In addition, those in the second group continue to be shielded from various employee actions which may arise as a result of the no fault principle in workers' compensation schemes. Workers' compensation premiums are the responsibility of employers; workers cannot be required to pay these premiums, either directly or indirectly. The workers' compensation board in each jurisdiction will determine an employer's premium by assessing the accident rate of that employer's industry. The higher the accident rate, the more likely it will be that the employer will pay a higher premium. Industries are classified into categories according to hazard, and each will be liable for the cost of accidents or diseases occurring within the category. Employers will be required to contribute

---

168 In Newfoundland and New Brunswick, the body is referred to as the Workplace Health, Safety and Compensation Commission, in Quebec it is called the Commission de la Santé at de la Sécurité du Travail, in Ontario it is the Workplace Safety and Insurance Board, and in the Yukon it is the Workers' Compensation Health and Safety Board.

169 Including Alberta, British Columbia, Manitoba, Newfoundland, Nova Scotia, Ontario, Quebec and the Northwest Territories.

according to the industrial category in which they belong and according to their payroll.

Jurisdictions such as Ontario allow their workers' compensation board to establish experience or merit ratings for assessing employers' individual contributions to the accident fund. These ratings serve to modify contribution assessments based on the employer's accident occurrence record. The merit system results in smaller assessments and payments for those employers who have a solid record in maintaining safe workplaces, and higher payments for those employers with higher accident histories. A number of jurisdictions without formal merit systems still base their compensation rates and assessments on an employer's accident record. An additional percentage or payment is often added where an employer has outstanding assessments or contribution payments owing.

Compensable Accidents or Injuries

"Accident" or "injury" is defined in workers' compensation legislation to include the intentional and wilful act of someone other than the worker, a fortuitous or chance event occasioned by a physical or natural cause, and any disablement or impairment arising out of or in the course of employment. Many jurisdictions also include occupational or industrial diseases in their definition of "accident" or "injury". In most jurisdictions, there are circumstances in which a worker's accident or injury will not be compensable, such as, for instance, where the accident is attributable solely to the worker's serious and wilful misconduct. A worker also may not be entitled to compensation for the day on which the accident occurred or for some period afterwards, although such waiting periods are being phased out in most jurisdictions.[170]

Where accidents occur outside of the jurisdiction in which workers seek benefits, workers may still be entitled to compensation. With regard to these accidents, workers may be entitled to compensation if any of the following apply:

1. The worker's place of residence or the usual place of the employer's work or business is in that province.
2. The worker is normally employed within the province or employed in an occupation which requires him or her to work both in and out of the province.
3. The worker is only employed outside of the province for a limited period of time.

---

170 In many jurisdictions, including British Columbia, Saskatchewan, Prince Edward Island, Manitoba, the Northwest Territories and the Yukon, the worker's compensation commences on the day following the compensable accident or injury. However, in jurisdictions such as Alberta, Ontario, Newfoundland, Nova Scotia and Quebec, the worker may be able to collect wages or compensation for the date of the accident.

Workers who are not residents of a particular jurisdiction will still generally be entitled to compensation in that jurisdiction, so long as benefits would be available to the worker had the accident occurred in the worker's home jurisdiction. Most provinces, including Alberta, British Columbia, Ontario, Quebec, Saskatchewan, the Northwest Territories and the Yukon, require that such non-resident injured workers elect the jurisdiction in which they wish to apply for benefits.

Payment for Disability

Under the workers' compensation scheme, three general categories of disability are recognized and compensated:

(1) temporary partial disability;
(2) temporary total disability; and
(3) permanent disability.

All benefits which a worker is entitled to receive are subject to periodic adjustment. In a number of jurisdictions, this adjustment is tied to the Consumer Price Index. Where a worker suffers a temporary partial disability, he or she will receive periodic payments calculated as a percentage of the difference in pre-accident earning capacity and post-accident earning capacity.[171]

For workers suffering from a temporary total disability, the compensation to which the worker is entitled is calculated as a percentage of the worker's gross or net earnings before the accident. All jurisdictions set minimum and maximum amounts of compensation for temporary disabilities.

Workers who are permanently disabled receive some form of monthly payment referred to as an "economic loss" payment, which is meant to compensate the worker for lost earnings. In some jurisdictions, permanently disabled employees may also receive a lump sum payment to represent their "non-economic loss", or payment for the disability or impairment they have suffered. Such awards represent the worker's lost opportunity and are often determined according to a rating schedule which attaches a monetary amount to an impairment or injury.

Jurisdictions such as Ontario also provide for injured employees to be compensated for the impact that their injury has on their pension contributions. For the purpose of ensuring that an impaired or disabled worker receives a retirement pension, in certain jurisdictions, a percentage of the payment made for loss of earning capacity may be put towards funding a pension which the worker will receive when he or she reaches the age of 65. In Ontario, the Workplace Safety and Insurance Board ("WSIB") will set aside an amount equal to 5% of all loss

---

171 These percentages vary depending upon the jurisdiction, and the calculations can be complex. As a result, any worker or employer wishing assistance in calculating benefits or determining compensation should contact the workers' compensation board or appropriate governing body in their jurisdiction.

of earnings benefits to pay for a worker's loss of retirement income benefits. This amount is over and above the worker's regular payments, but will not be paid to the worker until he or she turns 65 years of age. In addition, the worker may elect to make additional contributions by having the WSIB deduct a further 5% from his or her regular payments. Also, certain jurisdictions require an employer to continue a worker's fringe benefits after he or she becomes disabled. For example, Ontario's *Workplace Safety and Insurance Act, 1997* requires an employer to pay all fringe benefits to an employee during the first year of disability. In Quebec, an employee who is disabled continues to fall under the employer's retirement plan and to accumulate seniority during the period of disability.

Additional Compensation

All jurisdictions provide that a worker's medical expenses will be borne by the respective workers' compensation board and paid out of the accident fund. Workers are entitled to receive any amount necessary to compensate for medical expenses which arise as a result of the accident or injury. In addition, workers are entitled to any services required because of a permanent total disability. Such services may include medical, surgical, optometric, dental and nursing care, and the supply of artificial limbs where required. In certain jurisdictions, injured workers may be entitled to receive home care. Furthermore, most workers' compensation boards will provide a clothing allowance to injured workers who have additional wear to their clothing due to a compensable injury, the wearing of a prosthetic device, the wearing of orthotic braces or confinement to a wheelchair. By way of contrast, clothing damaged in an accident or destroyed during removal to attend to an injury is not typically reimbursable. Workers' compensation boards have the authority to determine what reasonable health care fees are and to make a majority of the health care arrangements, although in jurisdictions such as Alberta, Manitoba, British Columbia and Quebec, the legislation provides that workers are entitled to choose the doctor who will treat them.

If a worker dies as a result of an accident which arises out of and in the course of the worker's employment, all jurisdictions provide that the worker's dependants are entitled to compensation. A surviving spouse will be entitled to some periodic payment from the workers' compensation board, but continuation of the payment may be affected if the spouse reaches the age of 65 or remarries. These periodic payments are normally assessed on the basis of the worker's net average earnings before the injury or accident which caused his or her death. In certain jurisdictions, the spouse may also be entitled to immediate payment of a lump sum, equal to the amount which the worker would have received had he or she been totally disabled. A dependent spouse will receive an additional monthly sum for each dependent child that the worker and spouse have. These amounts generally continue until the dependent child reaches the age of majority. If a deceased worker leaves behind children but not a spouse, the children will generally receive any lump sum and/or periodic payment that the spouse would normally have received. A number of jurisdictions will also provide compensation for spouses who were separated from the deceased worker at the time of the accident if the deceased was required to pay the spouse support and maintenance payments. Most jurisdictions make provision for the worker's dependants to receive some compensation for burial expenses and for any costs to move the deceased from the site of the accident, and some jurisdictions provide educational benefits for the worker's children who are planning to attend post-secondary institutions.

Reinstatement and Rehabilitation

All jurisdictions recognize the value in a worker receiving rehabilitation which results in the worker returning to work as soon as possible. Provinces such as Ontario and Quebec have developed comprehensive rehabilitation schemes, providing injured workers with rehabilitation services. In other jurisdictions, such services are usually provided for in funds apportioned for general medical assistance.

Many jurisdictions require employers to reinstate and accommodate, to the extent possible, workers who are injured in the course of employment. However, not all jurisdictions impose this duty upon employers. In Ontario, the WSIB must first determine if the worker can perform the essential duties of his or her pre-injury job. If the worker is able to do so, then the employer is obligated to reinstate the worker to the same job or to a comparable job with comparable earnings. Where the worker is unable to perform the essential duties of the pre-injury occupation, the worker must still be offered suitable employment if and when it becomes available. Employers may also be required to accommodate a worker's injuries, impairments or disabilities up to the point of undue hardship if this is what is required to put the worker back to work. The duty to accommodate may be explicit in the relevant workers' compensation legislation or may be imposed by virtue of the common law or human rights legislation. In Ontario, the reinstatement obligation continues for a period of time after the worker has been put back to work. If an employee is terminated within six months of returning to work, this termination will be presumed to be in contravention of the reinstatement provisions. However, Ontario employers are not required to comply with the reinstatement provisions if they employ less than 20 workers.

Medical Examinations

To determine issues of compensation, workers' compensation boards may require injured workers to undergo medical examinations. Such examinations are usually conducted by practitioners or doctors recommended by the board and chosen from a list created by the province's Lieutenant Governor in Council.

Several jurisdictions, including Ontario, require workers to submit to medical examinations at the request of their employers. However, such requests may also be appealed. In addition, many jurisdictions provide for the existence of a medical review panel to deal with assessments and any medical disputes which may arise.

In the process of a workers' compensation claim, the workers' compensation board may collect much medical information regarding a worker. Employers and health care workers may have certain limited access to these records during the appeals process if they play a role in the worker's compensation claim.

Notice of the Accident or Injury

All jurisdictions require employers to provide the workers' compensation board with notice of employee accidents, although the requirements differ in each jurisdiction. In Ontario, for example, the employer must notify the WSIB of an accident involving a worker within three days from the time the employer learns of the accident. Workers' compensation legislation also provides that board reports remain confidential and that it is an offence to disclose information obtained from an inspection or inquiry. Confidentiality extends to any medical reports which are provided for a board's use.

PRIVACY LEGISLATION

The federal *Privacy Act*,[172] and provincial and municipal Acts dealing with freedom of information and protection of privacy, are statutes which control access to government information and the protection of personal information held by governments and government institutions. These statutes only apply to the public sector and have little impact upon privacy issues arising in the workplace, even with respect to employees working in the government.

As discussed earlier in this Part, there now exists legislation in the federal jurisdiction, and there is soon to exist legislation across the country, which governs the collection of, use of and access to personal information collected by employers. Naturally, this applies specifically to personal employee information. The federal *Personal Information Protection and Electronic Documents Act* ("PIPEDA"), which, until January 1, 2004, only applies to federally regulated employers, provides that individuals are entitled to access personal information collected by an organization. Individuals also have the ability to challenge the accuracy and completeness of such information and to have the information amended if it is found to be inaccurate or incomplete. By 2004, PIPEDA will apply to all remaining employers unless individual provinces have enacted similar legislation meant to govern their provincially regulated employers.

---

172 R.S.C. 1985, c. P-21 (as amended to SOR/2002-292).

The *Criminal Code* of Canada also makes it an offence for an employer to intercept a "private communication" by means of an "electro-magnetic, acoustic, mechanical or other device".[173] Therefore, if it is reasonable for an employee to expect that his or her email, voice mail, internet, or telephone communications will be kept private, the employer may be exposed to criminal liability in the event that any such communication is intercepted. Liability can be avoided if the employer obtains the employees' consent. In this regard, it is always recommended that employers develop and distribute policies notifying employees of the practice of any form of employee monitoring and surveillance, and obtain either the employees' express or implied consent.

In British Columbia, Manitoba, Newfoundland, Saskatchewan and Quebec, statutes have also been enacted which provide for a civil cause of action for "invasion of privacy". These statutes generally provide that a person may not wilfully, and without colour of right, violate the privacy of another. However, each statute also recognizes that the nature and degree of privacy to which a person is entitled in a given situation or in relation to a certain matter is that which is reasonable in the circumstances, giving due regard to the lawful interests of others. In the remaining jurisdictions, there exists no statutory right to privacy other than those specified earlier in this section. Accordingly, any privacy protection must be found in the common law or in an employment policy or contract. Where there exists no actionable right of privacy, courts may none the less demonstrate a willingness to recognize an actionable right of privacy in a situation where the privacy intrusion is substantial and would be regarded by a reasonable person as offensive and intolerable. Many such issues, as they arise between employer and employee, can be avoided through the effective implementation of privacy-related employment policies.

---

173 *Criminal Code*, s. 184.

Part 4

The Separation

INTRODUCTION

While many employment relationships continue on in a "blissful" married state for an indefinite period, many others do not. It is more likely that there may be times when the employment relationship does not proceed smoothly. These periods of disturbance are not unlike periods of discord or separation within a conventional marriage. Typically, such periods are precipitated by some event which causes a degree of upheaval in the relationship and results in the parties no longer having exactly the same interests. To the extent that employers and employees can plan for these events, recognize these disturbances when they arise, and ultimately find appropriate and creative ways to correct difficulties, the parties stand a much better chance of seeing these events end in a renewal of the relationship, as opposed to divorce.

CONSTRUCTIVE DISMISSAL[1]

General

In recent years, companies have faced increasing challenges in dealing with tough economic circumstances, technological change and consequent competitive marketplaces. This has resulted in rapid and unprecedented changes in the workplace. Individuals facing a change in their working conditions are increasingly consulting legal counsel, wondering if they have any rights when faced with such a change. Employers and employees should be aware of the legal concept known as constructive dismissal and how the imposition of such changes may have a significant impact on the present and future employment relationship.

---

[1] For a more comprehensive work on the subject of constructive dismissal, see R.S. Echlin and J.M. Fantini, *Quitting for Good Reason: The Law of Constructive Dismissal in Canada* (Aurora: Canada Law Book Inc., 2001).

The law of constructive dismissal developed soon after employers began to recognize that they might be liable for damages if their employees were wrongfully dismissed. Employers initially believed that a way around this liability might be to make the working environment so unbearable for the employee that he or she would be forced to resign. However, courts soon became aware of this underhanded tactic and began judicially recognizing the doctrine of constructive dismissal. An employer is seen to have constructively dismissed an employee if it unilaterally changes a significant and fundamental aspect of the employment relationship.[2]

The law of constructive dismissal has seen vast changes over the last several decades. What was once seen as a remote claim found extraordinary recognition in the 1980s, when courts were less sympathetic to changes in the workplace and the corresponding effects that these would have on employees. However, as more and more of these claims became successful, employees tried to use constructive dismissal claims as a way to resign from employment with a payout. As the 1990s proceeded, and as budgets got stretched and businesses were asked to provide more for less, judges appeared to become increasingly tolerant of changes in the workplace. Fewer and fewer constructive dismissal claims were recognized, and employers were granted considerable latitude to make changes to the employment relationship. However, as the turn of the millennium approached and the economy took a turn for the better, courts again became generally less sympathetic towards changes employers wished to implement where, to do so, would result in a fundamental change to an employee's contract. So is the cycle of constructive dismissal claims. When the economy does well, courts are perhaps more attuned to the needs of employees; when the economy is on a downturn, it seems more likely a court will grant some latitude to a company struggling to survive.

A 1995 decision of the Ontario Court (General Division) is a good example of the type of decision one might expect, coming towards the end of the recession of the early 1990s. In *Black v. Second Cup Ltd.*,[3] Mr. Black was hired by Second Cup in 1991 as Vice-President of Leasing and Franchising. Staying within the budget was critical to Second Cup and, by 1993, it became apparent that Mr. Black was having serious problems in achieving budgeted targets. In response to an emergency situation, Second Cup decided to separate the franchising and leasing functions. Mr. Black was placed in charge of leasing. He was told that he would remain a vice-president and would participate in the same bonus plan. Although his base salary was reduced by $10,000, he was to receive an additional incentive bonus to compensate for this. Mr. Black believed that he had been constructively dismissed and he resigned.

Madam Justice Macdonald held that the issue had to be dealt with from the perspective of the employer, who had to be able to deal with emergency situations

---

2   *Farber v. Royal Trust Co.* (1997), 145 D.L.R. (4th) 1 (S.C.C.).
3   (1995), 8 C.C.E.L. (2d) 72 (Ont. Ct. (Gen. Div.)).

such as that which arose in this case. Employers are entitled to require employees to accept new positions as part of a reorganization so long as they do not fundamentally alter the employment contract. No such alteration was found in this case. The Court was particularly persuaded by the fact that Mr. Black remained in management and was able to keep his title of vice-president. Additionally, Her Honour detected no bad faith on the part of Second Cup and observed:

> It is the right of The Second Cup, in protection of its own business interests, to propose the realignment of responsibility to Mr. Black, with the expectation that Mr. Black would not refuse to accept the proposal.[4]

The *Black* case can be contrasted with *Michaud v. RBC Dominion Securities*,[5] a case decided in better economic times. In *Michaud*, the plaintiff was a senior investment vice-president who held the joint position of director and regional manager for the defendant. In 1999, as part of a company reorganization, Mr. Michaud's position was eliminated, and he was told that he was to be removed from the board of directors and assigned to the position of branch manager. He was not required to relinquish the vice-presidency and was told that his remuneration would remain unchanged for a two-year period. Despite this, Justice Smith held that Mr. Michaud had been constructively dismissed since he went from being responsible for 14 branches to only one, and would be required to report to a regional manager at his own level. In addition, despite the concessions regarding compensation, it was held that Mr. Michaud would likely suffer a substantial reduction in compensation in the long term, and he would be stripped of the work he most enjoyed – the opening of new branches and the training of new brokers.

Once an employment contract has been formed, one party does not have the right to unilaterally change a term of the contract without obtaining the consent of the other party. If such a unilateral change is made to a fundamental term of the employment contract, this is known as constructive dismissal. In order to constitute constructive dismissal, such a change must seem to imply an intention on the part of the employer to end the employment relationship by repudiating the employment contract. Thus, it is not necessary to find that the employer actually intended to end the relationship, so long as the conduct shows some such intention. On the other hand, it is not enough for an employee to show that the employer has simply changed the employment contract. To establish that there has been a constructive dismissal, the employee must be able to show that the employer's alteration put the employee in a position of having to accept a change that an objective person, informed of all the facts, would find to be unreasonable, unfair and untenable in the circumstances, and therefore a repudiation of the employment contract.

---

4   *Supra*, at pp. 79-80.
5   2001 C.L.L.C. ¶210-032 (B.C.S.C.).

Whether or not a change amounts to a repudiation of the employment contract depends on the magnitude of the proposed change. To constitute constructive dismissal, the altered term of the contract must not be trifling. The change must be fundamental, in that it goes to the root of the contract. Employers are generally able to alter some terms and working conditions unilaterally, but a change to a fundamental term can only occur with the employee's consent. For example, requiring the employee to change work stations will not likely be considered a constructive dismissal, while cutting an employee's pay in half likely will. The question of whether constructive dismissal has occurred is a question of fact and depends upon the express or implied terms of the contract, as well as the parties' relationship. It will be up to the employee to prove to a court that the change was serious enough to constitute a repudiation of the employment contract.[6] A court making this decision will be less concerned with whether the employer intended to end the relationship by making the change and with the employee's perception of the action taking place, and more concerned with whether an objective person would have believed the change to imply an intention on the part of the employer to end the relationship. The employer must be responsible for some objective conduct which constitutes a fundamental change in the contract.[7] The leading English case of *Re Rubel Bronze & Metal Co., Ltd. and Vos*[8] noted:

> In every case the question of repudiation must depend on the character of the contract, the number and weight of the wrongful acts or assertions, the intention indicated by such acts or words, the deliberation or otherwise with which they are committed or uttered, and on the general circumstances of the case.

In the same way that it may be possible for an employer to avoid liability for damages for wrongful dismissal where it can successfully show that there existed just cause for the employee's actual dismissal from employment, it may also be possible for an employer to justify a demotion, transfer or reduction in pay on the principles of just cause. The employer will need to demonstrate that the employee either engaged in conduct sufficient to constitute just cause based on a one-time occurrence, or will have to show that the employee was satisfactorily warned that a failure to perform in the manner requested by the employer would result in the change ultimately implemented.[9]

---

6   *Jervis v. Raytheon Canada Ltd.* (1990), 35 C.C.E.L. 73 (Ont. Ct. (Gen. Div.)), affd 26 C.C.E.L. (2d) 101 (Ont. C.A.); *Grant v. Oracle Corp. Canada Inc.* (1993), 90 Man. R. (2d) 206 (Q.B.), affd 8 C.C.E.L. (2d) 1 (Man. C.A.).

7   *Smith v. Viking Helicopter Ltd.* (1989), 24 C.C.E.L. 113 (Ont. C.A.); *Lesiuk v. British Columbia Forest Products Ltd.* (1986), 33 D.L.R. (4th) 1 (B.C.C.A.), affg 56 B.C.L.R. 216 (S.C.).

8   [1918] 1 K.B. 315, at p. 322.

9   See *Kerr v. Canada Alloy Castings, Ltd.* (2000), 102 A.C.W.S. (3d) 739 (Ont. S.C.J.), where Justice Sills held that Mr. Kerr's demotion was not justified because he had never been warned of the consequences of a failure to comply with his boss's requests.

An employee who is faced with what might be a potential constructive dismissal would be well advised to seek legal advice as early as possible, given that a number of different alternatives are available to the employee, and his or her choice from amongst these alternatives can have a significant impact on the employee's legal rights in the future. Employees may continue to work or may resign. They are permitted a reasonable amount of time in which to decide whether to treat the employment contract as at an end.[10] In determining what constitutes a "reasonable" period of time, a court will consider a number of factors, including whether or not the employee expressed concern or dissatisfaction with the proposed change, the level of change being proposed, and the prejudice, if any, suffered by the employer when the employee did not decide within a given period of time. Whether the employee accepts the change or resigns can have significant legal ramifications for the employee.

If the employee is presented with a change and begins to work under the new conditions without first seeking legal advice, the employee may have limited his or her chance of pursuing a constructive dismissal action against the employer. If the change is found to be a constructive dismissal and the employee has commenced work under the new conditions, a court will likely hold that the employee condoned the change. Condonation acts as a bar to any later claim that the employee was constructively dismissed. In beginning work under the new conditions, the employee will be seen to have agreed to the unilateral fundamental change to the employment relationship and will have negated any potential legal claim against the employer. If the employer has proposed a number of changes, the employee is not entitled to choose which of the changes he or she will accept or reject; the employee must either accept or reject all such changes. However, employees are also entitled to a reasonable amount of time in the new position to determine whether it is a fundamental change, or to clarify or negotiate the change, before they will be seen to have condoned the change.

If the employee has determined that he or she has been constructively dismissed and does not want to resign, it may be possible to continue on in the employment without condoning the change; however, this should be approached with care. Employees may indicate to their employers that they have been constructively dismissed and refuse to do the new work or accept the change. Employees who are considering this course of action should be certain that they have been presented with a constructive dismissal; otherwise such a refusal could be construed as insubordination and may be cause for dismissal without notice. A scaled-down version of this alternative might see employees agreeing to take on the new position or recognizing the change under protest and never agreeing that the change has been accepted. Again, employees will want to be certain that the change constitutes constructive dismissal; otherwise such behaviour could similarly merit discipline or discharge.

---

10 *Farquhar v. Butler Brothers Supplies Ltd.*, [1988] 3 W.W.R. 347 (B.C.C.A.).

The other alternative available to an employee faced with a fundamental change to the employment relationship is to resign. A resignation brought about by a constructive dismissal differs in law from a legitimate resignation in that when an employee legitimately resigns, he or she makes an independent, voluntary decision to end the employment relationship. In the case of a constructive dismissal, the employee resigns because he or she feels that there is no reasonable alternative. An employee who is presented with a change that he or she believes to be a constructive dismissal is well advised to seek legal assistance to confirm this belief before resigning the employment. If the employee resigns and the resignation is accepted by the employer, and it is later determined that the change did not amount to constructive dismissal, the employee may not be able to regain the position. It may also be the case that, even if the employee was constructively dismissed, he or she had an obligation to mitigate the damages arising from the constructive dismissal by remaining in the altered position. By resigning, the employee could be limiting his or her potential recovery in a wrongful dismissal suit.[11] Generally speaking, an employee who has been presented with a change in employment and who is considering resignation is wise to consult an employment law specialist. Such a practitioner is qualified to set out the employee's alternatives and to assist the employee in recognizing the legal implications of taking any particular course of action, including resignation.

In challenging economic times, it is often necessary for employers to maintain the freedom to reorganize their operations, change job duties and titles, vary compensation schemes and even transfer employees to other locations if necessary. Such economic justification may assist a court in determining that an employer did not intend to end the employment relationship, which is necessary for a finding of constructive dismissal. However, this will not necessarily serve to avoid the prohibition against employers making unilateral changes to fundamental terms of the employment contract. For this reason, employers may wish to provide for such changes within the terms of a written employment contract. The employer can put employees on notice that such changes may be necessary, and it will then be difficult for an employee to later argue that he or she was not aware of the possibility that a change might occur. For example, if the possibility exists that the employee may someday be asked to geographically relocate, the employer may wish to include a contractual provision specifying this possibility. While this type of specific provision is likely to be upheld, employers should be cautious in their use of general provisions which attempt to give the employer discretion to make any changes to the employment relationship that it deems necessary. The inclusion of such provisions may not insulate employers from liability in the event they choose to make a change to an employee's contract if the alteration is so fundamental that the employee could not possibly have contemplated it when

---

11   The subject of mitigation is discussed in more detail under the heading "Mitigation" later in this Part.

the contract was entered into. In such circumstances, employers may still be exposed to potential liability for constructive dismissal.

If an employer wishes to bring about a change that could arguably constitute a constructive dismissal, but it has not provided in the employment contract for such a change, it will often want to know the best way to effect the change. The employer should obtain the employee's consent to the change. The current economic conditions may influence how accepting an employee is of changes to his or her job or working conditions, and how enthusiastic the employee is at the prospect of heading back into the job market. If the employee's consent is not forthcoming, the employer will want to put before a court as much evidence as possible showing that the change was necessary for legitimate business reasons. To this end, the employer should develop a file documenting the history of the decision and its economic justification. As a final alternative, the employer may avoid potential liability for constructive dismissal by providing the affected employee with reasonable notice of the change such that the employee is provided with sufficient time to seek and obtain alternate employment if he or she so chooses. When determining the length of notice which is "reasonable" under the circumstances, the employer should consider a number of factors, including the employee's age, length of service and position, and the availability of alternate employment.[12] To fulfil the reasonable notice requirement, the employer will need to provide certainty to the employee by setting a fixed date on which the change will take place. In many cases, the employer will not be in a position to put off such employment changes to a future date. If the change is likely to constitute a constructive dismissal, and the employee will not consent to the change, the employer may wish to offer the employee pay in lieu of reasonable notice as an alternative to requiring him or her to accept the change.

Changes Historically Considered to Be Constructive Dismissal

Theoretically, any change that an employer makes to a fundamental term of the employment contract could give rise to constructive dismissal. However, in the vast majority of cases, changes have fallen into four distinct categories:

(1) changes in remuneration;
(2) changes in job responsibilities;
(3) geographical relocations; and
(4) changes in working conditions.

---

12 The determination of reasonable notice is described in more detail under the heading "Reasonable Notice" in Part 5, "The Divorce".

Change in Remuneration

Compensation is one of the most fundamental terms of the employment contract. Any change to an employee's compensation scheme poses a significant risk of being interpreted as a constructive dismissal. The type of change which is usually considered by the courts involves a reduction in salary or a reduction in some other aspect of the employee's compensation scheme. A change in the method of computing remuneration may also amount to a constructive dismissal, such as where some portion of an employee's straight salary entitlement is converted to a commission-based compensation scheme or where changes are made to an employee's rate of commission. An indirect decrease in compensation, such as no longer reimbursing employees for expenses incurred in the course of their employment, may also amount to a fundamental change, so long as the reduction is significant in nature. Other examples of indirect changes could include a reduction in hours for an employee who is paid by the hour, a reduction in or elimination of the opportunity for overtime, and salary freezes. In determining whether the change constitutes a constructive dismissal, courts will consider whether the change is offset by some other aspect of the employee's remuneration package.

In addition to avoiding reductions in compensation, employers should be wary of making alterations to an employee's bonus entitlement or benefits package. For example, changing an employee's performance-based bonus to a purely discretionary one may be considered a constructive dismissal, as this takes away the employee's control over the ability to secure a portion of his or her compensation. Other alterations which could be construed as a constructive dismissal include the loss of a company vehicle, a reduction in or the elimination of Registered Retirement Savings Plan contributions, a reduction in vacation entitlement, the elimination of a profit sharing or stock option plan and the elimination of the personal use of travel points. Such alterations will only be considered a constructive dismissal if the employee can demonstrate that the changes were so significant as to affect a fundamental term of the employment contract. This will rarely be the case, as benefits are typically only collateral to the employment relationship.

Despite the fact that remuneration is considered to be a fundamental term of the employment contract, not every change to an employee's remuneration package will result in a constructive dismissal. Employers are entitled to make changes which do not have a significant impact upon the employee's overall compensation. For example, changing the employee's remuneration from salary plus bonus to straight salary may not be considered constructive dismissal if the salary figure is intended to provide the employee with a fair substitute for the salary/bonus combination. Across-the-board percentage pay reductions are also common in tough economic times and are often not considered to amount to constructive dismissal, given that such changes are usually made as a last resort in order to save the business, and affect all employees equally.

In *Pullen v. John C. Preston Ltd.*,[13] Mr. Pullen was hired by John C. Preston Limited in 1979 as regional marketing and sales manager for the Ottawa region, with remuneration of $30,000 per year, plus a small percentage of the Ottawa branch's profits. The company underwent a series of changes, which climaxed in 1981 when a revised compensation scheme was introduced and resulted in Mr. Pullen's base salary being reduced by $3,000 and his profit sharing scheme being replaced by a commission-based sales scheme. A new job description also accompanied the change in remuneration. Mr. Pullen took the position that he was being treated as a salesman and no longer as an equal member of the management team. He resigned and alleged that he had been constructively dismissed. The company had been forced to change Mr. Pullen's compensation scheme due to severe economic difficulties which it was suffering. The Court looked at all of the facts and held that the changes to Mr. Pullen's employment contract would only have amounted to a constructive dismissal if all of his management functions had been taken away, and this was not the case. Mr. Justice Walsh was also persuaded by the difficult times that the company was facing and by the fact that all employees were being forced to accept similar changes. The redirection was "genuinely required" and "necessitated by the company's financial needs".[14]

In *Lavergne v. Meloche Windows Ltd.*,[15] the plaintiff was a window salesman whose remuneration was commission-based. Before February 2000, it was estimated that 50% of the sales for which he was responsible and, as a result, 50% of his income were generated as a result of new business calls made to the company. Such calls were divided equally between the plaintiff and another salesman until February 2000, when a new salesman was hired and a change implemented requiring all new business calls to be directed to the new salesman. Based on this change, the plaintiff concluded that his income would drop by 50%, and he resigned. Justice Quinn agreed, holding that the withdrawal of all reference calls and the consequent reduction in income constituted a repudiation of a fundamental term of the employment contract and resulted in a constructive dismissal. If the reference calls had been divided equally among the three salesmen, or if the exclusive referral arrangement had been for a temporary period, Justice Quinn held that this would have been within the realm of the defendant's flexibility to manage its business.

Constructive dismissal, like any dismissal, is within an employer's discretion so long as the employee is provided with reasonable notice in law of the impending change. Thus, if a change in the employee's remuneration package is

---

13 (1985), 7 C.C.E.L. 91 (Ont. H.C.J.), affd 16 C.C.E.L. xxiii (Ont. C.A.).
14 *Supra*, at p. 96.
15 (2001), 103 A.C.W.S. (3d) 967 (Ont. S.C.J.).

proposed during salary negotiations, and notice of this is given far enough in advance to satisfy reasonable notice objections, the employer may be free to make the change regardless of whether it would normally be considered a constructive dismissal.

Change in Job Responsibilities

A change to some aspect of an employee's job can be considered a constructive dismissal, given that the employee was hired for a particular job and should not be required to perform one which is significantly different from that for which he or she was hired. Changes within this category which have been held to constitute constructive dismissal include a change from one job to another, a change in duties within the same position, a change in working conditions (such as hours of work or shifts), a change in job status or prestige, a change in supervisory capacity (whether it is being imposed or taken away), a change in the reporting structure, the imposition of a probationary period, and demotions or promotions.

Difficulty arises in determining when the change made to the employee's duties or position is fundamental enough to constitute constructive dismissal. Each case will turn on its individual facts, and the standard objective test will still be applied to assess whether there has been a unilateral change to a fundamental term of the employment contract which demonstrates an intention on the part of the employer to end the relationship. Courts have found constructive dismissal where an employee has been stripped of his or her duties and seen those duties reassigned to other employees.[16] Constructive dismissal has also been found where an employee who once acted in a supervisory capacity has had all of his or her subordinates taken away.[17]

A difficult economic climate normally means that employees are asked to do more for less. The result is that, rather than having duties taken away, many employees are assigned additional duties without additional corresponding compensation. Downsizing and mass terminations result in more work being done by fewer people. The extent to which a court will sanction this type of restructuring and afford employers any flexibility to alter and reassign employees' duties will depend upon the state of the economy, whether or not the future survival of the organization depends upon it, and whether or not changes are made in good faith and for legitimate business reasons. Any employees who expressly or impliedly agree to reassignments at the employer's discretion and take on the extra duties will likely be barred from bringing a constructive dismissal claim against their employers. This is especially true when the employer has merged with another

---

16 See *Lash v. Meriden Britannia Co.* (1883), 8 O.A.R. 680, and *Ally v. Institute of Chartered Accountants of Ontario* (1992), 42 C.C.E.L. 118 (Ont. Ct. (Gen. Div.)), affd 37 C.C.E.L. (2d) 212 (Ont. C.A.).

17 See *Cox v. Royal Trust Corp. of Canada* (1989), 26 C.C.E.L. 203 (Ont. C.A.), leave to appeal to S.C.C. refused 33 C.C.E.L. 224*n*.

company, the employee has a history of accepting reassignment, or the reassignment is required because of the employer's financial situation.

Generally speaking, courts will consider all of the factors surrounding the change made to a particular employee's job. What the employee may believe to be a constructive dismissal based on a perceived demotion or loss of status or prestige may actually be a lateral transfer, especially if the compensation scheme remains unchanged. Once all of the factors have been considered, a court will make a determination as to whether there has been a unilateral change to a fundamental term of the employment contract, and whether the change seems to imply an intention to end the relationship. If the employer's action is motivated by sound business reasons, is undertaken in good faith and does not have humiliating effects on the employee, courts may be sympathetic to the need for the change and may find in favour of the employer.

Geographical Relocation

Often, employees believe that they have been constructively dismissed when they are requested to geographically relocate within the employer's organization. The standard test for constructive dismissal applies here as well, and courts will strive to determine whether the request being made of the employee is such that the employee's contract has been fundamentally changed. However, there are a number of specific factors which courts may consider under this heading to determine whether the request for transfer was reasonable. These factors include the size of the employer's operation, the number of its branches, the area in which the employer operates, the location of the employer's headquarters, the number of employees working for the organization and the number being asked to transfer, whether the new position is a promotion or demotion, whether the employer is paying for relocation expenses, whether the transfer is related to a legitimate reorganization of the company, whether the transfer is temporary or permanent, whether the transfer will cause undue hardship to the employee and whether the employer is acting in good faith. In the case of a national or international company, courts will often find in the employment contract an implied term which provides that the employee agrees to accept reasonable transfers which do not involve a demotion or undue hardship.[18] The court may also look at the nature of the employer's business and the prevalence of employee transfers within the organization. Ultimately, the issue of reasonableness will be decided on the facts of the particular case.

In a leading case in this area, *Smith v. Viking Helicopter Ltd.*,[19] the Ontario Court of Appeal dealt with a situation in which an employee was asked to relocate

18 *Canadian Bechtel v. Mollenkopf* (1978), 1 C.C.E.L. 95 (Ont. C.A.); *Rose v. Shell Canada Ltd.* (1985), 7 C.C.E.L. 234 (B.C.S.C.).
19 (1989), 24 C.C.E.L. 113 (Ont. C.A.).

in the course of his employment. The Court commented that it did not understand employees to be entitled to jobs for life in a place of their choosing. As the following statement of Mr. Justice Finlayson demonstrates, the Court further indicated that, if an employee wishes to remain with a particular company, the employee must expect reasonable dislocations in that employment:

> It has never been my understanding that an employee is entitled to a job for life in a place of his choosing. If he wishes to remain an employee of a given company, he must expect reasonable dislocations in that employment including the place where it is to be performed.[20]

Change in Working Conditions

A constructive dismissal may also be found if there has been a fundamental change to an employee's conditions of work. For example, in *Bowen Estate v. Ritchie Bros. Auctioneers Ltd.*,[21] the plaintiff yard foreman found his duties split in two, and he was offered a position at the gatehouse on the company's property. The Ontario Court of Appeal found this change to be a constructive dismissal when it observed that the new position was to involve work at what could best be described as a "yard shack", a tiny structure with no heat, no washroom facility and no access to management or secretarial staff. As Justice MacPherson commented: "For an employee who had worked for several years in the main office almost adjacent to the manager, relegation to a tiny, unheated shed at the periphery of the premises was a clear signal that the company no longer valued Bowen's services and hoped he would quit."[22]

Courts have also been willing to consider whether an employee was constructively dismissed in a situation where the employee was the victim of sexual harassment.[23] This same logic would seem to apply equally in the case of any type of harassment, whether on the basis of some prohibited ground of discrimination established by human rights legislation or not. Complaints of bullying in the workplace appear to be on the rise, whether between co-workers, or between a tough manager and a subordinate. Employers who dismiss such conflicts as "playground antics" may find themselves facing liability. If an employee is subjected to treatment in the workplace which is humiliating and demeaning and ultimately forces the employee to resign, the employer may be found to have constructively dismissed the employee if the employer was aware of the conduct and took no steps to rectify it.

---

20 *Supra*, at p. 118.
21 (1999), 47 C.C.E.L. (2d) 232 (Ont. C.A.).
22 *Supra*, at para. 14.
23 *Alpaerts v. Obront* (1993), 46 C.C.E.L. 218 (Ont. Ct. (Gen. Div.)); *L'Attiboudeaire v. Royal Bank of Canada* (1996), 131 D.L.R. (4th) 445 (Ont. C.A.).

In the *Shah v. Xerox Canada Ltd.* case,[24] Mr. Shah was subjected to harassing behaviour at the hands of his manager. Mr. Shah was described by the trial judge as "gentle", "reticent" and "introspective", whereas his manager was considered "confident and assertive to the point of being combative". With such different temperaments, it was not surprising that Mr. Shah and his manager would experience conflict. Over a period of approximately six months prior to his resignation, Mr. Shah experienced unwarranted criticism and progressive discipline for matters which were determined to not be his fault. At the same time, Mr. Shah was experiencing significant personal and health problems, and was ordered by his doctor to take time off. When he did so, he was reprimanded despite his attempts to explain his situation. The stress of his circumstances eventually pushed Mr. Shah to resign his employment, and he sued Xerox, claiming he had been constructively dismissed.

At trial, Justice Cullity had no difficulty finding that Mr. Shah's manager had made his working conditions so intolerable that Mr. Shah was left with no alternative but to resign. It was held that the test is an objective one – whether the conduct of the manager was such that a reasonable person in the circumstances should not be expected to persevere in the employment. However, Xerox appealed this decision, claiming that a change in working conditions was not sufficient to constitute a constructive dismissal. Rather, it argued, there had to be an actual change to a particular term of employment. The Ontario Court of Appeal disagreed with Xerox and found that a change in working conditions was sufficient to constitute a constructive dismissal if the working conditions were such that the employee had no choice but to resign his or her employment. In the result, a finding was made in favour of Mr. Shah.[25]

Naturally, the *Shah* case may cause some concern to employers who are used to working their employees hard. As Justice Cullity pointed out in the trial decision:

> An employer is entitled to be critical of the unsatisfactory work of its employees and, in general, to take such measures – disciplinary or otherwise – as it believes to be appropriate to remedy the situation. There is, however, a limit. If the employer's conduct in the particular circumstances passes so far beyond the bounds of reasonableness that the employee reasonably finds continued employment to be intolerable, there will, in my view, be constructive dismissal whether or not the employee purports to resign.[26]

---

24 (1998), 49 C.C.E.L. (2d) 30 (Ont. Ct. (Gen. Div.)), affd 49 C.C.E.L. (2d) 166 (Ont. C.A.).

25 See also *Whiting v. Winnipeg River Brokenhead Community Futures Development Corp.* (1998), 159 D.L.R. (4th) 18 (Man. C.A.), where the trial judge concluded that an employee had been constructively dismissed because of a series of incidents culminating in the imposition of probation. The employer had unjustifiably criticized the employee, levelled vague and unfounded accusations against her, and created a hostile and embarrassing work environment. It was held that, viewed objectively, the plaintiff's continued employment in such an environment was no longer possible, and the Court of Appeal upheld this conclusion.

26 *Shah v. Xerox Canada Ltd.*, *supra*, footnote 24, at para. 38 (Ont. Ct. (Gen. Div.)).

Based on the foregoing, it seems clear that employers are still free to set reasonable standards for their employees and to expect those standards to be met. It is only in those egregious cases where a court might find that a constructive dismissal has taken place. For example, in *Menard v. Royal Insurance Co. of Canada*,[27] the plaintiff was an insurance adjuster who was put under pressure to explain a certain file where timelines had not been met. She failed to do so and instead resigned, claiming that she had been constructively dismissed. Justice Hennessey disagreed, and found that the letters to the plaintiff regarding the file were not unjustified criticism, the actions of the employer did not cause a hostile or embarrassing environment for the plaintiff, and none of the plaintiff's superiors had treated her in an abusive or authoritarian manner. Although Justice Hennessey commented that the employer had acted in an aggressive and non-constructive manner, it was none the less held that this did not demonstrate an intention on the part of the company to no longer be bound by the employment contract.[28]

Mitigation

One outstanding issue which typically arises in cases of constructive dismissal is what is required of the employee in terms of the fulfilment of the duty to mitigate. Employees who have been constructively dismissed are under a duty to mitigate their damages, as is the case in any wrongful dismissal action. This duty has prompted employers in many cases to allege that the constructively dismissed employee should have accepted the change to the employment contract and continued to work for the period of reasonable notice. If, for example, an employee refuses to be demoted, employers argue that the duty to mitigate contemplates the employee accepting the lower status job until he or she finds new employment or until the reasonable notice period has expired.

The case law is not entirely consistent as to whether an employee is required to accept the position being offered, even if to do so would, in effect, constitute condonation of a constructive dismissal situation. In *Mifsud v. MacMillan Bathurst Inc.*,[29] the Ontario Court of Appeal held that it seems reasonable to require an employee to fulfil the duty to mitigate by accepting the new position being offered within the company under the following circumstances:

(a) where the salary remains unchanged;
(b) where the working conditions are not substantially different nor the work demeaning; and
(c) where the personal relationships involved are not acrimonious.

---

27 (2000), 1 C.C.E.L. (3d) 96 (Ont. S.C.J.).
28 *Supra*, at para. 17.
29 (1989), 63 D.L.R. (4th) 714 (Ont. C.A.), leave to appeal to S.C.C. refused 68 D.L.R. (4th) vii.

In these instances, the employee would be required to work in the new position for the reasonable notice period or until the employee is able to secure alternate employment. The *Mifsud* case can be compared to *Furuheim v. Bechtel Canada Ltd.*,[30] where the Court held that an employer who has presented an employee with a change to the employment relationship must prove that the employee's rejection of this position is unreasonable in all respects.

The *Mifsud* case determined that employees may be required to work under circumstances which constitute constructive dismissal in order to fulfil their duty to mitigate. This case has been applied and followed in a number of subsequent decisions. However, many of these cases have qualified the finding in *Mifsud*. By virtue of these cases, we now have a better understanding of those circumstances where it would be unreasonable to expect an employee to remain in employment simply to fulfil the duty to mitigate. In the case of *Squires v. Stanley Hardware*,[31] the Court held that an engineer was not required to accept a unionized position with lower pay, in a different work location, on a different machine and on a different shift. Such work was found to be demeaning. In *Laakso v. Valspar*,[32] an employee, because of stomach problems which made shift work potentially hazardous to his health, was not required to assume a new position requiring shift work in order to fulfil the duty to mitigate. In *Davidson v. Allelix Inc.*,[33] the Court found it unreasonable to expect an executive to assume a new position when he had been hired from another company to fill a specific position. However, in *Michaud v. RBC Dominion Securities*,[34] the trial judge held that the plaintiff failed to mitigate his damages by refusing to accept a demotion from regional to branch manager, where the employee retained his vice-presidency and had his compensation maintained for a period of time, and where his superiors remained cordial and were anxious to have him continue with the company.

If a court does ultimately find that, in order to fulfil the duty to mitigate, an employee must accept a position in the organization which would otherwise constitute a constructive dismissal, this will not waive the employee's right to later claim that he or she was constructively dismissed, provided that the employee has clearly indicated a rejection of the proposed change and is simply fulfilling the obligation to mitigate by continuing to serve. Employers cannot have it both ways: they cannot argue that an employee should have accepted a new position in mitigation of the damages arising by virtue of the dismissal and, at the same time, argue that acceptance of the new position constitutes condonation. However, employees may waive their right to bring an action if they continue in the new employment after the expiration of the reasonable notice period.

---

30 (1990), 30 C.C.E.L. 146 (Ont. C.A.).
31 (1991), 36 C.C.E.L. 265 (Ont. Ct. (Gen. Div.)).
32 (1990), 32 C.C.E.L. 72 (Ont. Dist. Ct.), affd 35 C.C.E.L. 276 (Ont. Div. Ct.).
33 (1991), 86 D.L.R. (4th) 542 (Ont. C.A.).
34 2001 C.L.L.C. ¶210-032 (B.C.S.C.).

One important consideration which courts will make when examining constructive dismissal situations is the effective date upon which the employee was allegedly dismissed. The law is not entirely clear on whether the notice period begins to run from the time when the change is imposed or whether the period begins to run from the point at which the employee asserts constructive dismissal and resigns the employment. The weight of decisions appears to accept the former view that the notice period runs from the imposition of the change,[35] and this approach seems to best coincide with an employee having a potential obligation to accept the change in fulfilment of the duty to mitigate. It seems unlikely that an employee required to continue on in a position after a constructive dismissal in fulfilment of the duty to mitigate might later be prevented from claiming damages because the employee never resigned. If the notice period is seen to begin upon the imposition of the change, the employee can fulfil the duty to mitigate while the period of notice continues to run.

SALE OF A BUSINESS

Employers and employees often ask what impact a sale of the employer's business will have on existing employer-employee relationships. The legal impact which a sale of the business will have on the current relationship between employer and employee depends on the manner in which the transaction is effected. Although the owner or board of directors of an organization may change, it is entirely possible that the relationship between the employees and the business will remain unchanged, as is what normally happens when the transaction is one involving the sale of the shares of the business. In many sale of business situations, the purchaser makes known to existing employees that it has every intention of maintaining employment relationships with the current employees as it continues on in the business. Such an explicit communication of the intention to continue the relationship will make it difficult for the purchasing employer to later argue that there was an interruption in the service of these employees. However, in non-union settings, there is generally no obligation on the part of a purchaser to continue the employment of any of the existing employees. If the purchaser does not intend to continue the employment of any of the existing employees, the purchaser will wish to make this very clear to the employees,[36] and the employees should then recognize that they are being dismissed by the selling employer and are entitled to any notice, pay in lieu of notice or severance

---

35 *Bowie v. Motorola Canada Ltd.* (1991), 44 C.C.E.L. 307 (Ont. Ct. (Gen. Div.)); *Alpert v. Carreaux Ramca Ltée* (1992), 41 C.C.E.L. 276 (Ont. Ct. (Gen. Div.)).

36 This can be made clearer by providing an Employment Insurance Commission ("E.I.C.") Record of Employment to the employee in relation to his or her previous service with the selling employer. If the purchasing employer subsequently decides that it wishes to continue the service of the employee, it is advisable that it approach this as a new hiring by providing a letter of engagement with the purchasing employer and perhaps even conducting a job interview.

pay, whether statutory or otherwise, to which they would be entitled had they been dismissed in normal course. Any such claims must be made against the vendor and may not be effective against the purchasing employer if it was made clear to the employees that their employment would not be continued with the purchaser.

Purchasing employers who are considering retaining certain employees should proceed with caution. Sometimes such employers will allow the employees to continue working in their normal positions after the purchase, only to subsequently decide that such employees will be assigned to other positions within the new organization. Unless the employer in such a case has made it clear that the employee is being allowed to continue on in the old position on a "without prejudice" basis until a new position can be found, the employee may have a claim against the employer for constructive dismissal. In allowing the employee to continue on in the employment without any qualifications as to the nature of the continuation, the employer may be found to have accepted the transfer of the employee's existing employment contract, and any subsequent attempt to unilaterally change the fundamental terms of the contract will be seen as a constructive dismissal. Purchasing employers are well advised to ask that the vendor issue a clear blanket termination notice to all of the vendor's employees, thus clearly ending the employment relationship prior to the purchase. Even if these same employees then continue on with the purchasing employer, this may provide a basis to argue that they began under a new employment contract and that the parties were free to renegotiate any terms of the new contract at the time of hiring. Selling employers should be aware that any employees who continue on with the purchasing employer in the same or similar positions may be said to have mitigated their damages and, in such a case, the selling employer may be absolved (in whole or in part) from liability to these employees. However, selling employers should also be aware that if a new job offered by the purchaser to an employee constitutes a fundamental change to the employee's contract and, thus, could be a constructive dismissal, the employee may be within his or her rights to refuse the position and claim severance from the seller.

In addition to what has just been stated, most provincial employment standards legislation also deals with circumstances in which an employer sells its business. Generally, most Canadian jurisdictions provide that, in the event that an employer's business is sold (or something takes place which is akin to a sale, such as a lease, transfer, disposal or amalgamation), any employees whose employment is continued with the new employer will have their length of service with the previous employer recognized for the purposes of the legislation.[37] This may apply despite any effort on the part of the purchaser and the seller to terminate employment at the time of the transaction since it may be impossible to contract

---

37   All jurisdictions but Prince Edward Island and Quebec have a provision similar to this.

out of the employment standards legislation. Many employment standards referees in Ontario have considered what is meant by a "sale" for the purposes of the legislation, and there is general agreement that, while a share purchase will trigger the "sale" provision and require that previous service be recognized for employees who continue on, a mere asset purchase will not be considered a "sale" of the business. Employers can be certain that the substance of any transaction will be looked at in detail to determine whether a sale of the business has actually taken place, regardless of whether the transaction is referred to on paper as an asset or a share purchase.

BANKRUPTCY AND RECEIVERSHIP

As in the case of the sale of an employer's business, which may have a significant impact on the employment relationship, employees are often similarly concerned about the effect that the appointment of a receiver or a trustee in bankruptcy will have on the employment relationship.

The appointment of a receiver can generally arise in one of two ways. The first is through private or document appointment by a secured creditor of the debtor, pursuant to the terms of a security agreement. The second is through court appointment, usually on application by a secured creditor of the debtor. The appointment of a trustee in bankruptcy under the *Bankruptcy and Insolvency Act* (Canada) (the "BIA")[38] arises in one of three ways. The first is through a voluntary assignment in bankruptcy filed by the debtor. The second is through a receiving order made by a court on a petition by a creditor. The third way is through the failure of a proposal made by the debtor to its creditors.

At common law, the appointment of a receiver (whether by a court or under a security agreement), or the appointment of a trustee in bankruptcy has been held to terminate employees' contracts of service, and any continued service after the appointment is deemed to be under a new employment contract with the receiver or with the ultimate purchaser of the business.[39] Therefore, if employees are subsequently terminated by the receiver, the trustee in bankruptcy or a subsequent purchaser of the business, the employees' length of service should date back no further than the appointment of the receiver or trustee in bankruptcy for the purposes of the common law. The employees' length of service will be relevant in determining what, if any, reasonable notice or pay in lieu thereof the employees might be entitled to in the event of their dismissal.

In contrast to the common law situation, both receivers and trustees in bankruptcy may be considered to be employers for the purpose of the operation of the "sale of a business" provisions in employment standards legislation. Thus, if

---

38 R.S.C. 1985, c. B-3 (as amended to 2002, c. 8).
39 *Roche v. Battery Ltd.* (1985), 21 D.L.R. (4th) 94 (Nfld. S.C.); *Gresmak v. Yellowhead Town & Country Inn* (1989), 30 C.C.E.L. 85 (B.C. Co. Ct.).

employees continue in their positions after a receiver or trustee has taken control of the company, then their prior service may be recognized for the purposes of the legislation. As a result, any statutory notice to which employees might be entitled in the event of their dismissal due to the bankruptcy or receivership will be based on the employees' prior service as well as any service during the appointment of the receiver or trustee. Such prior service should also be recognized for employment standards legislation purposes in the event that a subsequent purchaser buys the business from the receiver or trustee. In such a case, the receiver or trustee in bankruptcy will be considered the selling employer. The quantum of these contingent liabilities becomes extremely important in any negotiations for the sale of a business in receivership or bankruptcy.

There used to be a difference in case law concerning the effect of bankruptcy on the ability of employees to file claims for termination or severance pay. The differences were settled by the Supreme Court of Canada decision in *Rizzo & Rizzo Shoes Ltd. (Re)*.[40] The Supreme Court held that the termination of employment by bankruptcy gives rise to claims by employees for termination pay and severance pay arising under relevant provincial legislation. Claims can also be filed for unpaid vacation pay. It should be noted, however, that only the vacation pay component will be afforded the limited preferred creditor status under s. 136(1)(*d*) of the BIA.

The *Employment Standards Act, 2000* (Ontario) (the "ESA")[41] makes it clear that the treatment afforded to employees in a bankruptcy as a result of *Rizzo* also applies in a receivership. The ESA provides that an employer shall be deemed, for the purposes of the termination and severance pay provisions of the legislation, to have terminated the employment of an employee as a result of insolvency, receivership or bankruptcy (whether or not the bankruptcy is initiated by the employer). Therefore, the law in Ontario as it regards entitlement to statutory termination and severance pay in insolvency-type situations now appears to be quite settled, and it remains to be seen if the remaining provinces will follow suit.

LAYOFFS

Another event which often takes place within the employment relationship is the laying off of employees. Layoffs often take place in cyclical or seasonal industries. Employees in these industries rarely question such layoffs and often welcome them to pursue other interests. However, employees faced with layoffs in other industries are not always as understanding. These employees are typically concerned about the effect that their layoff will have on the employment relationship and whether they have any rights in connection with being laid off.

---

40 (1998), 154 D.L.R. (4th) 193 (S.C.C.).
41 S.O. 2000, c. 41 (as amended to 2002, c. 18, Sch. J).

The term "layoff" usually means a period during which employees are not working but will be recalled when work is available for them, and those who have been laid off do not consider their employment to have ceased. Due to the presence of collective bargaining regimes, many employees in non-union settings have the perception that when they are laid off they have certain rights with respect to pay and recall. While employment standards legislation makes some provision for employees on layoff, most rights for laid off employees are negotiated within the terms of union collective agreements and do not apply to non-union employees. Unless the collective agreement provides otherwise, any employee can be laid off by his or her employer. Depending upon the nature of the layoff, the employee may or may not be entitled to statutory notice of termination or severance pay. An employer considering a layoff should consult the relevant employment standards legislation to determine whether the layoff will exempt the employer from providing the employee with statutory notice of termination or severance pay.

Employers cannot escape the requirement that they provide statutory notice to employees by attempting to lay them off indefinitely. Most provincial employment standards legislation deems a layoff to be a termination after a certain number of weeks, thereby activating the notice requirements of the statute.[42] In Ontario, this period is 13 weeks in any period of 20 consecutive weeks. Effectively, termination occurs when the layoff loses its temporary status. Among the factors which may be considered and which may assist a court in deciding that an employee has been dismissed, as opposed to having been temporarily laid off, are a lack of any indication that the employee will be recalled, no formal request for the employee to return, an E.I.C. Record of Employment or Separation Certificate indicating that the layoff is permanent or the recall date is unknown, and the payment of vacation pay. Whether or not an employee has been dismissed will not depend on the fact that the person remains an employee in the employer's records. In Ontario, employees will be deemed to have been "terminated" for the purpose of receiving statutory severance pay if they have been laid off as a result of a permanent discontinuance of all of the employer's business at an establishment or if they have been laid off for 35 weeks or more in any period of 52 consecutive weeks.[43]

In *Cagigal v. Mill Dining Lounge Ltd.*,[44] the general manager of a prestigious Ottawa restaurant was laid off along with the rest of the staff when the restaurant closed for renovations. The manager was told that this layoff was temporary and that he could expect to report for work eight months later when the restaurant

---

42 There are no such provisions in Prince Edward Island, Quebec and New Brunswick. However, in Quebec, an employer must provide written notice in the same form as notice of termination for layoffs which are longer than six months. In Nova Scotia, Saskatchewan and New Brunswick, the legislation contemplates layoffs of no more than six days.

43 *Employment Standards Act, 2000* (Ontario), s. 63.

44 (1991), 36 C.C.E.L. 21 (Ont. Ct. (Gen. Div.)), affd 3 C.C.E.L. (2d) 93 (Ont. C.A.).

reopened. Pursuant to the *Employment Standards Act*, the restaurant was able to lay off the manager for a period in excess of 13 weeks because it continued to make some form of payments to the manager. Approximately five months after the layoff, the manager was dismissed for cause, a claim for which the trial judge found no basis. At trial, the manager was awarded damages in lieu of notice of three months for wrongful dismissal and was also awarded salary for the five-month layoff period. The evidence demonstrated that the restaurant knew shortly after the layoff that the manager's employment would not be continued but failed to communicate this information to the manager. Since this time was unfairly lost to the manager, who had not made serious efforts to seek other employment due to the layoff status, the manager was compensated for this time. The Court of Appeal affirmed this decision and dismissed the appeal.

As can be seen from the *Cagigal* case, even if an employer is exempt from providing an employee with statutory notice of termination or severance pay in the event of a layoff, the employer may be liable to the employee for common law reasonable notice or pay in lieu thereof for having laid off an employee. It has been held that the term "layoff" in a non-union setting has no technical meaning and constitutes a euphemism for termination,[45] thereby entitling an employee to reasonable notice of termination in the absence of just cause.[46] In addition, *Cagigal* suggests that where there has been a layoff with a commitment to recall which went unfulfilled, the employee may be entitled to compensation for the loss of time which could have been dedicated to an alternate job search.

A layoff may also be viewed as a constructive dismissal at common law.[47] Generally speaking, a layoff often constitutes a change to a fundamental term of the employment contract, that being the provision of work on a regular basis. However, if the layoff is temporary and has been characterized as such in that the employee is subject to recall, it may be difficult for the employee to argue that he or she has been constructively dismissed, as the layoff does not demonstrate, on the part of the employer, an intention to end the employment relationship. The employee may be able to argue constructive dismissal if there is evidence that the employee should have been recalled and was not.[48]

Other circumstances in which an employee will have a difficult time arguing constructive dismissal after having been laid off are:

---

45 *Girling v. Crown Cork & Seal Canada Inc.* (1995), 127 D.L.R. (4th) 448 (B.C.C.A.).

46 It may be possible for an employer to argue that there was no obligation to provide notice of the layoff because this was the particular custom or usage in the industry. In such a case, it will be necessary to show both reasonableness and notoriety or universality: *Scapillati v. A. Potvin Construction Ltd.* (1999), 175 D.L.R. (4th) 169 (Ont. C.A.).

47 See, for example, *Stolze v. Delcan Corp.* (1998), 40 C.C.E.L. (2d) 70 (Ont. Ct. (Gen. Div.)).

48 *Petras v. Construction and General Workers' Union, Loc. 602* (1986), 4 A.C.W.S. (3d) 62 (B.C.S.C.).

(a) if the employee signed an employment contract which contemplated layoffs;

(b) if advance notice of the layoff was given which constituted reasonable notice in law;

(c) if the employee agreed to the layoff;

(d) if layoffs are standard in the industry (it being a cyclical or seasonal industry); and

(e) if a better qualified individual was hired while the person was laid off.[49]

Employees who work for organizations which are federally regulated may have another avenue available to them in the event that they believe that their layoff has resulted in an unjust dismissal. Employees with at least 12 months' service who are not subject to a collective agreement and who believe that they have been unjustly dismissed as a result of a layoff may bring a complaint under the *Canada Labour Code*[50] within 90 days of their "dismissal" (in this case the layoff would constitute the dismissal). Such a complaint may be heard by an adjudicator so long as the person was not laid off because of lack of work or because of the discontinuance of a function. In determining whether there was a lack of work, the adjudicator will be required to determine whether the actual operative and dominant reason for the termination was "lack of work".[51] A "discontinuance of a function" will be found to occur when the set of activities which forms an office is no longer carried out as a result of a decision of the employer acting in good faith.[52]

PROGRESSIVE DISCIPLINE

The doctrine of progressive discipline is most widely known for its application within arbitral jurisprudence. Generally, it refers to a system whereby an employer applies discipline for relatively minor infractions and misconduct on a progressive basis or in a series of steps. Each step carries a progressively more serious penalty until the last step, namely dismissal, is reached.[53] Progressive discipline is typically put in place within an organization by way of some formal policy and may include both verbal and written warnings and varying degrees of suspensions, up to the point of ultimate discharge.

Although progressive discipline systems are most common in unionized work-places, there is merit to having such a system in a non-union setting. Developing a progressive discipline policy forces employers to consider the level of performance which is required of all employees in order to determine some standard against

---

49 *Petras v. Construction and General Workers' Union, Local 602, supra.*

50 R.S.C. 1985, c. L-2 (as amended to 2002, c. 9).

51 *Sedpex Inc. v. Canada (Adjudicator of the Canada Labour Code)*, [1989] 2 F.C. 289 (T.D.), at p. 299.

52 *Flieger v. New Brunswick* (1993), 104 D.L.R. (4th) 292 (S.C.C.), at p. 314.

53 *Airport Inn and NAPE (Seward) (Re)* (1992), 28 L.A.C. (4th) 186 (Nfld. Arb. Bd.).

which to measure performance. To the extent that employees are involved in this developmental stage, this can also prove a useful means of communicating the governing standard to employees. Existence of such a policy ensures that misconduct will be dealt with in some uniform fashion. Workplaces without such a policy may find that different managers are effecting widely varying degrees of discipline for equal levels of misconduct. Such policies can also be useful for smaller-sized workplaces where employers may be reluctant to introduce discipline into their collegial environments. If they are "just following the rules" in effecting discipline, employees may not be as inclined to take the discipline personally. In developing a policy, employers should give careful thought to the types of conduct which they wish to be subject to progressive discipline. If an employer fails to set out the types of misconduct which will be subject to the policy, it may find that it will be forced to undertake progressive discipline for an employee whose misconduct might otherwise entitle the employer to dismiss for cause.

Evidence of progressive discipline is often put forth in support of an employer's allegations that there existed just cause for the dismissal of an employee. Depending upon the extent of the progressive discipline, it may be possible to satisfy a court that the employer was entitled to dismiss without notice or pay in lieu. However, employers that consider "building a case for just cause" might be wise to also consider the time and resources involved. Sometimes it makes more sense to simply let the employee go, without cause and with a severance package, than it does to invest time and energy in a process that the employer believes will likely fail in any event.

Employers that engage in progressive discipline are much less likely to be seen as having condoned an employee's behaviour if some form of discipline is taken against the employee. Also, regardless of the measure of discipline that an employer chooses, it will not be entitled to later dismiss an employee for the same misconduct for which the employee received a lesser penalty. Additional discipline, including dismissal, may be effected if the employee engages in further misconduct or if the employer learns of additional misconduct of which it was not aware when the original discipline was imposed.

The use of warnings as a means of progressive discipline is encouraged in all circumstances of employee misconduct where the employee is not dismissed for cause. The warning should detail the performance or behaviour problem, explain the standard expected of the employee and outline the actions necessary to improve. Where performance is in issue, the employer should also specify how long the employee will be given to improve and how and when performance will be reassessed. In doing so, employers should be careful that they do not guarantee employment until the end of the evaluation period.

More importantly, employers providing warnings should also explicitly state what the consequences will be if the employee fails to improve. If the warning being provided is a final one, the employee should be clearly told that this is the case. Increasingly, judges have shown an unwillingness to uphold a dismissal for just cause where an employer could not demonstrate that the employee knew his or her job was in jeopardy. Employers may not wish to threaten dismissal in every warning; otherwise the threat could be perceived as an empty one and may not be effective.[54]

It is not necessary for a warning to be in writing to be effective. Warnings can be given orally, so long as they are sharp, clear and understandable. In order to be effective, a warning must be understood. Therefore, to avoid a circumstance in which an employee denies ever having received an oral warning because he or she may not have understood the discussion to be a warning, written warnings are preferable in virtually all circumstances.

Employers may wish to impose a probationary period as a disciplinary measure. Employers who take this course of action run the risk of being seen as having constructively dismissed the employee in question. A court will be hesitant to interpret the imposition of a probationary period as a constructive dismissal so long as the probationary period is seen as a warning for poor behaviour or performance, as opposed to a unilateral change in the terms of the employment contract. When a regular employee is put on probation for the purpose of bringing performance back up to an acceptable standard, it has been held that the employee should be given the entire probationary period in which to achieve that standard.[55]

Employers in non-union settings occasionally use suspensions as disciplinary measures. In the same way that a layoff or the imposition of a probationary period can be seen as a constructive dismissal, so too can the suspension of an employee, depending on the circumstances. If the employment has never been subject to suspension, and if the suspension is not reasonable under the circumstances, then a court may hold that it was a change to a fundamental term of the employment relationship and therefore a constructive dismissal. Employers who wish to use suspensions in the workplace should ensure that they are only used in reasonable circumstances. An example of a suspension which a court held did not constitute a constructive dismissal involved an employee who was suspended with pay for three to four days while the employer investigated whether the employee had been involved in a fraudulent scheme in the workplace.[56] Since the employer's concern was that the employee had been involved in a fraud on the employer, it was reasonable to ask that the employee remove himself from the workplace. The length of the suspension was also reasonable under the circumstances, as was the continuation of pay until the employee's guilt or innocence could be determined.[57]

---

54   See *Cormier v. Hostess Food Products Ltd.* (1984), 52 N.B.R. (2d) 288 (Q.B.).
55   *Cox v. Royal Trust Corp. of Canada* (1989), 26 C.C.E.L. 203 (Ont. C.A.), leave to appeal to S.C.C. refused 33 C.C.E.L. 224n.
56   *Pierce v. Canada Trust Realtor* (1986), 11 C.C.E.L. 64 (Ont. H.C.J.).
57   However, this can be compared with *Haldane v. Shelbar Enterprises Ltd.* (1999), 179 D.L.R. (4th) 716 (Ont. C.A.), in which a suspension of the plaintiff for three days, without pay, for insubordinate conduct was found to be unreasonable. The plaintiff was awarded damages for wrongful dismissal when she was fired for refusing to accept the suspension.

BEHAVIOUR WHICH MAY CONSTITUTE JUST CAUSE[58]

Certain other behaviour, if engaged in by an employee, will cause problems within the workplace and, depending upon the nature and severity of the misconduct, may justify discipline or dismissal of the employee.[59] There are various categories of behaviour which may constitute just cause for the dismissal of an employee. Employers should be aware of these categories so that misconduct can be recognized when it occurs.

Dishonesty

Due to the requirement of openness and honesty in the employer-employee relationship, an employer is entitled to dismiss an employee summarily where the employee's dishonest conduct is seriously prejudicial to the employer's interests or reputation. A single, isolated incident of dishonesty has been held to be sufficient grounds for termination,[60] making dishonesty generally different from other categories of just cause. Similarly, an employee's dishonest conduct may remove the employer's duty to comply with its progressive discipline policy. Perhaps this is because dishonesty strikes at the root of the employment relationship, that is, the implied obligation of trust between the parties.

The employer must have proof that the employee has committed the dishonest act. Mere suspicion is not sufficient to warrant dismissal. It appears as though proof of intent to commit the dishonest act may also be required since any explanation showing an innocent intention may be sufficient to overcome the grounds for dismissal, as may some other reasonable explanation provided by the employee.[61]

Once the employer has established that a dishonest act has take place, it will next need to satisfy a court that the employee's dishonesty gave rise to a breakdown in the employment relationship. As the Supreme Court of Canada has held: "[J]ust cause for dismissal exists where the dishonesty violates an essential condition of the employment contract, breaches the faith inherent to the work relationship, or is fundamentally or directly inconsistent with the employee's obligations to his or her employer."[62] Simply proving the dishonesty is not sufficient.

---

58 For a more comprehensive discussion of the various types of behaviour which may constitute just cause, see R.S. Echlin and M.L. Certosimo, *Just Cause: The Law of Summary Dismissal in Canada* (Aurora: Canada Law Book Inc., 1998 – looseleaf).

59 Dismissal of an employee is discussed in more detail under the heading "Just Cause" in Part 5, "The Divorce".

60 *Stilwell v. Audio Pictures Ltd.*, [1955] O.W.N. 793 (C.A.); *Denham v. Patrick* (1910), 20 O.L.R. 347 (Div. Ct.); *Giberson v. J.D. Irving Ltd.* (1984), 59 N.B.R. (2d) 180 (Q.B.).

61 *Niwranski v. H.N. Helicopter Parts International Corp.* (1992), 45 C.C.E.L. 303 (B.C.S.C.); *Cooper v. Sears Canada Inc.* (1991), 40 C.C.E.L. 225 (N.S.S.C.).

62 *McKinley v. BC Tel* (2001), 200 D.L.R. (4th) 385 (S.C.C.), at para. 48.

Revelation of Character

An employer may be entitled to dismiss an employee summarily where the employee's misconduct, although less serious than dishonesty, reveals such an untrustworthy character that the employer is not bound to continue the employee in a position of responsibility or trust. Examples of this type of behaviour include an employee forging the signature of the company chairman without his knowledge,[63] padding an expense account, altering a document[64] and cheating on an examination required in the course of employment.[65] In these cases, it will be necessary to determine not only whether the employee has served the employer in a faithful manner, but whether the employee is capable of doing so in the future. It is not so much the employee's conduct, in these situations, which is cause for dismissal, but rather the fact that the employee was capable of such behaviour. Whether the employee's misconduct causes any harm to the employer's interest may be irrelevant to the determination of whether cause exists in a particular circumstance.

Insolence and Insubordination

Just cause based on insolence and insubordination stems from the principle that an employer has a right to direct employees to carry out lawful orders without extended debate and with respect shown. An employer may be entitled to dismiss an employee summarily if the employee regularly uses language or makes insolent remarks which are incompatible with the continuing employment relationship or if the employee deliberately refuses to follow an order given by the employer. A single instance of this type of conduct is not ordinarily sufficient to warrant dismissal without a warning. If the conduct is so serious that it is incompatible with the employee's duties and prejudicial to the employer's business, destroys harmonious relations between the parties and/or seriously undermines management's authority, it may be just cause for dismissal.[66]

A court should take into consideration a number of factors in assessing whether an employer is justified in dismissing an employee for insolence or insubordination. The context in which the employee has engaged in insolent or insubordinate behaviour is often relevant, as is whether the employee was provoked or aggravated by the employer, or whether the behaviour was caused by constructive dismissal. Other circumstances, such as where an employee acts out in a moment

---

63 *Jewitt v. Prism Resources Ltd.* (1980), 110 D.L.R. (3d) 713 (B.C.S.C.), affd 127 D.L.R. (3d) 190 (B.C.C.A.).
64 *Lake Ontario Portland Cement v. Groner* (1960), 23 D.L.R. (2d) 602 (Ont. C.A.), revd 28 D.L.R. (2d) 589 (S.C.C.).
65 *Takoff v. Toronto Stock Exchange* (1986), 11 C.C.E.L. 272 (Ont. H.C.J.).
66 *Clare v. Moore Corp.* (1989), 29 C.C.E.L. 41 (Ont. Dist. Ct.); *Neudorf v. Sun Valley Co-Op Ltd.* (1994), 6 C.C.E.L. (2d) 61 (Man. Q.B.); *Holden v. Metro Transit Operating Co.* (1983), 1 C.C.E.L. 159 (B.C.S.C.).

of temporary anger or is suffering from some type of emotional illness, may be relevant to a court's consideration of just cause.

Disobedience

While refusal to carry out the employer's reasonable orders will generally constitute cause for dismissal, typically a single act of disobedience will not be serious enough to justify dismissal without a warning. In order to justify dismissal on the basis of one act of disobedience, the act must be intentional, deliberate and serious enough to show that the employee has repudiated an essential condition of the employment contract. However, if the employee has a reasonable excuse for disobedience, such as some personal reason, this may eliminate the employer's right to dismiss for just cause without notice.[67]

The instructions given to an employee must be clear and unambiguous before the failure to follow them can be considered just cause to dismiss the employee. Unless an employee has expressly agreed to be bound by a particular rule, the employer's requests must be reasonable and within the scope of the employment contract. Employees must be aware of a rule before the act of disobeying it can amount to just cause.

Where less serious instances of disobedience have occurred, but they are frequent or are combined with other misconduct (such as insolence, incompetence, attitude problems or absence without permission), such instances may justify dismissal on the part of the employer. However, unless the cumulative effect of these instances of disobedience is serious, the employer will likely be required to have warned the employee. Failure to comply with the employer's rules or refusal to perform the job in the exact way specified may be considered to be just cause for dismissal in certain circumstances. If the employer's business is prejudiced by the refusal, if constant supervision would be required to ensure compliance or if the refusal is conduct incompatible with the faithful discharge of the employee's duties, just cause may be shown. Unless an employee has been warned, breach of a rule which has been inconsistently applied will rarely justify dismissal.

Lateness and Absenteeism

Generally speaking, an employer is entitled to expect an employee to report for work. An employee may breach the obligation to report for work if he or she is absent from work without leave. Depending on the circumstances, an employer may be entitled to summarily dismiss an employee who is frequently absent from work without the employer's permission. While a one-day absence or occasional

---

67   *Kozac v. Aliments Krispy Kernels Inc.* (1988), 22 C.C.E.L. 1 (Ont. Dist. Ct.); *Casey v. The General Inc. Ltd.* (1988), 24 C.C.E.L. 142 (Nfld. S.C.).

absences may not be sufficient, frequent unauthorized absence and unexplained absence or a brief unjustified absence at a critical time may constitute just cause and justify dismissal.[68] Circumstances in which dismissal of an employee on the basis of absenteeism may be justified include instances where the employer has been prejudiced by the employee's absence, where the employee's absence was wilful and/or where the employer provided the employee with warnings regarding past absenteeism problems.

There may be circumstances in which an employee believed that his or her absence was actually authorized by the employer. In these types of cases, where the employee seeks to establish that his or her absence was authorized by the employer, the onus of proving such authorization may fall on the employee.

An employee may also breach his or her obligation to report for work if the employee is late. Courts do not generally uphold dismissal for lateness where the employee has a valid excuse for being late, unless the lateness somehow interferes with the employee's ability to properly perform his or her duties. In considering the issue of lateness, courts typically consider whether the late time was ever made up, whether the reasons for being late were the fault of the employee, whether the lateness was chronic, whether the lateness had any prejudicial effect on the employer and whether the employee was ever warned about being late.

Employers considering dismissing due to lateness or absenteeism should be satisfied that the reason for the lateness or absenteeism is not tied in any way to a prohibited ground of discrimination under human rights legislation, such as where a single parent has child care obligations. In such cases, dismissal or discipline under the circumstances may bring with it human rights liability, and the employer may have an obligation to accommodate the employee up to the point of undue hardship.

Incompetence

Employers are generally not entitled to dismiss employees because of mere dissatisfaction with their work product. There must be actual incompetence, inability to carry out duties, or work which fails to meet a required standard, and such level of performance must continue even after warnings to improve. The difficulty in asserting incompetence as cause for dismissal, given that failure to meet employer goals is not sufficient, lies in establishing some objective standard of performance, below which the employee's performance has fallen. An employer's performance standard must be reasonable, fair and non-discriminatory.

It will be necessary for the employer to establish that the employee's substandard performance is his or her own fault. Any mitigating factors or any possible

---

68   However, in *Briant v. Gerber (Canada) Inc.* (1989), 17 A.C.W.S. (3d) 185 (Ont. H.C.J.), an
     employee was dismissed for refusing to change his long-standing, pre-authorized vacation plans
     on short notice. Although the employee's absence was to occur at a critical time for the employer,
     this was not found to be sufficient to justify dismissal for cause.

explanation for the performance will be considered, such as volume of business, working conditions or failure to provide proper training. An employer who knowingly hires an employee inexperienced in a particular area of work cannot rely on the employee's incompetence as grounds for dismissal. Employers will also find it difficult to dismiss for incompetency if a particular level of performance was condoned.

In general, a single mistake, an accident or some isolated incident of failing to maintain perfection will not justify dismissal without a warning. However, a single incident of incompetence or poor performance can justify dismissal without a warning if it shows gross incompetence or has serious consequences for the employer's business.[69] Similarly, a complete failure to display skills which the employee has claimed to possess can justify dismissal without a warning.

If an employer is alleging chronic substandard work rather than gross incompetence, there is a duty to warn the employee of the employer's concerns and the possible consequences. In order to be effective, a warning should:

    (a) state what the employee has done wrong;
    (b) set the desired standard for performance (*i.e.*, what the employee should be doing better);
    (c) specify the period of time the employee has in which to improve;
    (d) provide necessary support (such as training); and
    (e) indicate the specific consequences of a failure to improve.

The number of warnings required and the amount of time which must be allowed for improvement will depend upon the facts of each case, including the severity and consequences of the employee's unacceptable performance. A court will be less likely to uphold a dismissal for cause where the employee received mixed messages about his or her performance, or where the performance problems were overlooked by the employer for a period of time. It is not necessary for a warning to be in writing, although it is preferable. To be effective, the warning must be clear and unequivocal. Employers must ensure that the employee understands and appreciates the significance of the warning. To this end, employers should be especially cautious when giving warnings to employees whose first language is not English.

Conduct Outside of Normal Working Hours

An employer may dismiss an employee for just cause if the employee's conduct outside of working hours is wholly incompatible with the proper discharge of his or her duties or if real prejudice to the employer either has resulted or could likely

---

69 *Laws v. London Chronicle (Indicator Newspapers), Ltd.*, [1959] 2 All E.R. 285 (C.A.); *Kellas v. CIP Inc.* (1990), 32 C.C.E.L. 196 (B.C.S.C.); *Monaghan v. Utilase Canada Inc.* (1999), 85 A.C.W.S. (3d) 585 (Ont. Ct. (Gen. Div.)).

result from the employee's conduct. Whether or not just cause is found will depend on the seriousness of the conduct in relation to the exact nature of the job. The conduct will be judged objectively, not in the employer's subjective view, and in relation to the community's moral standards. In determining whether or not such conduct is sufficient to justify dismissal, courts will consider whether the conduct was in any way prejudicial to the business or reputation of the employer.

A good example of a situation in which the employer was justified in dismissing an employee for conduct outside of working hours is found in the case of a business professor at the University of Western Ontario who was convicted of fraud due to the improper filing of insurance claims.[70] On the other hand, one court has held that an employee's affairs with two female subordinates, where one affair was engaged in despite explicit instructions to the contrary from the president of the company, were insufficient to justify dismissal where the affairs had no adverse effect on the employer's business.[71] Lastly, the Ontario Court of Appeal[72] upheld a decision that a 30-day absence from work, caused by an employee's incarceration for offences completely unrelated to work, was not sufficient to constitute just cause to terminate a 23-year employee with an unblemished record. In particular, the trial judge was not persuaded that the employer would have suffered anything more than "minor inconvenience" in attempting to accommodate the employee during his jail time.

Illness and Disability

Terminating the sick or disabled employee is fraught with complexity and is one of the most challenging situations with which employers find themselves faced. However, if the illness or disability becomes or is of a permanent nature, termination of the employee may be justified based on the principle of frustration of contract,[73] rather than that of just cause. For what length of time are employers required to continue an employee's employment before the employee's illness or disability can be considered to be of a permanent nature? It has been held that the appropriate test to be applied in such circumstances is to consider the relationship between the term of the incapacity and the duration of the contract itself.[74] It is almost impossible to provide an accurate estimate of the length of time that an employer is required to continue the employment of a sick or disabled employee. Each case will depend on its own unique facts.

---

70 *Pliniussen v. University of Western Ontario* (1983), 2 C.C.E.L. 1 (Ont. Co. Ct.).
71 *Dooley v. C.N. Weber Ltd.* (1994), 3 C.C.E.L. (2d) 95 (Ont. Ct. (Gen. Div.)), affd 80 O.A.C. 234 (C.A.), leave to appeal to S.C.C. refused 89 O.A.C. 318*n*.
72 *Heynen v. Frito-Lay Canada Ltd.* (1999), 179 D.L.R. (4th) 317 (Ont. C.A.), leave to appeal to S.C.C. refused 188 D.L.R. (4th) vi.
73 See under the heading "Frustration of Contract" in Part 5, "The Divorce".
74 *Yeager v. R.J. Hastings Agencies Ltd.* (1984), 5 C.C.E.L. 266 (B.C.S.C.).

Terminating the sick or disabled employee due to frustration of contract may be attractive for an employer that wishes to avoid providing the employee with a payment of severance. However, dismissing the sick or disabled employee may be somewhat more straightforward if an employer has very deep pockets. An employer in such a circumstance should be prepared to provide the employee with a severance package based on the employee's entire length of service (including any period of illness or disability).[75] Working notice is illogical since it is meant to provide the employee with the time to find other comparable employment, and the sick or disabled employee is not in a position to do so. The employer should also be prepared for a court to see the dismissal as being engaged in in bad faith, entitling the employee to an extension of the reasonable notice period.[76]

All of what has been said thus far refers to the employer's obligation to the sick and disabled employee under the common law. Apart from that, the employer still always has an obligation not to discriminate against an employee on the basis of his or her disability or handicap. If an employer plans to dismiss an employee because his or her illness or disability has kept the employee from work for a period of time, the employer will likely be seen to have engaged in a *prima facie* case of discrimination, and it will then be up to the employer to show that the dismissal was justified, bearing in mind that the employer must, as part of this exercise, show that it would have been impossible to accommodate the employee without undue hardship.

Disruption of Corporate Culture

This category of just cause refers to conduct on the part of an employee which is so disruptive of the employer's business that it warrants dismissal. For example, where an employer's interests or image may be adversely affected by an employee's consistent neglect of personal hygiene, such neglect may provide just cause for dismissal (*i.e.*, the employer of a hair stylist may be entitled to dismiss the stylist if he or she fails to care for his or her own appearance,[77] or an employer who sells fragrances may be justified in firing an employee with body odour[78]). However, unless employees are sufficiently warned, dismissal for cause based on problems with the employee's personal appearance or habits may not be justified.

A minor personality conflict with a superior or member of staff will not usually justify dismissal. However, personality conflicts can be just cause for dismissal if they are evidence of behaviour which is inconsistent with the proper discharge of

---

75 See under the heading "Disability Insurance" in Part 5, "The Divorce", for a discussion of the impact that payments under a disability plan may have on such a severance payment.

76 See under the heading "Reasonable Notice" in Part 5, "The Divorce".

77 *Essery v. John Lecky & Co.* (1986), 60 Nfld. & P.E.I.R. 219 (P.E.I.S.C.).

78 *Bagnall v. Calvin Klein Cosmetics (Canada) Ltd.* (1994), 5 C.C.E.L. (2d) 261 (Ont. Ct. (Gen. Div.)).

the employee's duties or if they are unduly prejudicial to the employer's interests. Situations in which dismissal due to a personality conflict may be justified include those where the conflict:

   (a) results in total inability to get along with superiors or other staff;
   (b) substantially interferes with the proper functioning of the workplace; or
   (c) puts the employee into constant conflict in the workplace.

In small businesses though, good employee relations may be so crucial that an inability to get along may justify dismissal but, in such cases, a warning may still be required. It has also been held that an employee's poor attitude or personality conflict will not justify dismissal where the employee's attitude could be attributed to something brought on or about by the employer.[79]

Alcohol and Drug Use

In order for the employer to dismiss an employee for just cause on the grounds of intoxication, the employer must show that the intoxication has had some adverse effect on the job or is somehow prejudicial to the employer's business.

In dealing with cases of intoxication, courts are more willing to consider mitigating factors, such as situations in which employees drink or use drugs as a result of severe emotional problems or chronic alcoholism or a drug addiction. However, if the consumption of alcohol or drug use is causing serious performance problems or is otherwise seriously prejudicing the employer's business, the employer may be justified in terminating the employee for just cause. Courts may also consider whether, and the extent to which, an employee was warned about his or her behaviour and whether the employee was, in fact, capable of dealing with the problem.

Courts have a tendency to look upon intoxication more sympathetically now that drug and alcohol addiction have been recognized as disabilities by most human rights tribunals. The possibility exists that an employer may be freed from any liability surrounding the dismissal of an employee for incidents related to alcohol consumption or drug use but may then run into difficulty with the human rights commission for not attempting to accommodate what could be defined as the employee's disability. In addition, courts will look at whether the employer has urged or offered rehabilitation and tried to work with the employee to assist in treatment of the problem.

Employers should be wary of how alcohol consumption is looked upon in the workplace. If the consumption of alcohol is a regular occurrence at office functions or business meetings and lunches, or if employees are encouraged or required to "entertain" clients in the course of their employment, it may then be

---

79 *Macdonald v. Richardson Greenshields of Canada Ltd.* (1985), 12 C.C.E.L. 22 (B.C.S.C.).

more difficult to justify the termination of an employee for becoming intoxicated during work hours.

Conflict of Interest

Employees owe a duty of loyalty and good faith to their employers and are bound to protect the employer's interests by avoiding actual or potential conflicts of interest. Any employee breaching his or her fiduciary duty may be justly dismissed by the employer.[80] If an employer were to discover that an employee was running a business which was in direct competition with the employer's, such conduct could be considered a breach of trust and would justify summary dismissal of the employee. In cases involving potential conflicts of interest, the justification for the dismissal lies not in the actual damage to the employer's interests but rather in the revelation of disloyalty on the part of the employee. Conflicts of interest may also justify dismissal where, although not competitive, the employee's involvement in outside activities is incompatible with his or her employment or renders him or her unable to fulfil the duties of the employer. The principles of condonation apply to cases of conflict of interest, and an employer will not be justified in firing an employee for conflict of interest if the employer was aware of the conflicting behaviour and failed to complain or warn the employee that such behaviour was unacceptable.

Sexual Harassment

Sexual harassment in the workplace is "unwelcome conduct of a sexual nature that detrimentally affects the work environment or leads to adverse job-related consequences for the victims of the harassment".[81] Such conduct can certainly be found to constitute just cause for dismissal, since the employer bears a heavy responsibility to protect its employees from sexually harassing behaviour. If an employee is not aware that his or her conduct could be considered sexual harassment, the employee may be able to argue that he or she did not know that such conduct was unwelcome. To avoid such confusion, employers are encouraged to implement and enforce sexual harassment policies which include broad descriptions of sexually harassing conduct and which are presented to employees for signing either at the commencement of the employment relationship or at the time the policy is put into place. In the same way that an employee could argue that he or she was unaware that his or her conduct could be considered offensive, in the

---

80   See under the heading "Fiduciary Duties" in Part 5, "The Divorce", for a discussion of employees' fiduciary duties.

81   *Janzen v. Platy Enterprises Ltd.* (1989), 59 D.L.R. (4th) 352 (S.C.C.), at p. 375.

absence of an executed copy of the policy, an employee could argue that he or she was unaware of its existence.[82]

In determining whether an employer is entitled to dismiss for just cause based on sexual harassment, courts will consider the context or "fabric" of the workplace in which the sexually harassing behaviour took place. If an employee is fired for having engaged in sexually harassing behaviour within a workplace environment where such conduct is the norm, the employer may have a difficult time justifying the termination. Such an employee is in a position to make a strong argument that the conduct was not unwelcome, as others in the workplace encouraged and/or participated in it. However, such an argument is not likely to be successful for a supervisor or manager, in particular someone charged with the responsibility of overseeing the workplace.[83]

The following is a list of factors that courts have taken into account in determining whether certain conduct amounts to just cause for dismissal:

(a) whether the impugned conduct amounts to sexual harassment;

(b) the degree and nature of the conduct amounting to sexual harassment;

(c) the nature of the employment relationship between the offending employee and the victim(s), and whether the offending employee was in a position of authority over the victim, such that the degree and nature of the conduct was thereby exacerbated by a particularly offensive abuse of power;

(d) whether the offending employee was told that the impugned conduct was unwelcome or offensive;

(e) whether the offending employee continued or repeated the unwelcome or offensive behaviour after being told that the conduct was unwelcome;

(f) whether the employer warned the employee that the misconduct was inappropriate and that dismissal was a possible consequence of further similar misconduct;

(g) whether the employer had a formal, and known, sexual harassment policy, which was enforced;

(h) the nature of the employment relationship between the offending employee and the employer, including length of service and position, and whether there were implied or express terms of the employment contract which gave rise to additional obligations on the employer's part, such as with respect to warnings or the opportunity to respond; and

(i) whether the impugned conduct was condoned by the employer.[84]

---

82 See under the heading "Humiliation or Harassment of the Employee" in Part 3, "The Marriage", for additional discussion of harassment and harassment policies.

83 *Bannister v. General Motors of Canada Ltd.* (1998), 164 D.L.R. (4th) 325 (Ont. C.A.); *Simpson v. Consumers' Assn. of Canada* (2001), 209 D.L.R. (4th) 214 (Ont. C.A.), leave to appeal to S.C.C. refused 214 D.L.R. (4th) vi.

84 *Alleyne v. Gateway Co-operative Homes Inc.* (2001), 14 C.C.E.L. (3d) 31 (Ont. S.C.J.).

Part 5

The Divorce

INTRODUCTION

The sheer magnitude of this Part indicates that the final stage of the employment relationship, or the "divorce", carries with it the greatest number of legal implications. This is the stage at which lawyers are most likely to become involved in a company's employment matters. There are, however, many initiatives which an employer can take in the name of preventive maintenance to minimize its contact with lawyers in the final stages of an employment relationship.

This Part introduces the employer to many of the aspects of an employee dismissal and assists the employer in handling each dismissal in a sensitive and conscientious manner. Also detailed are the ways in which the employment relationship can be brought to an end, the employer's potential liability in such an event and many practical considerations which the employer might keep in mind, from the creation of a severance package to what can be expected if a matter proceeds to litigation. The more familiar an employer is with the legal implications and potential liabilities which arise by virtue of the conclusion of the employment relationship, the better prepared it will be to deal with all employees at the earlier stages of its employment relationships.

BRINGING THE EMPLOYMENT RELATIONSHIP TO AN END

The employment relationship can end in a number of ways, and the extent of the employer's obligations to the employee on termination of the relationship depends upon the particular circumstances surrounding the termination. Generally speaking, the most common ways that employment relationships end include:

(a) resignation;
(b) dismissal for just cause; and
(c) dismissal without cause.

195

Resignation

If the employee gives his or her resignation freely and voluntarily, and it is accepted, the employee will not be entitled to claim wrongful dismissal, and the employer will have no obligation to provide severance or pay in lieu of notice to the departing employee beyond accrued wages and vacation pay.

Simply because an employee offers to resign or tenders his or her resignation does not mean that the resignation is immediately effective. The employer must signify its acceptance before a binding resignation is enforceable. The employee maintains the right to withdraw his or her resignation at any time prior to acceptance. An employer wishing to end the employment relationship on the basis of an employee's resignation should be quick to communicate acceptance; otherwise the employee may take the time to reconsider and may withdraw the resignation before it is accepted.

If an employee wishes to claim wrongful dismissal in a situation where it could be argued that he or she voluntarily resigned, the onus will be on the employee to demonstrate, on a balance of probabilities, that he or she did not voluntarily resign from the employment relationship, but rather was wrongfully dismissed.[1] The test which will be applied in such a case is an objective one; the employee will be required to show that, given all of the circumstances, a reasonable person would not have understood the employee to have resigned from his or her employment.[2]

If the employer forces the employee into choosing between resigning or being fired, courts have held that such an act is effectively a dismissal.[3] Therefore, if an employee feels that he or she has no choice but to resign, as in the case of a forced resignation or in a case where the employee believed himself or herself to have been constructively dismissed, the employee's subsequent resignation will not necessarily bar an action in wrongful dismissal. However, at least one case has held that there are situations where the employer can give the employee a choice between resigning and being fired, and this will not constitute dismissal.[4] For instance, if the employee is sophisticated, a court may determine that, in choosing to resign over being fired, the employee was under no duress and was not subjected to the will of a stronger party.

It may not always be clear from the employee's words or language whether or not the employee has resigned. In these cases, courts have occasionally looked to the conduct of the employee to determine whether or not a resignation has taken

---

1   *Osachoff v. Interpac Packaging Systems Inc.* (1992), 44 C.C.E.L. 156 (B.C.S.C.).
2   *Assouline v. Ogivar Inc.* (1991), 39 C.C.E.L. 100 (B.C.S.C.), at p. 104.
3   *Smith v. Campbellford Board of Education* (1917), 37 D.L.R. 506 (Ont. C.A.); *Gillingham v. Metropolitan Toronto Board of Commissioners of Police* (1979), 101 D.L.R. (3d) 570 (Ont. Div. Ct.).
4   *Lane v. Canadian Depository for Securities Ltd.* (1993), 49 C.C.E.L. 225 (Ont. Ct. (Gen. Div.)), affd 29 C.C.E.L. (2d) 322 (Ont. C.A.).

place. Courts have considered the following conduct and have found that such conduct did not constitute resignation:

- The employee said, "Don't worry about me. I will be leaving when the appropriate time comes."[5]
- The employee wrote a letter to the president advising that he would be seeking other employment.[6]
- The employee said, "I quit", but apologized later in the day and told his employer that he did not mean to resign.[7]

Generally speaking, a court will examine all of the circumstances surrounding the alleged resignation. Unless a court can be satisfied that the resignation transaction was completed through both offer and acceptance, it is likely that voluntary resignation will not be found.[8]

In the same way that an employer is required to give reasonable notice of an employee's termination,[9] employees who resign may be under an obligation to provide their employers with reasonable notice of the termination of the employment relationship. In most circumstances, employers are not anxious to continue the employment of individuals who have tendered their resignations. Therefore, assuming the employer's business will not be unreasonably inconvenienced, employers will tend to waive this reasonable notice in the event of an employee's resignation or will require only a minimum amount of notice.[10]

There are circumstances in which an employee will be found to have "wrongfully resigned". These cases involve failure on the part of the employee to provide reasonable notice of the resignation to the employer.[11] It is generally thought that the amount of damages owed to an employer in the case of a wrongful resignation is lower than that owed to an employee in a wrongful dismissal situation. Such damage awards often follow statutory termination notice amounts. These lower amounts are based on the fact that it typically takes an employee a longer period of time to find alternate employment than it takes an employer to find a suitable replacement. However, in the case of *Tree Savers International Ltd. v. Savoy*,[12]

---

5   *Tolman v. Gearmatic Co.* (1986), 14 C.C.E.L. 195 (B.C.C.A.).

6   *Moore v. University of Western Ontario* (1985), 8 C.C.E.L. 157 (Ont. H.C.J.).

7   *Widmeyer v. Municipal Enterprises Ltd.* (1991), 36 C.C.E.L. 237 (N.S.S.C.).

8   *Maguire v. Sutton* (1998), 34 C.C.E.L. (2d) 67 (B.C.S.C.).

9   See under the heading "Reasonable Notice" later in this Part.

10 See *Oxman v. Dustbane Enterprises Ltd.* (1986), 13 C.C.E.L. 209 (Ont. H.C.J.), revd 23 C.C.E.L. 157 (Ont. C.A.); *Firemaster Oilfield Services Ltd. v. Safety Boss (Canada) (1993) Ltd.*, [2001] 4 W.W.R. 256 (Alta. Q.B.).

11 *Systems Engineering & Automation Ltd. v. Power* (1989), 90 C.L.L.C. ¶14,018 (Nfld. S.C.); *Henderson v. Westfair Foods Ltd.* (1990), 32 C.C.E.L. 152 (Man. Q.B.), vard 40 C.C.E.L. 81 (Man. C.A.); *Sure-Grip Fasteners Ltd. v. Allgrade Bolt & Chain Inc.* (1993), 45 C.C.E.L. 276 (Ont. Ct. (Gen. Div.)).

12 (1991), 37 C.C.E.L. 116 (Alta. Q.B.), vard but affd on this point 87 D.L.R. (4th) 202 (Alta. C.A.).

the Court awarded the employer damages in the amount of nine months' reasonable notice to compensate for the failure of two key senior employees to give reasonable notice of their resignation.

If the employee provides the employer with notice of his or her resignation the employer is obligated to accept this notice of resignation so long as it is reasonable. If the employer fails to do so and attempts to let the employee go immediately, it will have effectively turned the employee's quitting into the employer's firing, and this will entail providing the employee with pay in lieu of reasonable notice. For example, in the case of *Oxman v. Dustbane Enterprises Ltd.*,[13] Mr. Oxman gave his employer six months' notice of his leaving the company. Dustbane Enterprises turned the resignation into a firing by waiving this six-month period and accepting Mr. Oxman's resignation with one month's actual notice plus pay in lieu of one month's notice. Mr. Oxman rejected the company's severance offer and sued for repudiation of his resignation. The trial judge held that employers are entitled to waive an employee's notice of resignation, resulting in the employee's immediate dismissal, so long as the employee is then provided with reasonable notice. In this case, the Court found that Mr. Oxman had been offered a total of two months' notice and held that this was reasonable in the circumstances. The Court of Appeal held that, if an employer does not accept an employee's notice of resignation as given, then the resignation is not effective. The effect of any subsequent severance package would be a straight dismissal and would be measured as to whether it constitutes pay in lieu of reasonable notice. The Court of Appeal was of the view that Mr. Oxman should have received six months' notice of his dismissal from Dustbane Enterprises.

Mandatory Retirement

Under a mandatory retirement scheme, the employment relationship is brought to an end when the employee reaches a certain age, the employee attains a set number of years of service, or some prescribed combination of the two occurs. Employers are often of the view that all employees will voluntarily wish to retire upon reaching the age of 65 or earlier and are very surprised when this does not happen. In the event that an employee does not wish to retire as required under a company policy, the question which arises is whether the employee can be forced to do so. This depends on a number of applicable legal concepts, including the common law, provincial human rights legislation and the *Canadian Charter of Rights and Freedoms*.

If an employee does not wish to retire and the employer does not have a mandatory retirement policy, the employer may face some difficulty and potential liability if it wishes to end the employment relationship with the employee. In such a situation, the normal common law rules which apply to dismissal come

---

13   *Supra*, footnote 10.

into play, and the employer is required to provide the employee with reasonable notice of his or her dismissal. Given that employees approaching retirement often have long service records, liability for reasonable notice may be quite substantial, and employers sometimes seek ways to avoid this liability. In order to avoid the requirement that retiring employees be provided with reasonable notice, it is recommended that employers implement written mandatory retirement policies which are properly publicized and accepted and implemented with proper notice. Even in the absence of such a policy, it may be possible for employers to argue that mandatory retirement was an implied term of the employment relationship by pointing to evidence such as benefits plans or pension plans which conclude coverage or begin to provide benefits at a certain age. However, this may not remove the employer's potential liability. One way to avoid any potential liability is to put the employee on notice, by way of a policy or an explicit announcement, that the employment will end at a future retirement date. The period of time between the notice and the retirement can be considered reasonable notice of dismissal. To ensure maximum protection, at least 24 months should be provided.

Subject to the human rights considerations which are discussed in the pages that follow, employers are free to institute company policies which govern the mandatory retirement of employees. Mandatory retirement policies are like ordinary company policies in that, to be binding, they must be accepted by the employee as part of the employment contract. If such a policy is in existence when an employee joins the employer's organization, and the employee is made aware of the policy before joining, then the employee will be seen to have accepted the policy by commencing employment and entering into an employment contract with the employer. Should an employer seek to implement such a policy for workers who are already employed, then the employer must seek the agreement of the employees, or must provide the employees with reasonable notice of the implementation of the policy, so that those employees who do not wish to be bound by the policy have the option of seeking alternate employment. If an employer does not have a valid mandatory retirement policy and attempts to retire an employee at a certain age, the employer may be liable for damages for wrongful dismissal if reasonable notice of the employee's termination is not provided. Care should be used when drafting mandatory retirement policies, so as to avoid the use of language which, in providing that the employment relationship is to end at a certain point, may be seen as guaranteeing employment up to that date.

In *McLaren v. Pacific Coast Savings Credit Union*,[14] the British Columbia Court of Appeal held that a mandatory retirement policy was not applicable to the plaintiff, despite the fact that the plaintiff admitted that he knew of and understood the employer's policy to be that all employees would retire at the age of 65. In fact, there was evidence to suggest that, up until one year before retirement, the

---

14 (2001), 9 C.C.E.L. (3d) 273 (B.C.C.A.).

plaintiff had every intention of leaving. However, the employer's policy provided for some flexibility: an employee could request an extension of his or her employment beyond the normal retirement age. The plaintiff requested an extension less than one year before he turned 65. His request was rejected six months before his 65th birthday. The trial judge concluded, and the Court of Appeal agreed, that this was not sufficient notice. It was held that, since the retirement policy was not, on its face, an absolute one, the plaintiff was entitled to proper reasonable notice from the employer that the employer would *not* grant an extension in his case. Six months before the intended retirement date was not considered proper notice.[15]

Employers with established mandatory retirement policies can rely on such policies when looking to dismiss employees at a certain age or after a certain number of years of service. However, care should be taken not to allow employees to continue to work beyond the agreed-upon retirement date. If this occurs, the employer will no longer be shielded by the policy and will likely be required to provide the employee with notice or pay in lieu thereof. An employer would be wise, if it is considering an arrangement whereby an employee approaching mandatory retirement will continue to work past the retirement date, to set out the terms of such an arrangement in an employment contract. Such a contract can serve to limit the amount of reasonable notice or pay in lieu thereof, if any, to which such an employee would be entitled upon the conclusion of the stipulated working period.

Many employers consider the use of early retirement schemes as vehicles for effecting downsizing throughout their organizations. Employees who are required by their employers to take early retirement will be considered at common law to have been wrongfully dismissed, given that a court will view such a scheme as being no different than any termination of the employment relationship in the absence of just cause. Therefore, such schemes must be made voluntary to be lawful. However, voluntary schemes rarely result in weeding out undesirable employees. In implementing a voluntary early retirement scheme, the employer has no control over which employees will take advantage of early retirement, often loses many valuable employees in the process and fails to part company with the less valuable employees whom it sought to sever in the first place.

Although an employer may be free to implement a mandatory retirement policy at common law, the employer should be aware of the potential human rights implications in the implementation of such a policy. All human rights legislation

---

15   Compare with *Gerlitz v. Edmonton (City)* (1979), 11 Alta. L.R. (2d) 176 (Q.B.), where the plaintiff was forced to retire at age 60 notwithstanding that, for the majority of his employment, the mandatory retirement age had been 65. The employer had changed the policy two years before the plaintiff's retirement, and this notice was considered to be sufficient to make the new policy enforceable. Also, in *Coulthard v. Emil Anderson Construction Co.* (1997), 35 C.C.E.L. (2d) 88 (B.C.S.C.), the change in the employee's status after reaching retirement age was considered "predictable" in the employer's business. As a result, no notice of termination was owing to the employee.

prohibits employers from discriminating in employment on the basis of an employee's age. However, in some provinces,[16] "age" is defined as having upper and lower limits, with the upper limit being 65 years. In such provinces, an employee will not be protected by human rights legislation if the employer seeks to dismiss on the basis of age pursuant to a mandatory retirement policy which sets the retirement age at 65.

In those provinces which do not set an upper age limit on the protection which employees are afforded under human rights legislation, an employer may, in certain circumstances, avail itself of an exemption to the discrimination provisions of the legislation and justify a mandatory retirement policy on the basis that it is a *bona fide* occupational requirement (a "BFOR").[17] For example, fire and police departments have argued that such policies are necessary for public safety and to ensure that employees are capable of performing the essential duties of their positions. In those provinces where employees are not protected against mandatory retirement at age 65, an employer wishing to implement a mandatory retirement policy with a retirement age of *less* than 65 will also be required to establish a BFOR.[18] In comparison, the federal human rights regime is more flexible, allowing the employer and employee to negotiate any age of mandatory retirement, without the need to establish a BFOR, as long as the agreed-upon age is the norm for that industry.

Under human rights legislation, there exist two distinct types of mandatory retirement regimes. First, mandatory retirement pursuant to a valid policy may be statutorily permitted at age 65 by virtue of the definition of "age" in certain provincial human rights legislation. Otherwise, mandatory retirement on the basis of age must be justified as a BFOR. To establish a BFOR, an employer will need to show three things:

1. The policy was adopted for a purpose rationally connected to the performance of the job.
2. The policy was adopted in an honest and good faith belief that it was necessary to the fulfilment of that legitimate work-related purpose.
3. The policy was reasonably necessary for the accomplishment of that legitimate work-related purpose.

In order to fulfil the last of these criteria, the employer is also required to show that it was impossible to accommodate the individual employee(s) without imposing undue hardship on the employer.

---

16 Those provinces which do not include, in the definition of "age", any ages 65 years or older are Ontario (in employment circumstances only), British Columbia, Newfoundland and Labrador and Saskatchewan. Manitoba, Nova Scotia, the Northwest Territories, Prince Edward Island, Quebec and the Yukon do not specify any age groups protected, while Alberta protects all age groups 18 years and older and New Brunswick protects all those 19 years of age and older.

17 See the discussion under the heading "Discrimination" in Part 3, "The Marriage".

18 In all jurisdictions, the onus of proving the existence of a BFOR is on the employer; this is legislated in Prince Edward Island and Saskatchewan.

Since the three-part test was put in place by the Supreme Court of Canada in 1999 in the *Meiorin* case,[19] employers have found it increasingly difficult to justify any standard or policy in accordance with the test. In order to satisfy the third component, an employer will likely need to lead evidence concerning the relationship between the aging process and the safe, efficient performance of the duties of the job. Mere anecdotal evidence, consisting of personal impressions and opinions, is not likely to be sufficient. Employers will ideally be seeking to rely on compelling medical and statistical evidence.

Employers have often questioned why they must be concerned about human rights implications if they have a valid mandatory retirement policy in place. The confusion has arisen because employers assume that if they have a policy in place which all employees are aware of and have accepted, the human rights issue does not come into play. This is not the case. As the Supreme Court of Canada confirmed in *Etobicoke (Borough) v. Ontario (Human Rights Commission)*,[20] parties are not entitled to contract out of human rights legislation. If the employer's mandatory retirement policy constitutes a violation of human rights legislation, then it is irrelevant whether or not the employees have agreed to the policy. The employer with such a policy may face potential liability, unless it can be shown that it is exempt from the provisions of the legislation. Mr. Justice McIntyre stated in the *Etobicoke* case:

> Although the Code contains no explicit restriction on such contracting out, it is nevertheless a public statute and it constitutes public policy in Ontario as appears from a reading of the statute itself and as declared in the preamble. It is clear from the authorities, both in Canada and in England, that parties are not competent to contract themselves out of the provisions of such enactments and that contracts having such effect are void, as contrary to public policy . . . The *Ontario Human Rights Code* has been enacted by the Legislature of the Province of Ontario for the benefit of the community at large and of its individual members and clearly falls within that category of enactment which may not be waived or varied by private contract . . .[21]

Employers are permitted, on the basis of a mandatory retirement policy, to dismiss employees at age 65 or at an age established by a BFOR. However, if the employer seeks to rely on a BFOR, it must be aware that it bears the burden of proving that such a policy is necessary. In occupations involving legitimate public safety concerns, such as those of medical practitioners, firefighters and law enforcement officers, courts often appear to be more willing to uphold such policies.

---

19 *British Columbia (Public Service Employee Relations Commission) v. BCGSEU* (1999), 176 D.L.R. (4th) 1 (S.C.C.) (the "*Meiorin*" decision).
20 (1982), 132 D.L.R. (3d) 14 (S.C.C.).
21 *Supra*, at pp. 23-4.

Human rights legislation does potentially allow for discrimination against individuals on the basis of age. In Ontario, for example, the *Human Rights Code*[22] affords no protection against age discrimination to persons 65 years of age or older. The definition of "age" under the Code has been challenged as being inconsistent with s. 15 of the *Canadian Charter of Rights and Freedoms*, which guarantees to all individuals the right to equal treatment without discrimination based on a series of enumerated grounds, including age. It is arguable that the definition of "age" under the Code, and the mandatory retirement policies which are permitted by virtue of this definition, amount to discrimination on the basis of age in violation of s. 15 of the Charter. If this discrimination is a reasonable limit "prescribed by law as can be demonstrably justified in a free and democratic society", pursuant to s. 1 of the Charter, then such discrimination is permissible. In the Supreme Court of Canada decision, *McKinney v. University of Guelph*,[23] a majority of the Court held that the university's mandatory retirement policy did violate s. 15 of the Charter, but that the violation was justified under s. 1. Mr. Justice La Forest observed that the mandatory retirement policy was rationally connected to its objectives, those being to preserve excellence and academic freedom in higher education. Such policies also minimally impair the rights of individuals in achieving these objectives. Thus, it is possible for an employer to implement a mandatory retirement policy which violates the Charter so long as the measures adopted in the policy can be justified as being proportional to the achievement of its legitimate objectives.

Just Cause

The second major circumstance which can bring the employment relationship to an end occurs when an employee is dismissed for just cause. Dismissals for just cause constitute the exception to the rule that an employer is required to provide a departing employee with reasonable notice of his or her termination, or pay in lieu thereof. Where an employee has engaged in conduct which constitutes a breach of the employee's fundamental obligations to the employer or which is incompatible with the due or faithful discharge of the employee's duties to the employer, such conduct amounts to just cause and gives the employer the right to end the employment relationship without notice.[24] In effect, just cause is considered to be any conduct which is inconsistent with the employee's express or implied conditions of service. The law views such conduct as a repudiation of the employment contract sufficient to leave the employer with no further obligations to the employee beyond accrued wages, vacation pay and pension entitlements. Consistent with this definition, an employee cannot be dismissed for cause on the

---

22   R.S.O. 1990, c. H.19 (as amended to 2002, c. 18, Sch. C).

23   (1990), 76 D.L.R. (4th) 545 (S.C.C.), affg 46 D.L.R. (4th) 193 (Ont. C.A.).

24   See under the heading "Behaviour Which May Constitute Just Cause" in Part 4, "The Separation", for a discussion of the types of behaviour which may constitute just cause for dismissal.

grounds that his or her position has become redundant within the organization, as such redundancy is in no way attributable to conduct on the part of the employee.

Employers are not entitled to dismiss merely because they are dissatisfied with an employee's performance. In many circumstances, employers will be required to prove habitual patterns of misconduct, perhaps resulting in a culminating incident, and may be required to show some system of progressive discipline or written warnings.[25] In other circumstances, incidents of misconduct will be so serious that even an isolated incident will entitle the employer to dismiss the employee without notice.

Employers should be aware that they are entitled to dismiss employees for any conduct which constitutes just cause and occurs prior to the employee's dismissal. Conduct constituting just cause which occurred prior to the dismissal but of which the employer was unaware at the time of dismissal has been referred to as "after acquired cause" and may be relied upon by an employer looking to substantiate a dismissal for cause. An employer is not generally entitled to rely on any misconduct which occurs after dismissal, although there have been some limited exceptions.[26]

If a wrongful dismissal action, in which an employer is alleging just cause, proceeds to trial, the onus of proof will be on the employer to establish just cause for dismissal of the employee (*i.e.*, it will not be necessary for the employee to show that the employer did not have cause for dismissal). Wrongful dismissal cases are civil actions and, therefore, the standard of proof which applies to the employer in such a case is proof "on a balance of probabilities" (as opposed to the standard "beyond a reasonable doubt" which applies in criminal cases).[27] Essentially, the employer must show that it is more probable than not that the misconduct took place. In some circumstances, judges have held that, where the conduct engaged in by the employee, upon which the employer is relying to establish just cause, is of a criminal nature, such as theft or fraud, the standard of proof required may be higher than the "on a balance of probabilities" standard and may approach the level of "beyond a reasonable doubt".[28]

Are employers required to inform a departing employee of the reason for his or her dismissal? Some situations will require that the employee be provided with the allegations of his or her misconduct and be given an opportunity to respond

25   See the discussion under the heading "Progressive Discipline" in Part 4, "The Separation".

26   See *Aasgaard v. Harlequin Enterprises Ltd.* (1993), 48 C.C.E.L. 192 (Ont. Ct. (Gen. Div.)), affd 70 A.C.W.S. (3d) 80 (Ont. C.A.), where a division president was offered a severance package by the employer publishing company and told to close down his division. The president started his own publishing company during the close-down period and began transferring inventory, which belonged to the employer, to his new business. The employer rescinded its severance offer and asserted cause for dismissal. The Court upheld the employer's decision and found that the employment contract was still in place at the time of the misconduct, entitling the employer to assert just cause for dismissal. However, compare with *Letendre v. Deines Micro-Film Services Ltd.* (2001), 9 C.C.E.L. (3d) 296 (Alta. Q.B.).

27   *Matheson v. Matheson International Trucks Ltd.* (1984), 4 C.C.E.L. 271 (Ont. H.C.J.).

28   *Billingsley v. Saint John Shipbuilding Ltd.* (1989), 23 C.C.E.L. 300 (N.B.Q.B.).

to these allegations, as in the case of an internal employer policy or as required by certain statutes which govern employee dismissal. In other circumstances, courts have often looked with disfavour on employers who terminate employment without providing employees with an opportunity to respond to allegations of their misconduct.[29]

Since the Supreme Court of Canada's decision in *Wallace v. United Grain Growers Ltd.*,[30] it has been clear that employers owe a duty to employees, in the course of dismissal, to be "candid, reasonable, honest and forthright".[31] As part of this duty, it can easily be argued that employers have an obligation to advise employees in all circumstances of the reason for dismissal. That being said, in a situation where the employee is being dismissed without cause and the decision is irreversible, employers are not required to engage in a lengthy debate regarding the reasons. In fact, such a discussion in and of itself could be seen as engaging in bad faith and bring with it liability on the part of the employer for an extended notice period. Such might be the case if an employer chooses the dismissal meeting to have a lengthy discussion about performance problems when these have never been discussed with the employee previously. Employers should be prepared to provide a reason for dismissal, but should keep such reasons brief and present them in a sensitive fashion. Where an employee is to be dismissed due to misconduct, the duty to be "candid, reasonable, honest and forthright" most likely requires the employer to provide the employee with an opportunity to respond to the allegations of misconduct. Ideally, this is done in the context of an investigation into the allegations or suspicions, and the decision to dismiss is made only after the employee has been interviewed as part of this investigation. If the decision to dismiss is made as a result of the outcome of the investigation, the employee should be so advised.

Where an employer terminates an employee for reasons of just cause, the employer, in most cases, is not obliged to give the employee a severance offer or an offer of reasonable notice. This typically includes providing the minimum notice set out in the relevant employment standards legislation.[32] It has been held that to do so may preclude the employer from later taking the position that the employee was dismissed for cause.[33] Accordingly, while the employer may want to give the departing employee some offer of assistance, care must be exercised

29 *Reilly v. Steelcase Canada Ltd.* (1979), 103 D.L.R. (3d) 704 (Ont. H.C.J.); *Robarts v. Canadian National Railway* (1980), 2 C.C.E.L. 168 (Ont. H.C.J.). But see *Thompson v. Boise Cascade Canada Ltd.* (1994), 7 C.C.E.L. (2d) 17 (Ont. Ct. (Gen. Div.)).

30 (1997), 152 D.L.R. (4th) 1 (S.C.C.).

31 *Supra*, at p. 34.

32 Employers should bear in mind that the exemptions with respect to the provision of statutory notice and/or the provision of severance are not always identical. It is possible that an employer may have just cause, at common law, to dismiss with no notice or pay in lieu and none the less still have a minimum statutory notice/severance obligation to the employee.

33 *Tracey v. Swansea Construction Co.* (1964), 47 D.L.R. (2d) 295 (Ont. H.C.J.), affd 50 D.L.R. (2d) 130n (Ont. C.A.); *Cathcart v. Longines Wittnauer Watch Co.* (1980), 1 C.C.E.L. 287 (Ont. H.C.J.).

in so doing. It may be possible for an employer to provide an employee with payment while still protecting its right to assert just cause, if the offer explicitly states that it is being made on a "without prejudice" or on an *ex gratia* basis and that, in extending such an offer, the employer is in no way waiving its right to later rely on just cause as the reason for the employee's dismissal. Whether this is possible in a particular case will depend upon the unique circumstances of the case.

Condonation

If the employer is defending a wrongful dismissal action on the basis of just cause for dismissal, it may be open to the employee to argue that the employer condoned his or her behaviour. Condonation is not synonymous with approval of the behaviour, but rather typically refers to a situation in which the employer is aware of the employee's misconduct and fails to take any action to address it.

Condonation is always subject to an implied condition of continued good behaviour. Therefore, where an employer has forgiven previous misconduct but the conduct is repeated and the employee is summarily dismissed, the employer may, in certain circumstances, be entitled to rely on such behaviour despite the fact that it had previously been forgiven. An employer is also permitted a reasonable amount of time to consider what action will be taken upon the discovery of employee misconduct, without such a lapse of time being considered condonation.

"Near Cause"

Often an employee may be guilty of some misconduct but it is questionable as to whether this conduct is serious enough to justify dismissal for just cause. If just cause cannot be shown to the satisfaction of a court, the employer must provide the employee with reasonable notice or pay in lieu thereof. Not surprisingly, this often leaves employers questioning whether the obligation to provide reasonable notice is in any way reduced as a result of the employee's misconduct. On a psychological level, the prospect of providing a full severance package to an unsatisfactory employee, whose conduct has led the employer to a decision to dismiss, can be extremely distasteful. Unfortunately, however, the law does not endorse the payment of lesser severance, even to a less than stellar employee. In 1998, Mr. Justice Cory of the Supreme Court of Canada, writing for the entire Court, effectively struck down this principle of "near cause".[34] Since this decision, although it is no longer open for an employer to argue for a reduced notice period, an employer may be free to pursue a separate claim (or counterclaim) against an employee whose misconduct has caused the employer to suffer financial loss.

---

[34]   *Dowling v. Halifax (City)* (1998), 158 D.L.R. (4th) 163 (S.C.C.).

Dismissal Without Just Cause

The third circumstance in which the employment relationship comes to an end occurs when an employee is dismissed from his or her employment without cause. Similar to the circumstances previously discussed in which an employer might constructively dismiss an employee from his or her employment,[35] employees cannot be dismissed (unless it is for just cause) without being provided with reasonable notice of the termination or pay in lieu thereof. Without cause dismissals account for the vast majority of all dismissals in the workplace.

Reasonable Notice

An employer is required to give reasonable notice of the termination of its employment relationship with an employee in a contract of indefinite hire which does not specify a notice period. There are three options available:

1. The employee can be provided with "working notice", in which case the employee is expected to continue working throughout the notice period.
2. The employee may be asked to leave and should, in such a case, be paid an amount equivalent to what he or she would have received in compensation and benefits had he or she worked through the notice period.
3. The employee may be provided with some combination of the first two options.

If the employer gives "working notice" and the employee subsequently sues, claiming that the notice provided was insufficient, the employer will be credited with the amount of working notice actually given. This will be deducted from any greater notice period awarded to the employee. For example, if a court were to determine that a plaintiff employee should have received six months' notice, and the employer provided the employee with four months' working notice, the employee will most likely receive a damage award in the amount of two months' compensation only.

Working notice is obviously a less expensive alternative than providing an employee with a severance package. However, care should be used when considering whether to provide an employee with working notice. In cases where the employee works in a particularly sensitive area or works closely with clients, it might not be wise to allow the employee to continue working after he or she has been notified of the termination. If working notice is provided, then it is suggested that a generous amount of notice be given, that the employee be provided with ample opportunity to engage in a job search and that the employee be "kept in the loop" and not be ignored by the employer for the remainder of the period. If the employee continues to be treated as a productive member of the team, he or she

---

35   See under the heading "Constructive Dismissal" in Part 4, "The Separation".

is less likely to harbour resentment towards the employer, and hopefully less likely to sue on the dismissal.

When providing an employee with working notice, employers should also be careful in the wording of the notice itself. The notice should definitely be reduced to writing so there can be no future argument that the employee did not receive or understand the notice. The notice should also unequivocally state that the employee's position will terminate at some future date. Employers that make reference to only the possibility that a job might end, or that reference the possibility that another internal opportunity might become available for the employee in the intervening period, run the risk of the notice not being counted since it may not have been clear to the employee, under the circumstances, that he or she should actually have used the working notice period to start looking for other outside work.[36]

When dismissing, employers should give notice to the employee in language which is clear and unambiguous. No particular words are necessary in order to dismiss an employee. While notice may be given either verbally or in writing, it is preferable to provide employees with written notice of their dismissal. This way there can be no question of the effect of the dismissal and the date on which it is to commence. If confusion exists regarding the termination date, a court could find that the employer is required to provide the employee with a further payment of salary up to the date which the court determines to be the effective termination date.

It is not enough for an employer merely to provide an employee with notice of his or her termination. The employee must be given a "reasonable" amount of notice of such dismissal. If an employer does not provide the employee with sufficient advance working notice, then it is obligated to provide pay in lieu of notice. If an employee is not satisfied with the amount of notice provided or with the amount of the severance package offered by the employer, it is open to the employee to sue for damages for wrongful dismissal.

It is extremely difficult to estimate precisely the amount of reasonable notice to which each individual employee is entitled upon his or her termination. However, there are a number of factors which courts will consider in arriving at the reasonable notice period, the primary ones being the employee's age, his or her position, his or her length of service with the employer, his or her level of compensation and the likelihood that the employee will secure alternate employment.[37] Generally speaking, each factor will be evaluated with regard to the impact it might have on the employee's ability to find other work. For example,

---

36   *Jalbert v. University of British Columbia* (2000), 4 C.C.E.L. (3d) 285 (B.C.C.A.).

37   *Bardal v. Globe & Mail Ltd.* (1960), 24 D.L.R. (2d) 140 (Ont. H.C.J.), endorsed by the Supreme Court of Canada in *Machtinger v. HOJ Industries Ltd.* (1992), 91 D.L.R. (4th) 491 (S.C.C.). It is not unusual for a court to also consider other factors applicable to the determination of the appropriate notice period. For a comprehensive list, see H.A. Levitt, *The Law of Dismissal in Canada*, 2nd ed. (Aurora: Canada Law Book Inc., 1992), pp. 234-44.

it is generally thought that older workers face more barriers to employment than do younger workers. Therefore, the older a worker is, the lengthier the notice period to which he or she is entitled. Similarly, it is generally thought that it takes an individual longer to find work at a more senior level with a higher commensurate salary. This is because there are thought to be fewer of these jobs available. Essentially, a court will engage in the exercise of determining how long it would take a reasonable person in the employee's circumstances to find other comparable employment.

As the Supreme Court of Canada has noted,[38] the extent to which an employer has "induced" or "allured" an employee to leave a secure position with a former employer is also properly included among the considerations which can lengthen the amount of notice owed to an employee. Where an employee quit a secure, well-paying job, based on representations of length of tenure, promotion or security, it is not unusual for courts to make larger than expected damage awards.[39] For example, in *Cathcart v. Longines Wittnauer Watch Co.*,[40] a 54-year-old employee was induced to leave employment, after 11 years of service with another company, at a time when the employee was within months of a vested interest in the company pension plan and a likely promotion to vice-president. When the employee was dismissed after one year of service with the new employer, the court awarded damages in the amount of 12 months' notice, a much higher amount than an ordinary one-year employee would have received in the circumstances. The inducement claim often arises in situations where employees have been enticed away from their homes to take up employment in a different city or province. Generally speaking, the employee will need to show that he or she would not have left the secure employment were it not for the lucrative offer made by the hiring company. In a situation where the employee responded to an advertisement or was actively looking for employment, this will be more difficult to demonstrate. The extent of the inducement and the length of the employee's service with the new employer are factors that will be considered in determining the appropriate notice period.

When taking into consideration the employee's length of service, employers and courts are often required to consider the impact which an interruption in the employee's service should have on the employee's total length of service. Temporary layoffs, leaves of absence, short-term resignations (such as in the case of a pregnancy before the existence of statutory pregnancy leave) are all examples of possible interruptions in an employee's service. Courts will be asked to decide whether such interruptions constitute a break in or the end of the employment relationship, and the choice of categorization can have a significant impact on the length of notice to which the employee is entitled. For instance, a 20-year

38 *Wallace v. United Grain Growers Ltd.* (1997), 152 D.L.R. (4th) 1 (S.C.C.).
39 *Hooker v. Audio Magnetics Corp. of Canada Ltd.* (1984), 3 C.C.E.L. 288 (Ont. Co. Ct.); *Brisbois v. Casteel Inc.* (1983), 2 C.C.E.L. 35 (Ont. H.C.J.).
40 (1980), 1 C.C.E.L. 287 (Ont. H.C.J.).

employee may have taken a leave of absence at the 10-year mark. If the leave is viewed as an interruption, the employee's severance will be based on 20 years of service. If the leave is viewed as a resignation and an effective break in service, then the employee's seniority will be cut in half for the purpose of determining the length of the reasonable notice period. When determining the proper categorization, courts will consider the reasons giving rise to the break in service, its length, and the way in which the employee was treated by the company (*e.g.*, were benefits continued or was the benefits waiting period waived when the employee returned).

Another factor which both employers and employees often believe should have some impact on the period of reasonable notice is the current economic climate. Employers often argue that they should not be required to provide employees with lengthy notice periods if the current economic situation is such that they have been forced to terminate the employee and cannot afford a lengthy notice period. However, in the face of this argument, employees are equally entitled to argue that the current economic climate impairs their ability to secure alternate employment and therefore the length of reasonable notice should be greater in times of economic difficulty. Courts generally appear to give little weight to this argument and, when they have, it has been held that the effect of the current economic climate on both the employer and the employee had to be considered.[41] Courts will often engage in some exercise which seeks to achieve a balance between the effect the current economic state has on the employer and that which it has on the employee. In certain circumstances, some employers may be entitled to argue that the notice period should be shortened because it is the industry norm.

In addition to all of these factors, following the Supreme Court of Canada's decision in *Wallace v. United Grain Growers Ltd.*,[42] courts now also maintain the discretion to extend or lengthen the reasonable notice period in a situation where the employer is thought to have engaged in bad faith at the time of dismissal. As Justice Iacobucci wrote, on behalf of the majority:

> . . . I note that the loss of one's job is always a traumatic event. However, when termination is accompanied by acts of bad faith in the manner of discharge, the results can be especially devastating. In my opinion, to ensure that employees receive adequate protection, employers ought to be held to an obligation of good faith and fair dealing in the manner of dismissal, the breach of which will be compensated for by adding to the length of the notice period.[43]

Although Justice Iacobucci in *Wallace* stated that his intent was not to advocate in every case of dismissal anything akin to an automatic claim for damages under this heading,[44] in reality, this is close to what has happened. Dismissal is not

---

41 *Mann v. Andres Wines Ltd.* (1988), 19 C.C.E.L. 1 (Ont. Div. Ct.); *Bohemier v. Storwal International Inc.* (1982), 142 D.L.R. (3d) 8 (Ont. H.C.J.), vard 4 D.L.R. (4th) 383*n* (Ont. C.A.), leave to appeal to S.C.C. refused 3 C.C.E.L. 79*n*.

42 (1997), 152 D.L.R. (4th) 1 (S.C.C.).

43 *Supra*, at p. 33.

44 *Supra*, at p. 35.

pleasant, and employees who suffer through it are almost always able to spin some aspect of the exercise into a claim for an extension of the notice period due to bad faith dealings. Such an extension to the notice period is now commonly referred to as "*Wallace* damages".

It is difficult to say with any certainty the exact type of conduct which will warrant an extension of the notice period. In *Wallace*, it was held that, at a minimum, in the course of dismissal, employers ought to be candid, reasonable, honest and forthright with their employees, and should refrain from engaging in conduct that is unfair or is in bad faith as a result of the employer being, for example, untruthful, misleading or unduly insensitive.[45] Without providing an exhaustive list, the following specific examples of bad faith conduct were referenced in *Wallace*:

(a) maintaining unfounded accusations of just cause following the dismissal;

(b) intentionally withholding information from an employee regarding his or her status and/or impending dismissal, particularly where the employee has made inquiries or is in the process of taking steps in his or her personal life which could be profoundly impacted by dismissal (like purchasing a house),

(c) engaging in conduct which has a direct negative impact on an employee's ability to find other work; and

(d) dismissing an employee who is on a stress leave.[46]

The amount by which the reasonable notice period is extended will vary, and will be entirely dependent upon the circumstances of the case. However, at the time of publishing, it was fair to say that the vast majority of cases involving bad faith conduct resulted in extensions to the notice period in the range of one to three months.

Employers often question whether there exists any upper limit on the amount of reasonable notice which an employee might be awarded by a court. At one time, it was thought that 24 months represented this ceiling.[47] However, there have certainly been cases where this limit has been exceeded. It now appears

---

45 *Supra*, at p. 34.

46 See Appendix A, Table 11, for a list of cases in which notice periods were extended due to bad faith conduct.

47 *Kwasnycia v. Goldcorp Inc.* (1995), 10 C.C.E.L. (2d) 65 (Ont. Ct. (Gen. Div.)). In *Jolicoeur v. Hippodrome Blue Bonnets Inc.* (1990), 33 C.C.E.L. 284 (Que. S.C.), vard 15 C.C.E.L. (2d) 224 (Que. C.A.), the Court awarded damages in the amount of 36 months, but this was reduced to 18 months on appeal. In *Sorel v. Tomenson Saunders Whitehead Ltd.* (1985), 9 C.C.E.L. 226 (B.C.S.C.), vard 39 D.L.R. (4th) 460 (B.C.C.A.), the Court awarded 30 months, but this was lowered to 24 months on appeal. Similarly, in *Webster v. British Columbia Hydro & Power Authority* (1990), 31 C.C.E.L. 224 (B.C.S.C.), supp. reasons 19 A.C.W.S. (3d) 486 (B.C.S.C.), vard 91 D.L.R. (4th) 272 (B.C.C.A.), affd 118 D.L.R. (4th) 767 (S.C.C.), the Court awarded 26 months, but this was lowered to 18 months on appeal. In *Donovan v. New Brunswick Publishing Co.* (1996), 184 N.B.R. (2d) 40 (C.A.), the Court of Appeal increased an 18-month award to 28 months.

more accurate to say that, although there is no upper limit on the appropriate period of reasonable notice, it is only the exceptional case which will warrant a notice period in excess of 24 months.[48] Take, for example, the case of *Baranowski v. Binks Manufacturing Co.*,[49] where Mr. Baranowski was awarded 30 months (before a six-month extension for *Wallace* damages) since he had held a reasonable expectation that his employment was secure until retirement. Justice Maloney held in this case that this constituted an "exceptional case" which merited a notice period in excess of 24 months.

To further complicate matters, since the 1997 Supreme Court of Canada decision, *Wallace v. United Grain Growers Ltd.*,[50] courts have been extending notice periods to reflect both inducement and bad faith conduct engaged in on the part of the employer at the time of dismissal. Since *Wallace*, there have been an increasing number of decisions eroding the 24-month cap. Unlike *Baranowski*, where Justice Maloney made clear that the total award of 36 months reflected 30 months plus a six-month extension for bad faith, many judges simply state the overall award, with no explanation of its proper allocation. Therefore, in those cases involving awards in excess of 24 months, it is often difficult to tell whether the basic award of notice is in excess of 24 months, or whether it is the presence of some factor like inducement or bad faith which has pushed the award over the 24-month limit.[51]

Downsizing and Mass Terminations

During economic downturns, it is common for many employers to be faced with decisions to dismiss large numbers of employees within a short period of time. This phenomenon, known as "downsizing" (or "right-sizing" according to the politically correct), can be attributed to many factors:

   (a) Canadian employers attempting to become more competitive by cutting their corporate staff and endeavouring to develop more efficient employee production techniques;

---

48 *Veer v. Dover Corp. (Canada) Ltd.* (1997), 31 C.C.E.L. (2d) 119 (Ont. Ct. (Gen. Div.)), affd 45 C.C.E.L. (2d) 183 (Ont. C.A.); referred to in *Baranowski v. Binks Manufacturing Co.* (2000), 3 C.C.E.L. (3d) 107 (Ont. S.C.J.).

49 *Supra.*

50 *Supra*, footnote 42.

51 See, for example, *Kilpatrick v. Peterborough Civic Hospital* (1998), 36 C.C.E.L. (2d) 265 (Ont. Ct. (Gen. Div.)), supp. reasons 79 A.C.W.S. (3d) 685 (Ont. Ct. (Gen. Div.)), revd on other grounds 174 D.L.R. (4th) 435 (Ont. C.A.), where Mr. Kilpatrick was awarded 30 months for his six years of service, with inducement considered to be a factor. Compare with *Clendenning v. Lowndes Lambert (B.C.) Ltd.* (1998), 41 C.C.E.L. (2d) 58 (B.C.S.C.), vard 193 D.L.R. (4th) 610 (B.C.C.A.), where the British Columbia Court of Appeal overturned an award of 42 months (six months plus 36 months to reflect bad faith), and replaced it with an award of 12 months (six months plus six months).

(b) the poor economic conditions which Canada has weathered in recent years; or

(c) technological advancements which continue to eliminate positions once filled by people.

What employers should note is that downsizing does not bring into play any different legal rules than those which arise in the event of individual dismissals. Dismissals are what they are. Employers receive no special exemption from the obligation to provide statutory notice, severance or reasonable notice at common law just because the decision to terminate was made for justifiable business reasons. The only legal distinction to be made regarding downsizing occurs when a group of dismissed employees is large enough to trigger the "mass termination" provisions of the applicable employment standards legislation in a given jurisdiction.

When considering the termination of a large number of employees, employers are often motivated by economic factors. At law, such dismissals will still be subject to the requirement that an employer provide each employee with reasonable notice of the dismissal, given that any economic justification will not constitute just cause for dismissal. Although a court may take into account the economic circumstances of the company to some degree in assessing the reasonable notice periods of the affected employees, an employer will not be able to escape its liability for providing reasonable notice by pleading that it could not afford to provide notice.

Aside from the requirement that employees be provided with reasonable notice at common law, employers should also be aware that most employment standards legislation in Canada provides for the termination of mass numbers of employees. Many provincial and territorial governments have seen fit to impose certain extra notice and/or payment requirements on employers who are dismissing large numbers of employees at one time.[52] The following information dealing with mass terminations is not intended to be comprehensive. If an employer is preparing to engage in a mass termination, specific inquiries should first be made with provincial counsel in order to determine the particular requirements to be met in the given jurisdiction.

The employer should begin by determining the number of employees to be dismissed and should measure this against the minimum number of employees set out in the mass termination provisions of the relevant legislation. Although there are exceptions, many provinces have set this number at 50 employees.[53] The group must also be dismissed within a specific short-term period set out in the legislation. Generally, if the employer intends to fire the minimum number of

---

52   With the exception of Prince Edward Island. See Appendix A, Table 5.
53   Including Alberta, British Columbia, Manitoba, Newfoundland and Labrador, Ontario and the federal jurisdiction.

employees within a four-week period, it will trigger the mass termination provisions.[54]

Depending upon the number of employees being dismissed and the jurisdiction, the required statutory notice period can range from four to 18 weeks. Employers are usually required to provide written or posted notice to any or all of the applicable Ministry or Department of Labour, the union, if any, and/or the employees. Group notice is often not required when the employees are seasonal or employed for a definite term or task, or when the termination is the result of unforeseeable circumstances beyond the employer's control. The legislation may provide that the notice include a reason for the termination. In addition, particular employees may become disentitled to notice in situations where such employees are guilty of just cause or have refused a reasonable offer of alternate employment. Other reasons may be dictated by statute.

The Ontario *Employment Standards Act, 2000*[55] is a good example of how complicated some of the mass termination provisions can be. In Ontario, the mass termination provisions of the legislation do not apply if the number of employees being terminated (more than 50) does not represent more than 10% of the employees in the establishment and the termination is not caused by the permanent discontinuance of all or part of the employer's business. In determining the number of employees in an establishment for this purpose, those employed for less than three months are not taken into consideration. The employer conducting the mass termination will be required to provide the dismissed employees with the minimum notice set out in the mass termination provisions of the Act, plus any applicable common law reasonable notice. In addition, if the employer either has a payroll of $2.5 million or more, or dismisses 50 or more employees in a period of six months or less, *and* the terminations are caused by the permanent discontinuance of all or part of the employer's business at an establishment, the employer will be required to pay statutory severance pay to all dismissed employees who qualify.[56]

Those employers who are planning to terminate mass numbers of employees, and who are developing severance packages for those employees, may wish to consider doing more for them than just meeting the minimum statutory obligations. This will give the perception that the employer has fulfilled not only its legal but also its moral obligation to its employees and will help remaining employees to feel that their co-workers have been taken care of and dealt with fairly.

Employers may also wish to take advantage of several means of easing the transition for dismissed employees. An employer should arrange for on-site relocation counselling assistance. Employers may also consider providing on-site

---

54   See Appendix A, Table 5, for exceptions.
55   S.O. 2000, c. 41 (as amended to 2002, c. 18, Sch. J).
56   See under the heading "Severance Pay" in Part 3, "The Marriage", for a discussion of statutory severance pay.

Employment Insurance Commission ("E.I.C.") registration, financial counselling, relocation assistance, and resumé and job search clinics. Communication with all employees should be as honest and forthcoming as possible. This will serve not only to control negative feelings amongst the dismissed employees, but will also assist in allaying the fears of those employees who may have survived the initial "cut" but are worried about future job security. Employers wishing to rebuild morale among remaining employees might try meeting with employees or holding focus groups, re-evaluating responsibilities to reflect changes to the organization, holding training programs to assist employees in adjusting to the changes or conducting counselling or stress management seminars.

Frustration of Contract

In certain circumstances, employers may be entitled to dismiss employees who are permanently sick or disabled. The justification for such a dismissal is not based on just cause so much as on the principle of frustration of contract.

The basic test which has been applied in frustration of contract cases deals with whether the employee's incapacity, looked at before the dismissal, was of such a nature or appeared likely to continue for such a period that further performance of the employee's obligations would either be impossible or radically different from that to which the parties originally agreed.[57] The English decision, *Marshall v. Harland and Wolff Ltd.*,[58] which has been widely applied in Canada, lists factors which should be considered in determining whether this test has been met:

1. *The terms of the contract (including the provisions as to sick pay)* – The Court in *Marshall* contemplated that an employee on an annual salary is entitled to a longer period of sickness or disability than an employee who is employed on a week-by-week basis. In addition, if an employee is entitled to sick pay, his or her contract cannot be frustrated if the employee returns to work, or appears likely to return to work, during the period in which he or she is entitled to sick pay.

2. *The length of time the employment was likely to last in the absence of sickness or disability* – If the employment is of a temporary nature, the employer may be entitled to dismiss the employee for frustration of contract within a shorter period.

3. *The nature of the employment* – The employment relationship is more likely to survive the employee's incapacity if the employee is one of many in the same category, as others could be asked to substitute for the absent employee.

4. *The nature of the illness or disability* – A court will consider how long the injury or disability has already lasted, as well as the employee's prospects for recovery. The greater the degree of incapacity, and the longer the period

---

57 *Marshall v. Harland & Wolff Ltd.*, [1972] 2 All E.R. 715 (N.I.R.C.).
58 *Supra*, at pp. 718-19.

over which it has persisted and is likely to persist, the more likely it is that a court will consider the employment relationship to have been frustrated.

5. *The period of past employment* – A court will consider an employment relationship which has lasted for a longer period of time to be more difficult to sever than one of a shorter duration.

It is difficult to provide employers with advice regarding the length of time for which they must continue to employ sick or disabled workers. Each of the factors listed must be taken into account and carefully weighed. It is entirely possible that a court could rule that a line worker with a foot injury and one year's seniority could be dismissed after one month of disability leave on the basis of frustration of contract, while the same court could hold that an employer must continue to employ a manager with 20 years' seniority who has been absent for two years due to a mental illness.

Employers should remember that, even if they are certain that they are reasonably free from liability in dismissing an employee for frustration of contract, this does not eliminate the possibility that such a termination will have significant human rights implications. If an employee claims to have been discriminated against on the basis of disability, the employer typically argues that the employee was unable to perform the essential requirements of the job. However, the employer will not be entitled to use this defence unless it can be shown that the employee's disability could not be accommodated without undue hardship on the part of the employer. Employers should be aware that freedom from liability due to frustration of contract may not free them from liability under human rights legislation.

An employment contract can be frustrated in other circumstances, such as upon the death of the employee, in the event of an irreconcilable strike, lockout or labour dispute,[59] or upon the loss of an employee's professional status.[60] Courts have not been sympathetic to employers' arguments that employment relationships have been frustrated on the basis of a reduction in the employer's business caused by economic circumstances.[61] In such cases, courts have either held that frustration of contract does not apply when contracts merely become less profitable than the parties intended or that a reduction in business was within the contemplation of the parties at the time they entered into the contract.

Employers should be very cautious if they are considering dismissing an employee for frustration of contract. Such dismissals pose a high risk of litigation or human rights complaints. Employers should first satisfy themselves that they

---

59 *O'Connell v. Harkema Express Lines Ltd.* (1982), 141 D.L.R. (3d) 291 (Ont. Co. Ct.). But see *St. John v. TNT Canada Inc.* (1991), 38 C.C.E.L. 55 (B.C.S.C.).

60 *Thomas v. Lafleche Union Hospital Board* (1989), 27 C.C.E.L. 156 (Sask. Q.B.), affd 36 C.C.E.L. 251 (Sask. C.A.).

61 *Oxford v. Advocate Mines Ltd.* (1983), 56 Nfld. & P.E.I.R. 296 (Nfld. Dist. Ct.); *Misovic v. Acres Davy McKee Ltd.* (1985), 7 C.C.E.L. 163 (Ont. C.A.).

are on solid legal footing before taking any such action and would be wise to secure a legal opinion before dismissing an employee in these circumstances.

DAMAGES

General

Employees dismissed for reasons other than just cause, and other than in accordance with express contractual provisions, are entitled to damages in the event that they do not receive reasonable notice of their dismissal. Damages awarded in such situations are intended to compensate for the breach of the employment contract and to place employees in the position they would have been in had appropriate notice been given. Such damage awards should only reflect losses which flow directly from the lack of notice. In addition to wages or salary, and as part of the damages award, the employee should receive the value of all benefits and other compensation which would have been received during the relevant notice period.

An employee who works throughout his or her notice period, and receives compensation and benefits coverage, may not be entitled to damages, as the employee in such a situation is seen not to have suffered a loss. This is also true of an employee who, immediately upon termination, secures other work with remuneration equal to or greater than that which he or she was earning while with the original employer.

Employees who, themselves, voluntarily choose to leave their employment are often under the misconception that they are entitled to damages in the form of a severance package. This is generally not the case. Such an employee is considered to have resigned his or her employment and, upon the employee doing so, the employer's obligations to him or her cease.

Any damages to which an employee is entitled are normally computed from the time of the contract breach. In the case of an employee who is dismissed, this is the date upon which the employee received notice of the dismissal. If the employer continues to pay the employee in lieu of providing reasonable notice, these payments do not extend the period of employment. Any amount paid to the employee from the date of dismissal forward will be credited towards the employee's damages entitlement. In the case of a constructive dismissal, the notice period will typically run from the point at which the employer makes a unilateral change to a fundamental term of the employment contract.

Indefinite Term Employment Contracts

Employees who have been hired for an indefinite term, but whose employment is governed by an employment contract, may have included in their contracts provisions specifying the amount of notice to which they are entitled upon dismissal. In the event that such provisions do exist and are found to be valid and enforceable,[62] the employee will be held to the notice period set out by the provisions of the contract. If the employment is governed by a contract which contains a valid provision and the employee is dismissed, the employee will only be entitled to damages in the amount set out in the contract. It is easy to see the appeal of such clauses. They eliminate the necessity upon dismissal of trying to reach a consensus between employer and employee on the appropriate notice period. Employers seeking to rely on contracts entered into during the course of the employment relationship should ensure that the employee received something of value in exchange for execution of the contract. Mere continued employment is unlikely to be sufficient to form the "consideration" necessary to make the written contract valid.[63]

Unless the employment contract specifies that the amount of notice (or pay in lieu of notice) provided for in the contract includes any statutory entitlement to notice or severance, the employer may be required to provide such entitlement *in addition to* the notice required pursuant to the provisions of the contract. Although it is now generally accepted that damages payable to employees in lieu of reasonable notice of their termination pursuant to a contractual provision include notice or severance payments to which the employee is entitled under the relevant employment standards legislation, courts have also held that any ambiguities in an employment contract will likely be decided in the employee's favour.[64] Nevertheless, employers are well-advised to specify in the written contract that statutory entitlements are included in the contractually stipulated entitlements.

One issue which often arises when notice periods are predetermined within the provisions of an indefinite term employment contract is whether the employee's mitigation efforts have any effect on the notice period provided for in the contract. There have been cases which have held that a predetermined notice period or payment of a lump sum upon dismissal in lieu of a notice period is not affected by the employee's subsequent mitigation efforts. In such cases, it has been held that the parties have predetermined the amount of payment which the employee will receive upon dismissal, irrespective of his or her mitigation efforts following such dismissal.[65] However, employers will often wish to see their liability reduced in the event that an employee's mitigation efforts prove to be successful. An employer wishing to ensure that mitigation is taken into account should be sure to make some provision in the written contract to this effect.

As a way to incorporate an employee's mitigation efforts, employers will often include bridging clauses in the employment contracts which provide for payment to the employee of some percentage of the remaining payment in lieu of notice in

---

62 See under the heading "Enforceability of Contracts" later in this Part.

63 *Singh v. Y.M. Inc. (Sales)* (1999), 5 C.C.E.L. (3d) 73 (Ont. S.C.J.).

64 *Stevens v. Globe and Mail* (1996), 135 D.L.R. (4th) 240 (Ont. C.A.); *Christensen v. Family Counselling Centre of Sault Ste. Marie and District* (2001), 12 C.C.E.L. (3d) 165 (Ont. C.A.).

65 *Dho v. Patino Management Services Ltd.* (1984), 5 C.C.E.L. 11 (Ont. H.C.J.).

the event that the employee secures other employment during the relevant notice period. For example, if an employee who is being provided with four months' pay in lieu of notice finds other work after two months, the employment contract with a 50% bridging clause will provide that the employer need only pay to the employee 50% of that amount remaining pursuant to the contract, that is, 50% of the remaining two months' pay. This relieves the employer of some of its liability, in the event that the dismissed employee finds other work, and provides the employee with incentive to do so, in that the employee will receive a windfall of 50% from the previous employer after commencing work with a new employer, something to which the employee would not have been entitled at common law.

Expiration of a Definite Term Employment Contract

If an employee has entered into a fixed term employment contract with the employer, the parties have agreed, in entering into the contract, on the length of the employment and the conditions governing such employment. If, upon the expiration of the set term employment contract, the employer chooses not to renew the contract but rather to end its relationship with the employee, the employee may have no cause of action against the employer for wrongful dismissal. There has been no breach of the employment contract in such a case; the employment relationship has simply been allowed to run its due course, without further obligations between the parties.

In order to best ensure that a fixed term contract can be allowed to expire without any obligation on the part of the employer, care should be taken to see that the contract is really only used in circumstances where an indefinite term contract would not be appropriate. Employers that try to use short, fixed term contracts as a way to avoid severance obligations to an employee will likely find any attempt to rely on the fixed term contract thwarted by a court.[66] Courts will often apply the "smell test" to a situation where an employer uses annual, one-year contracts to avoid potential liability for reasonable notice based on length of service. Any such offending contract will be struck down, and reasonable notice awarded in its place. Use of fixed term contracts is not generally recommended unless the contractual arrangement is clearly for a temporary period. If the parties are unclear as to how long the relationship will last and, so, choose to use a fixed term contract at the outset, they should definitely consider entering into a new contract if it appears later that the contract will last for some extended period of time. Any such contract should then address the employee's entitlement to notice of dismissal.

In a situation where the parties' employment relationship has been governed by a fixed term employment contract, employers should be wary of permitting such contracts to expire and then allowing employees to continue on in the

---

66 *Ceccol v. Ontario Gymnastic Federation* (2001), 204 D.L.R. (4th) 688 (Ont. C.A.).

absence of entering into a new fixed term contract. In such a case, when the term contract expires, the employment relationship may no longer be governed by contractual terms but rather by the common law. The employee may be entitled to a longer notice period than that contemplated by the employer in the fixed term contract because the relationship will be seen as having evolved into an indefinite hire arrangement.

If an employer wishes to dismiss an employee prior to the expiration of a fixed term contract, careful attention must be paid to the terms of the contract. If the contract makes no provision for termination prior to the expiration of the contract, then, in the event of breach of contract, damages are generally calculated based on the unexpired portion of the employment term (*i.e.*, up to the end of the contract term), as opposed to what would be considered reasonable notice under all of the relevant circumstances. This is consistent with the concept that an employee is entitled to damages which equal his or her actual loss caused by virtue of the contractual breach. The employee will normally be entitled to damages which equal the compensation due to the employee under the remainder of the contract. Employers should ensure that their fixed term contracts make provision for immediate termination in the event of just cause for dismissal.

Types of Damages

The damages which an employee might expect if successful in a wrongful dismissal action in Canada are varied in scope but are limited to that which has befallen the employee as a result of the wrongful dismissal. As such, Canadian courts have largely avoided awards of the magnitude which might be seen in certain courts in the United States. Some of the damages which an employee might seek and recover include those set out in the following pages.

Compensation

(i) Salary

An employee who is entitled to damages for wrongful dismissal will usually find that salary comprises the largest portion of the damages award. Upon dismissal, employees are entitled to receive any remuneration which they would normally have received had they worked throughout the reasonable notice period. Such an award could, in certain circumstances, include overtime pay if the employee can demonstrate that he or she would likely have received overtime throughout the reasonable notice period, and may include tips or gratuities if the employee can demonstrate that these would have been earned.

Salaried employees are entitled to damages in the amount of the salary which the employee would have received during the reasonable notice period. However, employers often question whether they are obligated to include in the damages award scheduled increases or increases given to other employees during the notice period. Courts have generally agreed that, unless the employment is governed by a contractual provision to the contrary, such increases are purely discretionary and need not be given. One reason for this is that such increases are often performance driven, and it is probably unrealistic to expect that an employee who has been given notice of his or her dismissal would have performed to a level deserving of such an increase. However, if the employee is able to demonstrate that he or she would have received the increase had employment continued throughout the reasonable notice period, then an award of damages could include such an increase. A general rule of thumb is that such increases should be paid as part of damages awards if they form an integral part of the employee's salary structure. Across the board cost of living salary adjustments provided to all employees are an example of an increase which would likely be awarded.

If an hourly employee is dismissed, damages in lieu of reasonable notice will normally be assessed on the basis of the number of hours contained in the employee's notice period and on the basis of the employee's gross pay. If, however, the employment was such that the number of hours varied over the course of employment, and it is likely that they would similarly have varied over the notice period, the employer may wish to average the number of hours over an appropriate period in calculating the proper amount of damages.

(ii) Commission

Employees paid by straight commission, or some combination of salary and commission, are entitled to have their damages awards reflect to some degree the amount of commission that they would likely have earned throughout the notice period. The employee will be required to show that he or she would have earned commission during the notice period and must provide some basis on which to estimate what his or her commission would have been. The relevant factors considered in assessing the appropriate amount of commission may include the employee's average commission over a period of time prior to the dismissal, the history of the employee's earnings throughout his or her employment, general economic conditions affecting the employer's industry and the employee's projected income. Any expenses incurred by the employee in the earning of commissions throughout the notice period should be deducted from any payment representing commission which is made to the employee on dismissal. An employee will be entitled to any commissions earned prior to the dismissal, regardless of the fact that any such commission has not yet been paid, subject to the terms and conditions of the appropriate commission plan.

(iii) Bonuses

Dismissed employees often seek damages for payment of bonuses which they claim they would have earned or become entitled to during the reasonable notice period. In determining whether or not damages are payable for such bonuses, courts will consider whether payment of the bonuses was discretionary and whether the employee had any contractual right to a bonus. Bonuses which are gratuitous or intermittent and at the sole discretion of the employer are not generally recoverable, as these are considered to be voluntary payments made to the employee.

Employers should be careful if relying strictly upon language in employment contracts which refers to the fact that bonuses are paid at the sole discretion of the employer. Often employers immediately turn to such language to justify their non-payment of a bonus in the event of dismissal. However, if the employee is able to demonstrate a pattern whereby such bonuses were paid over an extended period of time in such a way that employees came to rely on their receipt as part of the overall compensation package, the employer may be required to provide a bonus payment despite a discretionary provision in the contract. As is the case with salary increases, the question which needs to be asked is whether or not the bonus was an integral part of the employee's compensation package.

In determining whether an employee is entitled to a bonus as part of the damages award, a court may consider evidence relating to the likelihood that the employee would have received a bonus had he or she worked for the reasonable notice period. To this end, a court may consider the employer's financial situation or general business conditions. Poor conditions might suggest that no bonus would have been paid despite any exemplary performance on the part of the employee. Certainly, if a bonus were guaranteed to an employee or somehow made part of his or her compensation package, it would be difficult for an employer to avoid payment in the event of that employee's dismissal.

Bonuses may also be payable if they are performance-based and, prior to dismissal, the employee fulfilled the criteria for the earning of such a bonus. In addition, a bonus will be payable if it is provided for contractually, and all contractual conditions have been met by the employee or would have been met during the employee's notice period.

In considering whether an employee is entitled to payment in the amount of a bonus upon dismissal, a court may also consider the explicit terms of the bonus plan. Often bonus plans require the employee to work for the full term for which the bonus would be paid before becoming entitled to the bonus. For example, employment contracts will often state that a performance bonus will be paid at the fiscal year end but only in the event that the employee continues to be employed throughout that period. In such a case, if the employee is dismissed prior to the date on which he or she would become entitled to the bonus, many plans do not contemplate a *pro rata* portion of the bonus being payable to the employee. However, courts have held that, in the event that the bonus comprises a substantial portion of the employee's total compensation package, and in the absence of a contractual term stating that the employee must remain an employee until the end of the term for which the bonus would be paid, the employee may be entitled to a *pro rata* portion of such bonus. Recognizing that courts are generally reluctant to deprive employees of their entitlement to a bonus, employers seeking to rely on a contractual (or bonus plan) provision which deprives employees of a bonus if they are unemployed on the payment date, would be wise to take steps to ensure that the employees are aware of, understand and agree to be bound by such a term.

Where it is clear that an employee is entitled to a bonus in the event of dismissal but the amount of such a bonus payment is unclear, employers will often engage in a form of averaging of past bonuses in order to arrive at an appropriate figure. In this way, the payment of bonuses is similar to the treatment accorded to commissions owed to employees on dismissal.

Insurance Benefits

Insurance benefits are considered to be part of an employee's total compensation package, and an employee is entitled to be compensated for all losses throughout the reasonable notice period. There are a number of different methods by which employers may compensate dismissed employees for insurance benefits (such as health, dental and life). One approach employers may take is to assume that they have no obligation to a departing employee until the employee obtains replacement insurance.[67] Once replacement insurance has been obtained, the employee has incurred an actual loss during the notice period for which he or she must be reimbursed. Employers may also take the approach that dismissed employees will be reimbursed for all claims which may arise during the notice period if the insurance would normally have covered such claims. In the case of reimbursement for a prescription drug claim, the costs might be nominal. In the event of a life insurance claim, the cost could be quite substantial.

Some courts have held, however, that these approaches are not satisfactory, and employees have been awarded damages for loss of insurance coverage even though such coverage was not replaced, nor was a loss sustained.[68] The logic here is that, in taking away the insurance coverage, the employer has deprived the employee of peace of mind throughout the notice period and deprived the employee of an asset previously possessed during employment. Another approach which is often taken with respect to insurance benefits has the employer determining its cost for the employee's coverage throughout the notice period, and this amount is then paid to the employee on dismissal as part of the employee's damages award. It may not be necessary to compensate the employee for lost

---

67 *McKilligan v. Pacific Vocational Institute* (1979), 14 B.C.L.R. 109 (S.C.), vard 28 B.C.L.R. 324 (C.A.); *Turner v. Canadian Admiral Corp.* (1980), 1 C.C.E.L. 130 (Ont. H.C.J.); *Plummer v. W. Carsen Co.* (1985), 10 C.C.E.L. 19 (Ont. Dist. Ct.).

68 *Christianson v. North Hill News Inc.* (1993), 106 D.L.R. (4th) 747 (Alta. C.A.), varg 39 C.C.E.L. 243 (Alta. Q.B.); *Dickinson v. Northern Telecom Canada Ltd.* (1985), 7 C.C.E.L. 139 (Ont. Dist. Ct.).

insurance coverage if the employee has sheltered under the coverage afforded by a spouse's plan.

Disability Insurance

It is unusual for a disability insurance carrier to allow for the maintenance of its coverage throughout the reasonable notice period for employees who are no longer employed. In Ontario, where employers are required by employment standards legislation to continue all employee benefits for the minimum notice period established in the legislation, disability insurance carriers are required to extend their coverage throughout this period. However, it is not easy to find a disability carrier which will continue coverage past this point.

Employers trying to compensate employees for lost disability insurance coverage throughout the notice period have two options. They can encourage employees to seek out and secure their own coverage and can then reimburse employees for the premium payments. Where the employer has offered to reimburse an employee for disability insurance premiums and the employee fails to secure coverage, subsequently suffers a disability and then claims against the employer for lost coverage, the employer may argue that the employee failed to mitigate the damages arising from the dismissal by failing to secure other coverage. Alternatively, the employer can refrain from compensating for such lost coverage unless the employee becomes disabled during the period, after which time the employer can commence disability payments until the conclusion of the disability or can immediately pay the employee the discounted present value of such payments in a lump sum.

Generally, it is not recommended that employees currently on disability leave be dismissed. If such employees are in receipt of benefits from the insurance carrier, the employer incurs minimal liability for keeping such employees on the rolls, and the employer will not be the target of a human rights complaint for having dismissed a person on disability leave. Similarly, the employer will not be open to an immediate claim for "*Wallace* damages" based on the dismissal having been conducted in bad faith.[69] Employers would be wise to wait until such an employee returns to work and until after some time and distance have been put between the employee's disability and the employee's subsequent dismissal. Handling the dismissal of any disabled employee is a very delicate task, and how to do so will depend largely on the circumstances of the individual case. Employers should seek legal advice before dismissing a disabled employee in order to minimize legal exposure.

When an employee becomes disabled during the reasonable notice period, there is often a question as to whether the employee is entitled to be provided with both the payments to which he or she is entitled under the disability benefits

---

69   See under the heading "Reasonable Notice" earlier in this Part.

plan in addition to damages for wrongful dismissal. The law on this point is not entirely clear. In a 1997 decision of the Supreme Court of Canada, *Sylvester v. British Columbia*,[70] it was held that whether or not an employee is entitled to both disability benefits and damages for wrongful dismissal depends upon the intention of the parties to the employment contract, namely, the employer and the employee. In the *Sylvester* case, the Supreme Court of Canada ultimately held that the employee's disability benefits were to be deducted from the amount to which the employee was entitled as pay in lieu of notice. However, it was noteworthy in this case that the disability benefits were paid by the employer, pursuant to a plan to which the employee did not contribute. Since *Sylvester*, other courts have considered the deductibility of disability benefits and have come to opposite conclusions. For example, in both *Sills v. Children's Aid Society of the City of Belleville and the County of Hastings and the City of Trenton*,[71] and *McNamara v. Alexander Centre Industries Ltd.*,[72] it was held that the dismissed employee was entitled both to the payment due under the disability plan and to pay in lieu of notice. In *Sills*, this was held despite the fact that the employee had actually been provided with working notice of her dismissal, and was unable to work the notice period as a result of her disability. It was also significant in each of these cases that the benefits were paid by third party insurance carriers and that the employees were seen in both cases to have contributed to the plan, either directly or indirectly. As can be seen, determining the deductibility of benefits in any given case is not easy and will be largely dependent upon the facts of the case and the intention of the parties.

If an employee sues for wrongful dismissal and subsequently becomes disabled during the notice period, the employer faces the potential of considerable exposure if the employee's disability insurance coverage is not continued and the employee ultimately succeeds at trial. The rationale will be that the employee should be compensated by the employer for that loss which would not have been suffered were it not for the wrongful dismissal. Recognizing that such an employee may be entitled to disability payments throughout the reasonable notice period *and* pay in lieu of reasonable notice of the dismissal, this can represent a significant liability for an employer that discontinues the benefits plan.

Canada Pension Plan

While some courts have refused to compensate an employee for contributions to the Canada Pension Plan which would have been made during the notice period, the employee should properly be compensated for such contributions, as the employee could then remit these additional contributions directly to the

---

70 (1997), 146 D.L.R. (4th) 207 (S.C.C.).

71 (2001), 198 D.L.R. (4th) 485 (Ont. C.A.).

72 (2000), 2 C.C.E.L. (3d) 310 (Ont. S.C.J.), affd 199 D.L.R. (4th) 717 (Ont. C.A.), leave to appeal to S.C.C. refused 204 D.L.R. (4th) vi.

Canada Pension Plan to increase eventual pension entitlement or invest them in a private pension plan. In the case of *McKilligan v. Pacific Vocational Institute*,[73] Mr. Justice Verchere awarded the plaintiff damages for loss of additional contributions to the Canada Pension Plan throughout the reasonable notice period. A dismissed employee will not be compensated for the fact that the employee's ultimate Canada Pension Plan entitlement may decrease due to his or her dismissal, as employers are entitled to dismiss employees as long as reasonable notice or pay in lieu of reasonable notice has been given. Given the current difficulties with the funding of the Canada Pension Plan and the proposed revisions to the plan, this area of claim may be modified in the future.

Registered Retirement Savings Plans

If the employer makes regular contributions to the employee's Registered Retirement Savings Plan ("R.R.S.P.") as part of the compensation package, such contributions are a compensable benefit and ought to be provided to the employee in the amount which would have been contributed during the period of reasonable notice.

Private Pension Plans

In the case of a private pension plan, it would seem, at the very least, that the employer is required to provide the dismissed employee with the amount of contributions which would have been made to the pension plan on the employee's behalf during the reasonable notice period. Some courts have held that, where the pension would not have vested within the notice period, the employee should not be entitled to damages unless the plan provides for repayment of contributions on the employee's behalf.[74] However, if the pension would have vested during the notice period, the employee should receive the present value of the pension to which he or she would have become entitled at the end of the notice period.[75] The employee is generally not entitled to damages for loss of vesting privileges unless the pension would have vested during the reasonable notice period.

In the event that the employee's pension plan entitlement has vested, there are a number of ways in which an employer may properly compensate the employee for the loss of the pension. The employer may pay the contributions which would have been paid or the benefits which would have been received by the employee during the notice period, and these may include both the employer's and the employee's contribution if the employee would have contributed during the notice period. Alternatively, the present value of the difference between the value of the

---

73 *Supra*, footnote 67.
74 *Dauphinee v. Bank of Montreal* (1985), 10 C.C.E.L. 36 (B.C.S.C.); *Hokanson v. SMW, Loc. 280* (1985), 12 C.C.E.L. 231 (B.C.S.C.).
75 *Zeggil v. Foundation Co. of Canada Ltd.* (1980), 2 C.C.E.L. 164 (Ont. H.C.J.).

pension at the time of the employee's termination and its value at the end of the notice period is another way to quantify the loss.[76] However, the employee will not be entitled to the difference in value of the pension plan at the time of dismissal and at the time of retirement had the employee continued to be employed until age 65. Employers may also offer to compensate the employee for the cost of a replacement plan for the period of notice or may agree to pay the difference between the amount of the benefit in new employment and the amount paid by the employer.

If the employee is able to demonstrate that he or she would have been offered the option of receiving early retirement benefits at a full or discounted pension during the notice period and, in addition, is able to show that he or she would likely have exercised this option, some courts have held that such employees should be awarded damages equal to the early retirement benefits of which they were deprived.[77] If the employee is offered the option of early retirement and chooses not to take it, he or she may be found to be in violation of the duty to mitigate.[78]

Automobile Benefits

In the event that an employee has received a car allowance, parking allowance or mileage allowance in the course of his or her employment for the purpose of discharging the duties of the position, it is generally accepted that such an allowance, in most cases, is not fully compensable at the time of dismissal. The reason for this is that the employee has no need to use his or her vehicle for business purposes during the notice period and therefore has not suffered that loss. However, if the parties anticipated that the allowance was to cover personal use of the car, or contemplated that this would be a benefit largely unrelated to the performance of the employee's duties, then damages may be awarded.

Employees who have been provided with the use of a company vehicle during their employment have typically been refused damages representative of the value of such vehicles upon dismissal for the same reason as that just discussed: a dismissed employee would no longer have a business need for the vehicle. However, the parties who agree to the provision of a company vehicle as a term of employment usually contemplate that the vehicle will be used for personal as well as for business purposes. In such cases, damages can be awarded to compensate the employee for the loss of the personal use portion of the company car. The same rationale would apply to denying an employee the use of a company-subsidized parking space during the notice period, or damages in lieu thereof, unless it was contemplated that the employee would have use of the space for

---

76 See *Peet v. Babcock & Wilcox Industries Ltd.* (2001), 8 C.C.E.L. (3d) 230 (Ont. C.A.), referred to therein as the "commuted value method".

77 *Harris v. Robert Simpson Co.* (1984), 7 C.C.E.L. 202 (Alta. Q.B.).

78 *Whillans v. Labatt Brewing Co.* (1985), 36 Man. R. (2d) 129 (Q.B.).

personal purposes. Some dismissed employees argue that a downtown parking space is a legitimate and necessary expense in discharging the duty to mitigate during the job search. There may also be circumstances where the use of the company car is part of the employee's compensation package, is meant entirely for personal use and is thus fully compensable.

Other Benefits

A dismissed employee is entitled to receive compensation for all benefits which he or she would have received had the employee worked throughout the reasonable notice period. Items which might be included in a plaintiff's recovery for benefits in the event of wrongful dismissal include club memberships, a company car or car allowance, pension entitlements, disability or medical insurance, rent-free residence, room and board, meal expenses, subsidized mortgages or loans, employee discounts and a host of other entitlements. The employer has a choice of either continuing the dismissed employee's benefits as they existed on the date of termination through to the end of the notice period, or paying the employee an amount in lieu of these benefits. Employers are not required to pay dismissed employees' work-related expenses which would only have been incurred had the employee worked throughout the reasonable notice period and therefore were not actually incurred.

Vacation Pay and Sick Leave

There has been some debate as to whether an employee is entitled to compensation for vacation pay or lost vacation for the duration of the reasonable notice period. Some courts have held that employees should be compensated for any vacation earned to the date of dismissal and during any statutory period, but not for the reasonable notice period.[79] However, other cases have held that, had the employee worked for the period of reasonable notice, he or she would have been entitled to take a paid vacation. Therefore, an award of salary made to a dismissed employee for the notice period would include any paid vacations, unless there was some indication that the employee would not have been allowed to take his or her vacation during the notice period.[80] It has been argued, however, that employees engaged in mitigation efforts throughout the reasonable notice period are not in a position to take a "vacation" from the reasonable notice period and

---

79 See *Scott v. Lillooet School District No. 29* (1991), 11 W.A.C. 254 (B.C.C.A.); *McNamara v. Alexander Centre Industries Ltd.* (2000), 2 C.C.E.L. (3d) 310 (Ont. S.C.J.), affd 199 D.L.R. (4th) 717 (Ont. C.A.), leave to appeal to S.C.C. refused 204 D.L.R. (4th) vi; *Cronk v. Canadian General Insurance Co.* (1995), 128 D.L.R. (4th) 147 (Ont. C.A.).

80 *Bohemier v. Storwal International Inc.* (1982), 142 D.L.R. (3d) 8 (Ont. H.C.J.), vard 4 D.L.R. (4th) 383*n* (Ont. C.A.), leave to appeal to S.C.C. refused 3 C.C.E.L. 79*n*.

should therefore be entitled to additional compensation for their not having been provided with a vacation.

With respect to sick leave, employees are generally paid full salary for the notice period and are thereby fully compensated for their right to take sick leave. As a result, no extra damages are usually payable for sick leave which was not taken during the notice period. If, however, the terms of the employee's contract allow him or her to be compensated for unused sick time, and there is no reason to suspect that such sick time would have been utilized during the reasonable notice period, this amount is compensable.

Stock Option Plans

The rise in the use of stock options as a form of compensation in the late 1990s has made compensation for lost options an issue which is increasingly being considered by courts in wrongful dismissal cases. Dismissed employees are often concerned about the lost opportunity to buy shares under a stock option plan or the forced resale of shares to the company which occurs upon dismissal. Typically, the employee's rights in such circumstances will depend on the interpretation of the particular plan involved, and the employee may be validly disentitled to benefits if the plan contains a condition limiting his or her rights upon dismissal.[81]

If the employee's right to compensation based on a lost opportunity to buy or sell shares is not limited by the terms of the relevant plan, the employee will generally be entitled to damages. Employees are often under the misconception that they are entitled to all stock options which they have earned. However, only those options which would otherwise become available during the reasonable notice period are the proper subject-matter of a compensable claim in this regard.

If the employee is a member of a stock option plan, the plan document will be looked at to determine the employee's rights following termination. Many plans use specific language to describe the fact that the employee's rights are normally restricted following termination. Usually the intent of such language is to limit the employee's ability to exercise any outstanding options to some short period following the actual date of termination. However, the law in this area is evolving, and courts are making clear their reluctance to deprive employees of their right to exercise options in cases where the employee is wrongfully dismissed. Where a typical plan might indicate that an employee has 30 days from termination in which to exercise his or her options, courts have increasingly been interpreting the term "termination" in such a case to mean the effective date of termination, that is, the end of the reasonable notice period, leaving the employee with 30 days following the *end* of the notice period in which to exercise his or her options.

---

81   *Brock v. Matthews Group Ltd.* (1991), 34 C.C.E.L. 50 (Ont. C.A.); *Veer v. Dover Corp. (Canada) Ltd.* (1999), 120 O.A.C. 394 (C.A.); *Gryba v. Moneta Porcupine Mines Ltd.* (2000), 5 C.C.E.L. (3d) 43 (Ont. C.A.), leave to appeal to S.C.C. refused 152 O.A.C. 199n.

Following the Ontario Court of Appeal decision in *Veer v. Dover Corp. (Canada) Ltd.*,[82] it was thought that, instead of making reference to the "termination" in the stock option plan, a reference to the date on which the employee "ceases to be employed" might preserve an employer's ability to restrict the employee's exercise of rights after termination. However, the Ontario Court of Appeal in *Gryba v. Moneta Porcupine Mines Ltd.*[83] held that even language which makes reference to ceasing to be employed may not be sufficient. As Justice Goudge was quoted in that case as saying: "Absent express language providing for it, I cannot conclude that the parties intended that an unlawful termination would trigger the end of the employee's option rights . . . *the parties must be taken to have intended that the triggering actions would comply with the law in the absence of clear language to the contrary.*"[84] Although it is possible to use language which preserves an employer's ability to limit the period of time in which an employee has to exercise options following termination, this must be done with great care.[85]

If an employee is found to have been deprived of a right to exercise options during the reasonable notice period, then it remains to be determined how the employee can be compensated for this loss. Damages will be assessed based on the difference between the option price and the market value of the shares. However, when it is held that the employee had the whole of the reasonable notice period in which to exercise the shares, it becomes difficult to determine at what point the shares should be valued. Some courts have held that shares should be valued as at the date of the employee's first available opportunity to exercise the shares.[86] It may also be possible to lead evidence in certain cases as to exactly when the employee would have exercised the shares. In most cases, it may make most sense for the court to measure damages by taking half of the difference between the option price and the highest value reached by the shares during the period in which the employee had to exercise the shares. It may also be necessary for the employee to lead evidence as to the number of options that he or she would have exercised.

Where the employee is forced to sell his or her shares, damages will be awarded in the amount of the difference in price between the date the employee was

---

82 *Supra*, footnote 81.

83 *Supra*, footnote 81.

84 *Supra*, at p. 51, citing *Veer v. Dover Corp. (Canada) Ltd.*, *supra*, footnote 81, at p. 396; emphasis added by the Court in *Gryba*.

85 *Brock v. Matthews Group Ltd.*, *supra*, footnote 81. See also *Kieran v. Ingram Micro Inc.* (2001), 109 A.C.W.S. (3d) 432 (Ont. S.C.J.), in which Justice Hawkins held that language which contemplates termination of employment occurring on the date the plan participant ceases to perform services for the company "without regard to whether participant continues thereafter to receive any compensatory payments therefrom or is paid salary thereby in lieu of notice of termination" is sufficient to prevent the employee from having the whole of the reasonable notice period in which to exercise his options.

86 *Hardie v. Trans-Canada Resources Ltd.* (1976), 71 D.L.R. (3d) 668 (Alta. C.A.); *Gilchrist v. Western Star Trucks Inc.*, 2000 C.L.L.C. ¶210-030 (B.C.C.A.).

dismissed and the date the resale agreement would properly have been terminated. Courts have refused to award damages for loss of the capital component but will compensate for the loss of income such shares will normally generate. An employee will also be entitled to any dividends which may have been payable under a stock option plan during the period in which the employee was entitled to hold the shares. In the rare case, employers have been successful in arguing that, having regard to the employee's past course of conduct, the stock options would not have been exercised.[87]

Staff Loans and Employee Discounts

Employees who were entitled to subsidized loans, mortgage assistance or employee discounts during their employment will be entitled to damages for the loss of these benefits in the event of dismissal. The damage award is calculated by determining the difference between the market value of the benefit and what the employee would have paid for the benefit during the notice period. For example, if a department store employee is entitled to a 25% discount, is dismissed and is able to demonstrate that he or she would have purchased a sofa, listed at $400, during the reasonable notice period, the employee will receive $100 representing the loss suffered. Similarly, if a bank employee was entitled to a low-interest mortgage or loan, the loss suffered will be the difference between interest at prevailing market rates and that which would have been paid at staff rates for the period of reasonable notice.

Interest

There is no question that an amount representing interest on a wrongful dismissal damages award is due and payable to an employee if the payment is not made upon dismissal. However, the decisions are not consistent as to the date from which interest should be calculated. Some courts have ordered that interest upon the entire damages award should run from the date of dismissal or the date on which the wrongful dismissal claim was commenced (the "lump sum approach").[88] Other courts have held that, because salary makes up a major component of the award and would ordinarily be paid periodically, interest should only be charged monthly on that amount of salary which the employee would have earned had he or she worked throughout the notice period (the "instalment approach").[89] Other courts, in attempting to establish some middle ground, have

---

87   *McCallion v. Canadian Manoir Industries Ltd.* (1991), 39 C.C.E.L. 269 (Ont. Ct. (Gen. Div.)).

88   *Morrell v. Grafton-Fraser Inc.* (1981), 44 N.S.R. (2d) 289 (S.C.), affd 51 N.S.R. (2d) 138 (C.A.); *Blackburn v. Coyle Motors Ltd.* (1983), 3 C.C.E.L. 1 (Ont. H.C.J.); *Stevens v. Globe and Mail* (1996), 135 D.L.R. (4th) 240 (Ont. C.A.).

89   *Rushton v. Lake Ontario Steel Co.* (1980), 112 D.L.R. (3d) 144 (Ont. H.C.J.).

held that interest should run from midway through the notice period[90] or from the date upon which the employee commences other employment.[91]

Other

The employee may also be entitled to compensation for other benefits to which he or she would have been entitled had employment not been terminated. These may include but are not limited to benefits representing the employee's participation in a profit sharing arrangement during the reasonable notice period, professional fees, lost expense accounts or meal allowances, room and board, clothing and cleaning allowances, and remote location compensation. Often, in providing compensation for these benefits, the employer will reduce the amount of the benefit by that portion which would have been attributable to expenses or allowances incurred in the course of employment, as the employee would not incur these expenses or allowances during the reasonable notice period.

Aggravated/Mental Distress/Punitive Damages

Mental distress damages are meant to compensate an employee for an intangible loss but will not simply be awarded because an employee believes that he or she has been aggrieved by his or her dismissal. Historically, damages for mental distress were only awarded if two preconditions were met. First, it was required that it had to be in the contemplation of the parties at the time of hiring that, if the dismissal occurred in the fashion it did, the plaintiff would suffer mental distress. Secondly, the mental distress had to flow from the failure to give adequate notice and not from the fact of the dismissal itself.[92] Aggravated damages were awarded in certain instances and were intended to soothe the employee's feelings after having been wounded by the quality of the employer's behaviour. Such awards are compensatory and are not meant to punish the employer for its behaviour. Quebec courts have made awards under this heading and referred to them as "moral damages".

The law now seems relatively settled as to those circumstances where aggravated damages (including damages for mental distress) and/or punitive damages are available in a wrongful dismissal case. The Supreme Court of Canada has said on several occasions that any award of damages beyond compensation for breach of contract for failure to give reasonable notice of termination must be

---

90 *Doucet v. Downey's Ltd.* (1991), 38 C.C.E.L. 90 (N.B.Q.B.); *Backman v. Hyundai Auto Canada Inc.* (1990), 33 C.C.E.L. 300 (N.S.S.C.).

91 *Ross v. Thorn Press Ltd.* (1982), 13 A.C.W.S. (2d) 285 (Ont. H.C.J.).

92 *Brown v. Waterloo (City) Regional Board of Police Commissioners* (1982), 136 D.L.R. (3d) 49 (Ont. H.C.J.), vard 150 D.L.R. (3d) 729 (Ont. C.A.).

founded on a separately actionable course of conduct.[93] In other words, to have a chance at recovering either aggravated or punitive damages, a wrongfully dismissed employee must also be able to show that the employer did something exceptional, at the time of dismissal, for which the employee could independently sue outside of the wrongful dismissal itself.[94] For a punitive damages award, it must also be shown that the employer's conduct was sufficiently "harsh, vindictive, reprehensible and malicious", and that compensatory damages are insufficient to express the court's repugnance at the employer's conduct; *i.e.*, the damages award will need to serve some rational purpose, such as punishment or deterrence.[95] The Supreme Court of Canada has, however, made it clear that, where an employer's conduct causes an employee to suffer mental distress or is deserving of condemnation, but none the less falls short of constituting an independently actionable wrong, it is now open to a court to extend the period of reasonable notice.[96]

Damages for Loss of Reputation or Opportunity

Damages for loss of reputation or opportunity have not historically been available, except in rare cases involving artists, entertainers or professional athletes who have lost the opportunity to perform and thereby enhance their reputation.[97] In these "loss of publicity" cases, the opportunity to perform or enhance reputation was the very subject-matter of the contract. Therefore, such damages were within the parties' contemplation when the contract was entered into and have been awarded. Courts have recognized that these relationships are often accompanied by promises of widespread publicity and advertisement which will probably lead to future opportunities following a successful performance. Damages for breach

---

93 *Vorvis v. Insurance Corp. of British Columbia* (1989), 58 D.L.R. (4th) 193 (S.C.C.); *Wallace v. United Grain Growers Ltd.* (1997), 152 D.L.R. (4th) 1 (S.C.C.), at p. 16, followed in *Noseworthy v. Riverside Pontiac-Buick Ltd.* (1998), 168 D.L.R. (4th) 629 (Ont. C.A.).

94 See, for example, *Haggarty v. McCullogh*, 2002 C.L.L.C. ¶210-022 (Alta. Prov. Ct.), in which $500 in aggravated damages was awarded to a wrongfully dismissed plaintiff when it was found that one of her employers had engaged in the independently actionable tort of intentional infliction of mental distress by treating her in a humiliating and demeaning fashion in the workplace. See also *Martin v. International Maple Leaf Springs Water Corp.* (1998), 38 C.C.E.L. (2d) 128 (B.C.S.C.), where the employee was awarded $35,000 as a result of slanderous allegations, and *Chahal v. Khalsa Community School* (2000), 2 C.C.E.L. (3d) 120 (Ont. S.C.J.), where the trial judge awarded $25,000 arising out of findings of conspiracy and defamation.

95 *Hill v. Church of Scientology of Toronto* (1994), 114 D.L.R. (4th) 1 (Ont. C.A.), affd 126 D.L.R. (4th) 129 (S.C.C.); *Marshall v. Watson Wyatt & Co.* (2001), 209 D.L.R. (4th) 411 (Ont. C.A.), supp. reasons 112 A.C.W.S. (3d) 834 (Ont. C.A.); *Whiten v. Pilot Insurance Co.* (2002), 209 D.L.R. (4th) 257 (S.C.C.).

96 See under the heading "Reasonable Notice" earlier in this Part.

97 *Withers v. General Theatre Corp.*, [1933] 2 K.B. 536 (C.A.); *Tolnay v. Criterion Film Productions Ltd.*, [1936] 2 All E.R. 1625 (K.B.).

of the relationship may properly compensate the employee for the loss of reputation which would have been acquired or for damage to the reputation already acquired.

Take for example, the case of *Cranston v. Canadian Broadcasting Corp.*,[98] where Mr. Justice Ferrier held that the Canadian Broadcasting Corporation had wrongfully terminated its contract with Toller Cranston, a notable Canadian figure skater who had been hired to provide colour commentary for a series of figure skating events. The Court awarded Toller Cranston $20,000 for loss of publicity, holding that the publicity lost had intrinsic value of which the parties were aware when they entered into the contract.

Outside of these loss of publicity cases, courts are generally reluctant to award damages for loss of reputation, although there have been cases in which such damages have been awarded.[99] This reluctance has been even more prevalent since the Supreme Court of Canada rendered its decision in *Wallace v. United Grain Growers Ltd.*[100] Since *Wallace*, most claims relating to damage to an employee's reputation have been framed as part of a defamation claim. Defamation is an independently actionable tort,[101] and so the employee avoids any argument that the loss of reputation cannot be sustained as a component of an aggravated damages award. It is then up to the employee to substantiate the claim by showing that his or her reputation has truly suffered as a result of the employer's dismissal-related conduct. It is not enough to say that the damage to reputation was caused by the dismissal itself.

Reinstatement

In general, courts cannot award the remedy of reinstatement for breach of an employment contract in a non-union setting. The common law does not envision specific performance of a personal service contract. The remedy available at common law is compensation. Reinstatement may be ordered if an employer has not complied with statutory provisions governing an employee's dismissal, so long as the governing statute specifically gives the power of reinstatement to the body enforcing the statute. For example, an employee who successfully claims unjust dismissal pursuant to the provisions of the *Canada Labour Code*[102] may be entitled to reinstatement.

---

98 (1994), 2 C.C.E.L. (2d) 301 (Ont. Ct. (Gen. Div.)).
99 See Appendix A, Table 14.
100 *Supra*, footnote 93.
101 See under the heading "Related Tort Claims" later in this Part.
102 R.S.C. 1985, c. L-2 (as amended to 2002, c. 9).

Ballpark Damages[103]

The "ballpark" theory of reasonable notice appears to have arisen, in part, as an attempt on the part of courts to encourage employers to voluntarily make severance offers which are "in the ballpark", and to discourage employees from suing over relatively small deficiencies in severance packages. The courts which have applied this theory endorse the amount of notice provided to departing employees on the basis that the amount falls within the range of what a court considers to be reasonable – typically, three months. A number of cases in the mid-1980s adopted the ballpark theory and were welcomed by employers who were finding it difficult to determine the exact amount of reasonable notice to which each individual employee was entitled.[104] However, since the 1980s, many courts have rejected this approach as inappropriate.[105] It is inconsistent with general damages principles, which call for an exact calculation of reasonable notice. In addition, in actual fact, the practical effect of the ballpark approach was that employers would typically make offers at the low end of what was considered to be a three-month range of reasonable notice, thereby shortchanging the employee of his or her true entitlement. Today, employers are wise to use their best efforts to strive for reasonable notice periods which are as close as possible to what a court would award, and not strive to simply land somewhere "in the ballpark".

MITIGATION

An employee who has been wrongfully dismissed has a duty to take all reasonable steps to mitigate his or her damages and reduce the amount for which the employer is liable upon dismissal. Dismissed employees are required to use reasonable efforts to seek out and find suitable and comparable alternate employment. If the employee is offered a substantially similar position during the reasonable notice period, he or she may be obligated to accept it. If the employee does not, then the refusal may reduce the plaintiff's entitlement to damages as of the date of the offer. If an employee obtains other employment in fulfilment of his or her duty to mitigate, the amounts earned by the employee from employment

---

103 Also referred to as the "threshold of fairness test".
104 *Perry v. Gulf Minerals Canada Ltd.* (1985), 30 A.C.W.S. (2d) 524 (Ont. H.C.J.); *McKee v. NCR Canada Ltd.* (1986), 10 C.C.E.L. 128 (Ont. H.C.J.), affd [1988] O.J. No. 420 (QL) (C.A.); *Rivers v. Gulf Canada Ltd.* (1986), 13 C.C.E.L. 131 (Ont. H.C.J.); *De Freitas v. Canadian Express & Transport Ltd.* (1986), 16 CC.E.L. 160 (Ont. H.C.J.), affd 18 C.C.E.L. xxx (Ont. C.A.).
105 *Garcia v. Crestbrook Forest Industries Ltd.* (1993), 2 C.C.E.L. (2d) 48 (B.C.C.A.); *Ward v. Royal Trust Corp. of Canada* (1993), 1 C.C.E.L. (2d) 153 (B.C.S.C.); *Rahmath v. Louisiana Land & Exploration Co.* (1989), 59 D.L.R. (4th) 606 (Alta. C.A.), supp. reasons 65 D.L.R. (4th) 150 (Alta. C.A.); *Hiltz v. Saskatchewan Property Management Corp.* (1995), 85 W.A.C. 316 (Sask. C.A.); *Battaja v. Canada Tungsten Mining Corp.* (1989), 29 C.C.E.L. 50 (N.W.T.S.C.).

during the notice period will be credited against any damages owed by the employer.[106]

A dismissed employee is only required to take "reasonable" steps to mitigate his or her damages. Courts have held that such employees are only obliged to take steps which a reasonable and prudent person would ordinarily take in the course of his or her business. It will not generally be considered reasonable for an employee to refuse a comparable job in his or her accustomed type of work, nor will it be considered reasonable for an employee to refuse to approach other employers, inquire about similar work with other employers or follow up on known job leads. Employees are allowed a reasonable amount of time to adjust to their circumstances and plan for the future before the duty to mitigate comes into effect.

The employee has the initial burden of proving that he or she made reasonable efforts to mitigate damages arising from the dismissal. If the employer wishes to argue that the employee has not satisfied his or her duty to mitigate, then the onus shifts to the employer to lead evidence demonstrating that the employee did not sufficiently mitigate the damages. Courts tend to place a heavy burden on such employers, given that they are already in breach of the employment contract.

In challenging a dismissed employee's mitigation efforts, employers are required to do more than merely suggest that the employee could have tried harder to secure other employment. The employer also needs to show the availability of comparable jobs during the relevant notice period. It may not be enough for an employer to merely introduce, at trial, newspaper advertisements for available positions, if the employer is unable to demonstrate that the jobs were comparable and appropriate and that the plaintiff had a reasonable chance of obtaining these positions.

If the employee has been provided with working notice, and the employee refuses to work throughout this period, the employee may be found to have failed to mitigate his or her damages. However, in circumstances where it would be humiliating or unreasonable to expect the employee to stay at his or her work throughout the notice period, this obligation may be waived.[107]

The law is unclear as to whether or not an employee is required to mitigate his or her damages in the event that a fixed term contract has been breached. Some judges have held that, in such a case, the employee has no obligation to mitigate his or her damages since the notice period has been contractually pre-set,[108] while other judges have held that the employee must still mitigate the damages, and any

---

106 Unless the employee obtains a higher paying job, in which case the clock on damages may simply stop ticking once the employee starts working again: see *LeBlanc v. Eurodata Support Services Inc.* (1998), 164 D.L.R. (4th) 763 (N.B.C.A.).

107 *Ahmad v. Procter & Gamble Inc.* (1987), 18 C.C.E.L. 124 (Ont. H.C.J.), affd 77 D.L.R. (4th) 515 (Ont. C.A.); *Mifsud v. MacMillan Bathurst Inc.* (1989), 63 D.L.R. (4th) 714 (Ont. C.A.), leave to appeal to S.C.C. refused 68 D.L.R. (4th) vii.

108 *McDowell v. Sunshine Coast Community Services Society* (1987), 15 C.C.E.L. 284 (B.C. Co. Ct.); *Paquin v. Gainers Inc.* (1990), 33 C.C.E.L. 80 (Alta. Q.B.), affd 37 C.C.E.L. 113 (Alta. C.A.).

sum of money earned by the employee within the remainder of the fixed term contract will be deducted from the employer's liability.[109]

Employees are not required to take any available job in fulfilment of the duty to mitigate. Their obligation involves looking for similar employment, and refusal of a materially dissimilar job will not be considered a failure to mitigate. If an employee chooses to look for dissimilar work, he or she could be found to be in breach of the duty to mitigate unless work of a similar nature is unavailable.

In determining whether an available position is substantially similar to the employee's past employment, courts will consider a number of factors, including the salaries of the positions, the locations of the jobs, the status of the positions and the skill or training required for the positions. An employee will not typically be required to accept a job beneath his or her skills or training, or of a lower status, and may be entitled to restrict the job search to positions with pay similar to that earned at the former job. However, if jobs at the employee's current pay level are no longer available, the employee may be entitled to accept a position with lower pay without breaching the duty to mitigate. If the job is substantially similar but located in a different city, the employee may still be required to accept the position, subject to a consideration of a number of factors, including the housing market, the employee's attachment to the community, the employee's family situation (spouse's employment, children's schooling, obligation to care for elderly relative) and the prospect of finding employment in the existing area.

The determination of whether an employee has made reasonable efforts to mitigate will depend on the circumstances of each case. It is entirely possible that an employee's efforts to search for work in a dissimilar area will be allowed, given the employee's interests and career objectives, while a court might also hold that an employee who had worked for a company for an extremely long period of time might not be required to search for dissimilar work even if employment in his or her area is no longer available. If, however, an employee chooses to change careers and take a job in a different industry at a lower salary when an equivalent job in the same industry was available and offered, the employee may be found to have failed to mitigate his or her damages.

Employers occasionally wish to offer dismissed employees alternate jobs within the workplace for the relevant notice period. If an employee were to refuse such an offer, it might be argued that the employee has failed to mitigate his or her damages. However, in those circumstances where the employer acted improperly in terminating the employee or where the alternate position would result in embarrassment, humiliation or loss of prestige for the employee, the employee may not be required to accept such a position in order to fulfil his or her duty to

109 *Neilson v. Vancouver Hockey Club Ltd.* (1988), 51 D.L.R. (4th) 40 (B.C.C.A.), leave to appeal to S.C.C. refused 22 C.C.E.L. xxxv; *Krell v. Truckers Garage Inc.* (1993), 3 C.C.E.L. (2d) 157 (Ont. C.A.); *Preston v. British Columbia* (1993), 47 C.C.E.L. 223 (B.C.S.C.), supp. reasons 81 B.C.L.R. (2d) 218 (S.C.), vard 116 D.L.R. (4th) 258 (B.C.C.A.).

mitigate.[110] It may be possible to apply the same reasoning in circumstances where the employer has had a change of heart after the dismissal and subsequently offers to re-employ the dismissed employee.[111]

An employee may satisfy the duty to mitigate by starting a business, regardless of whether the business succeeds or fails. However, starting a business will only qualify as mitigation for the purpose of reducing the employer's liability for wrongful dismissal if the company shows a profit or the employee receives an income from the business. Employees will not be entitled to claim that they have not received income from the business if the business is securing a healthy profit or if revenues are being pumped back into the business for the purpose of ongoing growth. In these circumstances, courts have typically designated some portion of this amount as the employee's income and have reduced the employer's liability accordingly.[112] No such deduction will usually be made if the business' profit position is in negative numbers. The employee will be entitled to deduct reasonable business expenses from the business' profit for the purpose of these calculations. In addition, some courts have viewed the start-up of a new business as an exercise in building a capital asset. In certain circumstances, a discount has been applied to reflect the value created.[113]

Although the concept of a dismissed employee spending the notice period retraining for a career change may appear to run against the principles of mitigation, courts have been sympathetic to such circumstances where it is reasonable for the employee to be pursuing a career change. The issue of retraining throughout the notice period often arises where job prospects in the industry are poor and the employee wishes to retrain for a position in a different field. In such cases, courts have held that such retraining is not a failure to mitigate damages, even if the employee does not become successfully employed after the training.[114] It may be possible to argue that there is a failure to mitigate where an employee refuses to retrain in economic conditions where it is not conceivable that he or she would be re-employed in a given area.[115]

Requiring an employee to accept a position with lower pay, status and responsibility in fulfilment of the duty to mitigate is fundamentally at odds with the law which relates to mitigation, as such an act on the part of the employer may be

---

110 *Johnstone v. Harlequin Enterprises Ltd.* (1991), 36 C.C.E.L. 30 (Ont. Ct. (Gen. Div.)).

111 See *Michaud v. Stroobants*, [1919] 3 W.W.R. 46 (Sask. C.A.). But see *Gould v. Hermes Electronics Ltd.* (1978), 34 N.S.R. (2d) 321 (S.C.), where the employee was found to have failed to mitigate the damages arising from his dismissal when he refused an offer of another position within the employer's organization.

112 *Larsen v. Saskatchewan Transportation Co.* (1992), 47 C.C.E.L. 238 (Sask. Q.B.), supp. reasons 38 A.C.W.S. (3d) 794 (Sask. Q.B.), vard 49 C.C.E.L. 165 (Sask. C.A.).

113 *Foster v. M.T.I. Canada Ltd.* (1992), 42 C.C.E.L. 1 (Ont. C.A.).

114 *Roberts v. Versatile Farm Equipment Co.* (1987), 16 C.C.E.L. 9 (Sask. Q.B.); *Kinsey v. SPX Canada Inc.* (1994), 2 C.C.E.L. (2d) 66 (B.C.S.C.).

115 But see *Tokawa v. Canadianoxy Industrial Chemicals Limited Partnership* (1993), 49 C.C.E.L. 247 (B.C.S.C.).

considered a constructive dismissal. Where it is questionable whether the employee has been constructively dismissed, and where there is no evidence to support a belief that it would be embarrassing or humiliating for the plaintiff to continue working for the employer, a court might require the employee to accept such a position.[116]

A dismissed employee may be entitled to claim from the employer reasonable out-of-pocket expenses incurred while fulfilling the duty to mitigate and seeking out and accepting alternate employment. These costs are considered to be expenses incurred in the mitigation of damages and are the responsibility of the employer. They may include career counselling, expenses incurred in travelling to interviews (gas mileage or transportation, hotel accommodation and meals if the interview is out of town), professional fees, retraining, costs of resumé preparation, photocopying, facsimile charges, postage, purchase of newspapers and telephone calls. Employees are well-advised to keep detailed records of all expenses incurred in the mitigation effort if a claim is to be made for such expenses.

As part of the job search expense reimbursement requirement, employers have been required to compensate employees for moving to a new location to accept other employment, where the relocation is reasonable and/or resulted in a new job.[117] In other cases, courts have viewed this claim as damage which would have been sustained even if proper notice had been given and have refused to make such an award.[118] In addition, it has yet to be resolved whether the dismissed employee is entitled to damages in the amount of the real estate agent's fees on the selling of the employee's old house, legal fees in relation to the employee's purchase of a new house and any loss sustained in the disposition of the property, where relocation is required to fulfil the employee's duty to mitigate.

ENFORCEABILITY OF CONTRACTS

General

Employment contracts are like any other contracts in that employers and employees are free to negotiate and include any terms in the contract so long as

---

116 *Zalusky v. Nestle Canada Inc.* (1992), 6 C.C.E.L. (2d) 73 (B.C.S.C.); *Guilbeault v. Centre d'Integration Socio-Professionel de Laval* (1989), 30 C.C.E.L. 149 (Que. C.A.); *Hulme v. Cadillac Fairview Corp.* (1993), 1 C.C.E.L. (2d) 94 (Ont. Ct. (Gen. Div.)), affd 81 A.C.W.S. (3d) 815 (Ont. C.A.), leave to appeal to S.C.C. refused 122 O.A.C. 381n.

117 *Erlund v. Quality Communication Products Ltd.* (1972), 29 D.L.R. (3d) 476 (Man. Q.B.); *West v. Jim Pattison Charters Ltd.* (1994), 6 C.C.E.L. (2d) 46 (B.C.S.C.); *Isaacs v. MHG International Ltd.* (1983), 2 C.C.E.L. 72 (Ont. H.C.J.), vard 7 D.L.R. (4th) 570 (Ont. C.A.).

118 *Lewarton v. Walters* (1985), 8 C.C.E.L. 86 (B.C.S.C.); *Pilon v. Great West Steel Industries Ltd.* (1985), 8 C.C.E.L. 270 (B.C.S.C.); *Paddon v. Kamloops Electric Motor Sales and Service Ltd.* (1994), 5 C.C.E.L. (2d) 191 (B.C.S.C.); *McCaw v. Dresser Canada Inc.* (1983), 2 C.C.E.L. 51 (Ont. H.C.J.).

the parties are careful to avoid any of the circumstances which might cause a court to later find that the contract is unenforceable or contrary to statutory requirements. There are a number of different matters which employers and employees should address when they are considering entering into an employment contract.

Unconscionability

Parties entering into an employment contract should ensure that no terms within the contract are particularly harsh or onerous, as a court may consequently find that the contract is unenforceable on this basis. For example, if an employer attempts to reduce the notice period set out in an employee's contract just before terminating the employee, such behaviour has been found to be unconscionable.[119] The doctrine of unconscionability can also apply in favour of the employer, as was the case in *Zielinski v. Saskatchewan Beef Stabilization Board*,[120] where a contractual term providing that the employee would receive an unusually high payment upon dismissal was found to be unconscionable and unenforceable.

Undue Influence or Unequal Bargaining Power

Courts will often find contracts to be unenforceable if they look at the circumstances surrounding the execution of the contract and find that the employee was pressured into or influenced to enter into the agreement. Courts have also recognized that employees often have much less bargaining power than employers at the time of entering into an employment contract; however, simply because an individual is unemployed and requires a job will not render a contract unenforceable due to unequal bargaining power. If a court determines that an employee felt that, in order to obtain the position, there was no alternative but to sign the employment contract presented by the employer, it is likely that the court will find the contract to be unenforceable.[121] This will obviously pose less of a potential problem if the employee in question is a sophisticated individual whom the employer is attempting to recruit.

For example, in *Burden v. Eastgate Ford Sales & Service (82) Co.*,[122] an employee mechanic, on his first day of work, was handed a form and asked to sign it. The employee did as he was told and did not read the form, which limited

---

119 *Baker v. British Columbia Insurance Co.* (1992), 41 C.C.E.L. 107 (B.C.S.C.), affd 46 C.C.E.L. 211 (B.C.C.A.); *Ballard v. Alberni Valley Chamber of Commerce* (1992), 39 C.C.E.L. 225 (B.C.S.C.).

120 (1992), 42 C.C.E.L. 24 (Sask. Q.B.), vard on other grounds [1994] 3 W.W.R. 44 (Sask. C.A.).

121 *Matthewson v. Aiton Power Ltd.* (1984), 3 C.C.E.L. 69 (Ont. Co. Ct.), revd 8 C.C.E.L. 312 (Ont. C.A.). The Court of Appeal held that simply because the employee was unemployed and needed a job did not mean that there was an inequality of bargaining power. It was held that the employee knew what he was signing, and the contract was found to be enforceable.

122 (1992), 44 C.C.E.L. 218 (Ont. Ct. (Gen. Div.)).

his notice upon dismissal to the minimum period prescribed by the employment standards legislation. When the employer sought to rely on this form, the Court held that the employer had an obligation to draw the employee's attention to this provision on the form and to explain it to the employee. In the absence of such an explanation, the employee could not be held to the clause. Compare, however, the case of *Wegg v. National Trust Co.*,[123] where the employee was hired as the vice-president of network services and was also required to sign a contract limiting his notice upon dismissal to the employment standards minimum. In Mr. Wegg's case, the Court held that the contract was enforceable, since he admitted that he had read and understood the agreement, and there was no evidence of undue influence or pressure to sign it.

To avoid allegations of undue influence or unequal bargaining power, employers should be wary of requiring employees to sign contracts immediately upon presentation. It is advisable to provide the employee, well in advance of the proposed start date of the employment relationship, with a copy of the contract and to allow the employee sufficient time to consider the terms and to consider whether or not he or she wishes to enter into the agreement. The employee may use this time to seek the advice of counsel regarding the terms of the contract, and this should be encouraged by the employer. In fact, some employers build provisions into their contracts requiring the employee to confirm that he or she has been provided with an opportunity to obtain the advice of counsel regarding the terms of the agreement.

Mistake and Non Est Factum

Courts are also disinclined to enforce the terms of an employment contract if it is clear that the employee did not fully understand the legal implications of the document which he or she signed. An employee may not be able to understand the terms of an employment contract because of a language barrier, a learning disability, illiteracy or some other reason and, unless the employer has ensured the employee's understanding or provided the employee with every opportunity to seek assistance in order to understand the contract, it is possible that the employee will not be held to the terms of the contract.

If an employer anticipates relying on the terms of an employment contract at some future date, the employer should make every effort to ensure that there can be no later suggestion, on the part of the employee, that he or she did not understand what was being signed. For the ordinary employee, this may simply involve drawing the employee's attention to any of the provisions within the contract which restrict the employee's rights (typically those which would later be challenged, such as provisions limiting the period of notice upon dismissal). However, in the case of an employee who may not be able to understand the

---

[123] (1993), 47 C.C.E.L. 104 (Ont. Ct. (Gen. Div.)).

employer's explanation, the prudent employer will wish to provide the employee with an opportunity to seek sufficient explanation. It is not necessary that the employer confirm that the employee actually does understand the contract. This responsibility lies with the employee. The employer is only responsible for ensuring that the employee has been provided with an opportunity to understand the contract or to seek the assistance of someone who can explain the contract. An employee is not likely to be excused from being bound by a contract if he or she did not read or understand the document after having been provided with an opportunity to do so.

Lack of Consideration[124]

Employers who wish to rely on their employment contracts should also pay particular attention to the timing of the execution of these contracts. For a binding contract to be formed, it is imperative that "consideration" passes at the time of the signature of the employment contract. This may be satisfied if the contract is signed under seal. Otherwise, the employer will want to ensure that, at the time of execution, some exchange for the parties' mutual benefit takes place. This will often not be the case if the employer waits until after the employee has commenced work before asking the employee to sign an employment agreement.[125] If, however, an employer wishes to enter into an employment agreement with an employee who has already been working for a period of time, the "consideration" requirement may be met if the employee is presented with the contract at a time when something new is being offered to the employee, such as a compensation increase or a promotion. Another way to avoid this problem is for the employer to present the employee with the contract far enough in advance that it could be said that the employee was provided with time to consider the agreement which was equivalent to reasonable notice. In this way, the employee may be asked to enter into the agreement regardless of what it contains, but will have sufficient time to seek alternate employment if he or she decides that the terms of the agreement are unacceptable.

Employment Standards Legislation

Many employers and employees enter into employment contracts for the purpose of choosing a predetermined notice period which will apply in the event that either party wishes to end the employment relationship. This introduces a level of certainty into the employment relationship and allows both parties to be aware of the consequences of ending the relationship. If including a predetermined notice

---

124 See under the heading "Drafting the Contract", in Part 2, "The Engagement", for a more detailed discussion of this issue.
125 *Francis v. Canadian Imperial Bank of Commerce* (1992), 41 C.C.E.L. 37 (Ont. Ct. (Gen. Div.)), vard 120 D.L.R. (4th) 393 (Ont. C.A.).

period in the employment contract, employers should be extremely careful to first check that the contract provides that, in the event of dismissal, the employee will receive at least the minimum amount of notice required under the applicable employment standards legislation. The Supreme Court of Canada has held that employers who do not provide for this minimum notice period in their contracts run the risk that the contracts will be held to be unenforceable.[126] If such a finding of unenforceability is made, employers who have attempted to keep their liability to a minimum by entering into the employment contract may find themselves exposed to the liability imposed by the common law. For example, if an employment contract states that an employee is entitled to two weeks' notice, and the applicable employment standards legislation requires that the employee be provided with three weeks' notice, then the contract provisions will be found to be unenforceable. It will not be enough, in such a situation, to provide the employee with three weeks' notice. Rather, the employee will be entitled to whatever period the court determines to be reasonable under the circumstances. Such amount could be well in excess of the three-week minimum mandated by statute, and the employer will have defeated the initial purpose of the contract, which was to reduce liability in the event of dismissal.

Outdated Contracts

If an employer is considering dismissing a long-term employee, it often searches its records for an ancient employment contract signed by the employee upon hiring. The employer is often surprised to discover that, in signing this contract, the employee limited his or her notice upon dismissal to some nominal amount, if any, and it may seek to enforce such a clause. Aside from the previously discussed problem of enforcing a contract which provides for less notice than that required by employment standards legislation, there exist other difficulties. Courts are often not inclined to enforce employment contracts entered into by employees at the beginning of the employment relationship if the contracts are no longer relevant to the employee's circumstances.

The case of *Lyonde v. Canadian Acceptance Corp.*[127] involved an employer which tried to rely on an application form signed by the employee when he joined the organization 21 years previously in a much different and lesser position. Since that time, the employee had worked his way up the corporate ladder, having reached the position of a senior-ranking officer prior to dismissal. When the employer tried to rely on this application form to limit the employee's notice upon dismissal, the Court held that, given that the substratum of the employment relationship which had existed at the time the application form was signed no

---

[126] *Machtinger v. HOJ Industries Ltd.* (1992), 91 D.L.R. (4th) 491 (S.C.C.), revg 55 D.L.R. (4th) 401 (Ont. C.A.).

[127] (1983), 3 C.C.E.L. 220 (Ont. H.C.J.).

longer existed, the employee could not be held to the terms of the application form.[128]

It is not only the mere passage of time which renders the employment contract unenforceable; it is the change in the nature of the employment or the change in position which causes the substratum of the contract to disappear and renders the contract unenforceable.[129] For this reason, employers are well-advised to keep their employment contracts current and to execute new contracts at the time of compensation or position changes.

RESTRICTIVE COVENANTS AND EMPLOYEE DUTIES

Restrictive Covenants

In addition to the question of reliance upon the terms of general employment contracts as the employment relationship draws to an end, employers are often particularly concerned with the enforceability of any restrictive covenants contained in their employment contracts. Restrictive covenants are agreements between the employer and employee which set restrictions on what the employee may do in the event that he or she leaves the employment relationship. Such covenants may take the form of non-competition agreements, non-solicitation agreements or other restrictions placed upon an employee after the conclusion of the employment relationship.

Employers often wish to utilize restrictive covenants if they are concerned that former employees will compete, solicit customers or employees, or disclose confidential business information. The potential stumbling block for employers wishing to use restrictive covenants is that such covenants have long been considered to be in restraint of trade and thus unenforceable. A restraint of trade is something which prevents an employee from running a new business or being able to be employed as he or she sees fit. Anything which restricts the former employee's freedom to work after he or she is no longer an employee is generally considered to be in restraint of trade and void.

Although restrictive covenants are in restraint of trade and are presumed unenforceable, it is possible to rebut this presumption by showing that the particular covenant in question is reasonable. The employer must show that the covenant does no more than protect those rights of the employer which are entitled to protection, and does not unduly restrain the employee. It will be up to the employer to show that the particular covenant is reasonable under the circumstances, and this determination will take into account both the employee's and the

---

128 Also known as the "changed substratum doctrine": see *Rasanen v. Lisle-Metrix Ltd.* (2002), 17 C.C.E.L. (3d) 134 (Ont. S.C.J.).

129 *Wallace v. Toronto-Dominion Bank* (1983), 145 D.L.R. (3d) 431 (Ont. C.A.), at p. 451, leave to appeal to S.C.C. refused 52 N.R. 157n.

employer's perspectives. Courts will typically try to strike a balance between the freedom of trade and freedom of contract.[130]

Determining the Reasonableness of a Restrictive Covenant

In determining whether a particular restrictive covenant is reasonable, courts will generally consider a variety of factors. They will look at whether the restriction constitutes a legitimate protection of the employer's proprietary interests. The scope of the protection offered by the restriction will be considered. The duration of the covenant and the geographic scope of the restriction upon the employee's activities will also be reviewed. Lastly, the covenant will be reviewed from the point of view of public policy in order to determine if it is unenforceable as being against competition generally. It should be noted that no one of these factors will, by itself, result in a finding that the employment contract is reasonable. The restrictive covenant must be reasonable with respect to each of the categories if enforceability is to be achieved.

(1) Protecting Employers' Legitimate Proprietary Interests

The employer may only impose restrictions on an employee's post-dismissal activities if there is a legitimate need to protect the employer's interests. Courts will look at the nature and extent of the business and the scope of the employee's duties within the organization, but what is considered reasonable will always depend on the individual facts of each case. For example, before a court will agree to uphold a non-competition covenant in an employee's contract, it must be demonstrated that the employer has some legitimate interest in remaining free from competition on the part of the employee. This may be obvious in a situation where the employer's business is client-driven and the employer has concerns that the employee will cross the street and set up his or her own shop and take the employer's customers along. However, this may not be as obvious in, for example, a manufacturing setting, where the employer already has a significant stakehold in the market. Here, a court may be inclined to hold that the employee should be provided with an opportunity to compete. Employers should use very specific language when defining what is restricted by the covenant. They may further try to enhance the enforceability of the covenant by setting out the justification for the covenant right in the contract. This may improve the chance that such a covenant will be seen as reasonable if challenged.

---

130 *Elsley v. J.G. Collins Insurance Agencies Ltd.* (1978), 83 D.L.R. (3d) 1 (S.C.C.), referred to in *Lyons v. Multari* (2000), 3 C.C.E.L. (3d) 34 (Ont. C.A.), leave to appeal to S.C.C. refused 150 O.A.C. 197*n*.

(ii) Scope of the Restriction

Employers will wish to ensure that, in drafting their restrictive covenants, they do not use language which is broader than that required to protect the employer's legitimate interests. For example, employers will want to ensure that employees are not restricted from using the skills or experience which they have acquired while working with the employer, as they are entitled to transfer these over to any new employment which they choose. Employers will also want to ensure that an employee is only being restricted from doing that which would have been within his or her job description while working with the employer. For instance, an employee cannot be restricted from dealing with customers or suppliers with whom he or she dealt before joining the former employer if these were not dealt with while at the former employer. Employers who attempt to design covenants which are more restrictive than is reasonably necessary to protect their legitimate interests run the risk of having their covenants found to be unenforceable.[131]

(iii) Duration of the Restriction

A restriction placed on an employee after the employment relationship has ended should only last long enough for the employer to protect its legitimate proprietary interests, and no more. What will be held by the courts to be reasonable as between the parties will generally be determined on the facts of each individual case. In the case of non-solicitation and non-competition situations, the length of time for which a restrictive covenant is to last can often be related to the length of time needed for the employer to solidify its position after the employee leaves. This may refer to the period of time required by the employer to cement relationships with its clients by introducing the replacement employee to the clients before the former employee has a chance to solicit these clients or seek their business through a competitive enterprise. The specific period will be largely determined on the facts of the case, but the prospects of obtaining a finding of enforceability increase if the period provided for is less than a year.

(iv) Geographic Restriction

The geographic area covered by the restrictive covenant must also be reasonable and not go beyond that required for the legitimate protection of the employer's interests. Often, the area defined in the covenant is the same as the area covered by the former employee in his or her duties. A restriction of this sort is often seen as reasonable, as this is where the former employee would likely cause the most damage to the employer's business after his or her departure. If the covenant does not explicitly set out a particular geographic restriction, it is

---

131 See, for example, *Lyons v. Multari*, *supra*, where a non-competition covenant was struck down by the Ontario Court of Appeal as being overly broad in a situation where a non-solicitation clause would have more appropriately protected the employer's business.

possible that a court will consider the restriction to apply broadly and to thus be unreasonable. It is advisable for employers to consider the geographic area with which they are particularly concerned and to limit any restriction on the employee, which will apply after the end of the relationship, to this specific area.

(v) In the Public Interest

Lastly, a court will often conclude its analysis by moving away from a consideration of the interests of the parties themselves, and towards a consideration of whether the covenant is in the broader public interest.

Types of Restrictive Covenants

(i) Non-Competition Agreements

To prevent a former employee from commencing employment with a competitor or starting a competitive enterprise, a non-competition clause is often written into the employment contract. Through the use of such a clause, the employer is able to protect its legitimate interests by contractually preventing the former employee from either talking to a competitor or using, in his or her own business, any employer-specific product information, knowledge of customers or business opportunities. Courts often do not look favourably on non-competition clauses since they may restrict the individual employee's right to use the skill and experience which he or she acquired while working with the former employer. However, as with all restrictive covenants, if the employer is able to show that the covenant is reasonable, then a court will be inclined to enforce the contract. In determining reasonableness, courts will consider the general factors previously discussed: the proprietary interest being protected, the scope, duration and geographic limitation of the restriction, and the public interest served by the restriction.

Many employers mistakenly use non-competition language as a way to prevent an employee from disclosing confidential proprietary information to a competitor. In such a case, it is much wiser for the employer to focus its energy on a non-disclosure/confidentiality agreement, which will be seen as narrower in scope since it does not limit an individual's employment opportunities. Courts have held that a non-competition clause should not be used if a non-solicitation clause would adequately protect the employer's interests.[132] The non-competition clause has been referred to as the "more drastic weapon in an employer's arsenal". Its focus is much broader than an attempt to protect the employer's client or customer base; it extends to an attempt to keep the former employee out of business.

---

132 *Lyons v. Multari, supra,* footnote 130; *Ash Temple Ltd. v. Croney* (2000), 7 C.C.E.L. (3d) 15 (Ont. C.A.).

If an employer attempts to include in the employment contract a general covenant for an employee not to compete, courts will typically find such a covenant to be too broad. However, these covenants are occasionally upheld if there is no other way for the employer to protect all of its legitimate interests. Employers should draft their contracts in the most reasonable manner possible so as to increase the chances that the contracts will be found enforceable. Employers should also remember that often the most effective result of a restrictive covenant is not its legal force but rather the deterring effect that it has on the possibility that an employee will enter into competition with the former employer.

One way in which an employer can strive to protect itself from the possibility that an employee will commence employment with a competitor, and can minimize the chance that a non-competition agreement will be viewed as unreasonable, is if the employer creates a short list of those competitors with which it is primarily concerned. For example, if the employer and employee agree that the employee will not join one of the employer's three main competitors within a period of one year after leaving the employer, a court may be inclined to consider such a restriction reasonable, given that it is narrower in scope. Employers considering the use of such agreements should be wary of a comprehensive list of every conceivable competitor, as this defeats the purpose of this type of an agreement and will probably be found not to be enforceable.

(ii) Non-Solicitation Agreements

Employers often wish to restrict a departing employee's ability to solicit the employer's clients, customers or other employees after leaving the employer. Even if a court were to determine that the employer is entitled to the protection of its employer-customer relationships, it would still place limits on the extent of non-solicitation which can be expected from a departing employee. For example, while an employer may be able to include a clause which prevents the employee from taking the employer's current customers to the new employment, the employer may not be able to include a clause preventing the employee from soliciting customers who became clients of the employer either after the employee left or before the employee even started.

Employees wishing to avoid a non-solicitation obligation may, in certain instances, be able to make a general solicitation to all customers on a public list or to the public generally, even if they know that former customers of the employer are contained within such groupings. The argument in favour of the employee, in such a situation, is that any individual entering into the marketplace is entitled to make such a solicitation, and thus the employee is not using any advantage or information gained in the course of having worked for the employer. The employee is merely engaging in healthy competition and may be free to do so.

In certain circumstances, employers might also wish to protect themselves from the possibility that employees may leave and take other employees with them. As in the case of other restrictive covenants, courts may be unwilling to uphold such prohibitions as reasonable unless the employer had a legitimate interest in protecting itself from the luring away of such employees. Employers should be aware that the inclusion of such a covenant in an employment contract will not necessarily prevent other employees from leaving to join a departing employee if this is done in the absence of solicitation on the part of the departing employee.

(iii) Non-Disclosure/Confidentiality Agreements

Employers are entitled to the protection of any of their confidential information and will often attempt to secure this protection by including in the employment contract covenants restricting the employee's use of confidential information after departure. In the absence of such agreements, employees still owe a common law duty not to disclose confidential information belonging to the employer. Despite the existence of this common law duty, many employers still include confidentiality agreements in their employment contracts in order to draw to the employees' attention the importance of confidentiality and to address any specific concerns which the employer may have.

Confidentiality covenants are not to be used to restrict an employee's right to take with him or her any general skills and/or knowledge acquired while with the employer, and any attempt to so restrict an employee may render the covenant unenforceable. Employers can typically only prevent former employees from giving away confidential information, such as secret formulas, customer lists, client records, marketing strategies, pricing information, computer programs, contract renewal dates and "trade secrets" of the employer. An employer may not be entitled to prevent its former employees from disclosing the employer's client list if that list is public or was already widely known by the employer's competitors.

Employers face a challenge in designing a confidentiality covenant which restricts the disclosure of trade secrets without limiting the use of the employee's "know-how" in a future job. Courts will uphold an employer's attempt to prevent the use of its legitimate confidential information but will not enforce a restriction upon the use of the employee's skills in competing with the former employer. Employers concerned about confidentiality should assess each new employee's duties and consider whether an employee will have access to information that the employer owns. If so, the employer may wish to include a restrictive covenant in the employment contract, which attempts to protect the employer's interest without infringing on the employee's use of personal skills or knowledge after he or she leaves the company.

Like other restrictive covenants, confidentiality clauses are subject to the same reasonableness requirements. It must be shown that the employer has a legitimate interest to protect, and the employer may wish to set out this reason within the terms of the provision. It is also helpful if the clause specifically sets out the information which is considered to be confidential. The clause should further state that if any of the information is made public by the employer, then that information is thereafter excluded from the confidentiality clause. These considerations will be useful in demonstrating to a court that the clause is reasonable in its application. The employer may wish to include in the clause that, upon termination, the employee is to return all documents and data belonging to the employer, including any copies which the employee may have made. Employers may also wish to combine confidentiality clauses with intellectual property or copyright clauses.

Unlike some other restrictive covenants, there is no need to limit the duration of, or geographic area covered by, a confidentiality clause since the information will be protected by the clause so long as it continues to remain confidential. Confidential information is generally confidential everywhere and for all time, until the employer releases it into the public domain.

Contractual Damages Provisions

Damages resulting from a former employee's breach of a restrictive covenant are often very difficult for an employer to prove. Given the current competitive nature of the business world, it is very difficult for an employer to prove, for example, that it would have kept a particular client if the former employee had not set out to compete with the employer. To protect against possible future restrictive covenant breaches, it is possible for employers to include clauses in their employment contracts which provide for the payment of compensation or damages in the event that the restrictive covenant is broken by either party. For example, such a provision might state that, during the specified non-competition period, the employee will repay to the employer any profits he or she earns by doing business with former clients of the employer in violation of the non-competition or non-solicitation provisions of the employment contract. Inclusion of a damages provision does not limit a court's right to alter such an arrangement or make a separate award if the matter proceeds to trial. However, when such remedies are included in employment contracts, they act as insightful indicators of what the parties contemplated as being a reasonable resolution to such a problem.

Employers considering the inclusion of such clauses should be very careful in their drafting because it is often difficult to distinguish between a genuine pre-estimate of damages, which is enforceable, and a penalty clause, which is not. Simply because a particular sum is referred to in the contract as a "penalty" or "liquidated damages" will not decide the issue; courts will carefully examine the contract and make this determination.[133] There are several principles which the

---

133 *Lozcal Holdings Ltd. v. Brassos Developments Ltd.* (1980), 111 D.L.R. (3d) 598 (Alta. C.A.).

courts have adopted in deciding the true nature of one of these clauses.[134] If the sum in question is extravagant and unconscionable as compared to the greatest loss which could possibly follow a breach of the contract, then it will likely be viewed as a penalty. If there is only one event on the happening of which the agreed sum is to be paid, then it will probably be considered liquidated damages. If a sum is to be paid upon the happening of any of a number of events, only some of which are serious, then there is a presumption that the clause is a penalty. It will be up to the party trying to invalidate the clause to demonstrate to a court that it is in the nature of a penalty. Even if the clause is determined to be a penalty, it will be open to the party, who sought to rely on the clause, to sue for the damages actually suffered as a result of the contract breach.[135]

Employees' Duties

All employees owe certain duties to their employers at common law. These duties exist even in the absence of particular provisions in the relevant employment contract, and employees are obligated to fulfil these duties. The nature and extent of each employee's duties will generally be dependent upon the employee's position within the employer's organization.

Duty of Fidelity

All employees owe to their employer a duty to be loyal and faithful.[136] Most of the cases which discuss this duty involve employees who owe a fiduciary duty to their employer. Other cases have held that this duty is owed even by general employees, and often the duty will be read into the employment relationship as an implied contractual term.[137] The full extent of the duty, by whom it is owed and the consequences of a breach of such a duty are always determined based on the particular facts of each case.

Duty of Confidentiality

All employees owe a duty of confidence to their employers regardless of whether or not the contract governing the employment relationship contains a provision dealing with protection of confidential information. The challenge facing a court will be to determine whether the information in question was actually confidential. Certain types of information, such as trade secrets (which

---

134 *Dunlop Pneumatic Tyre Co. v. New Garage and Motor Co.*, [1915] A.C. 79 (H.L.), at pp. 86-7.
135 *Charterhouse Leasing Corp. v. Sanmac Holdings Ltd.* (1966), 58 D.L.R. (2d) 656 (Alta. S.C.); *Caravan Trailer Rental Co. v. Westward Park Ltd.* (1990), 65 Man. R. (2d) 281 (Q.B.).
136 *Krell v. Truckers Garage Inc.* (1993), 3 C.C.E.L. (2d) 157 (Ont. C.A.).
137 *Durand v. Quaker Oats Company Canada Ltd.* (1990), 32 C.C.E.L. 63 (B.C.C.A.), revg 20 C.C.E.L. 223 (B.C.S.C.).

may include secret recipes, formulas and technical or manufacturing processes), customer lists, prices, new product developments and marketing strategies, have generally been held to be confidential information and thereby worthy of protection.

Some of the factors considered by the courts when attempting to determine whether certain information is of a confidential nature include:

(a) whether there is any way that the employer's competitors or the public could have had access to the information;

(b) whether the information is of such a nature that the employee should have been aware that it was meant to be kept confidential;

(c) whether the way in which the information was treated within the workplace was such that it could reasonably be concluded that the employer considered such information to be confidential; and

(d) whether the information was communicated to the employee in a manner which necessarily denoted its confidentiality.[138]

As can be seen, it is not always a simple matter to determine what information is protected as being confidential. It is generally thought that any information regarding the employer's organization or internal structure, or any personal skill or knowledge which the employee acquired while with the employer is information which is not confidential. Far from being helpful, these guidelines merely serve to create many grey areas when trying to assess whether particular information is confidential. For example, in the case of a customer list, if an employee has committed the employer's customer list to memory, then the question often arises as to whether the employee has appropriated proprietary information or is merely using knowledge acquired during employment. The confidentiality determination will most often depend on the facts of each particular case.

Fiduciary Duties

Particular employees may have duties which go beyond that of confidentiality. The Supreme Court of Canada has held that those employees classified as "fiduciaries" owe more extensive duties to their employers. Specifically, the fiduciary owes a duty of "loyalty, good faith and avoidance of a conflict of duty and self-interest".[139] More specifically, courts have considered fiduciary employees to be restricted from soliciting customers from their former employers and from divesting corporate opportunities belonging to their former employers. Once having left their employ, fiduciaries remain in a position of trust and may not enter into a conflict between self-interest and the interests of their former employer. However,

---

138 See, for example, *Molnar Lithographic Supplies Ltd. v. Sikatory* (1974), 14 C.P.R. (2d) 197 (Ont. C.A.).

139 *Canadian Aero Service Ltd. v. O'Malley* (1973), 40 D.L.R. (3d) 371 (S.C.C.), at p. 382.

the duration of the duty is limited and, while the actual length depends on the facts of each case, a typical duty may extend between six months and several years.

In *Canadian Aero Service Ltd. v. O'Malley*,[140] the Supreme Court of Canada considered the case of two senior officers of a company who spent a long period of time preparing a tender for a particular mining contract for their employer. Before the tender was made, the employees resigned their employment with the company, formed their own company, prepared a separate tender and secured the mining contract. The Supreme Court of Canada held that these employees were in a fiduciary relationship with the company, having acted as they did in senior capacities. The employees were held to have violated their fiduciary duties to the company when they resigned and pursued the corporate opportunity of which they only became aware by virtue of their position with the company. The employees were required to account to the company for all profits which they were to have realized as a result of completing the contract.

At one time, the definition of a "fiduciary" within the employment context was very restrictive and included only those very senior executives of an organization. The justification for this was that it was only these employees who held positions within the organization which contained the power and ability to direct and guide the affairs of the organization.[141] Thus, simply holding a management position was insufficient to impose a fiduciary duty if the position did not carry with it the power and ability to direct and guide the affairs of the company. The manager would have to act as an agent for the employer, not just as a mere employee, and the emphasis was really on the particular individual's role and function within the organization and not on his or her title or place in the hierarchy.

Some courts have now broadened the definition of "fiduciary" to include less senior employees within employer organizations, and the general trend has been an increase in the number of employees who have been found to owe fiduciary duties to their employers. Generally speaking, employees may now owe fiduciary duties to their employers if they play any key role within the organization (therefore considered to be "key employees"), although these cases will continue to be rare.[142] This does not necessarily denote only a senior position within the company; it means the employee must, in some way, be essential to the organization. In the case of *Canadian Aero Service Ltd. v. O'Malley*,[143] the Supreme Court of Canada observed that fiduciaries are not limited to the directors of a company, and it was not dispositive that the employees in question were under the direction of others. The Court also found that a fiduciary duty exists separate from the duty of confidentiality of information or copyright considerations. Therefore, a breach

---

140 *Supra.*
141 *R.W. Hamilton Ltd. v. Aeroquip Corp.* (1988), 65 O.R. (2d) 345 (H.C.J.).
142 *Barton Insurance Brokers Ltd. v. Irwin* (1999), 170 D.L.R. (4th) 69 (B.C.C.A.).
143 *Supra*, footnote 139.

of fiduciary duty does not necessarily require a breach of confidentiality or trade secrets.

Whether or not an employee is a fiduciary will be determined by a number of factors, including the position held by the employee, the employee's duties and responsibilities, the organizational structure of the employer with respect to the employee, the nature of the employer's business and whether or not the employee is an officer or director of the company. The determination of the issue will generally centre around the control exercised by the employee over the employer's confidential information, client lists and trade secrets. Courts will also look at whether the employee has independent authority over the employer's business. It is important to look at the whole relationship between the employee and employer, since fiduciaries have in the past included presidents, vice-presidents, general managers, directors, secretary-treasurers and other representatives.[144]

Employers thinking about hiring should consider whether the employee may have owed a fiduciary duty to his or her former employer. In the case of such an employee, the employer may wish to take precautions which will prevent the employee from violating his or her fiduciary duty while working for the new employer. The employer can obtain an agreement from the new employee that the employee will not use business opportunities discovered through the former employer. Employers can use the same type of agreement to require that new employees refrain from soliciting clients of the former employer and can make it clear to new employees that they are only to solicit the public at large.

Remedies

Employers whose employees violate restrictive covenants or their general or fiduciary duties will usually pursue one of the following remedies in seeking redress for the damage caused by an employee who has breached his or her duty or contract.

Damages

Employers are entitled to sue their employees or former employees for violations of the restrictive covenants contained in the employment contract, or for violations of the duties which the employees owed to the employer, be they fiduciary or otherwise. Damages are intended to put the employer in the position it would have been in had the breach of the contract or the violation of the duty not occurred. However, there is little judicial consensus on the nature of the compensation provided in the event of such a breach or violation. Some courts have held that the employee can be sued for all profits that the employee earned

---

144 For a more complete treatment of this subject, see M.V. Ellis, *Fiduciary Duties in Canada* (Scarborough: Carswell, 1993), Chapter 16.

by virtue of his or her conduct.[145] For instance, in the case of a fiduciary employee taking advantage of a corporate opportunity, the employee can be sued for any profits realized from this opportunity. Other courts have held that damages should be awarded for the actual loss suffered by the company, after deducting any expenses which the company would have incurred in pursuing the income for which it seeks reimbursement.[146] In the case of the employee who takes advantage of a corporate opportunity, this calculation of damages would allow the employee to show that the company would not have pursued the opportunity had it been provided the chance. In the case of solicitation of customers, the employee may have the opportunity to prove that certain customers would have come to the employee regardless of whether or not the employee solicited them in violation of the employment contract or his or her general duty. Courts will attempt to determine which of the available methods of assessing damages is appropriate in the circumstances and will then apply this approach.[147]

Injunctions

An award of damages is often insufficient to protect employers who are facing unlawful competition or the misappropriation of their confidential information. Such employers need immediate relief, and the damages they might receive at the end of a lengthy lawsuit may be insufficient to remedy their loss.

This has led to the use of the remedy of injunctive relief, which bars employees from continuing their improper behaviour. A court has the discretion to grant an interlocutory injunction where it is just and convenient for it to do so.[148] Although an injunction can be used to enforce a breach of either a fiduciary duty or a restrictive covenant, there is usually a greater readiness to grant such relief where a covenant exists.[149] The employer is required to apply for an injunction and will further be required to prove three things at the application hearing:

(1) that there exists a substantial issue which should proceed to trial;
(2) that irreparable harm to the employer is likely to occur if the injunction is not granted; and
(3) that granting the injunction will result in a balance of convenience in favour of the employer.

In order to meet the first criterion that there be a substantial issue for trial, the employer must be able to show quite clearly that it has a strong case. This is

---

145 *Canadian Aero Service Ltd. v. O'Malley, supra*, footnote 139.
146 *White Oaks Welding Supplies v. Tapp* (1983), 149 D.L.R. (3d) 159 (Ont. H.C.J.); *Edgar T. Alberts Ltd. v. Mountjoy* (1977), 79 D.L.R. (3d) 108 (Ont. H.C.J.).
147 *Moore International (Canada) Ltd. v. Carter* (1982), 40 B.C.L.R. 322 (S.C.), affd 56 B.C.L.R. 207 (C.A.); *McCormick Delisle & Thompson Inc. v. Ballantyne* (2001), 9 C.C.E.L. (3d) 50 (Ont. C.A.), leave to appeal to S.C.C. refused 158 O.A.C. 196n.
148 *Liberty National Bank & Trust Co. v. Atkin* (1981), 121 D.L.R. (3d) 160 (Ont. H.C.J.).
149 *Merrill Lynch Canada Inc. v. Pastro*, 2000 BCCA 243.

referred to as showing a *prima facie* case and is necessary because, if the employer is successful in being granted the injunction, the employee could effectively be prevented from competing for as long as it may take for the matter to proceed to trial. Courts will want to see fairly strong evidence of the employer's case before they are inclined to rule in favour of granting an injunction which might have this effect. This element is relatively easy to establish where, for example, the employee has breached a non-competition or other covenant in the employment agreement.[150]

Next, the employer is required to show that irreparable harm is likely to occur if the injunction is not granted. "Irreparable harm" is considered to be that which cannot be adequately compensated by damages at trial, such as damage to goodwill, loss of customers or loss of protection of trade secrets. Generally, there must be more than a suspicion of harm, and courts will carefully examine any employer's claim that damages would be difficult to quantify.

Finally, when looking at the balance of convenience, courts will generally favour the preservation of the status quo. For example, they will often order that the employee is prohibited from committing any more breaches of the employment contract or general duties but will not necessarily make an order regarding breaches that the employee has already committed. Generally, courts will consider whether the harm to the employee which is likely to result if the injunction is granted outweighs the harm to the employer which might result if the injunction is refused.

Courts are generally not inclined to limit employees' ability to earn a livelihood and, where an employer is likely to be able to withstand competition from its former employee, a court may be disinclined to grant an injunction. In granting an injunction, courts will require the employer to give an undertaking to pay such damages as may result from the injunction if, at the end of the day, it appears that the injunction should never have been granted.

Other

Other, but less commonly used, remedies available to employers are:

(a) *Mareva* injunctions, which freeze the assets of an employee where there are grounds for belief that those assets could be removed or disposed of before judgment is handed down; and

(b) *Anton Piller* orders, which allow the employer's representatives to enter an employee's premises to inspect or seize documents or property belonging to the employer (*e.g.*, client lists).

---

150 See *Towers, Perrin, Forster & Crosby, Inc. v. Cantin* (1999), 46 O.R. (3d) 180 (S.C.J.).

Such orders are obtained without notice to the employee, and therefore it must be established that there would be a significant risk of the documents or property being disposed of or hidden if notice were given to the employee.

If an employer is concerned about the possibility that it might be vulnerable to a particular employee in the event that the employee chooses to leave the organization, the employer may wish to attempt to limit its exposure by restricting the employee's post-departure activities within the provisions of an employment contract. While setting out the restricted activity may be important, it may be even more important from the point of view of deterrence to include, in the contract, the given remedy in the event of breach or non-compliance.

RELATED ISSUES

When an employer has reached the decision to dismiss an employee, assuming the employee is not being dismissed for just cause, the employer must consider the preparation of the employee's severance package. Employees are not necessarily entitled to a severance package *per se*. However, there are certain entitlements if the employee is dismissed without cause (statutory notice, common law reasonable notice and possibly statutory severance pay). Employees are also entitled to receive any accrued wages and vacation entitlements they may have pursuant to employment standards legislation. All of these entitlements can be worked into a severance package, which is prepared for the employee in the form of a letter thanking the employee for his or her service, and extending the company's best wishes to the employee in his or her future endeavours.

Preparation of a Severance Package

In addition to the statutory entitlements, the employer can include virtually anything else in the employee's severance package. The package is limited only by the bounds of the employer's creativity. Listed in this section are some of the main ingredients in a severance package. For other ideas, employers should review the earlier section on damages,[151] which covered the various entitlements which employees might have if their matter were to proceed to court. For example, although car allowances will not be dealt with in this section, the employer may wish to compensate the employee for a lost car allowance in the severance package. Otherwise, if the employee seeks legal advice and learns that he or she would be entitled to a lost car allowance during the relevant notice period, this may open up negotiations on the severance package or even prompt the employee to sue the employer if he or she feels that the employer is behaving unfairly.

---

151 See under the heading "Types of Damages" earlier in this Part.

Severance Amount

Determining a figure to offer to an employee by way of severance will typically involve some assessment of pay in lieu of reasonable notice, unless the employer is asserting just cause for dismissal. The employer will begin by determining the minimum payment to which the employee is entitled pursuant to the relevant employment standards legislation and will then proceed to assess whether the employee would be entitled to some greater amount of reasonable notice at common law. Suppose, for example, that the employer determines that the employee is entitled to four weeks' minimum pay in lieu of notice and is further advised that the employee might be entitled to between one and three months' notice at common law. The next question is: How does the employer decide what to offer? This will depend largely on the employer's strategy with respect to the dismissal. If the employee is one of many being dismissed over a period of time, then the employer may simply develop a formula for severance and apply that formula. Otherwise, the employer will make a decision based largely on its willingness to accept the risk of ensuing litigation, given what it knows about the individual employee. For example, if the employer believes that the employee will complain regardless of what is offered, then the employer might wish to offer a lesser amount and be prepared to increase its offer if the employee wishes to engage in negotiation. Many employers will make low severance offers as a rule because they are aware that many employees have an inherent need to negotiate and that many others will simply never challenge what they have been offered. If the employer adamantly wishes to avoid litigation, then the employer may wish to be more generous from the outset. The employer may also be concerned about the effect which the offer has on the workplace as a whole. If the other employees witness the former employee having to fight "tooth and nail" for a fair severance package, this sends a very different message to the workforce than does an employee being sent off with a generous package. Employers should also be wary of "lowballing" an employee's severance offer, as this often is now put forth as evidence of bad faith in support of a claim for an extended notice period based on a *Wallace* decision.

Once the employer has decided on the severance amount, it needs to consider whether to provide the employee with payment in the form of a lump sum or as a continuation of the employee's salary. In certain circumstances, it may be necessary to provide the employee with a portion of the severance in a lump sum, even where the employer decides to continue the employee's salary.[152] This would be the case for an Ontario employee with five years' or more service who works for an employer with a minimum $2.5 million payroll. This employee is entitled to statutory severance pay, and this must be paid upon dismissal unless the employee agrees to have it paid in instalments. The employer may wish to negotiate

---

152 See under the heading "Severance Pay" in Part 3, "The Marriage".

the structure of the severance package with the employee, as employees will occasionally have a preference between lump sum payments and salary continuance, for employment insurance or tax reasons.[153]

Pension and Other Benefits

The employer will want to establish whether it is required to provide the employee with any benefits upon dismissal. In Ontario, for example, the employer is required to continue the dismissed employee's benefits for the minimum period prescribed by statute. In other cases, the employer may be required to provide the employee with certain benefits upon dismissal, or compensation in lieu of such benefits, by virtue of the benefits plans themselves. The company stock option plan, for instance, may provide that the employee is entitled to a stock buyout upon dismissal or may be entitled to exercise his or her stock options for a limited period of time following the dismissal. The employer should be aware of any entitlements or options the employee may have at this stage, and these should be set out in the severance letter.

Even if the employer has no statutory or express contractual obligation to the employee in terms of benefits, the employer may wish to consider continuing the employee's benefits or pension entitlements for some period as a gratuitous term of the package or in fulfilment of its obligations at common law. Often, continuing the employee's benefits represents a minimal expense to the employer and may be all that an employee needs to smooth over a conservative severance amount.

Releases

In any case where an employer agrees to provide an employee with a severance package in order to avoid a lawsuit, or where the employer is attempting to settle a lawsuit, it is advisable for the employer to require the employee to sign a release, in which the employee agrees to refrain from bringing any further actions or proceedings against the employer. In exchange for the settlement of a wrongful dismissal action, an employer can insist upon the release of any dismissal claims. However, an employer cannot offer, in exchange for a release, any money already owed to the employee, such as by contract, or that to which the employee is statutorily entitled. The employer should beware of requiring an employee to sign a release where the employer has offered the employee only the minimum notice to which he or she is entitled by virtue of employment standards legislation, or where the employer is paying only that amount which the employee is owed pursuant to an employment contract, unless the contract specifies that a release will be provided by the employee in exchange for the payment.

---

153 See under the headings "Employment Insurance" and "Taxes" later in this Part.

A release is merely an agreement between the employee and the employer confirming that the employee will refrain from pursuing any legal or other action against the employer in exchange for a given settlement or severance package. Like other contracts, a release may be oral, given that a contract is formed as soon as the agreement is reached. However, it is rarely recommended that such a release be obtained verbally. Get it in writing. The party agreeing to refrain from pursuing any further action is referred to as the "releasor" and is usually the employee in a wrongful dismissal suit. The employer is the "releasee", having received the release from the employee.

Since a release is a contract, all of the terms relating to enforceability of contracts also generally apply to releases.[154] If a release is signed under duress, in the presence of inequality of bargaining power, in a case of mistake, while the releasor was operating without independent legal advice or in unconscionable circumstances, the release may be ineffective. Judges have ruled that releases were invalid and did not bar litigation when they were signed due to financial panic or under pressure, such as might occur where an employer threatens the employee that it will pay nothing unless the employee signs the release.[155] Similarly, if a truly inadequate severance package serves as the consideration for a release, the release could be struck down as unconscionable. In one case, an employee was dismissed for refusing to sign a release accepting a proposed settlement. The court held that the employee had been wrongfully dismissed.[156]

In *Blackmore v. Cablenet Ltd.*,[157] the plaintiff was a commissioned salesman who was dismissed without cause after three years' service. The employer offered the employee a package "in full satisfaction of all claims arising out of the termination of [his] employment".[158] In order to induce the plaintiff to sign the release, the employer withheld the employee's back pay and refused to provide a letter of reference. It was decided that the release should be set aside for unconscionability, since the defendant had used its position of superior bargaining power to obtain the executed release. The employee was awarded four months' pay in lieu of reasonable notice.

When drafting a release, an employer should ensure that it attempts to cover all claims, including those which may potentially exist under employment standards and human rights legislation. In order to do so, specific reference should be made to the legislation and the claims arising thereunder. However, depending upon the circumstances, this may not be foolproof in protecting against a future statutory claim, largely due to the fact that most such statutes provide that the parties cannot contract out of their provisions. The release should also cover

---

154 See under the heading "Enforceability of Contracts" earlier in this Part.
155 *Adamson v. Watts & Henderson (Atlantic) Ltd.* (1987), 16 C.C.E.L. 74 (Ont. H.C.J.), supp. reasons 21 C.P.C. (2d) 400 (Ont. H.C.J.); *Augustine v. Nadrofsky Corp.* (1986), 17 O.A.C. 297 (Div. Ct.).
156 *Van Smith v. M.F. Schurman Co.* (1992), 130 N.B.R. (2d) 129 (Q.B.).
157 (1994), 8 C.C.E.L. (2d) 174 (Alta. Q.B.).
158 *Supra*, at p. 177.

outstanding or unpaid wages, vacation pay, commissions or bonuses. The parties may wish to make the release conditional upon an agreement to keep the terms of the settlement confidential and upon there being no assumption of liability in connection with the dismissal. Employers should be aware that requiring an employee to sign a release, particularly a complicated one, may compel the employee to seek legal advice. Therefore, employers may not want to request the execution of a release if they are giving only minimal notice to an employee. If, however, employers are being more generous, they will want to do so only in exchange for an executed release.

Often, if an employer is wary of requesting that an employee sign a complicated release, the employer may attempt to obtain a "soft release". This is done by including a provision in the dismissal letter or severance letter which states that the employee, by cashing the enclosed cheque, agrees to refrain from pursuing any legal action against the employer in relation to the employee's employment. However, such releases are probably not specific enough to completely foreclose potential employment standards and human rights complaints, and a number of courts have held that they are not even effective as a general release between the parties.[159]

Employment Insurance

When an employment relationship ends, the employee may be entitled to employment insurance benefits.[160] An employee will be entitled to benefits if, during the "qualifying period", which is generally the 52 weeks prior to the application for benefits,[161] the employee had the requisite number of hours of insurable employment. For new entrants into the labour market, or for re-entrants, the eligibility requirements have been raised from 20 weeks to 910 hours, which is the equivalent of 26 weeks of work at 35 hours per week; for all other employees, the number of requisite hours ranges between 420 and 700 hours, depending on the regional rate of unemployment.[162]

For employment to be "insurable", an employee must have worked at least 15 hours per week or earned a certain minimum amount of income each week.[163] When collecting employment insurance, employees are entitled to 55% of their

---

159 For cases where soft releases were found not to be binding, see *Barrett v. Northern Lights School Division No. 113* (1986), 47 Sask. R. 251 (Q.B.), affd on other grounds 49 D.L.R. (4th) 536 (Sask. C.A.); *Woodlot Services Ltd. v. Flemming* (1977), 83 D.L.R. (3d) 201 (N.B.C.A.). But see also *Young v. Western Supplies Ltd.* (1985), 30 A.C.W.S. (2d) 437 (B.C.S.C.).

160 *Employment Insurance Act*, S.C. 1996, c. 23 (as amended to 2002, c. 9) (the "EI Act"), s. 7. The employee may also be so entitled in cases of other "interruptions in earnings", as defined in. s. 14 of the *Employment Insurance Regulations*, SOR/96-332 (as amended to SOR/2002-364) (the "EI Regulations").

161 The qualifying period may be a shorter period of time if it has been less than 52 weeks since the employee started his or her last employment insurance claim (EI Act, s. 8(1)).

162 EI Act, s. 7(3) and (2)(*b*).

163 EI Regulations, ss. 9 and 10.

weekly insurable earnings in the rate calculation period.[164] In certain circumstances, an employee will be entitled to 60% of average earnings, as is the case if the employee supports a dependant and falls below a certain income. The length of time for which an employee will be entitled to benefits will depend on the employee's length of service and the unemployment rate in the region in which the employee resides.[165]

For all dismissed employees, employers are required to complete a Record of Employment (an "ROE") form which can be obtained from the nearest Canada Employment Centre or from Human Resources Development Canada. According to the *Employment Insurance Regulations* (the "EI Regulations"),[166] the ROE must be issued within five days of the interruption of the employee's earnings as a result of his or her dismissal. Failure to do so could subject the employer to a fine of up to $2,000 or to imprisonment for a maximum of six months, or both.[167] Human Resources Development Canada encourages employees to apply for unemployment insurance as soon as possible after their dismissal, even if the ROE has not yet been issued. Employees will not be entitled to benefits for a "waiting period" of two weeks following their dismissal, but subsequent benefits will be received as soon as possible after the employee makes his or her application.[168] When completing section 19 of the ROE, which asks for the reason for the issuing of the ROE, employers should ensure that the reason indicated on the ROE is the same as that which might be later asserted for legal purposes. If employers are unsure as to which of the listed codes applies to the employee's situation, they should either seek legal advice or indicate the letter "K" (for "other") on the form, followed by a descriptive comment on the employee's situation. If the letter "K" is indicated on the form, Human Resources Development Canada will use its discretion, and make a decision regarding the employee's benefit entitlement, based on the circumstances of the dismissal.

Employees are disqualified from receiving employment insurance benefits if they lost their employment because of their own misconduct or if they voluntarily left employment without just cause.[169] The EI Act sets out a number of circumstances in which an employee will be justified for having voluntarily left employment. In such cases, the employee is considered to have left with "just cause" and may thereby be entitled to benefits. These circumstances include cases where an employee has been harassed or discriminated against (in violation of human rights or labour legislation), where an employee is obligated to follow a spouse or

---

164 EI Act, s. 14(1). An employee's insurable earnings are subject to a maximum, which is calculated according to a formula set out in s. 14 of the EI Act and, from 1997 to 2000, was $750 per week. If the claimant's benefit period begins in a subsequent year, the maximum weekly insurable earnings are equal to the maximum yearly insurable earnings divided by 52.

165 *Ibid.*, s. 12(2).

166 EI Regulations, s. 19.

167 EI Act, ss. 136 and 137.

168 *Ibid.*, s. 13.

169 *Ibid.*, s. 30.

dependent child to another residence, where the working conditions are unhealthy or unsafe, where the employer's practices are illegal, where the terms of employment (such as wages, salary or job duties) are changed significantly or where the employer requires excessive overtime or refuses to pay overtime.

The question often asked by employers is whether they are obligated to deduct from settlement or court awards for wrongful dismissal the amount received by the plaintiff during the period of reasonable notice on account of employment insurance. The case law on this issue is widely divergent, but employees have tended to rely on the Supreme Court of Canada decision, *Jack Cewe Ltd. v. Jorgenson*,[170] as authority for the fact that such deductions are not to be made. In that case, Mr. Justice Pigeon, writing for the Court, stated that the payment of employment insurance contributions by the employer is an obligation incurred by reason of the plaintiff's employment. Thus, to the extent that the payment of those contributions results in the provision of employment insurance benefits, these are to be considered a consequence of the employment contract and cannot be deducted from damages for wrongful dismissal.

What appears to have caused confusion in this area of law is the existence of ss. 45 and 46 of the EI Act. According to these sections, if an employee receives employment insurance benefits with respect to a period, and the employer subsequently becomes liable to pay and does pay earnings to the employee for that same period, the employee is obligated to remit to the Receiver General any overpayment of benefits which results. The amount of the overpayment is calculated as that amount which the employee would not have received by way of employment insurance if he or she had been paid the earnings at the time of receipt of the benefits. The EI Act sets out a corresponding obligation on the part of the employer to remit the amount of the overpayment to the Receiver General, so long as the employer has reason to believe that the employee is in receipt of employment insurance benefits.

For many years, the EI Act stated that the obligation to remit arose only when the employer became liable to pay to the employee "remuneration", as opposed to "earnings". A number of court decisions held that "remuneration" was not meant to include damages for wrongful dismissal obtained by a plaintiff by court order.[171] In *Jack Cewe Ltd. v. Jorgenson*,[172] the Supreme Court of Canada held that whether or not the employee was entitled to keep the benefits received from the government on account of employment insurance was not meant to impact on the employer's liability, but rather was meant to be a matter between the employee and the employment insurance authorities.

---

170 (1980), 111 D.L.R. (3d) 577 (S.C.C.), affg 93 D.L.R. (3d) 464 (B.C.C.A.).
171 *Peck v. Levesque Plywood Ltd.* (1979), 105 D.L.R. (3d) 520 (Ont. C.A.); *Olson v. Motor Coach Industries Ltd.*, [1977] 4 W.W.R. 634 (Man. Q.B.), affd 81 D.L.R. (3d) 132 (Man. C.A.); *R. v. Atkins* (1976), 68 D.L.R. (3d) 187 (F.C.A.), affg 59 D.L.R. (3d) 276 (F.C.T.D.); *Jack Cewe Ltd. v. Jorgenson, supra*, footnote 170.
172 *Supra*, footnote 170.

The EI Act was amended in 1990,[173] and now specifically states that earnings for which an employer may become liable, and pursuant to which the obligation to remit any employment insurance overpayment arises, include damages for wrongful dismissal. It seems clear that employers who have reason to believe that dismissed employees are in receipt of employment insurance benefits must ensure that any overpayment of employment benefits received by an employee during the reasonable notice period is remitted to the Receiver General. Generally, the best way to ensure that this is done is for the employer to remit this amount itself. Otherwise, it should be looking for confirmation from the employee that this amount has been remitted or the employer may find itself liable for the amount over and above the full damages award already paid to the employee.

The 1990 amendment to the EI Act appears to be consistent with the interpretation which the EI Regulations have received. Pursuant to the EI Regulations, earnings are to be allocated to the weeks of an employee's employment for the purpose of calculating the employee's employment insurance benefits. In *Canada (Attorney General) v. Walford*,[174] it was held that "earnings" for the purpose of the EI Regulations included a payment of damages for wrongful dismissal. This meant that any dismissed employee who received a payment upon dismissal representing damages for wrongful dismissal was to indicate that payment to the employment insurance authorities, where it would be allocated to the employee's period of unemployment for the purpose of calculating benefits. For example, an individual who, at the time of termination, was in receipt of a severance payment in the amount of one year's lump sum salary would be required to report such income as earnings under the EI Regulations and would not, as a result, be eligible for employment insurance benefits for a one-year period.[175] In such a case, the individual's entitlement to benefits would be deferred to the end of the severance period. Such an allocation of the severance funds will be made regardless of whether the payment is made in a lump sum or in the form of a salary continuance. In the case of a lump sum payment, the total amount will be divided into weeks and will disentitle the employee to employment insurance benefits for the resulting number of weeks.[176]

---

173 See *Unemployment Insurance Act*, R.S.C. 1985, c. U-1, ss. 37 and 38 (both rep. & sub. 1990, c. 40, s. 27). See now EI Act, ss. 45 and 46.

174 (1978), 93 D.L.R. (3d) 748 (F.C.A.).

175 EI Regulations, s. 36.

176 Please note, however, that a 2001 decision of the Federal Court of Appeal held that "earnings" do not include settlement moneys categorized as job search and training expenses, even if the expenses have not actually been incurred at the time of settlement. In order to exclude the payment from earnings, the moneys must be allocated for this purpose, and there must be a genuine intention that they be so used: *Canada (Attorney General) v. Radigan* (2001), 8 C.C.E.L. (3d) 44 (F.C.A.).

Taxes

Generally, amounts received by an employee as severance pay, or as damages for wrongful dismissal,[177] are considered income and are fully taxed.[178] Such amounts fall into the *Income Tax Act*'s definition of "retiring allowance",[179] which includes most amounts received on or after retirement in recognition of long service or in respect of loss of employment (whether or not the amount is received as, on account of, or instead of payment of damages or pursuant to an order or judgment of a competent tribunal). From a tax standpoint, it does not matter if the amount was received by way of judgment or in a negotiated settlement. Retiring allowances are not subject to deductions on account of the Canada Pension Plan or employment insurance premiums.

When employers pay retiring allowances, they are required to deduct and remit to the Receiver General of Canada a portion of the allowance in respect of income tax. This applies no matter when the amount is paid, be it at termination, at some later date when the parties settle the matter or when a court so orders. The employer is required to deduct the following:

- 10% for any payment of $5,000 or less;
- 20% for any payment over $5,000 but not more than $15,000;
- 30% for payments over $15,000.[180]

These withholdings are only estimates of the employee's liability for income tax, and more or less tax liability could arise for the employee at year end, depending on the level of other income and deductions available for the year. These withholding requirements only apply to resident Canadians. Non-residents are taxed differently. Taxes do not need to be deducted from any eligible portion of a retiring allowance which is paid directly to the administrator of an R.R.S.P. for the employee rather than to the employee,[181] if the employer has reasonable grounds to believe that the eligible amount is within the employee's R.R.S.P. deduction limit.

Employers who fail to withhold or remit an amount under the *Income Tax Act* are subject to penalties or prosecution, or both. Section 227(8) and (9) of the *Income Tax Act* provides a general penalty of 10% of the amount required to be withheld or remitted by the employer plus, in certain cases, the full amount

---

177 This is the case regardless of whether the amount is received pursuant to a settlement offer or is awarded by a court.

178 *Income Tax Act*, R.S.C. 1985, c. 1 (5th Supp.) (as amended to 2002, c. 9), s. 56(1)(*a*)(ii), which includes in income a "retiring allowance".

179 *Ibid.*, s. 248(1), definition "retiring allowance".

180 *Ibid.*, s. 153(1)(*c*), and *Income Tax Regulations*, C.R.C. 1978, c. 945 (as amended to SOR/2003-5), s. 103(4). Quebec administers its own taxes and imposes its own withholdings in addition to federal withholdings, so the corresponding combined federal and Quebec withholding rates are 25%, 33% and 38%.

181 See para. 15 of Interpretation Bulletin IT-337R3, *Retiring Allowances* (January 30, 1998).

required. The penalty is 20% where the failure occurs after an initial penalty has already been assessed. Added on to this will be an amount for interest on all amounts outstanding. Where an employer fails to withhold, it may be subject to prosecution, under s. 238(1) of the *Income Tax Act*, for an offence punishable on summary conviction by a fine ranging from $1,000 to $25,000 or by a fine and up to 12 months' imprisonment.

What is considered to be a "retiring allowance" has generally been interpreted rather strictly.[182] First, if an employee stops working pursuant to an early retirement program but continues to be paid until some later real retirement date, then the amount earned in the interim will not be seen as a retiring allowance. It is only when retirement formally begins that a retiring allowance can arise.[183] However, if it can be shown that a payment is in respect of a loss of an office or employment, the payment will constitute a retiring allowance, regardless of the fact that the individual's actual loss of office or employment may occur subsequent to his or her receipt of such payment.[184] Also, if an award or a settlement for wrongful dismissal includes an amount calculated for interest, such an amount is not viewed as part of the "retiring allowance".[185] Finally, in *Young v. M.N.R.*,[186] a taxpayer sought to exclude amounts received for exemplary and mental distress damages from the assessment of "retiring allowance". The Court concluded that there was insufficient evidence to show that these amounts were not connected to the dismissal. This leaves open the possibility that if such damages are received by virtue of a separate actionable tort, not connected with the dismissal itself, they might be excluded from the definition of "retiring allowance".

Employees are entitled to "roll over" (*i.e.*, transfer on a tax-deferred basis) amounts received as "retiring allowances" into their R.R.S.P.s, thereby deferring the tax payment on a wrongful dismissal award. Awards may be paid directly into an R.R.S.P., or the employee may simply make the R.R.S.P. contribution in the year in which the award is received. An employer who automatically directs an employee's retiring allowance into an R.R.S.P. will not be required to deduct income tax from that amount if the employer has reasonable grounds to believe that the amount transferred is within the employee's R.R.S.P. deduction limit and the amount eligible for transfer.

Employees receiving retiring allowances are only allowed to roll over certain amounts into their R.R.S.P.s. Each employee is allowed $2,000 for each year or

---

182 *Ibid.*

183 *Serafini v. M.N.R.*, [1989] 2 C.T.C. 2437 (Tax Ct. of Can.).

184 *Income Tax Technical News*, Issue 19 (June 16, 2000), "Retiring Allowances – Clarification to Interpretation Bulletin IT-337R3".

185 Technical Interpretation #9413245, *Retiring Allowance* (June 28, 1994). However, as stated in Technical Interpretation #9409870, *Canadian Payroll Association Conference – 3 Questions on Termination* (April 29, 1994), the Canada Customs and Revenue Agency (formerly known as Revenue Canada) may take a different view if such an amount is considered prejudgment or pre-settlement interest paid on an award or settlement for wrongful dismissal.

186 [1986] 2 C.T.C. 2111 (Tax Ct. of Can.).

part year in which the employee was employed up to and including 1995, and employees are entitled to an additional $1,500 for each year before 1989 when the employee was not entitled to participate in a pension plan or a deferred profit sharing plan.[187] The amount which is rolled over into an R.R.S.P. is not included in the definition of "earned income" for the purpose of the employee's annual fixed dollar R.R.S.P. contribution limit. Any amount which cannot be rolled over cannot be added to income for the purpose of an increased fixed dollar R.R.S.P. contribution limit for that year. To reduce the employee's remuneration on which source deductions are taken, the employer must have reasonable grounds to believe that the R.R.S.P. premium is deductible.[188] The Canada Customs and Revenue Agency (the "CCRA" – formerly Revenue Canada) advises that a copy of the employee's prior year's notice of assessment will normally suffice for this purpose, given that assessments usually contain a statement of the employee's contribution room. Employers wishing to be especially diligent might also seek written confirmation from the employee that no further contributions have been made to the R.R.S.P. since the conclusion of the year to which the assessment applies.

If an amount is paid to an employee upon dismissal pursuant to the terms of an employment contract, it will normally constitute income from employment rather than a retiring allowance. This would include salary, accrued vacation pay and any amount paid in lieu of notice of termination, whether statutory or otherwise. Statutory severance pay *is* a retiring allowance.[189] Both income and retiring allowances are taxable. Income will still constitute "earned income" for R.R.S.P. purposes.[190] Retiring allowances are taxed in the calendar year in which they are received. With respect to the receipt of golden parachutes,[191] the CCRA may take the position that an amount paid is not compensation for loss of employment or in recognition of long service but rather is deferred compensation and constitutes income.

The CCRA takes the position that payments made to dismissed employees as damages for wrongful dismissal will normally constitute deductible expenses to the employer, so long as.

---

187 *Income Tax Act*, s. 60(*j*.1). Years of employment after 1995 are not counted in calculating the amount of a retiring allowance that can be transferred under s. 60(*j*.1) since the application of that paragraph is being phased out: see Interpretation Bulletin IT-337R3, *op. cit.* footnote 181, at para. 12.

188 *Income Tax Regulations*, s. 100(3)(*c*).

189 The CCRA now states that, if an amount paid pursuant to the terms of an employment contract is for loss of employment or in recognition of long service, it will be a "retiring allowance". Therefore, employers will wish to word their employment contracts or negotiated settlement documents very carefully for income tax purposes.

190 Eighteen per cent of a taxpayer's income, subject to fixed limits and deductions for pension adjustments, may be deducted for contributions to a taxpayer's R.R.S.P. for the following tax year.

191 See under the heading "Golden Parachutes" in Part 2, "The Engagement", for a discussion of these benefits.

    (a) the payment is really a retiring allowance;

    (b) the moneys paid are reasonable; and

    (c) the employer did not terminate its business and unnecessarily and gratuitously pay an amount of money to an employee.[192]

To be a "retiring allowance", the payment must be received on or after retirement or be paid in connection with a loss of an office or employment. The CCRA accepts cessation of employment for any reason as being retirement or loss of income.[193] However, retirement or loss of employment does not include:

    (a) a transfer from one office or position to another with the same employer (or an affiliate), in a different capacity, including one with diminished responsibilities (however, the employee can continue as a corporate director receiving nominal compensation);

    (b) termination of employment with the employer, followed by employment with an affiliate of the former employer or re-employment with the employer pursuant to an arrangement made prior to the termination of employment;

    (c) termination of employment where salary and benefits continue to accrue.[194]

If, by virtue of a settlement, an employee is required to remit to the Receiver General an amount on account of an employment insurance overpayment, such an amount will be classified as a retiring allowance and is subject to income tax.[195] Since a total figure will need to be remitted on account of the overpayment, the amount will need to be grossed up to account for the income tax, and this grossed-up amount should be remitted on account of the income tax. For instance, if a wrongful dismissal suit settles for $10,000, and the employee has been in receipt of $8,000 worth of employment insurance which must now be deducted by the employer and remitted to the Receiver General, the employer will calculate that, using a 20% tax rate; the remaining $2,000 of the settlement will constitute income tax on a retiring allowance of $10,000 in order to result in the $8,000 overpayment figure. The $2,000 amount will be remitted on account of income tax. Such a gross-up is not necessary if the employment insurance overpayment is paid with after-tax dollars.

If, in settling a wrongful dismissal action, the parties designate a certain portion of the settlement funds as legal fees, and have evidence that such fees have been incurred, then such fees are not subject to source deductions. However, such

---

192 *Income Tax Act*, s. 67, and Interpretation Bulletin IT-467R, *Damages, Settlements and Similar Payments* (February 19, 1992). (Note: This bulletin, at the time of publication, was under review in order to reflect important court decisions.)

193 Interpretation Bulletin IT-337R3, *Retiring Allowances* (January 30, 1998), at para. 3.

194 *Ibid.*, at para. 3.

195 Technical Interpretation #9409870, *Canadian Payroll Association Conference – 3 Questions on Termination* (April 29, 1994).

amounts are meant to be included in income pursuant to the *Income Tax Act*.[196] Such amounts are not eligible to be transferred into an employee's R.R.S.P.[197]

Outplacement Services and Legal Fees

Increasingly, it seems, dismissed employees have an expectation that they will be offered, as part of their severance package, some form of outplacement or relocation support. Therefore, when preparing a severance package, every employer should consider whether it is prepared to make some offer of these services. There are a multitude of service providers available that can be retained to provide assistance to the employee at the time of or following dismissal. This assistance can include a great number of services designed to help the dismissed employee: counselling, resumé preparation, interviewing skills, networking opportunities, placement, etc.

It is not so much out of legal obligation that it is recommended that employers consider this form of assistance, although some counsel will argue that an employer's obligation to compensate an employee for expenses incurred in mitigating his or her damages will include compensating for the use of these kinds of services. Rather, it appears that most employees today expect to see some form of this assistance in their severance packages. As a result, even the most fair and reasonable severance package can appear to fall short if the employer has not included some form of outplacement assistance. Service providers in this area can offer a range of services, depending upon the amount the employer wishes to spend, and so it is often worth considering including something under this heading, especially if it represents a minimal cost to the employer.

In addition, where a severance package is structured in the form of a salary continuance, so that the employer financially benefits if the employee secures alternate employment or becomes self-employed (as is the case if the payments cease or some discounted lump sum is paid out at this time), an amount allocated to outplacement or relocation assistance can be seen as a worthwhile investment. Where the employer has the opportunity to save some of the overall severance package costs if the employee becomes re-employed, then providing this assistance makes inherent sense.

In formulating a severance package, a fixed amount for legal fees is sometimes also included. By including this amount, the employee is encouraged to seek legal advice on the reasonableness of the severance package. Again, such an amount is not mandatory but, if the employer is confident that it is offering a reasonable package, incurring this fee can help to ensure that the employee gets proper advice regarding the fairness of the package and that the employee's acceptance of the package is expedited, and may serve to avoid litigation. Employees in such

---

196 *Income Tax Act*, s. 56(1)(*l*.1).
197 Technical Interpretation #9409870, *op. cit.*, footnote 195.

a case are not inclined to believe that the employer is treating them unfairly if the employer is willing to pay for the employees to seek the advice of a lawyer. If such an amount is to be offered, it is strongly recommended that the package specify that the fee will be paid only if the employee obtains the advice of a lawyer specializing in employment law.

Reference Letters

When an employee is dismissed and offered a severance package, reference letters are often included in the package. When parties to litigation are settling a wrongful dismissal case, the reference letter may be used as a bargaining chip in the negotiations. In a case where an employee has been dismissed for just cause, the employer should ensure that it does not provide a letter of reference for the employee. This may seem to be an unnecessary caution; however, it is not unusual for an employee who has been dismissed for cause to seek and obtain a favourable letter from his or her immediate manager or supervisor, who was not involved in or did not endorse the dismissal. Sustaining a just cause claim in court in the face of such a letter can be extremely difficult.

Until the mid-1990s, it was generally thought that an employer was under no specific obligation to provide a reference to a departing employee. While a number of wrongful dismissal decisions had referred to the employer's failure to provide a plaintiff with a reference, very few definitive statements had been made regarding an employer's potential liability for failing to provide a reference. However, in the 1995 case of *Lim v. Delrina (Canada) Corp.*,[198] it was held that, if a particular situation dictates that a letter of reference ought reasonably to have been given, then the notice period can be increased for the failure on the part of the employer to provide one (subject to any satisfactory explanation). In the case, Justice LaForme observed that, in most circumstances, an employer's failure to provide a reference would be insignificant and, therefore, any consequent increase in the notice period would be minimal at best. In the case at hand, it was held that Mr. Lim was entitled to have his three-month reasonable notice period increased by one additional month to compensate for the employer's failure to provide a letter of reference.

Since the Supreme Court of Canada's decision in *Wallace v. United Grain Growers Ltd.*,[199] courts have been considering the failure to provide a letter of reference in relation to an employer's obligation to act in good faith at the time of dismissal. For example, in *Barakett v. Levesque Beaubien Geoffrion Inc.*,[200] Justice Gruchy increased the notice period on the basis that the employer had refused to provide the plaintiff with a letter of reference, noting that this had had

---

198 (1995), 8 C.C.E.L. (2d) 219 (Ont. Ct. (Gen. Div.)).

199 (1997), 152 D.L.R. (4th) 1 (S.C.C.).

200 (2001), 8 C.C.E.L. (3d) 96 (N.S.S.C.), affd 12 C.C.E.L. (3d) 24 (N.S.C.A.), leave to appeal to S.C.C. refused July 11, 2002.

a negative impact on the plaintiff's ability to find replacement employment. However, failure to provide a letter of reference will not always result in an increased notice period. In *Caers v. Usborne & Hibbert Mutual Fire Insurance Co.*,[201] the trial judge was critical of the employer's failure to provide the plaintiff with a letter of reference, noting that the failure was particularly insensitive for a 52-year-old employee who was terminated after a lengthy period of employment with only his second employer. However, the judge was not persuaded that the manner of dismissal as a whole was "unduly insensitive", as would have been required to support an increase to the notice period.

Assuming employers may now have some obligation to provide a letter of reference in certain circumstances, what type of reference is required? If the employee is dismissed on a without cause basis, then the employer may very well have a sound basis upon which to draft a positive reference for the employee and may be willing to do so as part of the employee's severance arrangement. However, in the case of an employee whose performance or attitude was unsatisfactory, but was not serious enough to justify a dismissal for cause, the employer is often hesitant to provide such a letter. One option might be to provide the employee with a factually based clinical letter, setting out the employee's position and responsibilities and the length of the employment relationship (the "name, rank and serial number" letter). Although this may not technically be considered a letter of "reference", as no positive reference is made to the employee's tenure, this type of neutral document may satisfy the employee's needs. Yet many employers feel compelled to address any problems they had with an employee in a reference, whether it be oral or written. For example, in a small industry made up of few employers who keep in close contact, "Oldco" may be concerned that, when asked by "Newco" for a reference regarding a potential employee, if Oldco fails to inform Newco that the employee had a very poor attitude and work ethic, Newco may be equally evasive the next time Oldco needs information.

With this in mind, the law has, for some time, provided protection to employers wishing to give honest references for departing employees. In the Ontario Court of Appeal decision, *Korach v. Moore*,[202] it was held that employers providing honest references could assert the defence of "qualified privilege" if their having provided an unfavourable reference interfered with the employee's ability to secure alternate employment. So long as the employer was honest in providing the reference and did not act in a manner which was malicious or intended to restrict the employee's ability to secure another job, and it was within the context of the reference giver's job to provide confidential information about employees, the employer and the reference giver may be protected.

Employers should, however, be aware of an English case, decided in the highest court, which held that employers may be liable for damages for interfering

---

201 (2000), 102 A.C.W.S. (3d) 121 (Ont. S.C.J.).
202 (1991), 76 D.L.R. (4th) 506 (Ont. C.A.), leave to appeal to S.C.C. refused 79 D.L.R. (4th) vii.

with departing employees' job searches if they provide damaging references. In *Spring v. Guardian Assurance plc.*,[203] the House of Lords held that an employer owes a duty of care to an employee in preparing a reference letter, and the employer may be liable for any economic loss suffered by the employee if the reference is negligently prepared. The employer has a duty not to negligently make untrue statements (even if such statements are honestly believed to be true) and a duty to avoid expressing unfounded opinions (even if those opinions are honestly held). To date, it does not appear that any Canadian court has applied *Spring* and, until a court does, it would seem that employers will still be entitled to the protection of the defence of qualified privilege in the giving of references. The reality is, though, that many employers will often use decisions like this as a basis on which to deny providing a reference and to even go so far as to adopt a standard company policy to this effect.

To minimize liability in the provision of references to departing employees, employers might seek to obtain agreement from the departing employee as to the content of the letter or may go so far as to seek a disclaimer of liability from the employee prior to providing any reference. Employers should also strive to ensure that all post-employment inquiries regarding the employee, whether oral or written, are directed to one company representative who has been given instructions with respect to the appropriate reference. In addition, employers might wish to consider a company policy on the provision of reference letters. The policy should set out whether references will be provided (either oral or written), the employees who will be entitled to references and the content of such references. The policy should then be applied consistently throughout the organization.

When the Dismissal Leads to Litigation

With employees becoming increasingly aware of their legal rights, it is not unusual for employees to consult legal counsel regarding their dismissals and any severance package they have been offered. Assuming that employees will seek some form of legal advice regarding their dismissal, employers can generally expect any of a number of different reactions to a dismissal or the offer of a severance package to an employee. First, it is possible that, after the dismissal, the employer will hear nothing further from the employee. In such a case, it is reasonable to assume that the employee either did not seek legal advice or, in fact, was advised that the dismissal was appropriate. Employers who have presented employees with a severance package may hear back from employees, either through legal counsel or not, in a case where an employee wishes to negotiate some aspect of the severance package. This can be distinguished from the next possible reaction, the writing of a "demand letter", because, in this case, the

---

203 [1994] 3 All E.R. 129 (H.L.).

employee appears generally accepting of the package and would likely agree to the package if the employer were to take the position that the package is non-negotiable. Such situations are usually resolved before lawyers need play any active role.

Lawyers will often become involved in more serious cases of employee dissatisfaction with dismissals or severance packages. Where the employee believes that he or she has been wrongfully dismissed (whether it be for just cause or in having been offered a deficient severance package), the employee's lawyer will typically take one of two courses of action. The lawyer may write a "demand letter", threatening a lawsuit in the event that the employer does not accept the employee's counter-offer, or the lawyer may simply omit this step in the process and proceed to issue a "statement of claim", thereby commencing a lawsuit against the employer.

"Demand letters" are written by a dismissed employee's lawyer, and set out a series of demands arising out of the employee's termination. The lawyer may be seeking pay in lieu of notice where an employee has received none, or the lawyer may simply be seeking an enhancement to the severance package already offered. In either case, such letters often indicate in some fashion whether the employee is simply "requesting" further assistance, or whether the employee is actually prepared to escalate and sue if his or her demands are not met. Employers are, however, cautioned to keep an eye out for hollow threats of litigation.

A demand letter is often recommended in a case where an employer has clearly engaged in a wrongful dismissal (the assumption being that the employer must simply not be aware of the law), or where an employee's case involves complex issues of law better left to a lawyer. In other cases, thought should be given to whether a demand letter is the best course of action. If an employee has some remaining goodwill with his or her former employer, he or she might better be able to capitalize on this rather than running the risk of irritating the employer by involving legal counsel. However, some employers will not take employee requests or demands seriously unless they come from a lawyer, and other larger and more sophisticated employers are often more comfortable dealing directly with counsel since they have legal or human resources departments with extensive experience in such matters.

It is not unusual for an employer to contact its lawyer only after a statement of claim has been served. The "statement of claim", as it is usually called, is an initiating process in civil litigation, and signals the commencement of a lawsuit. It is also a "pleading", in that it sets out the basis for the employee's case against the employer. The party who initiates a lawsuit is referred to as the "plaintiff", while the party against whom the action is commenced is referred to as the "defendant". Upon receipt of a statement of claim, the employer will have a limited amount of time in which to file a response, which is usually called a "statement of defence", and is also a "pleading". In Ontario, subject to certain exceptions, employers are required to file a defence within 20 days of being served with the statement of claim. It is imperative that an employer contact its lawyer immediately upon receipt of a statement of claim, and preferably before receipt if the employer has been alerted that an employee is planning to issue a claim.

In a wrongful dismissal case, the employer will generally be defending the case on the basis that the employee was either dismissed for just cause or was provided with notice or pay in lieu of notice which was reasonable. In entering a defence, the employer may also take the opportunity to enter any counterclaim which it may have against the employee, such as a claim for breach of fiduciary duty. Once the defence has been filed with the court, the employee may enter a "reply" if he or she wishes, after which the court considers the pleadings to be closed. The parties enter the next phase of the litigation process, which is "discovery".

Each party has an obligation to disclose to the other party all information and documentation which is relevant to the action. The general view of the courts today is that all parties to litigation should be forthcoming with all information or documentation which might in any way relate to the matters in issue. The parties are first required to provide written discovery in the form of an affidavit of documents. The parties must reveal all relevant documents to the other side and must swear an affidavit that this has been done. Employers will be required to undertake a full search of all records to locate relevant documentation and will be required to make reasonable inquiries with others who the employer believes may be in possession of relevant documents. Once the affidavits of documents have been filed by both parties, the matter proceeds to oral discovery.

Oral discovery is conducted by way of what are normally called "examinations for discovery". Gone are the days when parties to a lawsuit arrived at court, began the trial and commenced the examination of witnesses only to be surprised with information which was not disclosed by the other side. Such surprises resulted in countless adjournments and protracted proceedings. As a result, our civil legal system is now based on the principle that at least one representative of each party may be examined under oath prior to the trial to provide each party with an opportunity to ask questions and obtain full disclosure of the other party's case. The oral discovery stage of the lawsuit often provides an excellent impetus for settlement. Once the parties become aware of the case that they are required to meet, they may be inclined to settle, depending on the nature of the evidence. Discovery also provides an opportunity for each party to gauge the strength of the other side's witnesses. Many a case has been settled to avoid allowing a particular witness to testify in open court. All testimony given during examinations for discovery is recorded by an official examiner, and a transcript is prepared which can be used at trial.

Once discoveries have been conducted, and if the matter has not yet been settled, the case will typically be set down for trial, thereby being put on the respective court's trial list. Before a case goes to trial, the parties will be required to attend a pretrial before a judge, who is then precluded from going on to hear the trial of the matter. The pretrial judge will usually make some assessment of the case in an effort to induce the parties to settle the matter at this stage. The pretrial judge's comments are not binding and may be tailored to moving the parties towards a settlement.

If the matter is not settled at the pretrial stage, a trial date will be set. The length of time before a matter on the trial list reaches court varies greatly, depending on the jurisdiction and the current court backlog, but is likely to be anywhere from three to 18 months. Once this is added to the amount of time it takes the parties to get their case placed on the trial list, most litigants can expect that their matter will not go to trial for at least a year, and probably closer to between two and three years.

As if the amount of time it takes to litigate a case were not enough disincentive for parties considering litigating a wrongful dismissal matter, the issue of legal costs often settles the matter. Litigation exists to assist wronged parties in seeking justice and naturally one would assume that, if an employee is forced to sue an employer and proceed all the way to trial to achieve a fair result, he or she would be entitled to the legal costs required to make this happen. Similarly, an employer would be entitled to its legal costs where it was forced to defend a frivolous claim brought by a former employee. The system is designed to provide successful litigants with their legal costs; however, this is not a perfect system. In the vast majority of cases, the successful party will be awarded costs on a partial indemnity basis, which results in the party recovering only some percentage of the legal fees spent because the costs will be assessed based on tariffs for legal services set by the courts.[204] In certain exceptional cases, a court may award costs on a substantial indemnity basis and, in such a case, the party may be entitled to something more akin to full indemnification for legal fees incurred, subject to certain exceptions. The court usually maintains jurisdiction to fix the costs in an appropriate case and thereby provide the successful party with any extent of recovery that the court deems appropriate.

Courts have recognized that there will be circumstances where one party has made a fair offer to settle a case long before trial, only to have the offer rejected by the other party, resulting in an unnecessary trial. The rules of civil procedure typically provide that, if such an offer was made in accordance with the rules, and if the party who made the offer received a result equal to or better than the offer, that party should be in a better position in terms of recovery of costs because the trial could have been avoided had the opposing party accepted the offer when it was made. For example, in Ontario, if a plaintiff makes an offer to settle in accordance with the *Rules of Civil Procedure*,[205] and the plaintiff obtains a judgment as favourable as, or more favourable than, the offer, the plaintiff is

---

204 These are typically based on the average fees for such services throughout the jurisdiction and are likely to be only a percentage of what the parties are charged by their lawyers.

205 R.R.O. 1990, Reg. 194 (as amended to O. Reg. 206/02).

entitled to partial indemnity costs up to the date of the offer and substantial indemnity costs from that date forward.[206] Generally speaking, it is not unheard of for lawsuits to cost in the tens of thousands of dollars if they proceed through to the end of trial. It should thus come as no surprise that virtually all wrongful dismissal cases settle before trial.

One way in which a party may be able to control the exorbitant costs associated with litigation may be to come to some sort of contingency fee arrangement with his or her lawyer. Contingency fees are popular in the United States, where attorneys often agree to take cases on in exchange for a promise that they will be entitled to some percentage of any amount ultimately awarded to their client at trial. Such arrangements are gaining popularity in Canada as well, although they have not necessarily been sanctioned in all jurisdictions. Contingency fees hold great appeal for individuals with strong cases but little money to commence a lawsuit.

A further way to avoid the costs of taking a wrongful dismissal suit all the way to trial may be to take advantage of any available summary judgment or summary trial process. For example, in Ontario, the *Rules of Civil Procedure* provide that a party to a lawsuit may make a motion for summary judgment.[207] Such a motion can be made immediately after a statement of defence has been served. The judge hearing the motion may be required to determine whether there is a genuine issue which requires that the matter continue through to trial, unless the rules of civil procedure in the jurisdiction allow the parties to consent to proceeding by way of summary judgment. A summary judgment motion may only be appropriate in a case where there are no conflicting facts and where the judge is only required to make a decision on the applicable law. In a wrongful dismissal case where the parties are agreed on all relevant facts but cannot agree on the appropriate reasonable notice period, it may be possible to move for summary judgment. In fact, parties that do not take advantage of such summary procedures in appropriate cases may be chastised by the trial judge for having wasted judicial resources. On a summary judgment motion, evidence is introduced by way of affidavit, so that no testimony need be introduced through witnesses at the motion itself. This allows for a more expeditious procedure but highlights the fact that such a process is not necessarily appropriate where the facts are in dispute.[208]

The summary judgment or summary trial process allows the parties to potentially resolve their lawsuit judicially in a very short period of time. From the time the statement of claim is served upon the defendant, it may be possible to move for summary judgment and have a decision within three to six months. While

---

206 *Ibid.*, subrule 49.10(1).
207 *Ibid.*, Rule 20.
208 However, a summary judgment motion may be appropriate even where the facts are in dispute if the parties have an opportunity to cross-examine the individual who swore the affidavit in advance of the motion and if the judge is willing to make a ruling in the face of disputed facts.

obtaining a judgment in such a summary fashion is advantageous, it poses diffi-culties in terms of the plaintiff's duty to mitigate. Suppose, for example, that the plaintiff in a wrongful dismissal action obtained a favourable result on a summary judgment motion made within six months of the plaintiff's dismissal and the plaintiff was awarded 12 months' notice. If the plaintiff were to receive a lump sum at the six-month point, this would have the effect of eliminating the plaintiff's obligation to mitigate for the remaining six months. Judges have attempted to resolve this problem by building a contingency into their summary judgment awards to take into account that the plaintiff might find other work prior to the conclusion of the reasonable notice period.

Courts across Canada continue to struggle with a backlog of court cases, and are always searching for ways to bring matters to trial or resolution more quickly. In some jurisdictions, you might see cases governed by "case management", where measures are put in place to ensure that lawsuits proceed along at a certain pace and are not subject to undue delay. This can involve, for example, the parties in a case agreeing to adhere to a certain timetable, or the case being assigned to a particular judge or master who will meet with the parties on a regular basis to make sure the case keeps progressing. Elsewhere, we have seen initiatives such as the raising of the small claims court maximum recovery amount to $10,000 in Ontario, and the introduction of the "simplified procedure", which allows claims of less than $50,000 to proceed to trial without examinations for discovery. Initiatives such as these present options for plaintiffs looking to keep legal costs to a minimum and to move their matters to trial more quickly.

It may also be possible for a group of employees to commence a class action against their employer. Class proceedings legislation exists in some jurisdictions in Canada. It may allow a group of employees to participate in one joint lawsuit against their employer if their claims against the employer are related.[209] Central to a class action is the certification process, whereby a court decides if the proposed action is suitable to be tried as a class. In Ontario, in order for a class action to be certified as such, the group of employees would need to need to show the following:

1. The pleadings disclose a cause of action.
2. There exists an identifiable class of two or more persons that would be represented by a representative plaintiff.
3. The claim of the class members raises common issues.
4. The class proceeding is the preferable procedure for the resolution of the common issues.
5. There is a suitable representative plaintiff.[210]

---

209 See, for example, *Class Proceedings Act, 1992*, S.O. 1992, c. 6 (no amendments), as well as similar legislation in British Columbia and Quebec. See also *Kumar v. Sharp Business Forms Inc.* (2001), 9 C.C.E.L. (3d) 75 (Ont. S.C.J.).

210 *Class Proceedings Act, 1992* (Ontario), s. 5(1).

Assuming these or other similar criteria can be met, a class action may be an advantageous way for a large group of employees to proceed with their claims and keep legal costs to a minimum.

Employers have been the subject of certification in class proceedings in various employment cases, including wrongful dismissal actions where there has been a mass termination. For example, in *Webb v. K-Mart Canada Ltd.*,[211] after the Hudson's Bay Company announced that it would be purchasing several Kmart stores, it revealed that several of the stores would be closed across Canada. Plaintiffs' counsel took the position that the termination of employment of the store employees was a common issue, sufficient to ground a class action for common law damages for wrongful dismissal. The motions court judge agreed and certified the action as a class proceeding.

In order to minimize the risk of certification of a proceeding, it is recommended that employers try to individualize the process associated with terminating employees in a mass termination situation. The application of a formula in such a mass termination might, for example, lead a judge to conclude that the dismissal process may not have been representative of employees' proper entitlements to reasonable notice, and assist a judge in finding the common factual circumstances necessary to support the certification of a class. Another obvious circumstance in which it might be appropriate for employees to attempt to certify a class proceeding might be where the employer has failed to comply even with minimum statutory requirements in terms of notice of termination and severance pay. Overall, employers would be wise to avoid giving groups of employees common reason to bring action against the employer, as this may be easier and more viable for the group than it would otherwise be for one individual employee.

Alternate Dispute Resolution

Given the expense and time involved in the conduct of litigation, parties unwilling to settle are increasingly considering alternate methods of dispute resolution as means by which to come to a negotiated settlement. There are a variety of alternate dispute methods, but the most popular are arbitration and mediation. Today, more and more parties are seeing the value of such methods of dispute resolution and are considering them as alternatives to trial. Alternate dispute resolution ("ADR") is fast and relatively inexpensive when one considers the cost of taking a matter to court in the traditional way. ADR also allows the parties to choose a mediator or arbitrator and ultimately decide upon someone with experience in employment law who will have an excellent grasp of the fundamental principles. When parties utilize ADR to resolve their disputes, they also have the advantage of privacy and confidentiality.

---

[211] (1999), 45 C.C.E.L. (2d) 165 (Ont. S.C.J.).

Mediation is non-binding and involves the parties meeting in a neutral setting with a neutral mediator who acts only as a facilitator in helping the parties reach a negotiated settlement. The mediator's role is very different from that of an arbitrator or a pretrial judge. The mediator does not render a decision and will not normally provide an assessment of his or her view of the case. The mediator establishes negotiation ground rules and enforces them when they are infringed. The mediator ensures that communication is clear and effective, and will assist the parties in identifying the issues in dispute, in uncovering any underlying interests and in discovering options as to how the dispute might be resolved. Successful mediation involves a certain amount of trust and disclosure, on the part of each side, as to what the real concerns are, the idea being that there will be more options for settlement if each party's needs are known and attempts are made to meet them.

Arbitration, on the other hand, is binding and is more akin to a mini-trial, in that it is adversarial and the arbitrator ultimately renders a decision regarding the dispute. The parties to an arbitration are generally free to set the rules of procedure and may wish to hear testimony from witnesses. The most difficult hurdle for the parties to overcome before they agree to arbitration is the choice of an arbitrator. If the parties can both be satisfied with the choice of a neutral individual, they may wish to proceed by way of arbitration because of its speed and lessened expense. The parties should agree in advance as to whether there will be any means of appealing the arbitrator's decision. Parties contemplating arbitration should also check to see whether they would be bound by a provincial or territorial arbitration Act which may govern the manner in which their arbitration is conducted.

ADR is becoming so popular that many individuals and lawyers are entering into the dispute resolution business. Employers and employees considering the ADR option should have no difficulty finding someone in their jurisdiction who is in the business of providing ADR services. In fact, the advantages of ADR are becoming so widely accepted that, in some jurisdictions, including Toronto, all wrongful dismissal actions commenced (other than small claims matters and matters initiated under the simplified procedure)[212] are subject to mandatory mediation shortly after the lawsuit has commenced.[213] Given the tendency for wrongful dismissal matters to settle in advance of trial, mandatory mediation appears to have forced litigants to give serious consideration to whether they wish to incur additional legal expense to continue on with a matter which is most likely to settle in any event. If both parties are prepared to be reasonable and to consider the possibility of making concessions, there is a strong likelihood that the matter can be settled shortly after it has started. Naturally, this is typically considered desirable for both parties, but often more so for the unemployed plaintiff. On the

---

212 *Rules of Civil Procedure* (Ontario), Rule 76.
213 *Ibid.*, Rule 24.1.

other hand, the existence of mandatory mediation can sometimes leave employer and employee counsel less willing to discuss settlement outside the commencement of litigation, the risk being that they will be narrowing the parameters of settlement before a future settlement discussion to be held at the mandatory mediation session.

Litigation or Settlement?

Given that the vast majority of wrongful dismissal cases settle before trial, employers and employees are obviously deciding that it is more advantageous to attempt to settle these matters before they reach trial. What might prompt the parties to settle? Wrongful dismissal cases, like many family law cases, are often extremely emotionally charged. The employer and employee spent a period of time in a relationship, and there is often hostility on at least one side when the relationship comes to an end. Whatever the reason, many employers and employees allow their emotions to rush them into litigation, and they do not make any viable attempt to settle the matter at an earlier stage. For example, an employee who has been dismissed with notice might only feel vindicated if he or she initiates a wrongful dismissal suit against the employer, despite legal advice that there is probably not a great deal of merit to his or her claim. Similarly, some employers who do not provide their employees with reasonable notice become so offended at being sued that they defend the lawsuit instead of settling at an early stage, regardless of the fact that they are likely liable for significant damages. In such cases, as the litigation wears on and begins to take its toll on the parties in increasing legal fees, the parties become more anxious to settle and a settlement is usually reached at some stage prior to trial. In many other cases, the employee simply does not have the resources to fund litigation against the employer and may accept a settlement well below what the employee might receive if the matter were to proceed to litigation. In still other cases, an employer may recognize that the employee does not have a valid legal claim against it but may also realize that proceeding with the legal battle will cost more than it might to simply fulfil the employee's demands. The employer may also wish to avoid the adverse publicity associated with public litigation. In these cases, employers make a business decision to settle the matter, regardless of a potential lack of liability on their part. Whatever the reason, many employers and employees see the value of settling wrongful dismissal matters before or during the litigation process.

Reaching a Settlement

Preparing a settlement offer involves many of the same considerations as are involved in the preparation of a severance package.[214] In reaching a settlement,

---

214 See under the heading "Preparation of a Severance Package" earlier in this Part.

there will likely be discussion between the parties as to the settlement figure, the manner in which it will be paid (by lump sum, by instalments or in some other manner), the execution of a release, the provision of a letter of reference, and the employment insurance and income tax implications. By this stage, the employee and employer are "divorced" and the employee has indicated a willingness to proceed with litigation by virtue of having filed a statement of claim. If the employer wishes to settle, it must design a desirable settlement offer for the employee, and there is a good chance that the offer which the employee will require to settle the matter at this stage will be higher than what might have been accepted prior to the commencement of litigation. This is because, by this point, the employee is committed to litigation and has likely been informed by a lawyer that he or she has a reasonable chance of success. Where the employee might have accepted a lesser amount prior to litigation, the employee now has legal fees to recoup and has been forced to take an adversarial position. It is often more difficult and more expensive to move an employee from this position. The employee may be willing to accept a lesser settlement as the litigation drags on; however, the employer will have incurred additional legal fees by this stage, so it is worth considering settlement as early as possible. The settling of wrongful dismissal litigation is often restricted only by the parties' imaginations.

RELATED TORT CLAIMS

General

A tort is a civil wrong occasioned upon a plaintiff by a defendant, for which the defendant may be liable in damages. In the employment law context, there are a number of torts which can arise, and these may either form the basis for an independent action against the employer or accompany a wrongful dismissal suit. It is now well settled that employees are entitled to sue their employers in both contract and tort, that is, they can join one of the following tort claims with their wrongful dismissal action.[215] Those torts most often arising in the employment relationship are discussed in this section.

There are essentially two types of torts, intentional and negligent. An intentional tort involves a person deliberately inflicting some damage on another person, whether it be damage to the person or to the person's property. In the case of intentional torts, those responsible are generally required to make good the loss so inflicted. Examples of intentional torts which may arise within the employment relationship include defamation, intimidation, discrimination, inducing breach of contract, intentional infliction of nervous shock, and conspiracy. Generally, a

---

215 *Central Trust Co. v. Rafuse* (1986), 31 D.L.R. (4th) 481 (S.C.C.), vard on rehearing [1988] 1 S.C.R. 1206.

defendant will only be liable for an intentional tort if the conduct was both
voluntary and intentional.

The second type of tort is that involving negligence. Negligent torts can be
broken down into two classifications: negligence causing physical harm, and
negligence causing economic loss, such as negligent misrepresentation. A defendant will be liable for damages in negligence if the plaintiff can show that:

(a) the defendant owed a duty of care to the plaintiff;
(b) the duty of care was breached;
(c) the breach caused damage to the plaintiff; and
(d) the damage was not so remote a consequence of the breach that the
defendant should not be liable.[216]

Negligent Misrepresentation

Based on a 1993 Supreme Court of Canada decision,[217] employers must pay
particular attention to the representations they make to employment candidates
during the pre-employment process. It is possible for employees to found a claim
in negligent misrepresentation based on things told to them by the employer or
by the employer's representative, which do not prove to be true.

In the Supreme Court of Canada decision, *Queen v. Cognos Inc.*,[218] the Court
listed the required elements for a plaintiff to successfully found a claim in
negligent misrepresentation. First, there must be a duty of care based on a
"special relationship" between the representor and the representee. Secondly, the
representation in question must be untrue, inaccurate or misleading. Thirdly, the
representor must have acted negligently in making the misrepresentation.
Fourthly, the representee must have relied, in a reasonable manner, upon the
negligent misrepresentation. Fifthly, the reliance must have been detrimental to
the representee in the sense that damages resulted.

In *De Groot v. St. Boniface Hospital*,[219] Mr. De Groot was a surgeon in South
Africa applying for privileges, both general surgical and non-cardiac thoracic
surgical, at St. Boniface Hospital in Canada. While Mr. De Groot was still in
South Africa, he was told by the surgery department head that the general surgery
section had recommended granting him these privileges. However, at a later
meeting, it was decided that Mr. De Groot would not be extended general surgical
privileges, and this information was not communicated by the hospital until after
Mr. De Groot had arrived in Canada. In fact, after the decision was made, the
department head wrote to Mr. De Groot and asked him how he would like his

---

216 *Clark v. Canada* (1994), 3 C.C.E.L. (2d) 172 (F.C.T.D.).
217 *Queen v. Cognos Inc.* (1993), 99 D.L.R. (4th) 626 (S.C.C.).
218 (1993), 99 D.L.R. (4th) 626 (S.C.C.).
219 (1993), 48 C.C.E.L. 271 (Man. Q.B.), vard 3 C.C.E.L. (2d) 280 (Man. C.A.).

arrival announcement framed. Mr. De Groot sued the hospital for negligent misrepresentation.

At trial, Mr. Justice Scollin considered the five factors which must be met in a negligent misrepresentation case and found that these were present. There existed a special relationship between Mr. De Groot and the senior surgeon with whom he was dealing. Senior surgeons are looked upon as father figures, and this gives rise to a duty of care. The hospital had failed to communicate the full extent of Mr. De Groot's approved surgical privileges, and this was negligent. Further, it was held that it was reasonable for Mr. De Groot to have relied upon his communications with the hospital and that he clearly suffered damage in moving to Canada to accept the position. The hospital was found to be liable for negligent misrepresentation and was required to pay damages to Mr. De Groot.

Employers should also be aware that they may similarly be able to found a claim in negligent misrepresentation against an employee who negligently makes inaccurate representations during the pre-employment process. This might involve an employee misstating his or her qualifications, skills or education. It is likely that the most difficult aspect of proving the employer's case will be showing that the employer suffered damage as a result of the negligent misrepresentation. However, in a situation where an employee was hired for a particular purpose, and money was expended by the employer in preparing for the employee's work, the employer may very well be able to satisfy the requirements for negligent misrepresentation and successfully recover against the employee.

Intentional Infliction of Nervous Shock

Uttering false words or threats or engaging in conduct with the knowledge that it is likely to cause, and actually does cause, nervous shock and physical injury has long been recognized as actionable conduct. Not only must the defendant intentionally cause the mental suffering, there must be proof of actual harm in the form of a "visible and provable illness".[220] In the oft-cited English case, *Wilkinson v. Downton*,[221] the defendant told the plaintiff as a practical joke that her husband had been seriously injured in an accident. As a result, the plaintiff suffered nervous shock and mental and physical suffering. The Court found the defendant liable for the tort, having inflicted the nervous shock wilfully and in a manner calculated to cause harm to the plaintiff. It does not matter in a case of intentional infliction of nervous shock whether the defendant actually intended to cause the harm or not, so long as the harm was caused and was wilful. Generally speaking, it is only flagrant and extreme conduct inflicting mental suffering which will be found to have met this test.[222]

---

220 *Frame v. Smith* (1987), 42 D.L.R. (4th) 81 (S.C.C.), at p. 92.

221 [1897] 2 Q.B. 57.

222 *Rahemtulla v. Vanfed Credit Union* (1984), 4 C.C.E.L. 170 (B.C.S.C.).

Two cases, in particular, have dealt with claims for intentional infliction of nervous shock arising as a result of harassing behaviour. In the case of *Boothman v. Canada*,[223] Ms Boothman was treated in a deplorable manner by her supervisor. She was berated, yelled at, insulted, driven to tears, threatened with dismissal, threatened with bodily harm and subjected to other episodes of irrational behaviour. She issued a complaint with the Canadian Human Rights Commission and, as a result, her employer commenced an investigation into the supervisor's conduct and discovered severe impropriety. The supervisor was reprimanded and made to apologize to Ms Boothman, and a new system was put in place which avoided her having to report directly to the supervisor. However, the behaviour continued, and Ms Boothman was eventually let go. She subsequently filed a claim for, among other things, intentional infliction of nervous shock. The Court found that the supervisor had wrongfully exercised his authority to inflict mental pain and suffering and to harass, humiliate, interfere with and assault Ms Boothman. The employer was found vicariously liable for the supervisor's behaviour. As a result, Ms Boothman was awarded $5,000 for pain and suffering and $20,000 for loss of future earnings.

In *Clark v. Canada*,[224] Ms Clark was a former member of the Royal Canadian Mounted Police (the "R.C.M.P."), who alleged that sexual and other harassment by some of her male colleagues and supervisors had caused her severe stress and depression, leading to her resignation from the R.C.M.P. She brought an action for damages for wrongful dismissal, negligence and intentional infliction of nervous shock. The Court found the employer to be liable for intentional infliction of nervous shock, given that the conduct directed towards Ms Clark was extreme in nature and calculated to produce some effect of the kind which occurred. As well, Ms Clark suffered actual harm in the form of illness; her condition amounted to more than "mere anguish and fright". The tortious conduct occurred during the course of employment, occurred strictly within the confines of the working relationship and was occasioned by it. Ms Clark was awarded general damages for pain and suffering in the amount of $5,000, and special damages for lost earnings in the amount of $88,000.

Intimidation

The tort of intimidation occurs when someone coerces a person by unlawful threats into doing something or abstaining from doing something which he or she would otherwise have the right to do. In order for the claim of intimidation to be successful, the plaintiff will have to show that the defendant had intent to injure the plaintiff and there was unlawful interference with the plaintiff.

---

223 (1993), 49 C.C.E.L. 109 (F.C.T.D.).
224 *Supra*, footnote 216.

In the case of *Roehl v. Houlahan*,[225] the plaintiff was encouraged, at the age of 60, to join a company as vice-president and general manager. Houlahan was one of the other vice-presidents within the organization and resented the fact that the plaintiff had been hired from outside the company for a job which he believed he should have received. As a result, Houlahan engaged in a course of conduct, within the workplace, which was designed to result in the plaintiff's termination. As part of this conduct, Houlahan threatened to resign unless the plaintiff was removed from his position. Houlahan succeeded in securing the plaintiff's dismissal and, when Roehl sued for intimidation, the Court found in his favour. It was held that Houlahan had made unlawful threats with the intent to injure the plaintiff and had, in fact, caused such injury. Roehl was awarded $40,000 in damages for intimidation. This case was, however, overturned on appeal. A majority of the Court of Appeal held that, when Houlahan threatened to resign, he did not commit an illegal act as required for intimidation, and he did not threaten to take the middle management of the company with him.

The tort of intimidation does not often arise within the employment context, but the *Roehl* case demonstrates that it is possible to argue that intimidation has taken place. It appears as though it will be rare for the employer or other defendant to have committed the requisite unlawful act before an intimidation claim can be made out.

Conspiracy

There are two categories of civil conspiracy. The first does not require an unlawful act on the part of the conspirators, but must be based on an overt intent to cause harm to the plaintiff. In order for liability to be found within this category, it must be shown that:

(a) there was an agreement amongst conspirators;

(b) the predominant purpose of such agreement was to cause injury to the plaintiff (the means used to accomplish this purpose could be either lawful or unlawful); and

(c) actual damage was suffered by the plaintiff.

However, the second category of conspiracy focuses only on unlawful conduct. Actual intent to harm is not strictly necessary; rather, a court can rely on "constructive intent" on the part of the conspirators. This second category requires that the following elements be shown:

(a) there was an agreement amongst conspirators (although there does not have to be a predominant purpose to injure the plaintiff);

(b) the means used were unlawful;

---

225 (1988), 9 A.C.W.S. (3d) 308 (Ont. H.C.J.), supp. reasons 11 A.C.W.S. (3d) 417 (Ont. H.C.J.), revd 74 D.L.R. (4th) 562 (Ont. C.A.), leave to appeal to S.C.C. refused 79 D.L.R. (4th) vii.

(c) there was constructive intent, derived from the fact that the defendant should have known that injury to the plaintiff would follow; and

(d) actual damage was suffered by the plaintiff.[226]

In this second category, "unlawful acts" consist of conduct which amounts to an independent tort in itself or some other actionable wrong.

With respect to both types of conspiracy, the existence of an actual agreement must be shown, not in the sense of a binding contract, but rather in the sense of a joint plan or common design. The agreement may be proven by direct evidence or can be inferred from the actions of the defendants.

In the case of *Gallant v. Fenety*,[227] the plaintiffs, a husband and wife team employed at a special care home, alleged that the defendants had conspired to ensure that they were wrongfully dismissed from their employment. When the defendants had learned that Mr. Gallant had a criminal record, the Gallants were dismissed from their employment, based on what the defendants believed to be governmental standards which required that no staff person at a residential facility have such a criminal record. Following an extensive review of the law of conspiracy, Justice Russell held that the defendants had not conspired to terminate the plaintiffs' employment, but rather they were simply attempting to enforce governmental standards they believed to be appropriate. In addition, it was held that the defendants' actions did not have the predominant purpose of injuring the plaintiffs. As a result, the plaintiffs' action was dismissed.

Discrimination

For a short period of time, it was thought that the option of bringing a civil action in discrimination was available to victims of discrimination, in addition to those remedies available by virtue of human rights legislation.[228] In the case of *Seneca College of Applied Arts & Technology v. Bhadauria*,[229] the plaintiff, instead of filing a complaint under the Ontario *Human Rights Code*, sued for damages alleging discrimination on the ground of ethnic origin. The defendant applied to strike out the claim on the basis that it disclosed no cause of action. The defendant was successful at trial, but this ruling was overturned on appeal, where Madam Justice Wilson held that a cause of action for discrimination existed at common law. On further appeal to the Supreme Court of Canada, however, the trial judge's decision was restored, and the plaintiff's remedy was confined to that set out under the Ontario *Human Rights Code*, with Chief Justice Laskin noting that the civil courts do not provide an alternate route to recovery for violations of

---

226 *Canada Cement LaFarge Ltd. v. British Columbia Lightweight Aggregate Ltd.* (1983), 145 D.L.R. (3d) 385 (S.C.C.); *Chahal v. Khalsa Community School* (2000), 2 C.C.E.L. (3d) 120 (Ont. S.C.J.).

227 (2000), 4 C.C.E.L. (3d) 101 (N.B.Q.B.), affd 237 N.B.R. (2d) 133 (C.A.).

228 *Seneca College of Applied Arts & Technology v. Bhadauria* (1979), 105 D.L.R. (3d) 707 (Ont. C.A.), revd 124 D.L.R. (3d) 193 (S.C.C.).

229 *Supra.*

human rights. This reasoning was affirmed in the case of *A. (N.) v. C.F.P.L. Broadcasting Ltd.*,[230] where the plaintiff's claim, brought against her supervisor for sexual harassment, was struck out as disclosing no cause of action. The better view appears to be that no cause of action exists based on allegations of discrimination alone; however, this area of the law is not entirely free from doubt.[231]

Defamation

The law of defamation is primarily concerned with the protection of the good reputation of individuals in society. An appropriate definition of "defamation" is found in *Leenen v. Canadian Broadcasting Corp.*,[232] where Justice Cunningham for the Superior Court of Justice set out the test for defamation as follows:

> A defamatory statement is one which has a tendency to injure the reputation of the person to whom it refers, a statement which tends to lower that person in the estimation of right-thinking members of society generally and, in particular, to cause the person to be regarded with feelings of hatred, contempt, ridicule, fear, dislike or disesteem. The very essence of a defamatory statement is its tendency to injure reputation, which is to say all aspects of a person's standing in the community.[233]

To show defamation, the onus will be on the plaintiff to prove the following three elements:

(1) that the words complained of were published;
(2) that the words complained of refer to the plaintiff; and
(3) that the words complained of, in their natural and ordinary meaning, or in some pleaded extended meaning, are defamatory of the plaintiff.[234]

Based on this definition, it does not matter whether or not the defamation was intended, so long as it took place.

A statement must be published before it can be actionable in defamation, and publication takes place as soon as a statement is communicated to some third person. This can be done either verbally or in writing. Defamatory statements which are verbally communicated are referred to as "slander". While "libel" is most often associated with writing, it may also include pictures, films or conduct which implies a defamatory meaning. Publication of a defamatory statement will only be effected if the third person receiving the information heard it and/or

---

230 (1995), 9 C.C.E.L. (2d) 56 (Ont. Ct. (Gen. Div.)).
231 But see also *Lehman v. Davis* (1993), 1 C.C.E.L. (2d) 15 (Ont. Ct. (Gen. Div.)), and *Alpaerts v. Obront* (1993), 46 C.C.E.L. 218 (Ont. Ct. (Gen. Div.)), as examples of cases where wrongful dismissal actions were allowed to proceed despite the fact that the conduct at the heart of the claim was discriminatory conduct.
232 (2000), 48 O.R. (3d) 656 (S.C.J.), affd 54 O.R. (3d) 612 (C.A.).
233 *Supra*, at para. 40 (Ont. S.C.J.).
234 *Supra*, at para. 41 (Ont. S.C.J.).

understood it. It is the fact of the publication which makes the defamation actionable.

In the case of a libellous statement, it will not be necessary for the plaintiff to demonstrate that actual damage was suffered. It is presumed that damage will occur by virtue of the permanence of the written material and the possibility of reproduction and circulation. On the other hand, slanderous statements are not actionable *per se*, and an action will only lie if special damages arising from the slander can be shown. However, in circumstances where a person is slandered in relation to his or her business, trade, profession, occupation or employment activity, such proof is unnecessary.[235] Slander of such a nature is clearly calculated to cause pecuniary damage to the subject of the statement. In claiming aggravated or punitive damages, a plaintiff may rely on defamatory statements made by the defendant.[236] A tort claim in defamation can arise by virtue of statements made by a defendant upon or after the termination of an employee.

An employer or individual who is sued for defamation may be entitled to a number of defences to the claim. First, the defendant may avoid liability in defamation if it can be shown that the defamation was justified because it was true. Secondly, an absolute privilege may attach to statements made in circumstances where society's interests are better served by the fullest dissemination of information, regardless of accuracy and motive. Such an absolute privilege arises in relation to any statements made in the course of a proceeding of Parliament or in any judicial or quasi-judicial proceeding. Other statements may be subject to a qualified privilege if they were made pursuant to some moral, social or legal duty to communicate the information,[237] as in the case of the provision of an employment reference. As long as the information was provided in good faith, and the defendant had an honest belief in the truth of the statements and did not make the statements with malicious intent, the statements will be protected by qualified privilege.[238] Defendants are also entitled to make fair comments on matters of public concern. If such comments are given in the form of a personal opinion, then they will be protected, even if the opinion is not correct, so long as the information on which the opinion is based is correct. Also, the defendant in a defamation action may be entitled to a reduction in liability if it can be shown that a written apology or retraction was given, that the plaintiff already had a bad reputation or that the defendant was provoked.

Where a corporate employer was bankrupt but a director of the corporation defamed an employee by alleging criminal dishonesty before, during and after

---

235 *Ross v. Lamport* (1956), 2 D.L.R. (2d) 225 (S.C.C.); *Spong v. Westpress Publications Ltd.* (1982), 2 C.C.E.L. 228 (B.C.S.C.).

236 *Carson v. William W. Creighton Centre* (1990), 31 C.C.E.L. 31 (Ont. Dist. Ct.).

237 *Adam v. Ward*, [1917] A.C. 309 (H.L.), at p. 334.

238 *Korach v. Moore* (1991), 76 D.L.R. (4th) 506 (Ont. C.A.), leave to appeal to S.C.C. refused 79 D.L.R. (4th) vii; *Ahmad v. Ontario Hydro* (1993), 1 C.C.E.L. (2d) 292 (Ont. Ct. (Gen. Div.)), affd 72 A.C.W.S. (3d) 960 (Ont. C.A.); *Lipczynska-Kochany v. Gillham* (2001), 14 C.C.E.L. (3d) 304 (Ont. S.C.J.).

the dismissal, the director was personally liable for $25,000 in damages, in particular because there had been no retraction and no apology.[239] In another case,[240] the defendant employer issued a press release stating that the plaintiff employee had been reassigned due to difficulties completing his work. The defence of qualified privilege failed because the employer did not have a genuine belief in the statements made and because the Court found malice on the part of the defendant. The plaintiff was awarded $40,000 in damages for the harm to his reputation occasioned by the libel of the employer. In the case of *Stadler v. Terrace Corp. (Construction) Ltd.*,[241] an employer announced to other employees that a former employee was "a no good bum", "incompetent" and "ripped us off for hundreds of thousands of dollars". As a result, the Court awarded the employee $9,000 in damages for defamation. It may also be defamatory for an employer to put on an employment insurance ROE form as cause for discharge anything which constitutes just cause for dismissal if the employer has no reasonable basis for the opinion.

Since the decision in *Wallace v. United Grain Growers Ltd.*,[242] courts are reluctant to award punitive damages other than in cases where there exists an actionable wrong as distinct from the dismissal itself. Such was the case in *Martin v. International Maple Leaf Springs Water Corp.*,[243] where the president of the defendant company made allegations of dishonesty and abuse of alcohol against the plaintiff, leading to the plaintiff's dismissal. Because the accusations against the plaintiff amounted to the actionable wrong of slander, the plaintiff was awarded $35,000 in punitive damages. Since *Wallace*, however, courts have also seen defamatory statements as simply being evidence of bad faith, meriting an extension of the reasonable notice period.[244]

Inducing Breach of Contract

An employee who has been dismissed and who believes that a particular individual is responsible for the breach of his or her employment contract may have a cause of action in tort against that person for inducing breach of contract. Similarly, it is also possible for an employer to bring such a claim against another company or individual if it is the case that an employee was approached by that company or individual and induced to breach his or her employment contract.[245] An employee who has suffered a contract breach may bring a claim for inducing breach of contract against either the particular employee who intentionally and

---

239 *Havekes v. Listowel Feed Mill Ltd.* (1989), 17 A.C.W.S. (3d) 1076 (Ont. H.C.J.).
240 *Ahmad v. Ontario Hydro*, *supra*, footnote 238.
241 (1983), 41 A.R. 587 (Q.B.).
242 (1997), 152 D.L.R. (4th) 1 (S.C.C.).
243 (1998), 38 C.C.E.L. (2d) 128 (B.C.S.C.).
244 See, for example, *Musgrave v. Levesque Securities Inc.* (2000), 50 C.C.E.L. (2d) 59 (N.S.S.C.).
245 *Neal Bros. v. Wright*, [1923] 4 D.L.R. 998 (Man. C.A.).

knowingly sabotaged the employment relationship or against any third party who may have committed the same tort but who is outside of the employment relationship altogether.

To succeed in an action for inducing breach of contract, the plaintiff (whether employer or employee) will have to be able to prove that:

(a) a valid contract existed as between the parties;
(b) the defendant knew of the contract in existence between the parties;
(c) the defendant intended to wrongfully procure a breach of the contract;
(d) such a breach was, in fact, procured; and
(e) the plaintiff suffered damage as a result of the contract breach.[246]

Courts require the plaintiff to show that the defendant acted in bad faith or fraudulently in inducing the contract breach, and thus an individual defendant will have a valid defence against this claim if it can be shown that he or she acted *bona fide*, in the best interests of the company and within the authority of his or her position within the company.[247] Any plaintiff considering suing a fellow employee (or officer or director of the company) should first examine his or her employment agreement (or any other documentation he or she may have signed) to ensure that such an action is not prohibited by the terms of the agreement.

An action can also be commenced against a third party for inducing breach of contract if this third party has intentionally interfered with the employment relationship. While it is not necessary for the employee to show that the third party acted with malice (that is, that he or she intended to harm the employee), the employee will be required to show that the contract breach was induced knowingly and intentionally.[248] A rather extreme example might find an employer's client threatening to withdraw its business unless all employees of the employer refrain from shopping at the client's competitors. If a particular employee was dismissed for doing so, he or she might be able to make an argument that the client induced the breach of the employee's contract with the employer.

Any plaintiff considering suing in tort for inducing breach of contract should be aware that the damages which the plaintiff may be entitled to recover are not meant to be those which resulted from the breach of the contract. For this, the plaintiff should sue the party responsible for the actual breach of contract or wrongful dismissal. Rather, the successful plaintiff will be entitled to damages "at large" for the tort of inducing breach of contract. Such damages are based on impression, where the plaintiff is compensated for the invasion of the contractual

---

246 *Butler v. Dimitrieff* (1991), 38 C.C.E.L. 139 (Ont. Ct. (Gen. Div.)), revd 49 A.C.W.S. (3d) 1177 (Ont. C.A.). This case was overturned on appeal, on the basis that the facts did not support a finding of liability for inducing breach of contract. See also *McFadden v. 481782 Ontario Ltd.* (1984), 5 C.C.E.L. 83 (Ont. H.C.J.).
247 *Said v. Butt*, [1920] 3 K.B. 497.
248 *Posluns v. Toronto Stock Exchange* (1964), 46 D.L.R. (2d) 210 (Ont. H.C.J.), affd 53 D.L.R. (2d) 193 (Ont. C.A.), affd [1968] S.C.R. 330.

right and is not to be put to the strict proof of specific damage. Although courts have allowed recovery for the tort of inducing breach of contract only sparingly, where a plaintiff has also sued and recovered damages for the actual contract breach, such awards have been made.[249] It now appears settled that damages which can be recovered from a party found to have induced the breach of an employment contract can be in excess of those recoverable for the actual contract breach.[250] Such was the case, for example, in *Martin v. International Maple Leaf Springs Water Corp.*,[251] where damages in the amount of $25,000 were assessed against the president of the defendant company, who was found to have been responsible for having induced the wrongful dismissal of the plaintiff.

Retaliatory and Bad Faith Discharge

Retaliatory and bad faith discharge are claims which are currently recognized in the United States and which require proof that the dismissal was unlawful, against public policy or made in bad faith. While it was thought for some time that this sort of a claim might similarly be available to dismissed employees in Canada, it now appears that, at least for the time being, Canada's highest court has made clear its position on this issue.

In *Wallace v. United Grain Growers Ltd.*,[252] one of the issues on which the Supreme Court of Canada was asked to rule was whether Mr. Wallace was entitled to sue for damages for "bad faith discharge". When it was first argued that this might mean that an employer could not dismiss an employee without legitimate business reasons, this was quickly dismissed by the Court. It was confirmed that the law has long recognized the mutual right of both employers and employees to terminate an employment contract at any time provided there are no express provisions in the contract to the contrary. The Court went on to say that to allow for a new tort of bad faith discharge would constitute a "radical shift in the law" and was a step better left to be taken by the legislatures. Therefore, for now anyway, it appears that this is one claim which is not open to be made in Canadian courts.

PRACTICAL ADVICE REGARDING THE DISMISSAL

When conducting dismissals, employers are well-advised to approach the matter as if the employee being dismissed were their best friend. Stories continuously

---

249 See *Vale v. ILWU, Local 508*, [1979] 5 W.W.R. 231 (B.C.C.A.).

250 *Posluns v. Toronto Stock Exchange, supra*, footnote 248; *Ahmad v. Ontario Hydro* (1993), 1 C.C.E.L. (2d) 292 (Ont. Ct. (Gen. Div.)), affd 72 A.C.W.S. (3d) 960 (Ont. C.A.). But see also *Kepic v. Tecumseh Road Builders* (1987), 18 C.C.E.L. 218 (Ont. C.A.), wherein the Court of Appeal stated that the measure of damages for both the tort of inducing breach of contract and the actual contract breach should be the same.

251 (1998), 38 C.C.E.L. (2d) 128 (B.C.S.C.).

252 (1997), 152 D.L.R. (4th) 1 (S.C.C.).

circulate, in legal and human resources circles, about employers who have han-dled dismissals with very little sensitivity or thoughtfulness. If proper etiquette were the only concern, then a discussion of how to handle the dismissal meeting would probably be an inappropriate topic for this book. However, courts have often expressed displeasure with the manner in which employees have been dismissed and, if a dismissal has been handled in a way which appears high-handed or negatively impacts the employee's job search, or if the employer's conduct is so severe that it is actionable in its own right, then the employer might be liable for an extended notice period or an award of punitive or aggravated damages, due to its not having handled the dismissal with care. By paying attention to a few simple details, employers can conduct all dismissal meetings in a manner which minimizes resentment on the part of departing employees and, more importantly, minimizes legal liability.

It is preferable to have the employee's manager or supervisor conduct the dismissal meeting. Although this individual might be inclined to push this respon-sibility onto someone else in an effort to avoid the unpleasantness of having to "break the bad news", such manoeuvres do not go unnoticed by departing employ-ees, who often question why the more appropriate person "didn't have the guts" to conduct the interview. Sometimes, however, the employee's manager may be ill-equipped to handle a dismissal in a delicate manner. For this reason, it may be advisable to have one person within the firm who can be responsible for the conduct of interviews, who can participate in such interviews where appropriate and who can guide the manager through this difficult task.

It is always wise to have a second person present during the interview to act as a witness. Allegations of bad faith and unfair dealing very often arise out of the dismissal meeting. Since the Supreme Court of Canada decision in *Wallace v. United Grain Growers Ltd.*,[253] if a court agrees that an employer handled a dismissal badly, then the employee's entitlement to reasonable notice can be extended. In addition, if the employer, at the time of dismissal, engaged in conduct which constituted a separate actionable wrong, this can entitle the employee to an additional award of aggravated or punitive damages. The benefit of having two people present at the dismissal meeting is that it will not simply be up to a trial judge to assess the credibility of one person's word over another. The employer will have the advantage of an additional corroborative witness if there are allegations of culpable conduct.

Once the appropriate people have been selected to conduct the interview, a date and time should be chosen. The interview should be conducted as soon as possible after the decision has been made, to avoid word leaking out and the employee learning the news from someone indirectly. Naturally, such decisions should be kept strictly confidential so as to avoid the possibility of this happening. With regard to the date and time, it is recommended that interviews be conducted

---

253 *Supra.*

midday, early or midweek. Dismissal meetings may be conducted at the end of the day if the employer believes it may be advisable to ensure that the employee heads home to a full house. However, dismissal meetings conducted late in the day on a Friday are to be avoided in almost all cases. Although it may seem easier for an employer to conduct the interview just before a weekend, so that the employee will have an opportunity to "cool off", in fact, the result is typically the exact opposite. During the weekend, the employee rarely has access to those individuals whom he or she might contact to discuss the implications of the announcement, such as a lawyer, a relocation counsellor, a banking official or a financial planner. Take, for example, the long service employee who was called in at 5:00 p.m. on a Friday and provided with a very generous severance offer in the circumstances. Unfortunately, the employee was not aware of the employer's right to dismiss with pay in lieu of reasonable notice and could not reach his lawyer until Monday morning. By Monday, the employee had taken the entire weekend to stew about how poorly and unfairly he had been treated and, despite his lawyer's reassurances that the severance package was fair, the conclusion of the employment relationship left the employee full of resentment. This resentment could and should have been avoided.

The employer should next choose the location for the interview. Some employers wish to maintain as neutral a ground as possible and will arrange for the dismissal meeting to be held off site, perhaps in a hotel room. This is often unnerving for the employee and provides poor "optics". The person conducting the interview may wish to choose a place where he or she can leave once the interview is over, to avoid having to ask the employee to leave the office at the conclusion of the interview. Many dismissal meetings are conducted in the employee's own office. Such a meeting should never be conducted in the employee's office if the office is not private or if the employee can be seen by other staff members. An alternative is to conduct the interview in a neutral boardroom within the office, allowing the employee sufficient time to compose himself or herself before having to re-enter the workplace. This is another reason why midday meetings are often preferable. When the employee leaves the meeting, many of the other staff members will be on their lunch break, allowing the employee to exit the workplace gracefully.

Although dismissal meetings should be handled with sensitivity, they should also be short and to the point. There is generally no need for them to last longer than five to 10 minutes. The employer should begin the meeting by indicating that the company has reached a non-negotiable decision, followed by a brief but descriptive discussion of the employee's severance package. One particular aspect of the dismissal meeting which is often overlooked, but which is of great importance to the departing employee in a without cause dismissal circumstance, is the employer taking the opportunity to thank the employee for his or her service with the company. It might also be helpful to dispel any fear the employee may have that he or she was in some way responsible for the dismissal, if it is a without cause dismissal. This is particularly relevant in downsizing or redundancy situations.

Some minor inquiries into the employee's background can avoid any major pitfalls in the timing of the dismissal meeting. For instance, it is wise and often easy to ensure that the meeting is not being conducted on the employee's birthday or anniversary or another important day in the person's life. If the employer is aware that the employee has taken any time off for a significant death in the family, it may also be wise to ensure that the date chosen is not the anniversary of such a life event. This day will already be extremely difficult for the employee, and there is no reason to compound the problem if this can be avoided. Employers should also make discreet inquiries into the employee's personal calendar for that evening or the immediate future. Conducting the meeting on the day of a family reunion will be especially unpleasant for the employee. However, a similarly unpleasant incident for the employer occurred in a dismissal where the authors were retained after the fact. In that case, the employee had previously scheduled a dinner party at his home on the night of his dismissal and had invited most of the company's major clients. This created an awkward circumstance which could have been avoided had certain inquiries been made.

The employer should strive to provide assistance to the employee which will help to minimize or avoid embarrassment and humiliation. For example, if the employer is in a position to provide the employee with the company car which he or she has been using or to allow a buyout or assumption of the lease, this will avoid the possibility that the employee will have to explain immediately to neighbours and family members why the car has disappeared. Employers should be quick to explain whether benefits will be continued because this will often be of immediate concern to the employee's spouse and children. The employee may also be very concerned about how the dismissal will be announced to colleagues and business contacts. The employer can use the dismissal meeting to discuss with the employee the preferable wording for such an announcement.

The use of relocation counsellors has proven to be of great assistance to both employers and employees, and has even come to be expected by many employees. Inviting the counsellor to come on site for the dismissal meeting, introducing the counsellor to the employee at the conclusion of the meeting, and encouraging the employee to discuss the matter with the counsellor may help the employee to deal with the immediate trauma of the dismissal. The relocation counsellor might even wish to take the employee out to lunch (after a midday dismissal meeting) to assist him or her in overcoming the initial shock and to allow the employee to vent frustration in a controlled environment. The counsellor can act as a liaison between the employee and the company in tying up some of the loose ends which remain after the dismissal meeting, such as the handing over of keys and security badges and the cleaning out of the employee's desk and office. If the employer has any security concerns with respect to leaving the employee alone to collect his or her belongings, the presence of a relocation counsellor is likely to instill far less resentment than might the presence of the employee's superior or, even worse, a security guard. An employer who does not assist the employee in avoiding embarrassment in this process runs the risk of incurring the wrath of a trial judge who is sympathetic to the dismissed employee[254] and can subject the employer to additional *Wallace* damages.

Relocation counsellors are not always welcomed with open arms by dismissed employees. Many employees have an understandable tendency to be very shaken by the news of dismissal, and those who believe that they have been treated badly or unfairly are less likely to trust anyone appointed by the employer to assist them at this time. Recognizing that this might be the case, some employers offer the employee the option of seeking out his or her own relocation assistance in lieu of taking advantage of the assistance provided. This approach is not generally recommended because, with the multitude of immediate issues to be dealt with at the time of termination, the employee does not need to make yet another decision. Instead, it is recommended that the employer appoint a counsellor, while at the same time be prepared to accommodate a change in counsellors if valid reasons for such a change are made out by the former employee.

The need for a dismissal meeting in the case of an employee who is being dismissed is obvious. It is not always obvious that it might also be helpful to establish a practice of conducting exit interviews for all employees, even those who resign voluntarily. The purpose of the exit interview is to communicate information. In the case of a dismissed employee, the employer will want to communicate the terms of the severance package and/or the reasons for dismissal. In the case of a voluntary resignation, the employer may inquire as to the reasons why the employee is leaving and thereby gain some valuable insight into the employee's impressions of the company. All such meetings, regardless of whether they result from dismissals or resignations, should be documented at their conclusion and the documentation kept in the employee's personnel file.

In the end, the dismissal meeting should be conducted in a professional and business-like fashion. The employee should be treated with care, in a way which respects his or her dignity. This is likely to be the first time in the employee's life that he or she is experiencing this type of eventuality and, in most instances, it has been brought on through no fault of the employee. Recognizing this helps employers to anticipate the types of emotions that the employee will be feeling and allows employers to gauge their comments with this in mind. Employers are wise to avoid any protracted debate about the employee's abilities or the merits of the dismissal at this stage, since the decision has been made and will not be reversed. The focus should be on providing the employee with assistance in accepting the decision and making plans for the future.

---

254 In the case of *Speck v. Greater Niagara General Hospital* (1983), 2 D.L.R. (4th) 84 (Ont. H.C.J.), appeal abandoned and cross-appeal dismissed 19 D.L.R. (4th) 576 (Ont. C.A.), the Court looked with disfavour on the fact that the employee was forced to pack up her belongings into a green garbage bag and carry them out of the hospital in the presence of all of her co-workers.

Conclusion

Throughout this book, the natural parallel between employment relationships and personal relationships has been drawn as the various stages of the employment relationship have been examined. These included "courting" (the search for employees), "engagement" (hiring employees), "marriage" (maintaining relationships with employees), "separation" (dealing with employee problems) and "divorce" (employee dismissals). However, it must be emphasized that, while there are similarities, employment relationships are *not* personal relationships and cannot always be treated as such. These relationships are different, and an overview of their differences will serve to remind employers that ultimately their relationships with their employees are unique.

One of the most significant differences between employment relationships and personal relationships is the difference in purpose. Personal relationships are most often entered into for the simple purpose of creating and maintaining a relationship. There are secondary reasons, such as companionship, support, shared interests, and often procreation, but these all really go towards achieving the greater purpose. The parties' energies are expended in working at the relationship and trying to keep it together in the face of adversity. Employment relationships, on the other hand, are entered into for any number of different reasons, but one would likely be hard-pressed to find a company with a mission statement based on maintaining relationships with its employees. Perhaps it is for this reason that employment relationships appear to have lost much of their permanency over the years. As companies struggle with increased competition and budgetary constraints, there is often less time left to deal with employee problems. The contents of this book are intended to assist employers in becoming more aware of their rights and obligations. This may have some positive effect on their relationships with employees and, although it may not affect the length of employment relationships, it may improve the parties' satisfaction with the relationships into which they enter.

Typically, when personal relationships are entered into, it is with a view (perhaps idealistic) that they will last forever. Increasingly, employees are learning that such an expectation in an employment relationship may be unrealistic. It is likely that, at least once during their lifetime, individuals will experience each of the stages of the employment relationship discussed in this book. Many may experience them several times. This is changing employees' attitudes in the workplace and has resulted in more and more employees becoming aware of their rights. Employers need to be well-informed of their obligations in the face of such employee awareness.

Employment relationships also differ from personal relationships in that individuals do not necessarily enter into employment relationships with the best interests of the company in mind. Unlike personal relationships, where two people commit themselves to working as a team, the reality in employment relationships is that the parties may have their own agendas which they seek to advance. Circumstances which arise and force the parties to choose between their respective interests are often catalysts for a "separation" or even a "divorce" in an employment relationship. Where the parties' interests are no longer compatible, fewer attempts to work out these differences are made than might be the case in a personal relationship. For example, an employee may be interested in the employment relationship as a means by which to support his or her family, while an employer may only be concerned with profit. These interests may be compatible for a period of time, until the employer decides that the employee will no longer receive discretionary bonuses. This may improve the company's bottom line but inherently conflicts with the employee's interest in maintaining a certain income. In a personal relationship, the parties may have incentive for working through this difference, whereas in the employment relationship, it is likely that such incompatibility will simply bring the relationship to an end. Knowing in advance that these types of situations will arise helps employers to prepare when making decisions within the organization which will have a significant impact on employees.

There are other obvious differences between employment relationships and personal relationships, such as the fact that employment relationships are platonic and do not involve children. This is not meant to be a facetious observation, but rather helps to put the employment relationship in perspective. Marriage is often referred to as an "institution" because of the important role that it and other similar personal relationships play in our society. This should not demean the importance of our employment relationships. Work is fulfilling and self-defining, and is one of the most important facets of people's lives. Appreciating the role that employment plays in society helps employers recognize how best to deal with employees who rely on their work for self-esteem, self-confidence and, sometimes, pure survival. However, employers should also remember that, for many individuals, employment is not necessarily the most important thing in life. Recognizing this, and recognizing that many employees do not wish to be "married" to their jobs, should serve to enlighten employers as to what expectations are realistic and how best to achieve corporate goals while maintaining successful employment relationships.

Appendix A

Tables

TABLE 1
PAID PUBLIC HOLIDAYS

	Fed.	Alta.	B.C.	Man.	N.B.	Nfld.	N.S.	Ont.	P.E.I.	Que.	Sask.	Nunavut	N.W.T.	Yukon
New Year's Day (January 1st)	X	X	X	X	X	X	X	X	X	X	X	X	X	X
3rd Monday in February		X[5]												
Good Friday	X	X	X	X	X	X	X	X	X	X[8]	X	X	X	X
Victoria Day	X	X	X	X				X		X[2]	X	X	X	X
St. Jean Baptiste Day (June 24th)										X				
Canada Day (July 1st)	X	X	X	X	X	X[1]	X	X	X	X	X	X	X	X
1st Monday in August			X[7]		X[7]			X[3]			X[7]	X		
3rd Monday in August													X[6]	
Labour Day	X	X	X	X	X	X	X	X	X	X[9]	X	X	X	X
Thanksgiving Day	X	X	X	X				X		X[10]	X	X	X	X
Remembrance Day (November 11th)	X	X	X	X[11]		X	X[4]				X	X	X	X
Christmas Day (December 25th)	X	X	X	X	X	X	X	X	X	X	X	X	X	X
Boxing Day (December 26th)	X							X						
National Aboriginal Day (June 21st)													X	

[1] Referred to as "Memorial Day".

[2] Referred to as "Dollard Day".

[3] In Ontario, the August Civic Holiday (referred to as "Simcoe Day") is a customary public holiday but is not set out in the legislation.

[4] In Nova Scotia, employers are only required to provide those employees who work on Remembrance Day with a paid holiday at another time.

[5] Referred to as "Family Day".

[6] Referred to as "Discovery Day".

[7] Referred to as "British Columbia Day", "New Brunswick Day" and "Saskatchewan Day" in each of the respective provinces.

[8] Good Friday or Easter Monday, at the option of the employer, or Easter Sunday for employees working in a commercial establishment that is ordinarily open on Sundays but to which the public cannot be admitted on Easter Sunday.

[9] First Monday in September.

[10] Second Monday in October.

[11] In Manitoba, employees who work on Remembrance Day must be paid the same as for a general holiday. Employees who do not work on this day do not have to be paid.

TABLE 2
MINIMUM WAGE AS OF APRIL 2003

	Regular	Other
Federal	Refer to provincial minimum wages	
Alberta	$5.90	
British Columbia	$8.00	
Manitoba	$6.75	
New Brunswick	$6.00	
Newfoundland and Labrador	$6.00	
Nova Scotia	$6.00[1]	Inexperienced: $5.35
Ontario	$6.85	Student under 18 working < 28 hours: $6.40 Student employed during school holiday: $6.40 Hunting or fishing guide < 5 consecutive hours: $34.25 Homeworker: $7.54 Serving liquor: $5.95
Prince Edward Island	$6.25[2]	
Quebec	$7.30	With gratuities: $6.25
Saskatchewan	$6.65	
Northwest Territories	If living in community: $6.50 If not living in community: $7.00	Under 16: If living in community: $6.00 If not living in community: $6.50
Yukon	$7.20	
Nunavut	$8.50	

[1] On October 1, 2003, the wage will rise to $6.25, and in April 2004, it will rise to $6.50.
[2] On January 1, 2004, the wage will rise to $6.25, and on January 1, 2005, it will rise to $6.80.

TABLE 3
HOURS OF WORK

	Overtime Hours	Maximum Daily Hours	Maximum Weekly Hours	Daily Minimum Rest/Eating Period	Overtime Rates
Federal	over 8 hrs./day or 40 hrs./wk.		48 hrs.		1.5 × regular wages
Alberta	over 8 hrs./day or 44 hrs./wk.	12 hrs.		30 min. ea. 5 hrs.	1.5 × regular wages
British Columbia	over 8 hrs./day or 40 hrs./wk.	16 hrs. in any 24 hrs.		30 min. ea. 5 hrs.	1.5 × regular wages[1]
Manitoba	over 8 hrs./day or 40 hrs./wk.		40 hrs.	30 min. ea. 5 hrs.	1.5 × regular wages
New Brunswick	no limit[4]	no limit[4]	no limit[4]	30 min. ea. 5 hrs.	1.5 × minimum wage[2]
Newfoundland and Labrador	over 40 hrs./wk.	16 hrs. in any 24 hrs.		1 hr. ea. 5 hrs.	1.5 × regular wages[2]
Nova Scotia	over 48 hrs./wk.				1.5 × minimum wage
Ontario	over 44 hrs./wk.	13 hrs.	48 hrs.[3]	30 min. ea. 5 hrs.	1.5 × regular wages
Prince Edward Island	over 48 hrs./wk.			30 min. ea. 5 hrs.	1.5 × regular wages
Quebec	over 40 hrs./wk.			30 min. ea. 5 hrs.	1.5 × regular wages
Saskatchewan	over 8 hrs./day or 40 hrs./wk.	16 hrs. in any 24 hrs.	44 hrs.	For a 6+ hr. shift:[3] 30 min. ea. 5 hrs.	1.5 × regular wages
Northwest Territories and Nunavut	over 8 hrs./day or 40 hrs./wk.	10 hrs.	60 hrs.	30 min. ea. 5 hrs.	1.5 × regular wages
Yukon	over 8 hrs./day or 40 hrs./wk.	16 hrs. in any 24 hrs.		30 min. ea. 5 hrs. For a 10+ hr. shift: 30 min. ea. 6 hrs.	1.5 × regular wages

[1] An employee will receive 2 × regular wages for all hours worked in excess of 11 per day or 48 per week.

[2] In New Brunswick, the actual overtime rate is set out as a dollar figure which is equivalent to 1.5 × minimum wage.

[3] An employer may permit an employee to work up to a specified number of hours in excess of 48 hours per week if the employee agrees to work those hours and the employee will not work more than 60 hours or such other number of hours as are prescribed in a work week.

[4] This does not apply to "children", as defined.

TABLE 4
INDIVIDUAL STATUTORY NOTICE PERIODS

AFTER:	Fed.	Alta.	B.C.	Man.	N.B.	Nfld.	N.S.	Ont.	P.E.I.	Que.	Sask.	N.W.T.	Nunavut	Yukon
1 Month[1]	Nil	Nil	Nil	1 pay period	Nil	1 wk.	Nil	Nil	Nil	Nil	Nil	Nil	Nil	Nil
3 Months[2]	2 wks.	1 wk.	1 wk.	1 pay period	Nil	1 wk.	1 wk.	1 wk.	Nil	1 wk.	1 wk.	2 wks.	2 wks.	Nil
6 Months	2 wks.	1 wk.	1 wk.	1 pay period	2 wks.	1 wk.	1 wk.	1 wk.	2 wks.	1 wk.	1 wk.	2 wks.	2 wks.	1 wk.
1 Year	2 wks.	1 wk.	2 wks.	1 pay period	2 wks.	1 wk.	1 wk.	2 wks.	2 wks.	2 wks.	2 wks.	2 wks.	2 wks.	2 wks.
2 Years	2 wks.	2 wks.	2 wks.	1 pay period	2 wks.	2 wks.	2 wks.	2 wks.	2 wks.	2 wks.	2 wks.	2 wks.	2 wks.	2 wks.
3 Years	2 wks.	2 wks.	3 wks.	1 pay period	2 wks.	2 wks.	2 wks.	3 wks.	2 wks.	2 wks.	4 wks.	3 wks.	3 wks.	3 wks.
4 Years	2 wks.	4 wks.	4 wks.	1 pay period	4 wks.	2 wks.	2 wks.	4 wks.	2 wks.	2 wks.	4 wks.	4 wks.	4 wks.	4 wks.
5 Years	2 wks.	4 wks.	5 wks.	1 pay period	4 wks.	2 wks.	4 wks.	5 wks.	4 wks.	4 wks.	6 wks.	5 wks.	5 wks.	5 wks.
6 Years	2 wks.	5 wks.	6 wks.	1 pay period	4 wks.	2 wks.	4 wks.	6 wks.	4 wks.	4 wks.	6 wks.	6 wks.	6 wks.	6 wks.
7 Years	2 wks.	5 wks.	7 wks.	1 pay period	4 wks.	2 wks.	4 wks.	7 wks.	4 wks.	4 wks.	6 wks.	7 wks.	7 wks.	7 wks.
8 Years	2 wks.	6 wks.	8 wks.	1 pay period	4 wks.	2 wks.	4 wks.	8 wks.	4 wks.	4 wks.	6 wks.	8 wks.	8 wks.	8 wks.
9 Years	2 wks.	6 wks.	8 wks.	1 pay period	4 wks.	2 wks.	4 wks.	8 wks.	4 wks.	4 wks.	6 wks.	8 wks.	8 wks.	8 wks.
10 Years	2 wks.	8 wks.	8 wks.	1 pay period	4 wks.	2 wks.	8 wks.	8 wks.	4 wks.	8 wks.	8 wks.	8 wks.	8 wks.	8 wks.

[1] 30 days in Manitoba.
[2] 90 days in the Northwest Territories and Nunavut.

TABLE 5
NOTICE PERIODS FOR MASS TERMINATION

	Number of Employees											
	10+		11+		25+		50+		100+		101+	
	Minister	Employee	Minister	Employee	Minister	Employee	Minister	Employee	Minister	Employee	Minister	Employee
Federal[1]		*		*		*	16 wks.	16 wks.	16 wks.	16 wks.	16 wks.	16 wks.
Alberta[1]		*		*		*	4 wks.	*	4 wks.	*	4 wks.	*
British Columbia[2]		*		*		*	8 wks.	8 wks.	8 wks.	8 wks.	12 wks.	12 wks.
Manitoba[1]		*		*		*	10 wks.	10 wks.	10 wks.	10 wks.	14 wks.	14 wks.
New Brunswick[3]		*	6 wks.	6 wks.	6 wks.	6 wks.	6 wks.	6 wks.	6 wks.	6 wks.	6 wks.	6 wks.
Newfoundland and Labrador[1]		*		*		*	8 wks.	8 wks.	8 wks.	8 wks.	8 wks.	8 wks.
Nova Scotia[4]	8 wks.	8 wks.	8 wks.	8 wks.	8 wks.	8 wks.	8 wks.	8 wks.	12 wks.	12 wks.	12 wks.	12 wks.
Ontario[1 and 5]		*		*		*	8 wks.	8 wks.	8 wks.	8 wks.	8 wks.	8 wks.
Prince Edward Island		*		*		*		*		*		*
Quebec[6]	2 mos.	*	2 mos.	*	2 mos.	*	2 mos.	*	3 mos.	*	3 mos.	*
Saskatchewan[4]	4 wks.	4 wks.	4 wks.	4 wks.	4 wks.	4 wks.	8 wks.	8 wks.	12 wks.	12 wks.	12 wks.	12 wks.
Northwest Territories[7]		*		*	4 wks.	*	8 wks.	*	12 wks.	*	12 wks.	*
Nunavut		*		*	4 wks.	*	8 wks.	*	12 wks.	*	12 wks.	*
Yukon[7]		*		*	4 wks.	*	8 wks.	*	12 wks.	*	12 wks.	*

Footnotes on next page

TABLE 5 — *Continued*

	Number of Employees									
	200+		300+		301+		400+		500+	
	Minister	Employee	Minister	Employee	Minister	Employee	Minister	Employee	Minister	Employee
Federal[1]	16 wks.	16 wks.	16 wks.	16 wks.	16 wks.	16 wks.	16 wks.	16 wks.	16 wks.	16 wks.
Alberta[1]	4 wks.	*	4 wks.	*	4 wks.	*	4 wks.	*	4 wks.	*
British Columbia[2]	12 wks.	12 wks.	12 wks.	12 wks.	16 wks.	16 wks.	16 wks.	16 wks.	16 wks.	16 wks.
Manitoba[1]	14 wks.	14 wks.	18 wks.	18 wks.	18 wks.	18 wks.	18 wks.	18 wks.	18 wks.	18 wks.
New Brunswick[3]	6 wks.	6 wks.	6 wks.	6 wks.	6 wks.	6 wks.	6 wks.	6 wks.	6 wks.	6 wks.
Newfoundland[1]	12 wks.	12 wks.	12 wks.	12 wks.	12 wks.	12 wks.	12 wks.	12 wks.	16 wks.	16 wks.
Nova Scotia[4]	12 wks.	12 wks.	16 wks.	16 wks.	16 wks.	16 wks.	16 wks.	16 wks.	16 wks.	16 wks.
Ontario[1 and 5]	12 wks.	12 wks.	12 wks.	12 wks.	12 wks.	12 wks.	12 wks.	12 wks.	16 wks.	16 wks.
Prince Edward Island		*		*		*		*		*
Quebec[6]	3 mos.	*	4 mos.	*	4 mos.	*	4 mos.	*	4 mos.	*
Saskatchewan	12 wks.	12 wks.	12 wks.	12 wks.	12 wks.	12 wks.	12 wks.	12 wks.	12 wks.	12 wks.
Northwest Territories[7]	12 wks.	*	16 wks.	*	16 wks.	*	16 wks.	*	16 wks.	*
Nunavut	12 wks.	*	16 wks.	*	16 wks.	*	16 wks.	*	16 wks.	*
Yukon[7]	12 wks.	*	16 wks.	*	16 wks.	*	16 wks.	*	16 wks.	*

*Same as in case of individual termination.
[1] 50 or more employees in a 4-week period.
[2] 50 or more employees in a 2-month period.
[3] More than 10 employees in a 4-week period, where the number of employees is at least 25% of the employer's workforce.
[4] 10 or more employees in a 4-week period.
[5] Where the number of employees is less than 10% of the employees at the establishment, and there is no permanent discontinuance of all or part of the employer's business, this is not a mass termination and individual notice periods apply.
[6] 10 or more employees in 2 consecutive months.
[7] 25 or more employees in a 4-week period.

TABLE 6

TIMING OF PAYMENT OF WAGES UPON TERMINATION

	When Payment Is Due
Federal	Within 30 days of termination.
Alberta	Within 3 days when employer terminates (within 10 days if employment is terminated and employer has no obligation to provide notice or pay in lieu).
British Columbia	Within 48 hours when employer terminates; within 6 days when employee terminates.
Manitoba	Within 10 working days of termination.
New Brunswick	Next regular payday — no later than 21 days after termination.
Newfoundland and Labrador	Within 1 week of termination.
Nova Scotia	Upon the expiry of the notice period.
Ontario	Within 7 days of termination or the day that would have been the employee's next payday, whichever is later.
Prince Edward Island	No later than the last day of the next pay period following termination.
Quebec	Legislation does not specify.
Saskatchewan	Within 14 days of termination.
Northwest Territories	Within 10 days of termination.
Nunavut	Within 10 days of termination.
Yukon	Within 7 days of termination — can be paid in instalments.

TABLE 7
PREGNANCY LEAVE

	Service Requirement Before Eligible for Leave	Length of Leave	Notice to Employer	Earliest Start Date Before Delivery
Federal	6 mos.	17 wks.	4 wks.	11 wks.
Alberta	12 mos.	15 wks.	6 wks.	12 wks.
British Columbia	No requirement	17 wks.	4 wks.	11 wks.
Manitoba	7 mos.	17 wks.	4 wks.	17 wks.
New Brunswick	No requirement	17 wks.	4 mos. notice of intention to take leave; 2 wks. notice of commencement of leave	11 wks.
Newfoundland and Labrador	20 wks.	17 wks.	2 wks.	17 wks.
Nova Scotia	12 mos.	17 wks.	4 wks.	16 wks.
Ontario	13 wks.	17 wks.	2 wks.	17 wks.
Prince Edward Island	20 wks.	17 wks.	4 wks.	11 wks.
Quebec	No requirement	18 wks.	3 wks.	16 wks.
Saskatchewan	20 wks. ir last 52 wks.	18 wks.	4 wks.	12 wks.
Northwest Territories and Nunavut	12 mos.	17 wks.	4 wks.	17 wks.
Yukon	12 mos.	17 wks.	4 wks.	6 wks.

TABLE 8
PARENTAL AND ADOPTION LEAVE

	Service Requirement Before Entitlement	Length of Leave	Notice to Employer	When Leave Must Be Taken Relative to Birth or Adoption
Federal (parental/adoption)	6 mos.	37 wks.	4 wks.	Completed within 52 wks.
Alberta (adoption)	12 mos.	37 wks.	6 wks.	Completed within 52 wks.
British Columbia (parental/adoption)	No requirement	35 wks. if pregnancy leave; 37 wks. otherwise	4 wks.	Completed within 52 wks.
Manitoba (parental/adoption)	7 mos.	37 wks.	4 wks.	Commenced within 52 wks.
New Brunswick (child care — including adoption)	No requirement	37 wks.	4 wks. for parental; 4 mos. before expected adoption placement	Completed within 52 wks.
Newfoundland and Labrador (parental/adoption)	20 wks.	35 wks.	2 wks.	Commenced within 35 wks.
Nova Scotia (parental/adoption)	12 mos.	35 wks. if took pregnancy leave and child arrived home during that time; 52 wks. otherwise	4 wks.	Completed within 52 wks.
Ontario (parental/adoption)	13 wks.	35 wks. if took pregnancy leave; 37 wks. otherwise	2 wks.	Commenced within 52 wks.
Prince Edward Island (parental/adoption)	20 wks.	35 wks. for natural mother or father; 52 wks. for adoptive parent or legal guardian	4 wks. for parental; for adoption, when employee is notified of child placement	Commenced within 52 wks.
Quebec (parental/adoption)	None	52 wks.	3 wks.	Completed within 70 wks.

TABLE 8 — *Continued*

	Service Requirement Before Entitlement	Length of Leave	Notice to Employer	When Leave Must Be Taken Relative to Birth or Adoption
Saskatchewan (parental/adoption)	20 wks. of the 52 wks. before leave	34 wks. if took pregnancy leave; 37 wks. otherwise	4 wks.	Completed any time between 1 mo. before and 8 mos. after
Northwest Territories and Nunavut (parental/adoption)	12 mos.	37 wks.	4 wks.	Completed within 52 wks.
Yukon (parental/adoption)	12 mos.	37 wks.	4 wks.	Completed within 1 yr.

TABLE 9
ANNUAL VACATION AND VACATION PAY

	Completed Years of Service									
	1 year	2 years	3 years	4 years	5 years	6 years	7 years	8 years	9 years	10 years
Federal	A	A	A	A	A	B	B	B	B	B
Alberta¹	A	A	A	A	B	B	B	B	B	B
British Columbia	A	A	A	A	B	B	B	B	B	B
Manitoba	A	A	A	A	B	B	B	B	B	B
New Brunswick	A	A	A	A	A	A	A	B	B	B
Newfoundland and Labrador	A	A	A	A	A	A	A	A	A	A
Nova Scotia	A	A	A	A	A	A	A	A	A	A
Ontario	A	A	A	A	A	A	A	A	A	A
Prince Edward Island	A	A	A	A	A	A	A	A	A	A
Quebec	A	A	A	A	B	B	B	B	B	B
Saskatchewan	3 wks. at 3/52 of annual earnings	3 wks. at 3/52 of annual earnings	3 wks. at 3/52 of annual earnings	3 wks. at 3/52 of annual earnings	3 wks. at 3/52 of annual earnings	3 wks. at 3/52 of annual earnings	3 wks. at 3/52 of annual earnings	3 wks. at 3/52 of annual earnings	3 wks. at 3/52 of annual earnings	4 wks. at 4/52 of annual earnings
Nunavut and Northwest Territories	A	A	A	A	A	B	B	B	B	B
Yukon	A	A	A	A	A	A	A	A	A	A

A = 2 weeks at pay of 4% of annual earnings
B = 3 weeks at pay of 6% of annual earnings
¹ Workers in Alberta who are paid monthly receive their normal monthly wage divided by 4 1/3 for each week of vacation entitlement.

TABLE 10
PROHIBITED GROUNDS OF DISCRIMINATION

	Fed.	Alta.	B.C.	Man.	N.B.	Nfld.	N.S.	Ont.	P.E.I.	Que.	Sask.	N.W.T.	Nunavut	Yukon
Race	X	X	X	X	X	X	X	X	X	X	X	X	X	
Religious Beliefs/Religious Creed	X	X	X	X	X	X	X		X	X	X	X		X
Colour	X	X	X		X	X	X	X	X	X	X	X	X	
Sex/Gender[1]	X	X	X	X	X	X	X	X	X	X	X	X	X	X
Physical and/or Mental Disability	X	X	X	X	X	X	X	X	X	X	X	X	X	X
Marital Status	X	X	X	X	X	X	X	X	X		X	X	X	X
Family Status	X		X	X			X	X			X	X	X	X
Civil Status										X				
Sexual Orientation[2]	X		X	X	X	X	X	X	X	X	X	X		X
Age[3]	X	X	X	X	X	X	X	X	X	X	X	X	X	X
Political Beliefs/Opinions			X	X		X	X		X	X				X
Language										X				
Creed							X	X	X		X	X	X	X
Ancestry		X	X	X⁴	X	X		X			X	X	X	X
Nationality/National Origin	X			X	X	X			X	X	X	X	X	X
Place of Origin		X	X		X		X	X			X	X	X	X

Footnotes on next page

TABLE 10 — Continued

	Fed.	Alta.	B.C.	Man.	N.B.	Nfld.	N.S.	Ont.	P.E.I.	Que.	Sask.	N.W.T.	Nunavut	Yukon
Ethnic Background/Ethnic Origin	X			X		X		X	X	X				X
Social Origin/Social Condition						X				X				
Source of Income				X			X				X			
Citizenship								X						
Criminal/Summary Offences[5]	X		X					X						X

[1] Sex or gender as a prohibited ground of discrimination includes pregnancy in Alberta, Manitoba, New Brunswick, Nova Scotia, Ontario, Saskatchewan and the Yukon and under the *Canadian Human Rights Act*, R.S.C. 1985, c. H-6 (as amended to 2002, c. 7). In Quebec, pregnancy is listed as a separate ground of discrimination.

[2] Sexual orientation as a prohibited ground has been read in by the courts: see *Vriend v. Alberta* (1998), 156 D.L.R. (4th) 385 (S.C.C.).

[3] In Alberta, age as a prohibited ground of discrimination is applicable to individuals 18 years of age or older. In British Columbia and Newfoundland, age is defined as between 19 and 65 years of age. In Saskatchewan and Ontario, the age range is between 18 and 65 years of age.

[4] In Manitoba, ancestry includes colour and perceived race.

[5] This category includes offences unrelated to employment, convictions for which a pardon has been granted and the record of offences.

TABLE 11
WALLACE DAMAGES

Case Name	Court	Date	No. of Months	Reasoning
Robertson v. Red Robin Restaurants of Canada Ltd. (unreported)	B.C. Prov. Ct. (Small Claims Ct.)	February 25, 1998	2	• Employer maintained that claimant had left by his own choice. Position of employer found to be high-handed, offensive and indefensible. Combined with public nature of termination meeting, this resulted in loss of self-esteem, public humiliation, and loss of confidence for employee.
Nagy v. Metropolitan Toronto Convention Corp. (1998), 35 C.C.E.L. (2d) 209	(Ont. Ct. (Gen. Div.))	March 12, 1998	1	• Mental distress suffered as result of termination.
Whiting v. Winnipeg River Brokenhead Community Futures Development Corp. (1998), 159 D.L.R. (4th) 18, [1998] 9 W.W.R. 584, 167 W.A.C. (3d) 176, 126 Man. R. (2d) 176	(Man. C.A.)	April 23, 1998	6	• Manner of termination found to be callous, improper and totally without sensitivity. As a result, mental stress was induced.
Zimmerman v. Kindersley Transport Ltd. (1998), 80 A.C.W.S. (3d) 336	(Sask. Prov. Ct.)	May 5, 1998	1	• Employee not given pay in lieu of notice to which she was entitled. Employee treated in shabby and humiliating manner, including abrupt firing without explanation, and being watched as she cleaned out desk.
Stolle v. Daishinpan (Canada) Inc. (1998), 37 C.C.E.L. (2d) 18, 98 C.L.L.C. ¶210-028	(B.C.S.C.)	May 14, 1998	3	• Employer withheld employee's statutory severance payment in order to obtain execution by employee of release protecting employer from any action by employee pursuant to *Employment Standards Act* and *Human Rights Act*.

TABLE 11 — Continued

Case Name	Court	Date	No. of Months	Reasoning
Boule v. Ericatel Ltd. (1998), 80 A.C.W.S. (3d) 85	(B.C.S.C.)	June 8, 1998	4	• Employer accused employee of fraudulent conduct. Accusations held to be unfounded and should not have been made. Allegations caused distress to employee and his family and constituted bad faith conduct.
Birch v. Grinnell Fire Protection (1998), 80 A.C.W.S. (3d) 1190	(B.C.S.C.)	July 2, 1998	2	• Employee's position as manager of his own department abolished when employee was on vacation. Employer alleged that employee dismissed for just cause as a result of insubordination.
Martin v. International Maple Leaf Springs Water Corp. (1998), 38 C.C.E.L. (2d) 128	(B.C.S.C.)	July 10, 1998	3	• Employee accused of dishonesty and abuse of alcohol. Held that actions of employer made it difficult for employee to obtain employment insurance benefits.
Cassady v. Wyeth-Ayerst Canada Inc. (1998), 163 D.L.R. (4th) 1, 38 C.C.E.L. (2d) 171, 99 C.L.L.C. ¶210-006, [1999] 3 W.W.R. 74, 178 W.A.C. 277, 54 B.C.L.R. (3d) 68	(B.C.C.A.)	August 11, 1998	3	• Mental distress suffered as result of termination.
Budd v. Bath Creations Inc. (unreported)	(Ont. Ct. (Gen. Div.))	September 18, 1998	3	• Employer was less than forthright and candid about employee's prospects. Employee should have been told he was there for the transition and given opportunity to look for other work in a reasonable time.

TABLE 11 — Continued

Case Name	Court	Date	No. of Months	Reasoning
McGeady v. Saskatchewan Wheat Pool (1998), 40 C.C.E.L. (2d) 218, 174 Sask. R. 110 (Q.B.), vard 49 C.C.E.L. (2d) 1, 205 W.A.C. 309, 180 Sask. R. 309 (C.A.)	(Sask. Q.B.)	December 11, 1998	6 (reduced to 1 month by Court of Appeal)	• Statutory payment of wages in lieu of notice withheld despite demand for payment. Threats made to employee in absence of her solicitor. • Court of Appeal reduced damages from 6 months to 1 month – conduct considered to be borderline, given its relative impact on employee.
Squires v. Corner Brook Pulp & Paper Ltd. (1999), 44 C.C.E.L. (2d) 246, 175 Nfld. & P.E.I.R. 202	(Nfld. C.A.)	May 10, 1999	6	• Employer knew or should have known from beginning that there was no just cause, but attempted to arrive at settlement by threatening to use false claim of just cause. Employee also never given any reason to doubt he was considered a valued employee doing a good job.
Kissner v. Goodall & Hills (1999), 89 A.C.W.S. (3d) 1194	(Ont. S.C.J.)	June 25, 1999	3	• After 21 years of service, employee found to be entitled to proper warning that persistence in her course of conduct could result in dismissal. Employee also entitled to opportunity to respond to any concerns expressed.
Truong v. British Columbia (1999), 178 D.L.R. (4th) 644, 47 C.C.E.L. (2d) 307, 2000 C.L.L.C. ¶210-004, [2000] 1 W.W.R. 61, 208 W.A.C. 240, 67 B.C.L.R. (3d) 234	(B.C.C.A.)	September 13, 1999	2	• Employee dismissed for cause based on allegations that were not properly investigated, were unsubstantiated, and in some cases were false.
Hampton v. Thirty-Five Charlotte Ltd. (1999), 48 C.C.E.L. (2d) 96, 2000 C.L.L.C. ¶210-006, 218 N.B.R. (2d) 109	(N.B.Q.B.)	September 30, 1999	2½	• Employer found to have played game with letter of recommendation. Employer also acted in bad faith by alleging just cause when there was no basis for doing so.

TABLE 11 — Continued

Case Name	Court	Date	No. of Months	Reasoning
Baranowski v. Binks Manufacturing Co. (2000), 49 C.C.E.L. (2d) 170, 2000 C.L.L.C. ¶210-016	(Ont. S.C.J.)	January 12, 2000	6	• Employee informed of dismissal by taxi driver who delivered note to employee's home on night of employee's son's graduation. Employer also made spurious allegations at trial that employer knew or ought to have known were baseless.
Daley v. Golden Child Care Society (2000), 94 A.C.W.S. (3d) 79	(B.C.S.C.)	January 13, 2000	approx. 1-2	• Employer not candid, reasonable, honest and forthright with employee. Employee terminated without explanation or warning that there was dissatisfaction with her employment.
Robinson v. Fraser Wharves Ltd. (2000), 5 C.C.E.L. (3d) 81, 2000 BCSC 199	(B.C.S.C.)	February 2, 2000	3	• Employer's decision to maintain allegations of illegal activity against employee, especially after criminal charges stayed, succeeded in intensifying employee's injuries. Employer's allegations made known to potential employers and to people in the industry, resulting in employee being unable to obtain reference letters from individuals in the industry or interview from employer's competitor.
Sjerven v. Port Alberni Friendship Center (2000), 3 C.C.E.L. (3d) 71	(B.C.S.C.)	March 27, 2000	6	• Employer clearly ignored procedural fairness and its own internal procedures and basic principles of fair dealing when it terminated employee. Employee terminated because she continued to associate herself with Mr. S.M. in a personal relationship, which was found to be an inappropriate reason for termination.
Khan v. Fibre Glass-Evercoat Co. (2000), 97 A.C.W.S. (3d) 468	(Ont. S.C.J.)	May 30, 2000	5	• When employee terminated, employer insisted that he abide by 5-year non-competition agreement which would have seriously impeded availability of similar employment and would have made it more difficult for him to find such employment.
Hamer-Jackson v. McCall Pontiac Buick Ltd. (2000), 3 C.C.E.L. (3d) 20, 229 W.A.C. 101, 77 B.C.L.R. (3d) 214, 2000 BCCA 416	(B.C.C.A.)	July 4, 2000	6	• Actions by employer (false allegations) damaged reputation of employee and caused him intangible injuries sufficient to merit compensation.

TABLE 11 — *Continued*

Case Name	Court	Date	No. of Months	Reasoning
Clendenning v. Lowndes Lambert (B.C.) Ltd. (2000), 193 D.L.R. (4th) 610, 4 C.C.E.L. (3d) 238, 2001 C.L.L.C. ¶210-013, 237 W.A.C. 188, 82 B.C.L.R. (3d) 239, 2000 BCCA 644	(B.C.C.A.)	November 27, 2000	18	• Employer found to have acted in bad faith when making serious unfounded allegations against employee. Employee's opportunity to find new employment adversely affected as a result. • Notice period reduced from 36 months to 18 months by Court of Appeal.
Baughn v. Offerski (2001), 5 C.C.E.L. (3d) 283	(Ont. S.C.J.)	January 22, 2001	5	• Dismissal based on accusation of theft which was not investigated prior to termination. Held that, after 10 full years of service, employer had duty to investigate further before acting.
Sawyer v. Rab Energy Group Inc. (unreported)	(Y.T.S.C.)	September 21, 2001	1	• Employee handed termination letter to read at meeting of new board. Failure to pay her any severance allowance some two months after her termination added further distress.
Marshall v. Watson Wyatt & Co. (2002), 209 D.L.R. (4th) 411, 16 C.C.E.L. (3d) 162, 2002 C.L.L.C. ¶210-019, 57 O.R. (3d) 813, 155 O.A.C. 103 (C.A.), supp. reasons 112 A.C.W.S. (3d) 834 (Ont. C.A.)	(Ont. C.A.)	January 17, 2002	3	• Employer maintained allegations of just cause until shortly before trial began, refused to pay commissions owing, and delayed several months before sending record of employment required for employment insurance benefits.
Danaher v. Moon Palace (2000) Ltd. (2002), 15 C.C.E.L. (3d) 305, 248 N.B.R. (2d) 331, 2002 NBQB 86	(N.B.Q.B.)	March 12, 2002	4	• Employee not told about sale of restaurant. Employee led to believe that lease would not be signed until she was happy. Lease signed behind her back, copies of which were subsequently destroyed.

TABLE 11 — *Continued*

Case Name	Court	Date	No. of Months	Reasoning
Buchanan v. Geotel Communications Corp. (2002), 18 C.C.E.L. (3d) 17	(Ont. S.C.J.)	May 14, 2002	3	• Employee not provided with opportunity to respond to allegations made against him, and not even told complainant's name or circumstances of complaint. Employer also did not provide written reasons for dismissal, and sent employee a fax wrongfully stating that he had resigned.

TABLE 12
POST-WALLACE PUNITIVE DAMAGES

Case Name	Court	Date	Amount Awarded	Reasoning
David v. Congregation B'Nai Israel (1999), 44 C.C.E.L. (2d) 302, 99 C.L.L.C. ¶210-031	(Ont. Ct. (Gen. Div.))	April 12, 1999	$20,000	• Conduct was cruel, abusive, insolent and hurtful to plaintiff. Particulars of cause unfounded and a personal attack on plaintiff and his family to hurt them. Defendant dismissed plaintiff's wife to exacerbate hurt to plaintiff. Conduct in informing plaintiff that he was no longer welcome at synagogue was malicious.
Dixon v. British Columbia Transit (1995), 13 C.C.E.L. (2d) 272, 95 C.L.L.C. ¶210-049, 9 B.C.L.R. (3d) 108	(B.C.S.C.)	September 5, 1995	$75,000	• Employer informed media that plaintiff dismissed after performance review, which was not true. • Publication of that information by employer was actionable wrong which came after firing and was separate from it. Such contact by public servants had to be deterred.
Martin v. International Maple Leaf Springs Water Corp. (1998), 38 C.C.E.L. (2d) 128	(B.C.S.C.)	July 10, 1998	$35,000	• Employee wrongfully accused of dishonesty and taking a secret commission, as well as misuse of alcohol, where there was no foundation for any of these accusations. Accusations amounted to actionable wrong, being slander.
Chahal v. Khalsa Community School (2000), 2 C.C.E.L. (3d) 120	(Ont. S.C.J.)	June 30, 2000	$25,000	• School made allegations against Chahal which were defamatory, and school's representatives conspired to injure Chahal, which justified award of punitive damages.

TABLE 13

**AGGRAVATED AND/OR MENTAL DISTRESS DAMAGES
(PRE-WALLACE CASES)**

Date	Case	$	Brief Description
July 4, 1990	*Legorburu v. Det Norske Veritas* (1990), 32 C.C.E.L. 126, 97 N.S.R. (2d) 250 (S.C.)	$500	Naval architect dismissed after 12 years' service. Suffered from anxiety and depression and received medical treatment. Damages awarded for emotional trauma which was short in duration and responded to treatment.
August 7, 1991	*Dickinson v. Radio Atlantic (CFNB) Ltd.* (1991), 38 C.C.E.L. 123, 123 N.B.R. (2d) 361 (Q.B.)	$1,500	40-year-old production manager dismissed after 20 years' service. Defence of cause abandoned before trial. Because career in narrow field, whole life upset by dismissal. Experienced stomach problems and sleepless nights. Damages for mental distress awarded.
October 9, 1991	*Linkson v. UTDC Inc.* (1991), 40 C.C.E.L. 305, 92 C.L.L.C. ¶14,037 (Ont. Ct. (Gen. Div.))	$5,000	43-year-old middle manager dismissed after $7\frac{1}{2}$ years' service. Unacceptable that employer did not provide minimum notice required by employment standards legislation. Employee suffered significant stress and mental anguish as a result. Amount awarded as either aggravated or punitive damages.
December 13, 1991	*Johnson v. Famous Players Inc.* (1991), 77 Man. R. (2d) 25 (Q.B.)	$5,000	Manager dismissed due to suspicion he was involved in thefts. Court found no evidence of theft. Manager devastated and experienced headaches and sleepless nights. Fact that manager was actually accused of theft independently actionable. Amount awarded as aggravated damages, but Court held amount could equally have represented punitive damages.
April 10, 1992	*Leonard v. Wilson* (1992), 41 C.C.E.L. 226 (Ont. Ct. (Gen. Div.))	$4,000	Manager of a horseback-riding operation summarily dismissed without reasons. Had employer thought about dismissal at time of hiring, would have realized that to do so in such a brutal manner would have profound emotional impact. Manager developed migraines and hives, reported

Date	Case	$	Brief Description
	Leonard v. Wilson (cont'd)		dizziness and numbness in her hands, slept poorly and had a tendency to weep readily. Doctor prescribed tranquillizers and anti-depressants. Separate and actionable wrong resulted from manner and timing of firing. Mental distress damages awarded.
August 26, 1992	*Kaniewski v. Key Property Management (1986) Inc.* (1992), 44 C.C.E.L. 136, 92 C.L.L.C. ¶14,050 (Ont. Ct. (Gen. Div.)), supp. reasons 35 A.C.W.S. (3d) 656 (Ont. Ct. (Gen. Div.))	Nil	Supervisor dismissed for alleged theft and fraud. Employee suffered from increase in migraine headaches as result of wrongful dismissal and was naturally depressed. Mental distress damages denied because no evidence that employee required any medical attention.
November 23, 1992	*Ribeiro v. Canadian Imperial Bank of Commerce* (1989), 24 C.C.E.L. 225, 89 C.L.L.C. ¶14,033, 67 O.R. (2d) 385 (H.C.J.), vard 44 C.C.E.L. 165, 13 O.R. (3d) 278 (C.A.), leave to appeal to S.C.C. refused 65 O.A.C. 79*n*, 157 N.R. 400*n*	$20,000	Bank officer dismissed for dishonesty in loans to customer. Employer's inspector did not investigate in good faith and fabricated information. Was within contemplation of parties that employee would suffer mental distress if terminated in given manner. Trial judge's award of $10,000 for mental distress damages increased by Court of Appeal to $20,000 due to seriousness of reactive depression and duration of symptoms.
December 2, 1992	*Hughes v. Gemini Food Corp.* (1992), 45 C.C.E.L. 113, 93 C.L.L.C. ¶14,034 (Ont. Ct. (Gen. Div.)), supp. reasons 42 A.C.W.S. (3d) 383 (Ont. Ct. (Gen. Div.)), affd 27 C.C.E.L. (2d) 204, 97 O.A.C. 147 (C.A.)	$75,000	President/CEO dismissed for alleged conflict of interest and inattention to duties. Employer failed to investigate allegations. Dismissal very public and humiliating, with information being communicated to Premier and legislature of P.E.I. Aggravated damages awarded as a result.
March 15, 1994	*Ashton v. Perle Systems Ltd.* (1994), 2 C.C.E.L. (2d) 243 (Ont. Ct. (Gen. Div.))	$5,000	Employee transferred from U.K. to Canada for position which differed from that promised. Employee dismissed, and employer breached agreement to pay expenses for move back to U.K. Fact that aggravated damages not claimed did not preclude award if evidence so warranted. When employee returned to U.K., he was

Date	Case	$	Brief Description
	Ashton v. Perle Systems Ltd. (cont'd)		distressed by inability to find suitable accommodation. Failure to pay moving costs found to be separate actionable wrong and merited aggravated damages award.
August 12, 1994	*Crawford v. Rory's Mountain Motel (1988) Ltd.* (1994), 6 C.C.E.L. (2d) 99, 151 N.B.R. (2d) 272 (Q.B.)	$1,000	Head cook fired upon return from maternity leave. Offered lesser position, which was held to be wrongful dismissal. Employee suffered mental distress, broke out in a rash and was prescribed anti-anxiety drugs. Combined effect of manner of dismissal, distress suffered and need for medical attention gave rise to claim for mental distress damages.
August 18, 1994	*Rock v. Canadian Red Cross Society* (1994), 5 C.C.E.L. (2d) 231, 94 C.L.L.C. ¶14,048 (Ont. Ct. (Gen. Div.)), supp. reasons 7 C.C.E.L. (2d) 146 (Ont. Ct. (Gen. Div.))	$25,000	Medical director dismissed for alleged misappropriation of funds and mismanagement. She was found only to have breached policy and this was not cause for dismissal. Employee treated like common criminal at time of termination, had research and personal files withheld and was frustrated when attempting to transfer grants. Aggravated damages awarded as a result.
November 23, 1994	*Francis v. Canadian Imperial Bank of Commerce* (1994), 120 D.L.R. (4th) 393, 7 C.C.E.L. (2d) 1, 95 C.L.L.C. ¶210-022, 21 O.R. (3d) 75, 75 O.A.C. 216 (C.A.), varg 41 C.C.E.L. 37, 92 C.L.L.C. ¶14,014 (Ont. Ct. (Gen. Div.))	Nil	Branch manager charged for involvement in pyramid scheme, for which he received absolute discharge. Learned of termination only after could not access his account with his VISA card. He was never told reason for termination, and employer did not withdraw defence of termination for cause until "11th hour". Trial judge's award of $15,000 for mental distress set aside because no medical evidence presented to support claim.
December 2, 1994	*Engel v. Krug Furniture Inc.* (1994), 8 C.C.E.L. (2d) 91 (Ont. Ct. (Gen. Div.))	$1,500	20-year employee dismissed despite being fully capable of fulfilling duties. Employer breached promise not to dismiss senior employees at age 65. Aggravated damages awarded because employee emotionally shattered, stigmatized and mentally distressed.

Date	Case	$	Brief Description
December 14, 1994	*Greenwood v. Chilliwack Christian School Society* (1994), 8 C.C.E.L. (2d) 122 (B.C.S.C.)	$500	School board dismissed teacher for reasons not amounting to just cause and sent letter to parents hinting at matters too serious to mention. Employer's actions caused great embarrassment and affected employee's reputation and relationships in closely knit Christian community. Nominal aggravated damages awarded given circumstances.
January 23, 1995	*Jeffrey v. Purolator Courier Ltd.* (1995), 8 C.C.E.L. (2d) 205 (Ont. Ct. (Gen. Div.)), affd 79 A.C.W.S. (3d) 950 (Ont. C.A.)	$6,000	Manager replaced while on leave of absence. Offer of transfer was demotion and constructive dismissal. Award of aggravated damages for mental distress arising out of lack of notice, given that mental distress was reasonably foreseeable by parties when they entered into employment contract.
March 22, 1995	*Trask v. Terra Nova Motors Ltd.* (1995), 9 C.C.E.L. (2d) 157, 127 Nfld. & P.E.I.R. 310 (Nfld. C.A.), affg 35 C.C.E.L. 208, 89 Nfld. & P.E.I.R. 130 (Nfld. S.C.)	$4,000	Car salesman dismissed for alleged theft. Employer informed prospective employers that employee had committed theft. No theft proven. Employee wrongfully dismissed. Slanderous accusations of theft were independent actionable wrong, and there was evidence of mental distress. Damages awarded for mental distress.
May 4, 1995	*Deildal v. Tod Mountain Development Ltd.* (1995), 10 C.C.E.L. (2d) 202 (B.C.S.C.), affd 28 C.C.E.L. (2d) 1, [1997] 6 W.W.R. 239, 148 W.A.C. 214, 33 B.C.L.R. (3d) 25 (C.A.), leave to appeal to S.C.C. refused 166 W.A.C. 239n, 225 N.R. 398n	$25,000	President unjustly accused of misappropriating company funds. Aggravated damages for mental distress not awarded for breach of contract because no distress suffered as result of breach. Aggravated damages awarded because of slanderous conduct of employer which constituted actionable wrong, caused employee mental distress and forced him to sell his home and leave community.
September 5, 1995	*Dixon v. British Columbia Transit* (1995), 13 C.C.E.L. (2d) 272, 95 C.L.L.C. ¶210-049, 9 B.C.L.R. (3d) 108 (S.C.)	$50,000	President/CEO of Crown corporation dismissed without cause, but defendant misrepresented that cause existed. Court found that defendant had committed tort of deceit and that unwarranted allegation of cause had humiliated and

Date	Case	$	Brief Description
	Dixon v. British Columbia Transit (cont'd)		frustrated plaintiff. Plaintiff awarded aggravated damages for defendant's malicious conduct.
September 29, 1995	*Campbell v. Wellfund Audio-Visual Ltd.* (1995), 14 C.C.E.L. (2d) 240 (B.C.S.C.)	$20,000	Vice-president of audio and television equipment manufacturer dismissed after he refused to fabricate reason for dismissing sexual harassment complainant. Court found that plaintiff was harassed and intimidated by his superiors for failing to "support the company", and this conduct aggravated plaintiff's migraines and caused him to experience panic attacks, nightmares, claustrophobic incidents and inability to concentrate. Plaintiff awarded damages for tort of intentional infliction of mental suffering.

TABLE 14
LOSS OF REPUTATION DAMAGES
(PRE-WALLACE CASES)

Date	Case	$	Brief Description
January 7, 1983	*Multivision Films Inc. v. McConnell Advertising* (1983), 69 C.P.R. (2d) 1 (Ont. H.C.J.)	$5,000	By virtue of breach of employment contract, producer/director lost screen credit for remaining episodes of television program. Loss of enhancement of reputation equivalent to loss of publicity, but differs from claim for injury to existing reputation. Amount awarded for loss of publicity.
September 4, 1987	*Carle v. Comité Paritaire du Vêtement Pour Dames* (1987), 22 C.C.E.L. 281, [1987] R.J.Q. 2553 (S.C.)	$3,000	Corporate counsel dismissed without cause. Required to leave immediately, and police escorted him from building. Employee was expelled, humiliated and treated like criminal who could not be trusted. Damages awarded for loss of reputation and "moral damages".
February 9, 1989	*Ribeiro v. Canadian Imperial Bank of Commerce* (1989), 24 C.C.E.L. 225, 89 C.L.L.C. ¶14,033, 67 O.R. (2d) 385 (H.C.J.), vard 44 C.C.E.L. 165, 13 O.R. (3d) 278 (C.A.), leave to appeal to S.C.C. refused 65 O.A.C. 79*n*, 157 N.R. 400*n*	Nil	Bank officer dismissed for dishonesty in loans to customer. Employer's inspector did not investigate in good faith and fabricated information. Damages for loss of reputation are like those for mental distress in that it must have been in contemplation of parties at time of hiring that wrongful breach of employment relationship and wanton and reckless conduct relating thereto could cause loss of reputation. Exception exists where claim represents one for defamation, in which case it should be advanced as such. Any compensation for loss of reputation here was included in mental distress damages for "hurt feelings" and humiliation.
November 25, 1991	*Murphy v. Canadian Tire Corp.* (1991), 39 C.C.E.L. 205 (Ont. Ct. (Gen. Div.))	Nil	Cashier dismissed for dishonesty and, despite her acquittal on criminal charges, evidence established that she was dishonest. Employer gave poor reference to prospective employer after employee acquitted. Damages assessed at $1,500 for loss of reputation as result.

Date	Case	$	Brief Description
	Murphy v. Canadian Tire Corp. (cont'd)		However, not awarded after Court held that employee not wrongfully dismissed.
March 29, 1994	*Cranston v. Canadian Broadcasting Corp.* (1994), 2 C.C.E.L. (2d) 301 (Ont. Ct. (Gen. Div.))	$20,000	Television colour commentator dismissed. Damages awarded for loss of publicity or loss of opportunity to enhance reputation due to breach of contract. Contract contemplated maintenance and potential increase of employee's exposure to public. Publicity lost by employee had intrinsic value, and parties knew this when they entered into employment agreement.
August 18, 1994	*Rock v. Canadian Red Cross Society* (1994), 5 C.C.E.L. (2d) 231, 94 C.L.L.C. ¶14,048 (Ont. Ct. (Gen. Div.)), supp. reasons 7 C.C.E.L. (2d) 146 (Ont. Ct. (Gen. Div.))	Nil	Medical director dismissed for alleged misappropriation of funds and mismanagement. She was found only to have breached policy, and this was not cause for dismissal. Loss of reputation only applies to very distinct and unique classifications, such as artists, entertainers and professional athletes (not doctors and scientists).
May 4, 1995	*Deildal v. Tod Mountain Development Ltd.* (1995), 10 C.C.E.L. (2d) 202 (B.C.S.C.), affd 28 C.C.E.L. (2d) 1, [1997] 6 W.W.R. 239, 148 W.A.C. 214, 33 B.C.L.R. (3d) 25 (C.A.), leave to appeal to S.C.C. refused 166 W.A.C. 239*n*, 225 N.R. 398*n*	$50,000	President unjustly accused of misappropriating company funds. Employer announcing to shareholders that president had been fired, had misappropriated funds and was poor manager. Amount awarded for injury done to employee's reputation and represented 12 months' salary.

TABLE 15
PUNITIVE DAMAGES
(PRE-WALLACE CASES)

Date	Case	$	Brief Description
February 16, 1990	*Lippert v. Barkingside Investments Ltd.* (1990), 29 C.C.E.L. 257 (Ont. Dist. Ct.)	$2,500	Nurse administrator dismissed without notice or cause and told to leave immediately. Although no actionable wrong, manner of dismissal unnecessarily harsh and reprehensible. Punitive damages awarded to punish employer.
May 10, 1990	*Moffatt v. Canso Pharmacy Ltd.* (1990), 30 C.C.E.L. 22, 96 N.S.R. (2d) 399 (S.C.)	$2,500	Pharmacist transferred without being informed while on maternity leave. This amounted to constructive dismissal. Higher standard of behaviour expected in professional setting. Punitive damages awarded because employer's conduct was unacceptable, unnecessarily insensitive, humiliating and wrong.
October 9, 1991	*Linkson v. UTDC Inc.* (1991), 40 C.C.E.L. 305, 92 C.L.L.C. ¶14,037 (Ont. Ct. (Gen. Div.))	$5,000	43-year-old middle manager dismissed after 7 1/2 years' service. Unacceptable that employer did not provide minimum notice required by employment standards legislation. Employee suffered significant stress and mental anguish as result. Amount awarded as either aggravated or punitive damages.
December 13, 1991	*Johnson v. Famous Players Inc.* (1991), 77 Man. R. (2d) 25 (Q.B.)	$5,000	Manager dismissed due to suspicion that he was involved in thefts. Court found no evidence of theft. Manager devastated, and experienced headaches and sleepless nights. Fact that manager was actually accused of theft independently actionable. Amount awarded as aggravated damages, but Court held amount could equally have represented punitive damages.
January 13, 1992	*Anderson v. Peel Memorial Hospital Assn.* (1992), 40 C.C.E.L. 203, 92 C.L.L.C. ¶14,026 (Ont. Ct. (Gen. Div.))	$5,000	Director of pharmacy demoted after critical report issued regarding performance. Director demoted despite officials' knowledge that criticism unfounded. All medical staff told director dismissed due to inability. Punitive damages

Date	Case	$	Brief Description
	Anderson v. Peel Memorial Hospital Assn. (cont'd)		appropriate because no honest belief in truth of statements. Employer's actions unfair and reprehensible.
February 28, 1992	*Ballard v. Alberni Valley Chamber of Commerce* (1992), 39 C.C.E.L. 225, 65 B.C.L.R. (2d) 378 (S.C.)	$3,000	Employee signed contract with understanding that employer would provide continued, secure, long-term employment. At time of signing, employer had already decided to terminate employee, but withheld information because this would have material effect upon employee's decision to sign. Conduct constituted civil fraud and actionable wrong; therefore punitive damages awarded.
August 26, 1992	*Kaniewski v. Key Property Management (1986) Inc.* (1992), 44 C.C.E.L. 136, 92 C.L.L.C. ¶14,050 (Ont. Ct. (Gen. Div.)), supp. reasons 35 A.C.W.S. (3d) 656 (Ont. Ct. (Gen. Div.))	$5,000	Supervisor dismissed for alleged theft and fraud. Punitive damages awarded because, despite fact that reasonable investigation would have revealed employee's innocence, it took employer until opening of trial (over 2 years) to withdraw allegations of impropriety. Also awarded because employer engaged in character assassination of employee and intimidation to dissuade him from continuing wrongful dismissal action.
November 23, 1992	*Ribeiro v. Canadian Imperial Bank of Commerce* (1989), 24 C.C.E.L. 225, 89 C.L.L.C. ¶14,033, 67 O.R. (2d) 385 (H.C.J.), vard 44 C.C.E.L. 165, 13 O.R. (3d) 278 (C.A.), leave to appeal to S.C.C. refused 65 O.A.C. 79n, 157 N.R. 400n	$50,000	Bank officer dismissed for dishonesty in loans to customer. Employer's inspector did not investigate in good faith and fabricated information. Actions of employer arrogant and outrageous and called for condemnation. Trial award of $10,000 insufficient for punishment and deterrence, so Court of Appeal increased award to $50,000.
December 8, 1992	*Conrad v. Household Financial Corp.* (1992), 45 C.C.E.L. 81, 118 N.S.R. (2d) 56 (S.C.A.D.)	$5,000	Employer dismissed employee for theft one day before scheduled transfer. Employer did not explain reason for dismissal while criminal investigation underway, even though employee clearly not guilty. Employer breached duty of care not to injure employee and engaged in reprehensible conduct towards employee. Punitive

Date	Case	$	Brief Description
	Conrad v. Household Financial Corp. (cont'd)		damages awarded as warning to other employers not to abuse relatively advantageous positions over employees.
April 29, 1993	*Boothman v. Canada*, [1993] 3 F.C. 381, 63 F.T.R. 48, 49 C.C.E.L. 109 (T.D.)	$10,000	Clerical worker assaulted and harassed by supervisor who also intentionally inflicted nervous shock. Employer placed supervisor in position of trust, and supervisor used authority to harass, intimidate and assault employee. Given reprehensible conduct, outrageous and unacceptable behaviour of supervisor, punitive damages awarded for purpose of deterrence.
August 23, 1993	*Pollinger v. Bergman Graphics Ltd.* (1993), 18 O.R. (3d) 31 (Gen. Div.)	1 month's wages	Employee dismissed for threatening to complain to Ministry of Labour about co-worker smoking in restricted area. Employer's conduct in selecting employee for termination because he had threatened to complain under important legislation merited censure by Court.
March 15, 1994	*Ashton v. Perle Systems Ltd.* (1994), 2 C.C.E.L. (2d) 243 (Ont. Ct. (Gen. Div.))	$10,000	Employee transferred from U.K. to Canada for position which differed from that promised. Employee dismissed, and employer breached agreement to pay expenses for move back to U.K. Employer's conduct high-handed, reprehensible and breaching obligation to carry out dismissal in open, honest manner and avoid harm to employee. Punitive damages appropriate.
August 18, 1994	*Rock v. Canadian Red Cross Society* (1994), 5 C.C.E.L. (2d) 231, 94 C.L.L.C. ¶14,048 (Ont. Ct. (Gen. Div.)), supp. reasons 7 C.C.E.L. (2d) 146 (Ont. Ct. (Gen. Div.))	Nil	Medical director dismissed for alleged misappropriation of funds and mismanagement. She was found only to have breached policy, and this was not cause for dismissal. Employee treated like common criminal at time of termination, had research and personal files withheld and was frustrated when attempting to transfer grants. Conduct not malicious; therefore punitive damages not awarded.

Date	Case	$	Brief Description
November 23, 1994	*Francis v. Canadian Imperial Bank of Commerce* (1994), 120 D.L.R. (4th) 393, 7 C.C.E.L. (2d) 1, 95 C.L.L.C. ¶210-022, 21 O.R. (3d) 75, 75 O.A.C. 216 (C.A.), varg 41 C.C.E.L. 37, 92 C.L.L.C. ¶14,014 (Ont. Ct. (Gen. Div.))	$40,000	Branch manager charged for involvement in pyramid scheme, for which he received absolute discharge. Learned of termination only after could not access his account with his VISA card. He was never told reason for termination, and employer did not withdraw defence of termination for cause until "11th hour". Punitive damages awarded for manner in which employee terminated and devastating effect this had on him. Court of Appeal increased award from $15,000 to $40,000.
March 16, 1995	*Lenarduzzi v. P.B.N. Publishing Ltd.* (1995), 9 C.C.E.L. (2d) 238 (Ont. Ct. (Gen. Div.))	$15,000	Employees enticed into joining employer by negligent misrepresentations. Dismissed without warning, cause or notice after 1 month. Punitive damages awarded for this high-handed, cavalier and deceitful conduct.
May 4, 1995	*Deildal v. Tod Mountain Development Ltd.* (1995), 10 C.C.E.L. (2d) 202 (B.C.S.C.), affd 28 C.C.E.L. (2d) 1, [1997] 6 W.W.R. 239, 148 W.A.C. 214, 33 B.C.L.R. (3d) 25 (C.A.), leave to appeal to S.C.C. refused 166 W.A.C. 239n, 225 N.R. 398n	Nil	President unjustly accused of misappropriating company funds. Employer announced to shareholders that president had been fired, had misappropriated funds and was poor manager. Employer's slanderous conduct merited punitive damages award, but amount of $25,000 awarded to compensate for aggravated damages held to be sufficient to also punish employer. No additional damages awarded.
September 5, 1995	*Dixon v. British Columbia Transit* (1995), 13 C.C.E.L. (2d) 272, 95 C.L.L.C. ¶210-049, 9 B.C.L.R. (3d) 108 (S.C.)	$75,000	President/CEO of Crown corporation dismissed without cause, but defendant misrepresented that cause for dismissal existed. Defendant also provided media with false information about circumstances of plaintiff's dismissal. Court found that defendant had committed tort of defamation and that such conduct was harsh and reprehensible. Plaintiff entitled to punitive damages since general and aggravated damages were insufficient to achieve goal of punishment and deterrence.

Date	Case	$	Brief Description
January 16, 1996	*Williams v. Motorola Ltd.* (1996), 18 C.C.E.L. (2d) 74 (Ont. Ct. (Gen. Div.)), affd 38 C.C.E.L. (2d) 76 (Ont. C.A.)	$20,000	Marketing representative dismissed by employer without notice or prior warnings that her work was unsatisfactory. Shortly after termination, she was escorted off employer's premises and offered patently inadequate severance package, but was not provided with reason for her abrupt dismissal. At trial, defendant maintained that termination was due to down-sizing. Court held that plaintiff was dismissed to relieve employer from potential obligation to pay large bonus and to reduce tender price on major project. Plaintiff awarded punitive damages as result of these factors.

Appendix B
Legislation

EMPLOYMENT STANDARDS LEGISLATION

Federal

Canada Labour Code, R.S.C. 1985, c. L-2

Alberta

Employment Standards Code, R.S.A. 2000, c. E-9

British Columbia

Employment Standards Act, R.S.B.C. 1996, c. 113

Manitoba

Employment Standards Code, S.M. 1998, c. 29 (C.C.S.M. c. E110)

New Brunswick

Employment Standards Act, S.N.B. 1982, c. E-7.2

Newfoundland and Labrador

Labour Standards Act, R.S.N.L. 1990, c. L-2

Nova Scotia

Labour Standards Code, R.S.N.S. 1989, c. 246

Ontario

Employment Standards Act, 2000, S.O. 2000, c. 41

Prince Edward Island

Employment Standards Act, S.P.E.I. 1992, c. 18

Quebec

"Act respecting labour standards", R.S.Q., c. N-1.1

Saskatchewan

Labour Standards Act, R.S.S. 1978, c. L-1

Northwest Territories

Labour Standards Act, R.S.N.W.T. 1988, c. L-1

Nunavut

Labour Standards Act, R.S.N.W.T. 1988, c. L-1

Yukon

Employment Standards Act, R.S.Y. 1986, c. 54

HUMAN RIGHTS LEGISLATION

Federal

Canadian Human Rights Act, R.S.C. 1985, c. H-6

Alberta

Human Rights, Citizenship and Multiculturalism Act, R.S.A. 2000, c. H-14

British Columbia

Human Rights Code, R.S.B.C. 1996, c. 210

Manitoba

Human Rights Code, S.M. 1987-88, c. 45 (C.C.S.M. c. H175)

New Brunswick

Human Rights Act, R.S.N.B. 1973, c. H-11

Newfoundland and Labrador

Human Rights Code, R.S.N.L. 1990, c. H-14

Nova Scotia

Human Rights Act, R.S.N.S. 1989, c. 214

Ontario

Human Rights Code, R.S.O. 1990, c. H.19

Prince Edward Island

Human Rights Act, R.S.P.E.I. 1988, c. H-12

Quebec

Charter of Human Rights and Freedoms, R.S.Q., c. C-12

Saskatchewan

Saskatchewan Human Rights Code, S.S. 1979, c. S-24.1

Northwest Territories

Fair Practices Act, R.S.N.W.T. 1988, c. F-2

Nunavut

Fair Practices Act, R.S.N.W.T. 1988, c. F-2

Yukon

Human Rights Act, S.Y. 1987, c. 3

EQUITY LEGISLATION

Equal Pay for Equal Work/Work of Equal Value

Federal

Canadian Human Rights Act, R.S.C. 1985, c. H-6

Alberta

Human Rights, Citizenship and Multiculturalism Act, R.S.A. 2000, c. H-14

British Columbia

Human Rights Code, R.S.B.C. 1996, c. 210

Manitoba

Employment Standards Code, S.M. 1998, c. 29 (C.C.S.M. c. E110)

New Brunswick

Employment Standards Act, S.N.B. 1982, c. E-7.2

Newfoundland and Labrador

Human Rights Code, R.S.N.L. 1990, c. H-14

Nova Scotia

Labour Standards Code, R.S.N.S. 1989, c. 246

Ontario

Employment Standards Act, 2000, S.O. 2000, c. 41

Prince Edward Island

Human Rights Act, R.S.P.E.I. 1988, c. H-12

Quebec

Charter of Human Rights and Freedoms, R.S.Q., c. C-12

Saskatchewan

Labour Standards Act, R.S.S. 1978, c. L-1

Northwest Territories

Fair Practices Act, R.S.N.W.T. 1988, c. F-2

Nunavut

Fair Practices Act, R.S.N.W.T. 1988, c. F-2

Yukon

Employment Standards Act, R.S.Y. 1986, c. 54
Human Rights Act, S.Y. 1987, c. 3

Pay Equity

Manitoba

Pay Equity Act, S.M. 1985-86, c. 21 (C.C.S.M. c. P13)

New Brunswick

Pay Equity Act, S.N.B. 1989, c. P-5.01

Nova Scotia

Pay Equity Act, R.S.N.S. 1989, c. 337

Ontario

Pay Equity Act, R.S.O. 1990, c. P.7

Prince Edward Island

Pay Equity Act, R.S.P.E.I. 1988, c. P-2

Quebec

Pay Equity Act, R.S.Q., c. E-12.001

Employment Equity

Federal

Employment Equity Act, S.C. 1995, c. 44

Quebec

"Act respecting equal access to employment in public bodies and amending the Charter of Human Rights and Freedoms", R.S.Q., c. A-2.01

OCCUPATIONAL HEALTH AND SAFETY LEGISLATION

Federal

Canada Labour Code, R.S.C. 1985, c. L-2

Alberta

Occupational Health and Safety Act, R.S.A. 2000, c. O-2

British Columbia

Industrial Health and Safety Regulation, B.C. Reg. 585/77 (made under the *Workers Compensation Act*, R.S.B.C. 1996, c. 492)
Occupational Health and Safety Regulation, B.C. Reg. 296/97 (made under the *Workers Compensation Act*, R.S.B.C. 1996, c. 492)

Manitoba

Workplace Safety and Health Act, R.S.M. 1987, c. W210 (C.C.S.M. c. W210)

New Brunswick

Occupational Health and Safety Act, S.N.B. 1983, c. O-0.2

Newfoundland and Labrador

Occupational Health and Safety Act, R.S.N.L. 1990, c. O-3

Nova Scotia

Occupational Health and Safety Act, S.N.S. 1996, c. 7

Ontario

Occupational Health and Safety Act, R.S.O. 1990, c. O.1

Prince Edward Island

Occupational Health and Safety Act, R.S.P.E.I. 1988, c. O-1

Quebec

"Act respecting occupational health and safety", R.S.Q., c. S-2.1

Saskatchewan

Occupational Health and Safety Act, 1993, S.S. 1993, c. O-1.1

Northwest Territories

Safety Act, R.S.N.W.T. 1988, c. S-1

Nunavut

Safety Act, R.S.N.W.T. 1988, c. S-1

Yukon

Occupational Health and Safety Act, R.S.Y. 1986, c. 123

WORKERS' COMPENSATION LEGISLATION

Federal

Government Employees Compensation Act, R.S.C. 1985, c. G-5

Alberta

Workers' Compensation Act, R.S.A. 2000, c. W-15

British Columbia

Workers Compensation Act, R.S.B.C. 1996, c. 492

Manitoba

Workers Compensation Act, R.S.M. 1987, c. W200 (C.C.S.M. c. W200)

New Brunswick

Workers' Compensation Act, R.S.N.B. 1973, c. W-13

Newfoundland and Labrador

Workplace Health, Safety and Compensation Act, R.S.N.L. 1990, c. W-11

Nova Scotia

Workers' Compensation Act, S.N.S. 1994-95, c. 10

Ontario

Workplace Safety and Insurance Act, 1997, S.O. 1997, c. 16, Sch. A

Prince Edward Island

Workers Compensation Act, S.P.E.I. 1994, c. 67

Quebec

"Act respecting industrial accidents and occupational diseases", R.S.Q., c. A 3.001

Saskatchewan

Workers' Compensation Act, 1979, S.S. 1979, c. W-17.1

Northwest Territories

Workers' Compensation Act, R.S.N.W.T. 1988, c. W-6

Nunavut

Workers' Compensation Act, R.S.N.W.T. 1988, c. W-6

Yukon

Workers Compensation Act, S.Y. 1992, c. 16

Appendix C
Government Contacts

EMPLOYMENT STANDARDS INQUIRIES

Federal

Human Resources Development Canada
For Labour Program Regional Offices, District Offices, Services Centres and
General Information Numbers
http://info.load-otea.hrdc-drhc.gc.ca/common/offices.shtml

Alberta

Alberta Human Resources and Employment
Employment Standards Branch
Sterling Place, Main Floor
9940 – 106th Street
Edmonton, Alberta
T5K 2N2
General Inquiries: (780) 427-3731 / 427-8837
www3.gov.ab.ca/hre/employmentstandards

British Columbia

British Columbia Employment Standards Tribunal
890 – 360 West Georgia Street
Vancouver, British Columbia
V6B 6B2
Toll Free: 1-800-663-3316
Fax: (604) 775-3372
www.labour.gov.bc.ca/esb

Manitoba

Manitoba Labour and Immigration
Employment Standards Division
   401 York Avenue, Room 604
   Norquay Building
   Winnipeg, Manitoba
   R3C 0P8
   General Inquiries: (204) 945-3352
   Toll Free: 1-800-821-4307
   www.gov.mb.ca/chc/archives/L/L3.html
   www.gov.mb.ca/labour/standards

New Brunswick

Department of Training and Employment Development
Central Employment Standards Office
   470 York Street
   P.O. Box 6000
   Fredericton, New Brunswick
   E3B 3P7
   General Inquiries: (506) 453-3902
   www.gnb.ca/0308/0001e.htm

Newfoundland and Labrador

Newfoundland and Labrador Labour Standards
Labour Standards Division
   3rd Floor, Beothuck Building
   20 Crosbie Place
   P.O. Box 8700
   St. John's, Newfoundland
   A1B 4J6
   General Inquiries: (709) 729-2742
   www.gov.nf.ca/labour/labour/labour_standards.asp

Nova Scotia

Nova Scotia Labour Standards Tribunal
   5151 Terminal Road, 7th Floor
   P.O. Box 697
   Halifax, Nova Scotia
   B3J 2T8
   General Inquiries: (902) 424-6730
   www.gov.ns.ca/enla/labstand

Ontario

Ministry of Labour
Employment Practices Branch
    400 University Avenue, 9th Floor
    Toronto, Ontario
    M7A 1T7
    General Inquiries: (416) 326-7160
    Toll Free: 1-800-531-5551
    www.gov.on.ca/LAB/es/ese.htm

Prince Edward Island

Prince Edward Island Employment Standards Board
    31 Gordon Drive
    P.O. Box 2000
    Charlottetown, Prince Edward Island
    C1A 7N8
    General Inquiries: (902) 368-5550
    www.gov.pe.ca/commcul/csb-info/index.php3

Quebec

Labour Standards (Commission des normes du travail)
    2 Complexe Desjardins
    East Tower, 24th Floor
    P.O. Box 730, Succursale Place Desjardins
    Montreal, Quebec
    H5B 1B8
    General Inquiries: (514) 873-7061
    www.cnt.gouv.qc.ca/en/index.asp

Minimum Wage Commission
    400 Blvd. Jean-Lesage, 6th Floor
    Quebec City, Quebec
    G1K 8W1
    Toll Free: 1-800-265-1414

Saskatchewan

Department of Labour
Labour Standards
    1870 Albert Street, 4th Floor
    Regina, Saskatchewan
    S4P 3V7
    General Inquiries: (306) 787-2438
    Toll Free: 1-800-667-1783
    www.labour.gov.sk.ca/standards/index.htm

Northwest Territories

Labour Standards Board of the Northwest Territories
P.O. Box 2804
Yellowknife, Northwest Territories
X1A 2L9
General Inquiries: (867) 873-7294
www.justice.gov.nt.ca/publicservices/labourboard.htm

Yukon

Department of Justice
Labour Services (J-8)
P.O. Box 2703, Government of the Yukon
Whitehorse, Yukon
Y1A 2C6
General Inquiries: (867) 667-5944
Toll Free: 1-800-661-0408
www.gov.yk.ca/depts/community/labour/esa.html

HUMAN RIGHTS INQUIRIES

Federal

Canadian Human Rights Commission
344 Slater Street
Canada Building, 8th Floor
Ottawa, Ontario
K1A 1E1
General Inquiries: (613) 995-1151
www.chrc-ccdp.ca

Alberta

Human Rights and Citizenship Commission
800 Standard Life Centre
Suit 1600
10405 Jasper Avenue
Edmonton, Alberta
T5J 4R7
Calgary Tel.: (403) 297-6571
Edmonton Tel.: (780) 427-7661
Toll Free: 1-800-310-0000
www.albertahumanrights.ab.ca

British Columbia

British Columbia Human Rights Commission
844 Courtney Street, 2nd Floor
Victoria, British Columbia
V8W 9J1
General Inquiries: (250) 387-3710
www.bchrc.gov.bc.ca

British Columbia Human Rights Tribunal
306 – 815 Hornby Street
Vancouver, British Columbia
V6Z 2E6
General Inquiries: (604) 660-6811

Manitoba

Human Rights Commission
175 Hargrove Street, 7th Floor
Winnipeg, Manitoba
R3C 3R8
General Inquiries: (204) 945-3007
www.gov.mb.ca/hrc

New Brunswick

Human Rights Commission
751 Brunswick Street
P.O. Box 6000
Fredericton, New Brunswick
E3B 5H1
General Inquiries: (506) 453-2301
www.gnb.ca/hrc-cdp

Newfoundland and Labrador

Human Rights Commission
345 Duckworth Avenue
P.O. Box 8700
St. John's, Newfoundland
A1B 4J6
General Inquiries: (709) 729-2709
www.gov.nf.ca/hrc

Nova Scotia

Human Rights Commission
  Lord Nelson Arcade, 7th Floor
  5675 Spring Garden Road
  P.O. Box 2221 (Halifax South Postal Station)
  Halifax, Nova Scotia
  B3J 3C4
  General Inquiries: (902) 424-4111
  www.gov.ns.ca/humanrights

Ontario

Human Rights Commission
  180 Dundas Street West, 8th Floor
  Toronto, Ontario
  M7A 2R9
  General Inquiries: (416) 314-4500
  www.ohrc.on.ca

Prince Edward Island

Human Rights Commission
  98 Water Street
  P.O. Box 2000
  Charlottetown, Prince Edward Island
  C1A 7N8
  General Inquiries: (902) 368-4180
  www.gov.pe.ca/humanrights

Quebec

Human Rights Commission (Commission des droits de la personne et des
droits de la jeunesse)
  360 St. Jacques Street West, 2nd Floor
  Montreal, Quebec
  H2Y 1P5
  General Inquiries: (514) 873-5146
  Toll Free: 1-800-361-6477
  Fax: (514) 873-6032
  www.cdpdj.qc.ca

Saskatchewan

Human Rights Commission
  Sturdy Stone Building, 8th Floor
  122 – 3rd Avenue North
  Saskatoon, Saskatchewan
  S7K 2H6
  General Inquiries: (306) 933-5952
  Toll Free: 1-800-667-9249
  www.gov.sk.ca/shrc

Northwest Territories

Fair Practices Office
  3rd Floor, Panda II Mall
  P.O. Box 1920
  Yellowknife, Northwest Territories
  X1A 2P4
  General Inquiries: (867) 920-8764
  Fax: (867) 873-0489
  Toll Free: 1-800-661-0760
  www.justice.gov.nt.ca/publicservices/fairpractices.htm

Yukon

Human Rights Commission
  201 – 211 Hawkins Street
  Whitehorse, Yukon
  Y1A 1X3
  General Inquiries: (867) 667-6226
  www.yhrc.yk.ca

**OCCUPATIONAL HEALTH AND SAFETY AND WORKERS'
COMPENSATION INQUIRIES**

Federal

Human Resources Development Canada
For Labour Program Regional Offices, District Offices, Services Centres and
General Information Numbers
  http://info.load-otea.hrdc-drhc.gc.ca/common/offices.shtml

Canadian Centre for Occupational Health and Safety
  250 Main Street East
  Hamilton, Ontario
  L8N 1H6
  General Inquiries: (905) 572-4400
  Toll Free: 1-800-263-8466
  www.ccohs.ca

Hazardous Materials Information Review Commission
  427 Laurier Avenue West, 7th Floor
  Ottawa, Ontario
  K1A 1M3
  General Inquiries: (613) 993-4331
  www.hmirc-ccrmd.gc.ca

Alberta

Alberta Workplace Health & Safety Partnership Program
  9th Floor, Labour Bldg.
  10808 – 99th Avenue Northwest
  Edmonton, Alberta
  T5K 0G5
  General Inquiries: (780) 427-8842
  www3.gov.ab.ca/hre/index.asp

Workers' Compensation Board
  9912 – 107 Street
  P.O. Box 2415
  Edmonton, Alberta
  T5J 2S5
  General Inquiries: (780) 498-3999
  www.wcb.ab.ca

British Columbia

Workers' Compensation Board
  P.O. Box 5350
  Station Terminal
  Vancouver, British Columbia
  V6B 5L5
  General Inquiries: (604) 279-2266
  www.worksafebc.com

Ministry of Skills Development and Labour
  634 Humboldt Street
  P.O. Box 9594
  Stn. Prov. Govt.
  Victoria, British Columbia
  V8W 9K4
  www.gov.bc.ca/sdl

Manitoba

Manitoba Labour and Immigration
Workplace Safety and Health Division
  200 – 401 York Avenue
  Winnipeg, Manitoba
  R3C 0P8
  General Inquiries: (204) 945-3602
  www.gov.mb.ca/labour/safety/index.html

Advisory Council on Workplace Safety and Health
  200 – 401 York Avenue
  Room 200
  Winnipeg, Manitoba
  R3C 0P8
  General Inquiries: (204) 945-3744
  www.gov.mb.ca/labour/safety/health/index.html

Workers Compensation Board
  333 Broadway
  Winnipeg, Manitoba
  R3C 4W3
  Toll Free: 1-800-362-3340
  Fax: (204) 954 1999
  www.wcb.mb.ca

New Brunswick

Department of Training and Employment Development
  Chestnut Complex
  3rd Floor, 470 York Street
  P.O. Box 6000
  Fredericton, New Brunswick
  E3B 5H1
  General Inquiries: (506) 453-5342
  www.gnb.ca/0105/index.htm

Workplace Health, Safety and Compensation Commission
1 Portland Street
P.O. Box 160
Saint John, New Brunswick
E2L 3X9
General Inquiries: (506) 632-2200
Toll Free: 1-800-222-9775
www.whscc.nb.ca

Newfoundland and Labrador

Department of Labour
Occupational Health and Safety Branch
Confederation Building, West Block, 2nd Floor
P.O. Box 8700
St. John's, Newfoundland
A1B 4J6
General Inquiries: (709) 729-2706
Toll Free: 1-800-563-5471
www.gov.nf.ca/labour

Workplace Health Safety and Compensation Commission
146 – 148 Forest Road
P.O. Box 9000, Station B
St. John's, Newfoundland
A1A 3B8
General Inquiries: (709) 778-1000
Toll Free: 1-800-563-9000
www.whscc.nf.ca

Nova Scotia

Department of Environment and Labour
Occupational Health and Safety Division
5151 Terminal Road, 6th Floor
P.O. Box 697
Halifax, Nova Scotia
B3J 2T8
General Inquiries: (902) 424-4125 / 424-5400
Toll Free: 1-800-952-2687
www.gov.ns.ca/enla/ohs

Workers' Compensation Board
  5668 South Street
  P.O. Box 1150
  Halifax, Nova Scotia
  B3J 2Y2
  General Inquiries: (902) 491-8000
  Toll Free: 1-800-870-3331
  www.wcb.ns.ca

Ontario

Ministry of Labour
  400 University Avenue, 14th Floor
  Toronto, Ontario
  M7A 1T7
  General Inquiries: (416) 326-7400
  www.gov.on.ca/lab/main.htm

Workplace Safety and Insurance Board
  Simcoe Place
  200 Front Street West
  Toronto, Ontario
  M5V 3J1
  General Inquiries: (416) 344-1000
  Toll Free: 1-800-387-5540 or 1-800-387-0750
  Claims: (416) 344-1011
  www.wsib.on.ca

Prince Edward Island

Department of Community and Cultural Affairs
Labour and Industrial Relations Division
  31 Gordon Drive
  P.O. Box 2000
  Charlottetown, Prince Edward Island
  C1A 7N8
  General Inquiries: (902) 368-5550
  www.gov.pe.ca/commcul/lair-info/index.php3

Workers' Compensation Board
  14 Weymouth Street
  P.O. Box 757
  Charlottetown, Prince Edward Island
  C1A 7L7
  General Inquiries: (902) 368-5680
  Toll Free: 1-800-237-5049
  www.wcb.pe.ca

Quebec

Ministry of Labour (Ministère du travail)
200 Chemin Sainte-Foy, 6th Floor
Quebec, Quebec
G1R 5S1
www.travail.gouv.qc.ca

Workers' Compensation Board
Commission of Occupational Health and Safety (Commission de la santé et de la sécurité du travail)
1 Complexe Desjardins
Tours du Sud
CP 3 Succursale Place Desjardins
Montreal, Quebec
H5B 1H1
General Inquiries: (514) 906-3000
Fax: (514) 906-3131
www.csst.qc.ca

Saskatchewan

Department of Labour
Occupational Health and Safety Division
1870 Albert Street, 6th Floor
Regina, Saskatchewan
S4P 3V7
General Inquiries: (306) 787-4496
Toll Free: 1-800-567-7233
www.labour.gov.sk.ca

Workers' Compensation Board
1881 Scarth Street
Suite 200
Regina, Saskatchewan
S4P 4L1
General Inquiries: (306) 787-4370
Toll Free: 1-800-667-7590
www.wcbsask.com

Northwest Territories

Department of Education, Culture and Employment
Occupational Health and Safety
P.O. Box 1320
Yellowknife, Northwest Territories
X1A 2L9
General Inquiries: (403) 873-7078
No website available

Workers' Compensation Board
  P.O. Box 888
  Yellowknife, Northwest Territories
  X1A 2R3
  General Inquiries: (403) 920-3888
  Toll Free: 1-800-661-0792
  www.wcb.nt.ca/home.htm

Nunavut

Workers' Compensation Board
  P.O. Box 888
  Yellowknife, Northwest Territories
  X1A 2R3
  General Inquiries: (403) 920-3888
  Toll Free: 1-800-661-0792
  www.wcb.nt.ca/home.htm

Yukon

Workers' Compensation Health and Safety Board
  401 Strickland Street
  Whitehorse, Yukon
  Y1A 5N8
  General Inquiries: (403) 667-5645
  Toll Free: 1-800-661-0443
  www.wcb.yk.ca

Additional Resources

GENERAL

Audet, G., *Wrongful Dismissal in Quebec* (Montreal: Editions Y. Blais, 1990)

Ball, S.R., *Canadian Employment Law* (Aurora: Canada Law Book Inc., 1996)

Bonhomme, R., D. Kaufer and G. Rosen, *Labour and Employment Law: Frequently Asked Questions* (Toronto: Carswell, 2002)

Christie, I.M., G. England, and W.B. Cotter, *Employment Law in Canada*, 2nd ed. (Toronto: Butterworths, 1993)

Corry, D., and J. Petrie, *Conducting a Wrongful Dismissal Action* (Scarborough: Carswell, 1996)

Echlin, R., and M.J. MacKillop, *Creative Solutions: Perspectives on Canadian Employment Law*, 2nd. ed. (Aurora: Canada Law Book Inc., 2001)

Elliott, C.J., and S.D. Saxe, *Employment Contracts Handbook*, 2nd ed. (Aurora: Canada Law Book Inc., 1997)

England, G., and I. Christie, *Employment Law in Canada*, 3rd ed. (Toronto: Butterworths, 1998 – looseleaf)

Fox, H.G., *The Law of Master and Servant in Relation to Industrial and Intellectual Property* (Toronto: University of Toronto Press, 1950)

Franklin, J., *Employment Law: Constructive Dismissal* (Edmonton: Legal Education Society of Alberta, 1997)

Grosman, B.A., and J.R. Martin, *Employment Law in Ontario: A Guide for Employers and Employees* (Aurora: Canada Law Book Inc., 1991)

Harris, D., *Wrongful Dismissal* (Don Mills: DeBoo, 1984)

Levitt, H.A., *The Law of Dismissal in Canada*, 2nd ed. (Aurora: Canada Law Book Inc., 1992)

Mole, E., *Butterworths Wrongful Dismissal Practice Manual*, 2 vols. (Markham: Butterworths, 1984)

Saxe, S., *Ontario Employment Law Handbook: An Employer's Guide*, 6th ed. (Markham: Butterworths, 2002)

Sproat, J.R., *Employment Law Manual: Wrongful Dismissal, Human Rights and Employment Standards in Ontario* (Toronto: Carswell, 1990)

Wilson, P., and A. Taylor, *The Corporate Counsel Guide to Employment Law* (Aurora: Canada Law Book Inc., 1998)

Young, B., *Beyond Discharge* (Toronto: Canada Labour Views Co., 1984)

PART 1 — THE COURTING

Advertisements and Job Applications

A Recommended Personnel Policy Regarding Employment-Related Sexual Harassment (Toronto: Law Society of Upper Canada, 1992)

Aggarwal, A.P., *Sex Discrimination: Employment Law and Practices* (Markham: Butterworths, 1994)

Bowland, A., T.C. Nakatsu, and J.W. O'Reilly, *The 1996 Annotated Ontario Human Rights Code* (Scarborough: Carswell, 1995)

Grosman, B.A., and J.R. Martin, *Discrimination in Employment in Ontario* (Aurora: Canada Law Book Inc., 1994)

Human Rights Legislation: An Office Consolidation (Toronto: Butterworths, 1991)

Keene, J., *Human Rights in Ontario*, 2nd ed. (Toronto: Carswell, 1992)

Kelly, J.G., *Human Resource Management and the Human Rights Process* (Don Mills: CCH Canadian, 1991)

McDowell, L., *Human Rights in the Workplace: A Practical Guide* (Scarborough: Carswell, 1995)

Interviewing

Bota, A.N., *Employment Related Drug Testing: The Legal Implications for Employers* (Kingston: Industrial Relations Centre, Queen's University, 1989)

Butler, B., M. Huberman, and R. Townshend, *The Drug Testing Controversy: Imperial Oil and Other Lessons* (Scarborough: Carswell, 1997)

Drug Testing and Privacy (Ottawa: Privacy Commissioner of Canada, 1990)

Medley, H., *Sweaty Palms: The Neglected Art of Being Interviewed* (Berkeley: Ten Speed Press, 1984)

Report on Drug and Alcohol Testing in the Workplace (Toronto: Ontario Law Reform Commission, 1992)

Report on Mandatory Drug-Testing (Toronto: Canadian Bar Association, Ontario Branch, 1987)

Venne, R., *Psychological Testing in Personnel Selection* (Kingston: Industrial Relations Centre, Queen's University, 1987)

PART 2 — THE ENGAGEMENT

Hiring — Breach of Contract

Pitch, H.D., and R.M. Snyder, *Damages for Breach of Contract*, 2nd ed. (Toronto: Carswell, 1989)

The Broken Contract: Contract Termination and Remedies (Toronto: Canadian Bar Association, Ontario Branch, Continuing Legal Education, 1984)

Types of Employees — Agents

Bowstead, W., *Bowstead and Reynolds on Agency*, 16th ed. (London: Sweet & Maxwell, 1996)

Fridman, G.H.L., *Fridman's Law of Agency*, 6th ed. (London: Butterworths, 1990)

Types of Employees — Partners

Cases and Materials on Partnerships and Canadian Business Corporations (Agincourt: Carswell, 1989)

Lindley, N., *Lindley & Banks on Partnership*, 17th ed. (London: Sweet & Maxwell, 1995)

Manzer, A., et al., *A Practical Guide to Canadian Partnership Law* (Aurora: Canada Law Book Inc., 1994)

Types of Employees — Crown Employees

Grosman, M.N., *Federal Employment Law in Canada* (Agincourt: Carswell, 1990)

The Employment Contract

Aust, A.E., and L. Charette, *The Employment Contract*, 2nd ed. (Cowansville: Editions Y. Blais, 1993)

Bowlby, B., P. Jarvis, and E. Mole, *Employment Contracts — An Employer's Guide* (Markham: Butterworths, 1991)

Canadian Bar Association, *Advising Information Technology Business, Part II: IT Contract Information, Employment and Intellectual Property Issues* (Toronto: Canadian Bar Association – Ontario, Continuing Legal Education, 2001)

Elliott, C.J., and S.D. Saxe, *Employment Contracts Handbook* (Aurora: Canada Law Book Inc., 1990)

International Handbook on Contracts of Employment (Deventer, Boston: Kluwer Law and Taxation Publishers, 1988)

Executive Employment Contracts

Bernstein, J., *Tax Planning for Professionals and Executives* (Don Mills: CCH Canadian, 1993)

Chartier, R., *The Management of Professional Employees* (Kingston: Industrial Relations Centre, Queen's University, 1968)

Executive Pensions: Balancing the Interests of Executives, the Corporation and Shareholders (Toronto: Canadian Institute, 1994)

Executives on the Move: Tax Implications (London: Binder, Dijker, Otte, 1985)

Gordon Group, *Dismissal of Management Personnel* (Toronto: Gordon Group, 1986)

Grosman, B.A., *The Executive Firing Line: Wrongful Dismissal and the Law* (Toronto: Carswell/Methuen, 1982)

Stikeman, Elliott, *Executive Employment Law* (Toronto: Butterworths, 1993)

Tax Planning for Executive and Employee Compensation and Retirement (Toronto: Canadian Tax Foundation, 1985)

Tax Planning for Executive Compensation (Toronto: CCH Canadian Conference Division, 1990)

Taxation of Executive Compensation and Retirement (Montreal: Federated Press, 1989)

Executive Employment Contracts — Immigration

Immigration Practice and Procedure under the North American Free Trade Agreement (Washington, D.C.: American Immigration Lawyers Association, 1995)

Issues Affecting Transborder Relocation of Business Persons and the Free Trade Agreement (Mississauga: Insight, 1989)

Waldman, L., *Immigration Law and Practice*, 2 vols. (Toronto: Butterworths, 1992)

Wydrzynski, C.J., *Canadian Immigration Law and Procedure* (Aurora: Canada Law Book Inc., 1983)

PART 3 — THE MARRIAGE

Considerations During the Employment Relationship

Adler, N.J., *Human Resource Management in the Global Economy* (Kingston: Industrial Relations Centre, Queen's University, 1993)

Chartier, R., *The Management of Professional Employees* (Kingston: Industrial Relations Centre, Queen's University, 1968)

Kelly, J.G., *Human Resource Management and the Human Rights Process* (Don Mills: CCH Canadian, 1991)

Kumar, P., *Personnel Management in Canada: A Manpower Profile* (Kingston: Industrial Relations Centre, Queen's University, 1975)

Rozovsky, L.E., and F.A. Rozovsky, *The Canadian Law of Patient Records* (Toronto: Butterworths, 1984)

Stockdale, A., *Administering Wage and Salary Programs: Some Problems and Issues* (Kingston: Industrial Relations Centre, Queen's University, 1978)

Wood, W., *Personnel Administration and Professional Employees* (Kingston: Industrial Relations Centre, Queen's University, 1970)

Employment Standards Legislation

Employment Standards Legislation in Canada (Ottawa: Labour Canada, 1989)

Mehmet, O., *Theoretical Aspects of Severance Pay: A Human Capital Theory Approach* (Kingston: Industrial Relations Centre, Queen's University, 1975)

Ontario Ministry of Labour, Employment Practices Branch, *Employment Standards Act 2000: Policy and Interpretation Manual* (Scarborough: Carswell, 2001)

Parry, R.M., *Employment Standards Handbook*, 3rd ed. (Aurora: Canada Law Book Inc., 2002 – looseleaf)

Roher, E., *Employment Standards Guide* (Scarborough: Carswell, 1997 – looseleaf)

Whittingham, F., *Minimum Wages in Ontario: Analysis and Measurement Problems* (Kingston: Industrial Relations Centre, Queen's University, 1970)

Williams, C., *Family Related Benefits in Canada* (Kingston: Industrial Relations Centre, Queen's University, 1981)

Working Times: Report of the Ontario Task Force on Hours of Work and Overtime (Toronto: Ministry of Labour, 1987)

Human Rights Legislation

Aggarwal, Dr. A.P., *Sex Discrimination: Employment Law and Practices* (Markham: Butterworths, 1994)

Aggarwal, Dr. A.P., *Sexual Harassment — A Guide for Understanding and Prevention* (Markham: Butterworths, 1992)

Aggarwal, Dr. A.P. and M.M. Gupta, *Sexual Harassment in the Workplace*, 3rd ed. (Toronto: Butterworths, 2000)

Bowland, A., T.C. Nakatsu, and J.W. O'Reilly, *The 1996 Annotated Ontario Human Rights Code* (Scarborough: Carswell, 1995)

Brodsky, G., and S. Day, *Canadian Charter Equality Rights for Women: One Step Forward or Two Steps Back?* (Ottawa: Canadian Advisory Council on the Status of Women, 1989)

D'Andrea, J.A., D.J. Corry, and H.I. Forester, *Illness and Disability in the Workplace: How to Navigate Through the Legal Minefield* (Aurora: Canada Law Book Inc., 1995)

Grosman, B.A., and J.R. Martin, *Discrimination in Employment in Ontario* (Aurora: Canada Law Book Inc., 1994)

Human Rights Legislation: An Office Consolidation (Toronto: Butterworths, 1991)

Keene, J., *Human Rights in Ontario*, 2nd ed. (Toronto: Carswell, 1992)

Kelly, J.G., *Human Resource Management and the Human Rights Process* (Don Mills: CCH Canadian, 1991)

McDowell, L., *Human Rights in the Workplace: A Practical Guide* (Scarborough: Carswell, 1995)

Mendes, E., *Racial Discrimination: Law and Practice* (Scarborough: Carswell, 1995)

Ontario Human Rights Commission, *Human Rights Policy in Ontario*, 3rd ed. (Toronto: CCH Canadian Limited, 2001)

Tarnopolsky, W.S., *Discrimination and the Law: Including Equality Rights under the Charter* (Toronto: DeBoo, 1985)

The Duty to Accommodate: The Legal and Practical Aspects of Integrating People with Disabilities into Your Workforce (Mississauga: Insight, 1991)

Vizkelety, B., *Proving Discrimination in Canada* (Toronto: Carswell, 1987)

Equity Legislation

Bevan, L., *The Employment Equity Manual* (Toronto: Carswell, 1992)

Burkart, M.L., *Implementing Pay Equity in Ontario* (Kingston: Industrial Relations Centre, Queen's University, 1990)

Coates, M.L., *Pay and Employment Equity* (Kingston: Industrial Relations Centre, Queen's University, 1989)

Elliott, C.J., *Employment Equity Handbook* (Aurora: Canada Law Book Inc., 1994)

Elliott, C.J., *Ontario's Equity Laws: A Complete Guide to Pay and Employment Equity* (Aurora: Canada Law Book Inc., 1992)

Elliott, C.J., and S.D. Saxe, *Pay Equity Handbook: A Step-by-Step Guide to Implementing Equal Pay for Work of Equal Value in Ontario*, rev. ed. (Aurora: Canada Law Book Inc., 1992)

Employment Equity: A Guide for Employers (Ottawa: Employment and Immigration Canada, 1992)

Gordon Group, *Pay Equity: The Impact of New Equal Pay for Work of Equal Value Legislation* (Toronto: Gordon Group, 1986)

Kelly, J.G., *Pay Equity Management* (Toronto: CCH Canadian, 1988)

Marcotte, M., *Equal Pay for Work of Equal Value* (Kingston: Industrial Relations Centre, Queen's University, 1987)

Pay Equity Commission of Ontario, *Questions and Answers: Pay Equity in the Workplace* (Toronto, 1988)

Pay Equity: Means and Ends (Kingston: John Deutsch Institute for the Study of Economic Policy, 1991)

Weiner, N., *Employment Equity: Making It Work* (Toronto: Butterworths, 1993)

Occupational Health and Safety Legislation

Canadian Employment Safety and Health Guide, 3 vols. (Don Mills: CCH Canadian, 1980)

Grossman, M., *The Law of Occupational Health and Safety in Ontario*, 2nd ed. (Markham: Butterworths, 1994)

Keith, N.A., *Ontario Health and Safety Law: A Complete Guide to the Law and Procedures, with Digest of Cases* (Aurora: Canada Law Book Inc., 2002 – looseleaf)

McKenzie, G., *Report on the Administration of the Occupational Health and Safety Act* (Toronto: Ministry of Labour, 1987)

Nash, M.I., *Canadian Occupational Health and Safety Law Handbook* (Don Mills: CCH Canadian, 1983)

Occupational Health & Safety: Legal and Practical Advice (Toronto: Centre for Professional Learning, 1988)

Simon, P., *Handbook of Occupational Health and Safety Law Reform in Ontario* (Don Mills: CCH Canadian, 1989)

Stones, I., *The Extended Workday: Health and Safety Issues* (Hamilton: Canadian Centre for Occupational Health and Safety, 1987)

Workers' Compensation Legislation

Dee, G., N. McCombie, and G. Newhouse, *Butterworths Workers' Compensation in Ontario Service* (Markham: Butterworths, 1993)

Dee, G., N. McCombie, and G. Newhouse, *Workers' Compensation in Ontario* (Toronto: Butterworths, 1987)

Gilbert, D.G., J. Mastoras, and L.A. Liversidge, *A Guide to Workers' Compensation in Ontario*, 2nd ed. (Aurora: Canada Law Book Inc., 1995)

Ison, T.G., *Workers' Compensation in Canada*, 2nd ed. (Toronto: Butterworths, 1989)

Johnson, V., *Comparison of Workers' Compensation Legislation in Canada* (Mississauga: Association of Workers' Compensation Boards of Canada, 1999)

Legge, B., *The Canadian System of Workmen's Compensation* (Toronto: Workmen's Compensation Board, 1972)

Workers' Compensation (Toronto: Canadian Institute, 1988)

PART 4 — THE SEPARATION

Sale of Business

Acquiring or Selling the Privately Held Company (New York: Practicing Law Institute, 1986)

Employment Issues on the Purchase and Sale of a Business (Toronto: Canadian Bar Association, Ontario Branch, 1988)

Bankruptcy and Receivership

Bennett, F., *Bennett on Bankruptcy*, 2nd ed. (Don Mills: CCH Canadian, 1991)

Employee Issues in Downsizing and Bankruptcy: Managing the Human Side of Corporate Retrenchment (Mississauga: Insight, 1991)

Houlden, L.W., and C.H. Morawetz, *Bankruptcy and Insolvency Law of Canada*, 3rd ed., 2 vols. (Toronto: Carswell, 1992)

Lazar, S., *The Law of Bankruptcy and Insolvency in Canada* (Montreal: Jewel Publications, 1997)

PART 5 — THE DIVORCE

Bringing the Employment Relationship to an End

Audet, G., *Wrongful Dismissal in Quebec* (Montreal: Editions Y. Blais, 1990)

D'Andrea, J.A., D.J. Corry, and H.I. Forester, *Illness and Disability in the Workplace: How to Navigate Through the Legal Minefield* (Aurora: Canada Law Book Inc., 1995)

Grosman, B.A., *Fire Power: The Positive Approach to the Dilemma Faced by Every Employer and Employee* (Markham: Penguin Books, 1989)

Grosman, B.A., *Fire Proofing: Protecting Your Job in the 90s* (Toronto: Key Porter Books, 1992)

Grosman, B.A., *The Executive Firing Line: Wrongful Dismissal and the Law* (Toronto: Carswell/Methuen, 1982)

Harris, D., *Wrongful Dismissal* (Don Mills: DeBoo, 1984)

Heenan, R.L., *Wrongful Dismissal of Non-Union Employees: Arbitral Remedies* (Kingston: Industrial Relations Centre, Queen's University, 1992)

Insight Press, *Cutting the Costs of Wrongful Dismissal* (Toronto: Insight Press, 1998)

Levitt, H.A., *The Law of Dismissal in Canada*, 2nd ed. (Aurora: Canada Law Book Inc., 1992)

Mole, E., *The Wrongful Dismissal Handbook*, 2nd ed. (Markham: Butterworths, 1997)

Mole, E., *Wrongful Dismissal Practice Manual*, 2 vols. (Markham: Butterworths, 1984)

Rubin, J., *A Practical Guide to the Law of Termination in Ontario* (Aurora: Aurora Professional Press, 1995)

Sproat, J.R., *Wrongful Dismissal Handbook*, 2nd ed. (Toronto: Carswell, 2002)

Young, B., *At the Point of Discharge* (Toronto: Canada Labour Views Co., 1980)

Damages

Defense Research Institute, *The Case Against Punitive Damages: Practice and Procedure* (Milwaukee: DRI, 1969)

McGregor, H., *McGregor on Damages*, 15th ed. (London: Sweet & Maxwell, 1988)

Pitch, H.D., and R.M. Snyder, *Damages for Breach of Contract*, 2nd ed. (Toronto: Carswell, 1989)

Punitive Damages in the Modern Civil Justice System: An Anomaly in Need of Change (Los Angeles: American College of Trial Lawyers, 1988)

Waddams, S.M., *The Law of Damages*, 2nd ed. (Aurora: Canada Law Book Inc., 1991)

Restrictive Covenants and Employee Duties

Ellis, M.V., *Fiduciary Duties in Canada* (Don Mills: DeBoo, 1988)

Grosman, B.A., *Corporate Loyalty: A Trust Betrayed* (Markham: Penguin Books, 1989)

Related Issues

Alternative Dispute Resolution Practice Manual (North York: CCH Canadian, 1996)

McLaren, R.H., and J.P. Sanderson, *Innovative Dispute Resolution: The Alternative* (Scarborough: Carswell, 1994)

Mehmet, O., *Theoretical Aspects of Severance Pay: A Human Capital Theory Approach* (Kingston: Industrial Relations Centre, Queen's University, 1975)

Rudner, K.L., *The 1996 Annotated Unemployment Insurance Act* (Scarborough: Carswell, 1995)

Related Tort Claims

Clerk, J., *Clerk & Lindsell on Torts*, 18th ed. (London: Sweet & Maxwell, 2000)

Fleming, J., *The Law of Torts*, 8th ed. (Sydney: Law Book Company, 1992)

Fridman, G.H.L., *The Law of Torts in Canada*, 2nd ed. (Toronto: Carswell, 2002)

Klar, L., *Tort Law* (Calgary: Carswell, 1991)

Linden, A.M., *Canadian Tort Law*, 5th ed. (Toronto: Butterworths, 1993)

Salmond, J., *Salmond and Heuston on the Law of Torts*, 20th ed. (London: Sweet & Maxwell, 1992)

Employment law has given rise to a number of terms relating to dismissal and layoff.* In the 1990s, these have been referred to as follows:

Euphemisms for Dismissal — decruited, dehired, deselected, destaffed, discontinued, disemployed, dislocated, downsized, excessed, involuntarily separated, new career opportunity, non-retained, severed, surplused, transitioned and vocationally relocated

Euphemisms for Layoff — downsizing, employee culling, payroll adjustment, personnel adjustment, personnel surplus reduction, reduction in force ("R.I.F."), redundancy elimination, refocusing of the skill mix, resource reallocation, rightsizing and workforce imbalance correction

---

* Source: "Firing by Every Other Name", *The Globe and Mail* "Report on Business", March 8, 1996, p. B6.

Index